AL-GHAZĀLĪ
THE ISLAMIC REFORMER

Al-Ghazālī
The Islamic Reformer

*An evaluative study of the attempts of
Imam al-Ghazālī at Islamic reform (Iṣlāḥ)*

Mohamed Abu Bakr A. Al-Musleh

IBT
Islamic Book Trust
Kuala Lumpur

Published by
Islamic Book Trust
607 Mutiara Majestic
Jalan Othman
46000 Petaling Jaya
Selangor, Malaysia
www.ibtbooks.com

Islamic Book Trust is affiliated with The Other Press.

Perpustakaan Negara Malaysia   Cataloguing-in-Publication Data

Al-Musleh, Mohamed Abu Bakr A.
    Al-Ghazali the Islamic reformer : an evaluative study of the attempts of Imam
    al-Ghazali at Islamic reform / Mohamed Abu Bakr A. Al-Musleh.
    Includes index
    Bibliography: p. 285
    ISBN 978-967-5062-82-7
    1. Ghazzali, 1058-1111. 2. Scholars, Muslim. 3. Islam--Doctrines.
    I. Title. II. Series.
    297.61

To the one who has sacrificed
much for me; to the one who has added
a sweet taste to my unsettled life;
to my wonderful and supportive wife,
Aisha al-Emadi.

Contents

Acknowledgement

Praise be to Allah, without Whose help nothing can be accomplished.

I am grateful to my supervisor Dr Bustami Khir for his valuable feedback throughout the four years of my PhD programme, and for treating me as a younger brother, not just a student. Thanks also to Abū Faṭimah, Shihab al-Mahdawi, for introducing me to Dr Khir.

I am also thankful to all who have helped or encouraged me, in any way, in the course of preparing the present work. They include my respected teacher at the University of Qatar, Dr ʿAbd al-ʿAẓīm al-Dīb, who suggested that I should base my thesis on al-Ghazālī; Mr Muhammad Hozien, the webmaster of al-Ghazālī website, to whom I owe a great deal for making my research on al-Ghazālī easier by providing materials online. Discovering his website has been truly invaluable; my friend Mokhtar Ben Fredj deserves warm thanks for always being forthcoming.

I want to also thank Dr Abdulla al-Shamahi for lending me some useful references; Dr Eve Richard and Mr David Oakey, from the English for International Students Unit at the University of Birmingham, for reading parts of my thesis and for their useful comments on my English. Special thanks to Mr Elfatih Ibrahim, who proofread the entire thesis.

My deepest gratitude to my family and relatives, namely my respected parents and my parents-in-law for their continuous prayers and sincere wish for my success.

Finally, my heartfelt thanks to my dear wife for her continuous support and patience throughout my exhausting higher education life.

Glossary

'ādah: habitual act.

'adālah: righteousness, uprightness.

'ādātahum wa ālātahum: their rule of conduct and their method of approach.

ad'iyā' al-'ilm: claimers of knowledge.

Aḍud al-Dawlah: the Strong Arm of the State.

afsaṭah: sophistry.

aḥādīth: (pl. of *ḥadīth*) Prophetic sayings.

aḥkām: Islamic rules.

aḥkām nujūmiyyah: astrological rules.

ahl al-ibāḥah: the Latitudinarians.

ahl al-sunnah: people of sunnah.

akhlāq khabīthah: evil character.

'alā'iq: worldly attachments or involvements.

'ālim: scholar.

'amal: action.

a'māl al-qulūb: the knowledge dealing with the activities of the hearts.

'āmī: an ordinary man.

amīr: (lit. prince) one who rules with absolute authority over his lusts and passions.

amīr al-juyūsh: head of the troops.

amrāḍ al-qulūb: sickness of the heart.

amwāl: (pl. of *māl*) wealth.

al-Andalus: Muslim Spain.

al-'aqā'id al-īmāniyyah: the articles of faith.

aqāma: to set right or correct. *'āqibah*: aftermath.

'aql: intellect, reason.

aqwiyā': (pl. of *qawī*) strong.

al-aqwiyā' fī al-dīn: the strong in religiousness.
arbāb al-'ibādah: worshippers.
arbāb al-aḥwāl: masters of real ecstatic experiences.
arbāb al-amwāl: wealthy people.
'ārif: gnostic.
arkān: (pl. of *rukn*) pillars.
asānīd: (pl of *sand*) chains of narrators by whom the book was transmitted.
asās kul nuqṣān: the root of all deficiency.
asbāb: means.
ashrār: (pl. of *shirīr*) wicked.
aṣlaḥa: to reform.
aswāq: markets.
'atf al-khāṣ 'alā al-'ām: joining the particular to the general.
āthār: (pl. of *athar*) Prophetic *exempla* (lit. traces).
aṭibbā': (pl. of *ṭabīb*) doctors, physicians.
aṭibbā' al-dīn: the doctors of religion.
'awāmm: the ordinary people or general folks.
awrād: (pl of *wird*) specified parts.
āyah: Qur'anic verse.
āyāt: (pl .of *āyah*) Qur'anic verses.
'ayn al-baṣīrah: the eye of insight.
'ayn al-sukhṭ: the hostile eye.
azāla: he removed.
bā'ith al-dīn: the impulse or motive of religion.
bā'ith al-hawā': the motive of passion.
baddala: to transform, to convert, to change.
bahīmiyyah: wildness.
bahīmiyyah: wildness.
baḥth: investigation.
baqā' lā fanā' lah: life without death.
baṭala: became false, invalid or of no avail.
bāṭin: inner.
bi al-adillah al-'aqliyyah: with rational proofs.
bi dalīl: by evidence.
bi ḍarūrah: by common sense.
bi nafsih: in itself.
bid'ah: innovation.
bilā: the state of becoming shabby or worn out.
burhānī: apodictic.
da'wah: religious preaching.
dā': malady.
ḍarūrīyah: axiomatic (lit. necessary).
dawā': remedy.
dhamm: dispraise.

dhawq: spiritual taste.
dīn: religion or religiousness.
ḍiyā': illumination.
Ḍiyā' al-Dīn: the light of the religion.
ḍiyāfah: hospitality.
ḍu'afā': (pl. of *ḍa'īf*) weak ones.
dunyā: world.
faḍīlah: a virtuous knowledge but not obligatory.
fāḥishah: fornication.
falāsifah: (pl .of *faylasūf*) philosophers.
falayughayyirānna: so they will change.
falsafah: philosophy.
faqīh: jurist.
faqr: poverty.
farḍ 'ayn: must.
farḍ kifāyah: Islamically ordained on the Muslim community as a whole.
fasād: corruption.
fasada: became false, invalid or of no avail.
fasādah: its corruption.
fāsiq: transgressor.
fāsiqūn: (pl. of *fāsiq*) transgressors.
fatāwā: (pl .of *fatwā*) jurisprudence views.
fatwā: jurisprudence view.
fawāḥish: (pl. of *fāḥishah*) disgraceful deeds.
faylasūf: philosopher.
Faylasūf al-'Arab: philosopher of the Arabs.
fi'l al-mubāḥāt: doing permissible acts.
fiqh: jurisprudence.
fiqhī: jurisprudential.
firaq: (pl. of *firqah*) groups.
fitnah: temptation.
fiṭrah: disposition.
fuqahā': (pl .of *faqīh*) jurists.
furū ': (pl. of *far'*) the branches of religion.
ghaḍab: anger.
ghanẓ: a psychological disease largely appears among those who are of extreme religious course.
gharīzah: instinct.
ghayb: unseen.
ghayyara: to transform, to convert, to change.
ghinā: richness.
ghinā lā faqr ba'dah: wealth without poverty.
ghufl: innocent.
ghurabā': (pl. of *gharīb*) strangers.

ghurūr: self-delusion.
hadī: mode.
Ḥajj: the Muslim pilgrimage.
ḥāl: the state of real ecstasy, condition.
ḥalāl: lawful.
ḥammāmāt: (pl. of *ḥammām*) bath-houses.
ḥaqā'iq al-umūr: the actual reality of things.
ḥarām: unlawful.
ḥasartuhu: I weakened him or I fatigued him.
hawā: base desire.
hawas: mania.
ḥawwala: to transform, to convert, to change.
hidāyah: right guidance.
ḥijāb: veil.
ḥijāj: arguing.
ḥikmah: wisdom.
ḥujjah: proof.
ḥujjah al-islām: the Proof of Islam.
ḥulūl: inherence or incarnation.
'ibād: worshipers.
'ibādah: worship.
al-idṭirāb wa al-khalal: disorder and deficiency.
ifsād: spreading or causing corruption.
ijmā': consensus.
ijmā' al-ṣaḥābah: the consensus of the Companions.
al-ijmā' mun'aqid: a consensus has been reached.
ijtihād: reasoned opinion.
ilhām: inspiration.
ilḥāq al-ḍarar: inflicting detriment.
'ilm: (religious) knowledge.
'ilm al-a'māl: the knowledge of practical religion.
'ilm al-ākhirah: the knowledge of the next world.
'ilm al-bāṭin: the knowledge of the inward, the knowledge of the inner self.
'ilm al-dalīl: the science of reasoning.
'ilm al-dunyā: worldly knowledge.
'ilm al-fiqh: the Discipline of Islamic Jurisprudence.
'ilm al-kalām: Islamic theology.
'ilm al-mu'āmalah: the knowledge of the Praxis.
'ilm al-mukāshafah: the knowledge of the Unveiling.
'ilm al-taṣawwuf: the knowledge of the Islamic Mysticism.
'ilm al-yaqīn: the knowledge of certitude.
'ilm al-ẓāhir: the perceptible knowledge, the outward knowledge.
'ilm a'māl al-jawāriḥ: the knowledge of actions done by bodily members.
'ilm lā jahl ma'ah: knowledge without ignorance.

imāmah: supreme leadership of the Muslims.
īmān: Islamic faith.
insān muṭlaq: absolute man.
al-insihāb wa al-'awdah: withdrawal and return.
iqtiṣād: moderation.
irādah: will.
ishārah al-shayāṭīn: the direction of devils.
'ishq: love.
iṣlāḥ: reformation.
iṣlāḥī: reformatory.
Islām muttafaq 'alayh: a consensus Islam.
istibṣār: insight.
istiqāmah: righteousness.
i'tidāl: moderation.
i'tidāl al-amr: equilibrium.
itiḥād: unity.
ittibā': imitation, the following (of the *'ulamā'* or the *muftīs*).
i'yā': fatigue, jadedness, or tiredness.
al-jadb wa al-qahṭ: barrenness and drought.
jaddad: revived.
jāh: fame, status.
jahl: Ignorance.
jiddah: newness.
jihād: struggle.
jizyah: a tax imposed on non-Msulims.
al-jumlah: in short.
junūd: (pl. of *jundī*) soldiers.
kabā'ir: major sins.
kalām: Islamic theology.
kamāl: perfection.
kāna nāfi'an: being beneficial.
kanz: a psychological disease largely appears among those who are of extreme religious course.
khaliq: the state of becoming shabby or worn out.
khalq: creation.
khānqāh: sojourn.
kharāj: land tax.
khāṭir: suggestion.
khawāṣ: the select few.
khawāṭir: (pl. of *khāṭir*) involuntary suggestions (lit. thoughts).
khayr: good.
al-khilāf wa al-jadal: jurisprudential polemics and dialectics.
khuluq: character, morality.
khusrān: loss.

khuṭbah: sermon.
kiswah: dress.
kitāb: book.
kufr: unbelief.
kul mutadayyin: every religious person.
kutub: (pl. of *kitāb*)books.
lā khayra fīh: in whom there is no goodness or benefit.
lā tufsidū: do not cause corruption.
lahum: for them.
laṭīfah: divine subtlety.
madāris: (pl. of *madrasah*) religious institutions of learning.
madhāhib: (pl. of *madhhab*) schools of thought.
madhhab: school of thought (lit. religious brotherhood or community).
madhmūmah: blameworthy.
madrasah: religious institution of learning (lit. school).
maḥmudah kulluhā: all praiseworthy.
maḥsūsāt: sense-perception.
māl: wealth.
mā lā ʿahda laka bih: a thing of which you have had no knowledge.
man: the one or those who.
manāzil: (pl. of *manzil*) stations.
manbaʿ kul fasād: the source of all corruption.
manzilah: status.
maqāṣid: (pl. of *maqṣid*) aims.
marḍā al-qulūb: those sick in the heart.
maʿrifah: gnosis.
maʿrūf: right (lit. know).
maṣdar: infinitive noun.
al-mashāhid al-muʿaẓẓamah: the venerated sanctuaries.
mashāyikh: (pl. of *shaykh*) (religious) leaders.
maskan: home.
mathārāt al-dhunūb: sins.
mawāʾiẓ: (pl. of *mawʿiẓah*) exhortations.
mazāj: disposition.
millah: religious community.
min afḍal al-ʿibādāt: one of the best types of worship.
mubāḥ: Permissible.
mubāḥ: permissible .
mubāyaʿah: paying homage.
mubtadiʾ: innovators.
mubtadiʿah: (pl .of *mubtadiʾ*)innovators.
mudāhanah: flattery.
muḍāriʿ: aorist.
mudrakāt khāṣah: certain perceptibles.

mufsid: corrupter.
mufsidāt: (pl .of *mufsid*) corrupters.
mufsidūn: those who do mischief.
muḥaqqiqīn: (pl. of *muḥaqqiq*) earnest ones.
mujaddid: revivalist.
mujāhadah: spiritual struggling, spiritual disciplining.
mujtahidūn: (pl. of *mujtahid*) practitioners of *ijtihād*.
mukallaf: charged.
mulk: state.
mulk al-qulūb: to dominate the hearts.
mulūk al-ṭawā'if: kings of parties or factions.
munkar: wrong.
munkarāt: (pl. of *munkar*) wrongs.
al-munkarāt al-ma'lūfah fī al-'ādāt: common wrongs in customs.
muqallid: a conformist or uncritical follower of authority.
al-Murābiṭūn: Almoravids.
murāghamah: being away from (lit. abandonment).
muṣālaḥah: conciliation.
mushahadah: seeing.
muṣliḥ: Islamic reformer.
muṣliḥ ijtimā'ī: social reformer.
muṣliḥūn: (pl .of *muṣliḥ*) Islamic reformers.
muta'aṣibūn: (pl. of *muta'aṣib*) fanatical followers.
mutakalimūn: (pl. of *mutakallim*) theologians.
mutakallim: theologian.
mutakallimūn: Muslim Theologians.
mutarassimūn: (pl. of *mutarasssim*) those who apparently resemble *'ulamā'*.
mutaṣawwifah: (pl. of *mutaṣawif*) mystics.
al-nahy 'an al-munkar: forbidding wrong.
nafs: self or soul.
naẓar: penetration.
ni'mah: blessing.
nifāq: hypocrisy.
nubuwwah: prophesy.
nūr: light.
qābiliyyah al-hazīmah: becoming disposed to defeat.
qāḍī al-qud'āh: the Chief Jurist.
qadhf al-muḥṣanāt: accusing chaste women of fornication.
qaḍī: judge.
qalb: heart.
qāṣidīn: seekers of guidance.
qāṣir: deficient.
qaṭ': cut.
qawī: strong.

qawl: opinion.
qiyās: analogy.
qudāh: (pl. of *qāḍī*) judges.
qūt: food.
quwwah al-ʿadl: the faculty of making a just equilibrium.
quwwah al-ʿilm: the faculty of rationalness.
quwwah al-ghaḍab: the faculty of anger.
quwwah al-irādah: the will-power.
quwwah al-shahwah: the faculty of desire.
raʿiyyah: subjects.
raʾs al-khaṭāyā al-muhlikah: the fountain-head of destructive sins.
raʾs kul khaṭīʾh: the beginning of all misdeeds.
raʾy: reasoning.
rabbāniyyah: superiority.
rajāʾ: hope.
rashwah: bribery.
riyāḍah: self-training.
riyāḍah al-nafs: disciplining of the soul.
rubʿ: quarter.
rūḥ: spirit.
rukn al-dīn: pillar of religion.
rushd: rectitude.
ruʾyah: naked eye (lit. looking).
sabʿiyyah: bestiality.
sabab: cause.
salaf: early Muslims.
ṣalāh: prayer.
ṣalāḥ: righteousnes, goodness.
al-salāmah min al-ʿayb: being free from defect.
ṣāliḥ: good, righteous.
ṣāliḥūn: (pl. of *ṣāliḥ*)righteous men.
samāʿ: hearing.
sawdāʾ: melancholy.
shādhah: deviators.
shahādah: i.e., there is no god but Allah and Muḥammad is the Messenger
    of Allah.
shahwah: desire.
shahwāt: (pl. of *shahwah*) desires.
shaqāwah: misery.
sharʿ: Islamic revealed Law.
sharʿī: religious (lit. jural).
sharʿiyyah: religious.
sharīʿa: law.
sharr: evil.

shaṭaḥ: ecstasy.
shaṭaḥāt: (pl. of *shaṭaḥ*) ecstatic utterances.
shawāriʿ: (pl. of *shāriʿ*) streets.
shayʾ: thing.
shaykh: (religious) leader.
shayṭāniyyah: devilry.
shirk: unbelief.
shurūṭ: (pl. of *sharṭ*) conditions.
silm: peace.
sūʾ: evil.
subḥānī: praise be to me.
sufahāʾ: (pl. of *safīh*) foolish ones.
ṣūfiyyah: (pl. of *ṣūfī*) sufis.
suḥt: unlawful.
ṣulḥ: conciliation, peace.
sulūk: actual disciplining.
al-suqūṭ min al-safar: travel-weariness.
surūr lā ghamm fīh: joy without sorrow.
taʾālīq: (pl. of *taʿlīqah*) lectures and works.
taʿaṣṣub: fanaticism.
ṭabʿ: nature.
tafakkur: reflection.
taghyīr: change.
taḥrīr al-addillah: formulating evidence.
ṭāiʾfah: community.
tajdīd: renewal or restoration.
takhārīj: citation of *ḥadīth*.
takhmīn maḥḍ: purely conjecture.
takhmīnī: conjectural.
takhrīj: verification (lit. interpretation).
al-talaf wa al-ʿaṭab: destruction and ruin.
ṭalāḥ: wickedness.
ṭalāḥah: fatigue, jadedness, or tiredness.
ṭālibīn: disciples.
ṭāliḥ: wicked.
taʿlīm: authoritative instruction.
taʿlīqah: lecture and work (lit. comment).
ṭāmāt: (pl. *ṭāmah*) heresies.
tamyīz: discernment.
tanaṭuʿ: extravagance.
taqdīm: preference.
taqlīd: imitation.
taqlīd maḥḍ: blind imitation.
taqwā: piety.

ṭarīq maʿrifah al-ḥaq: the way to get at truth.
ṭarīqah: method or way.
taṣāluḥ: reconciliation.
taṣawwuf: sufism.
tawakkul: having trust in God.
tawātur: impeccable transmission.
tawbah: repentance.
taʾwīl: exegesis.
thawbun jadīd: a new garment.
ʿulamāʾ: (pl .of *ʿālim*) scholars.
ʿulamāʾ al-ākhirah: otherworldly scholars.
ʿulamāʾ al-dunyā: worldly scholars.
ʿulamāʾ al-sūʾ: evil scholars.
al-ʿulūm al-ʿaqliyyah: intellectual knowledge.
ʿulūm maḥmūdah: praiseworthy knowledge.
ʿulūm muktasabah: acquired knowledge.
ummah: nation.
ummahāt dīnihim: their religion.
ʿumūm: generality or general character.
umūr burhāniyyah: demonstrated facts.
uṣūl: principles of Islamic jurisprudence.
ʿuyūb nafsih: the faults which acquire his soul..
wahmī: fancied.
waraʿ: scrupulousness.
wasaṭ: mean.
wasāṭah rūḥiyyah: Sufi spiritual mediating.
wasīṭ: mediator.
wazn: grammatical stem form (lit. weight).
wiswās: whispering.
yaqīn: certainty.
yufsidūn: they causing corruption.
yughayyiru: to change it.
yujaddid: to renew.
yuṣliḥu: to correct.
ẓāhir: outward.
ẓawāhir: (pl. of *ẓāhir*) outwards.
zāwiyah: hospice.
zuhd: asceticism, abstinent.

Introduction

"Yet thy Lord would never destroy communities for doing wrong while as its members were *muṣliḥūn*" (Qur'an, 11:117). This translated Qur'anic *āyah* (verse)[1] reveals one of the Divine norms relating to the life of communities; the efforts of the *muṣliḥūn*,[2] i.e., those who fulfil *iṣlāḥ* which may be translated roughly as reform,[3] are safeguards for the whole of their communities from general destruction.[4] This signifies, from a Qur'anic point view, the necessity of ongoing *iṣlāḥ* in any community. This necessity increases when *ifsād* (spreading or causing corruption), the opposite of *iṣlāḥ*, increases, because the spread of *fasād*[5] (corruption) in a community is a real threat to all its members, as the Qur'an warns.[6]

Furthermore, the mission of the prophets, according to the Qur'an, is to fulfil the duty of *iṣlāḥ*, as Prophet Shu'ayb clearly stated: "I desire only *al-iṣlāḥ*, as far as I am able" (Qur'an, 11:88). Thus, *iṣlāḥ* is an essential duty in the Islamic doctrine.

By attempting to correct the aspects of *fasād*, the *muṣliḥūn* undertake a prophetic mission and fulfil a vital Islamic duty. Therefore, it is not surprising to see that in every generation along the history of the Islamic *ummah*, there were a number of devoted Muslims working towards the fulfilment of the duty of *iṣlāḥ*, though every one in his own way.[7] These continuous efforts of the *muṣliḥūn* throughout Islamic history resulted in what can be called the 'legacy of the *muṣliḥūn*,' which includes their *iṣlāḥī* teachings, as well as their *iṣlāḥī* actions.

Although there have been continuous attempts at *iṣlāḥ* along the Islamic history[8] and the 'legacy of the *muṣliḥūn*' is so rich, the study of *iṣlāḥ* as a separate topic is somewhat new and the knowledge gap in the literature of *iṣlāḥ* is noticeably wide. The available studies that deal with *iṣlāḥ* as a separate topic are relatively few, and are mainly limited within the views and the achievements of a number of distinguished *muṣliḥūn* of the eighteenth, nineteenth and early twentieth centuries, who are considered the main contributors to the early modern movement of *iṣlāḥ*.[9]

The study of *iṣlāḥ*, I believe, should not be limited to the contribution of these *muṣliḥūn*, and should not ignore the earlier efforts of distinguished persons, who richly contributed to the 'legacy of the *muṣliḥūn*.' This is particularly because *iṣlāḥ*, as Merad justifiably puts it, "is deeply rooted in the basic soil of Islam, and cannot therefore be viewed solely in relation to the intellectual trends that appeared in the Muslim world at the beginning of the modern period."[10]

New scholarship studies on the *muṣliḥūn* in a wider scope are needed in order to discover their rich 'legacy' in depth, and shed more light on the topic of *iṣlāḥ*, as a distinctive Islamic duty. This is very important, particularly in the contemporary age in which the calls for *iṣlāḥ* have become very popular in the Islamdom, and led to an ongoing debate over various aspects of the projects of *iṣlāḥ*. By such new studies, it is hoped that much of these controversial issues would be treated systematically.

The present work is one step towards discovering part of the rich 'legacy of the *muṣliḥūn*' and is a conscious effort to shed some fresh light on the topic of *iṣlāḥ* as a distinctive Islamic duty by introducing the Imam Abū Ḥāmid Muḥammad al-Ghazālī (450/1059-505/1111) as a *muṣliḥ* (Islamic reformer), whose name 'springs to mind' among the long and honourable chain of the *muṣliḥūn*,[11] and by studying his main efforts and teachings, from an *iṣlāḥ* perspective.

This study may very likely meet some immediate objections, and in fact I have already experienced this. For those who may raise such abrupt objections at the outset, I would like to say right at the beginning that a fair judgment should be based on evaluating the methodology and the findings of the study rather than simply judging by the title.

The literature on al-Ghazālī

Numerous studies have been done on al-Ghazālī, in almost all the major languages of the world.[12] This is partially because he has been regarded as a highly respected thinker, and his thoughts have been fully appreciated by countless Muslims and non-Muslims alike. Masses of Muslims over the centuries since his time have regarded him as the *mujaddid*[13] (revivalist) of the 5th century AH as well as *ḥujjah al-islām*[14] (the Proof of Islam) and thus for them he is a leading authoritative figure and a unique Imam. At the same time, a number of well-known non-Muslim scholars have paid tribute to al-Ghazālī, and have heaped lavish words of praise on him, such as the following: "one of the greatest intellectuals of the Islamic society,"[15] "a great writer,"[16] "one of the most renowned and influential writers in the history of Muslim religious thought,"[17] "the greatest of all Muslims since the day of the Prophet,"[18] and "one of the greatest thinkers Islam [has] ever produced."[19]

The vast number of studies on this highly distinguished man is also due to the fact that he has contributed richly to various fields of thought, to the extent that he has been considered "a composite of great personalities [and] a master of various disciplines."[20] This explains why he has been introduced in a number of studies as a Sufi (Muslim mystic),[21] as a *faqīh* (jurist),[22] as a *mutakallim* (theologian),[23] as a critic of *kalām* (Islamic theology),[24] as a *faylasūf* (philosopher)[25] and as a critic of philosophy[26] at the same time.

Another reason which contributed to the considerable increase in the studies on al-Ghazālī is that his very complex course of life, as well as a number of his views and works, both the genuine ones and those whose authenticity has been questioned, have sparked off ongoing debates amongst scholars and have provoked sharp criticism among his critics since his age up to the present time.[27]

This fact about the number of the studies on al-Ghazālī has led some to say that it is difficult to find any element of originality in a new study on him, because he has been given all the deserved attention in academic research.[28] On the contrary, it has been argued that al-Ghazālī is far greater than to be fully covered in the studies to date, and that there is still much need for more studies on him.[29]

Although it is true that with this significant amount of studies, it is very challenging to display originality in a fresh study, I side with the second view. Moreover, I would add that there are various aspects of his life and thought, which have still not been adequately studied yet, and thus they deserve to be studied further. One of these, in my view, is the aspect of *iṣlāḥ*, which, despite its special importance, does not seem to have gained enough concern from researchers. As Ṣāliḥ al-Shāmī has rightly noticed, due to the blinding glare of the two famous honorific titles of al-Ghazālī, i.e., *ḥujjah al-islām* (the Proof of Islam) and the *mujaddid* (revivalist) of the 5th century AH, other titles are less well known, if at all, including the title *muṣliḥ* (Islamic reformer).[30]

To the best of my knowledge, there is as yet no detailed and focused study on al-Ghazālī as a *muṣliḥ*, but there are relatively few studies which have partially dealt with this crucial aspect. For example, in a chapter entitled *al-Imām al-Muṣliḥ*, al-Shāmī, in his well-presented general book about al-Ghazālī, gives just a few representative examples of his *iṣlāḥī* role.[31] Similarly, al-Nadwī, in a section of his book *Rijāl al-Firkr wa al-Daʿwah fī al-Islām*, presents him as a *muṣliḥ ijtimāʿī* (social reformer), and briefly discusses his social reform as represented in al-Ghazālī's most celebrated work, *Iḥyā' 'Ulūm al-Dīn*.[32] In a more interesting way, al-Kīlānī devotes a section in his unique book, *Hākadhā Ẓahr Jīl Ṣalāḥ al-Dīn wa Hākadhā 'Ādat al-Quds*, to al-Ghazālī's *iṣlāḥī* efforts.[33] The purpose of that section of the book was to briefly show al-Ghazālī's role in the *iṣlāḥī* movement, which, according to al-Kīlānī, developed over the 5th-6th century AH and resulted in a reformed Muslim generation, to which the Muslim leader Ṣalāḥ al-Dīn (Saladin, d. 589/1193) belonged, which could defeat the Crusaders.[34] Al-Ghazālī, al-Kīlānī argues, was the founder of that fruitful movement.[35] However, it was not intended in al-Kīlānī's book to study closely the *iṣlāḥī* efforts of al-Ghazālī. As a result, there are important relevant points, which have not been covered by al-Kīlānī, that deserve to be studied. Furthermore, some of his arguments, though positively presented, are questionable, and thus need to be examined. Moreover, he completely ignores the controversy over al-Ghazālī. It is hoped that the present study overcomes these shortcomings.

The problem

Besides the absolutely positive picture of al-Ghazālī as a *muṣliḥ* created in the above studies, a remarkably conflicting image of al-Ghazālī has been given by other writers. A good representative of these is al-Mahdāwī who considered al-Ghazālī as a representation of the backwardness of the Muslim *ummah* at that time, and that he reflects the defeat of the Muslims before the Crusaders,[36] totally opposite to al-Kīlānī's argument mentioned previously.

In a similar way, there have been two contrary positions on the worth of al-Ghazālī's thought. In the view of Lazarus-Yafeh, for example, al-Ghazālī's "ideas about religion, faith, the relationship between God and man and between man and man have always seemed extremely "modern" to me and are expressed so convincingly that they crossed the barriers of time and religion."[37] Yet according to al-Mahdāwī, his views are outdated and only deserve to be stored in "museums of thoughts."[38]

Such great controversy leads us to raise the following two central questions at the outset: (1) how far is it justified to consider al-Ghazālī as a *muṣliḥ* and (2) to what extent do al-Ghazālī's teachings of *iṣlāḥī* nature withstand criticism and prove worthy over time.

As a deliberate attempt to answer these controversial and challenging questions in a balanced way, I suggest the following positive hypothesis, and I will do my best to verify it in the course of subsequent chapters.

The hypothesis

The present study attempts to verify the following positive hypothesis:

At a late period of his life, al-Ghazālī sincerely devoted his career to *iṣlāḥ*. During this period, he made serious *iṣlāḥī* efforts, and effectively conveyed his *iṣlāḥī* teachings. These teachings have various great strengths, which withstand criticism highly and have proven useful over the centuries, as well as some serious weaknesses, which are potentially of negative influence, and are very open to criticism. As a result, his teachings have had two contrary effects: one is positive and favourable and the other is negative and unappreciative. Despite such weaknesses, and regardless of their negative consequences, al-Ghazālī can still be properly classified as a *muṣliḥ*.

It is difficult to claim that by determinedly attempting to prove this hypothesis, I would resolve the problem concerning the conflicting images of al-Ghazālī illustrated above, but it is hoped that valid interpretation of the causes of this phenomenon will be given, and that some possible partial solutions will be proffered.

The methodology and the structure

Hoping to verify the above hypothesis, I have taken the following methodological steps:

1. Constructing an analytical definition of *iṣlāḥ*: To correctly judge whether al-Ghazālī was a *muṣliḥ* necessitates that we first define the term *iṣlāḥ*. In addition, the definition of *iṣlāḥ* shall provide us with essential prerequisites and important tools for systematically studying al-Ghazālī as a *muṣliḥ*. Since I, with the best of my ability in literature search, have not been able to find a definition of the term which is sufficient for the purpose of the present study, I have had to construct a provisional definition in Chapter One. To achieve this, I have analysed the morphology of the term *iṣlāḥ* and its lexical explanation. In addition, because it is an Islamic concept, I have also analysed its usages in the Qur'an and the Ḥadīth. In addition to defining it, I have taken the following two steps to further clarify the term: firstly, I have examined the extent to which the English term 'reform', which is usually used as a rendering of *iṣlāḥ*, is an equivalent translation of it. Secondly, I have examined the similarities and differences between *iṣlāḥ* and each of the following concepts which are sometimes connected to it, whether justifiably or not: *tajdīd* (renewal or restoration), *taghyīr* (change), and *al-amr bi al-maʿrūf wa al-nahy ʿan al-munkar* (commanding right and forbidding wrong).

2. Setting the historical context: In the belief that it is important to bear in mind the historical context in which al-Ghazālī lived, in order not to misunderstand and misjudge his efforts and teachings, I have presented an overview of his age in Chapter Two. The overview focuses on the political setting and the religio-intellectual life at that time, which shall provide sufficient background and an essential foundation for the unfolding discussion.

3. Discussing the life-experience of al-Ghazālī: To clearly and justifiably show in which period of his life, he really sought *iṣlāḥ*, and which of his works represent that period, I have discussed in Chapter Three, at considerable length, his life-experience, relying primarily on his own account about his spiritual and

intellectual progression in his genuine book *al-Munqidh min al-Ḍalāl* (Deliverance from Error), and also on the primary available biographies of al-Ghazālī. Since the truthfulness of al-Ghazālī's account has been the object of doubt, I have closely dealt with such doubt throughout the chapter.

4. Surveying al-Ghazālī's *iṣlāḥī* efforts: Since it is essential to determine the extent of al-Ghazālī's *iṣlāḥī* efforts, in order to be able to fairly justify the classification of al-Ghazālī as a *muṣliḥ*, I have tried to objectively survey his main *iṣlāḥī* efforts in Chapter Four. The survey is based on a careful study of al-Ghazālī's major authentic works, which belong to his *iṣlāḥī* period, namely the *Iḥyā'*.

5. Assessing al-Ghazālī's *iṣlāḥī* teachings: For the purpose of discovering the main strengths and weaknesses of al-Ghazālī's *iṣlāḥī* teachings and judging how far they stand criticism, I have devoted Chapter Five to the assessment of his *iṣlāḥī* teachings in general, and to a discussion of the main criticisms levelled against his views and teachings. The assessment in this chapter is based on the following major criteria: (1) originality, (2) clarity, (3) deepness, (4) balance between individualism and collectivism, (5) realism and practicality, and (6) Islamic-justification. By judging with this range of criteria, though apparently limited, the assessment has, I hope, covered the key points which serve the intended purpose.

6. Studying the effects of al-Ghazālī's attempts at *iṣlāḥ*: To evaluate the consequences of al-Ghazālī's attempts at *iṣlāḥ*, I have discussed in Chapter Six a number of phenomena which have been regarded as effects of al-Ghazālī's efforts and I have assessed the main controversy surrounding the evaluation of these effects.

Despite their limitations, which seem unavoidable in a timed study like the present, these steps have been reasonably fruitful in verifying the suggested hypothesis, as shall be illustrated in the following chapters.

Notes

1. For translating this and other Qur'anic quotations, I have consulted the following translations of the Qur'an: (1) Arberry J. Arberry, *The Koran: Interpreted*, Oxford: Oxford University Press, 1982; (2) A. Yusuf Ali, *The Holy Qur'an: Text, Translation and Commentary*, Bierut: Dār al-Qur'ān, n.d.; (3) M.A.S. Abdel Haleem, *The Qur'an: A New Translation*, Oxford: Oxford University Press, 2004; and (4) N.J. Dawood, *The Koran: Translated with Notes*, London: Penguin Books Ltd, 1999. My translation, however, largely follows Arberry's most poetic translation, but with frequent amendments to this, especially when I think there is misunderstanding of the original text.

2. Sing. *muṣliḥ*.

3. More about the meaning of *iṣlāḥ*, and its English equivalent, will be discussed in Chapter One.

4. This is based on the *tafsīr* (Exegesis) of the Prophet's renowned companion, Ibn 'Abbās (d. 68/687f), see Ibn 'Abbās, *tafsīr*, Qur'an, 11:117, online version: *http://altafsir.com/Tafasir.asp?tMadhNo=0&tTafsirNo=10&tSoraNo=11&tAyahNo=117&tDisplay=yes&UserProfile=0*, visited on 11/07/2007.

5. More about this term will be discussed below.

6. Read, for example, Qur'an, 17:16.

7. For a brief discussion of the historical continuity of *iṣlāḥ* in the Islamic history, see: A. Merad, *Iṣlāḥ, EI²*, Leiden: E.J. Brill, 1978, Vol. 4, pp. 141f.

8. Cf. al-Sayyid Abū al-Ḥasan 'Alī al-Nadwī, *Rijāl al-Fikr wa al-Da'wah fī al-Islām*, Damascus: Dār al-Qalam, 2002, Vol. 1, p. 93.

9. For an informitive outline of the contributers to this movement, though within the Arab nationalist dimension, see: Basheer M. Nafi, *The Rise and Decline of the Arab-Islamic Reform Movement*, London: The Institute of Contemporary of Islamic Thought, 2000.

10. Merad, *Iṣlāḥ, EI²*, Vol. 4, p. 141.

11. Ibid, p. 142.

12. To gain a rough idea about this interesting phenomenon, visit the following website, which contains hundreds of books and articles about al-Ghazālī in various languages: *http://www.ghazali.org*.

13. See, for example, Muḥammad b. Muḥammad al-Ḥusaynī al-Zabīdī, known as Murtaḍā al-Zabīdī (d. 1205/1791), *Itḥāf al-Sādah al-Muttaqīn bi Sharḥ Iḥyā' 'Ulūm al-Dīn*, Beirut: Dār al-Kutub al-'Ilmiyyah, 2005, Vol. 1, pp. 35-37.

14. See, for instance, Tāj al-Dīn al-Subkī (d. 771/1370), *Ṭabaqāt al-Shāfi'iyyah al-Kubrā*, Cairo: al-Maṭba'ah al-Ḥusayniyyah, 1906, p. 101.

15. W. Montgomery Watt, *Muslim Intellectual: A Study of al-Ghazali*, Edinburgh: The University Press, 1963, p. 1.

16. Margaret Smith, *al-Ghazali the Mystic*, London: Luzac and co., 1944, p. 5.

17. R.M. Frank, *al-Ghazālī and the Ash'arite School*, Durham: Duke University Press, 1994, p. 1.

18. Samuel M. Zwemer, *A Moslem Seeker After God*, p. ii.

19. Hava Lazarus-Yafeh, *Studies in al-Ghazali*, p. 3.

20. Aḥmad Z.M. Ḥammād, "Abū Ḥāmid al-Ghazālī's Juristic Doctrine in *al-Mustaṣfā min 'Ilm al-Uṣūl* with a translation of Volume one of *al-Mustaṣfā min 'Ilm al-Uṣūl*," a PhD dissertation, the University of Chicago, March 1987, Vol. 1, p. 2, available online in PDF: *http://www.ghazali.org/books/azhmd-p1.pdf*.

21. As in the book of Smith, *al-Ghazali the Mystic*, London: Luzac and co., 1944.

22. As in the study of Ḥammād, "Abū Ḥāmid al-Ghazālī's Jurist Doctrine in al-Mustaṣfā."

23. As in the study of M.A.R. Bisar, "al-Juwayni and al-Ghazali as theologians with special reference to al-Irshad and al-Iqtisad," a PhD thesis submitted to Edinburgh University in 1953.

24. As in the book of Richard M. Frank, *al-Ghazālī and the Ash'arite School*, Durham: Duke University Press, 1994.

25. As in the study of 'Abd al-Amīr al-A'sam, *al-Faylasūf al-Ghazālī: I'ādah Taqwīm li Munḥanā Taṭwwrih al-Ruḥī*, Amzil (Tonisia): al-Dār al-Tūnisiyyah li al-Nashir, 1988.

26. As in the book of Iysa A Bello, *The Medieval Islamic Controversy between Philosophy and Orthodoxy: Ijmā' and Ta'wīl in the Conflict between al-Ghazālī and Ibn Rushd*, Leiden: E.J. Brill, 1989.

27. For an outline of a number of the critics of al-Ghazālī over the centuries and a brief discussion of their main criticisms, see Yusuf al-Qaradawi, *al-Imām al-Ghazālī bayn Mādiḥīh wa Nāqidīh*, Beirut: Mu'assasah al-Risālah, 1994, pp. 117-186.

28. As in the book of al-A'sam, *al-Faylasūf al-Ghazālī*.

29. Farīd Juḥā, *Abū Ḥāmid al-Ghazālī*, Damascus: Ṭilās li al-Dirāsāt wa al-Tarjamah wa al-Nashir, 1986, p. 13.

30. Ṣāliḥ Aḥmad al-Shāmī, *al-Imām al-Ghazālī: Ḥujjah al-Islam wa Mujaddid al-Mi'ah al-Khāmisah*, Damascus: Dār al-Qalam, 1993, pp. 7f.

31. Al-Shāmī, *al-Imām al-Ghazālī*, pp. 195-256.

32. Al-Nadwī, *Rijāl*, Vol. 1, pp. 295-315.

33. Mājid 'Irsān al-Kīlānī, *Hākadhā Ẓahr Jīl Ṣalāḥ al-Dīn wa Hākadhā 'Ādat al-Quds*, Dubai: Dār al-Qalam, 2002, pp. 101-174. This

34. Al-Kīlānī, *Hākadhā Ẓahr Jīl Ṣalāḥ al-Dīn*, pp. 101 &174.

35. Ibid, p. 101.
36. Ismāʿīl al-Mahdāwī, *Abū Ḥāmid al-Ghazālī: al-Falsafah al-Taṣawwuf wa ʿIlm al-Kalām*, Marrakesh: Tansift, 1993, p. 6.
37. Hava Lazarus-Yafeh, *Studies in al-Ghazzali*, Jerusalem: The Magnes Press, The Hebrew University, 1975, p. 3.
38. Al-Mahdāwī, *Abū Ḥāmid al-Ghazālī*, p. 7.

1

Analytical definition of *iṣlāḥ*

*D*efining the concept of *iṣlāḥ* is an essential and practical start for studying al-Ghazālī as a *muṣliḥ* (Islamic reformer). The definition is a form of reference for the topic. To judge correctly whether al-Ghazālī was a *muṣliḥ* or not, depends initially on what is meant by *iṣlāḥ*.

Moreover, a number of basic elements, which form a sound and logical foundation for the topic, are expected to be obtained by dealing with this essential question. A list of key words on the topic of *iṣlāḥ* is developed through the activity of defining it. The scope of *iṣlāḥ* are also very likely to be specified in its definition. In addition, the definition, when precisely constructed, provides proper parameters for limiting the topic, and excluding that which does not relate to it. Similarly, the distinguishing characteristics which clarify *iṣlāḥ* and separate it from other topics, with which it might be confused, is provided by the definition. Furthermore, the criteria by which an occurrence of *iṣlāḥ* is determined are invoked in its definition. Based on all these necessary elements, it can be decided what aspects of al-Ghazālī's thought and efforts are related to the topic of *iṣlāḥ*, and thus should be considered in the present study.

Since it does not seem that there is a ready-made definition of *iṣlāḥ* to satisfy the purpose of the present study in the available related literature,[1] there is a special need to construct a satisfactory definition of the term at the very beginning of the present study.

Having stated this, the following question arises: which method of defining can fulfil the present need? Among the various possible methods of defining,[2] the analytical method appears to be the most useful and thus it is chosen here to define *iṣlāḥ*. In addition to the fact that it is broadly considered the best method of defining,[3] the analytical method is very fruitful in the context of the present study. Defining *iṣlāḥ* by giving a detailed analysis of it provides much-needed elaboration of the concept and not just a simple introduction to its meaning.[4]

The approach taken in this analysis is semantic. This approach, "as the name itself reveals, literally means to analyse the structure of [a] word along the lines indicated by the articulation of its meaning."[5] This method of semantic analysis, as Toshihiko Izutsu clearly explains, "consists in applying a careful procedure of linguistic analysis to the meaning structure of [a] word, in splitting up its complex structure of meaning into a number of well-defined constituents."[6]

The choice of this method leads to another logical question: what data should be considered in this analysis in order to attain the previously stated essential and practical result? Since *iṣlāḥ* is essentially an Arabic term, the first obvious piece of data which needs to be considered here is the available meaning and usages of the term in the Arabic language. This is done in two steps described in page 3: the first is analysing the morphological description of *iṣlāḥ*, and the second is analysing the available explanation of the term in a number of leading and celebrated Arabic lexicons.[7]

In addition to this essential type of data, the original Islamic perspective of *iṣlāḥ* also has to be considered in defining the concept. This is because firstly *iṣlāḥ* is an Islamic concept, as "it is deeply rooted in the basic soil of Islam."[8] Secondly, the topic of the this book lies within an Islamic context—al-Ghazālī is studied as an Islamic reformer—and thus the definition of *iṣlāḥ* is employed particularly in this context. For these reasons, the usages of the term *iṣlāḥ* in the Qur'an and the Ḥadīth—the two essential Islamic resources which provide the basis of the Islamic conception of the term—are analysed in page 7.

Based on the findings of all these analysed dimensions of the concept, the definition of *iṣlāḥ* is practically formulated in page 15.

Other than the first essential aim of defining *iṣlāḥ*, this chapter has two more objectives, which shall contribute in clarifying the concept of *iṣlāḥ*. The first is to examine the extent to which the English term "reform," which is usually used as a rendering of *iṣlāḥ*,[9] is an equivalent translation of the Arabic term *iṣlāḥ*. In page 16, this examination is done in the light of the constructed definition of *iṣlāḥ*, and the meanings of the term "reform" as well as its usage.

The last objective of the present chapter is to understand the differences and similarities between *iṣlāḥ* and other concepts which are sometimes connected to it, justifiably or not. Since "it is not often that one can analyse a concept without also considering other concepts which are related to it, similar to it, or in some way importantly connected with it,"[10] *iṣlāḥ* is compared and contrasted with each of the following concepts in page 17: *tajdīd* (renewal or restoration), *taghyīr* (change), and *al-amr bi al-maʿrūf wa al-nahy ʿan al-munkar* (commanding right and forbidding wrong).

Iṣlāḥ in the Arabic language

To satisfactorily analyse the meaning of the term *iṣlāḥ* in Arabic, at least two essential pieces of linguistic information have to be studied: the morphological description of the term and the available lexical explanation of it. The former gives the basics and provides some useful hints for consulting the Arabic lexicons, while the lexicons themselves provide the literal meanings of the term, and also cross-refer to the related words and demonstrate their usage by Arabs. This will be evident in the following two sub-sections.

Morphological description of iṣlāḥ

The term *iṣlāḥ* is the *maṣdar* (infinitive noun) of the transitive verb *aṣlaḥa* since the *wazn* (stem form) of its verb is *afʿala*, as is known in Arabic morphology. The basic root of this transitive verb is *ṣalaḥa*, an intransitive verb which is derived from its *maṣdar ṣalāḥ*. And the epithet from *ṣalāḥ* is *ṣāliḥ*, whereas the epithet from *iṣlāḥ* is *muṣliḥ*. All these derivatives share the same three basic radical letters, which are *ṣ-l-ḥ*.

From this basic morphological explanation, four essential general conclusions emerge. First, *iṣlāḥ* denotes the same phenomenon as that indicated by its verb *aṣlaḥa* but it is free from time or tense, unlike the verb. Second, *iṣlāḥ* is a causative term, the outcome of which is *ṣalāḥ* or a *ṣāliḥ* thing/person. Third, the performer of *iṣlāḥ* is called *muṣliḥ* or in other words a *muṣliḥ* is one who conducts *iṣlāḥ*. Fourth, all these derivatives are related and thus studying them should all help in clarifying the idea of *iṣlāḥ*.

Before proceeding to the next sub-section, an important limitation of the topic should be presented at once. According to al-Jawharī, the *maṣdar* of *ṣulḥ*—a noun which means *silm*[11] (peace) and *taṣāluḥ*[126] (reconciliation)—is not *ṣalāḥ*, but rather *ṣilāḥ*,[125] which means *muṣālaḥah*[14] (conciliation). On the basis of this precise lexical explanation, two main divisions of *iṣlāḥ* can be differentiated here in respect of their outcome: the first causes *ṣalāḥ*, while the second brings *ṣulḥ*. Consequently, it can be stated that the latter does not lie within the scope of this study, though it is called *iṣlāḥ* and the epithet derived from it is *muṣliḥ*.

By studying al-Ghazālī as a *muṣliḥ*, it is not intended to study him as one who makes *ṣulḥ* (reconciliation) between disputants. Therefore, whatever is related to the topic of *ṣulḥ* is not part of the concern of the present study, and in the interests of conciseness, is not even considered in the proposed definition of *iṣlāḥ*.

Lexical explanation of iṣlāḥ[15]

The term *iṣlāḥ*[16] is defined as the opposite of *ifsād* in the consulted Arabic lexicons, which explicitly mention the term,[17] and no further interpretation is given. Supposedly, studying the meaning of *ifsād* in its respective location[18] in the lexicons sheds some light on the meaning of *iṣlāḥ* in a contrary way; however, no direct definition is given there. This makes it a necessity to study the other related derivatives of *iṣlāḥ*, as well as *ifsād*, in order to find clues for more clarification of the idea of *iṣlāḥ*.

Starting with the transitive verb *aṣlaḥa*, two related senses of the term are given in two different contexts. The phrase *aṣlaḥa al-shay'* (a thing) means *azāla fasādah*[19] (He removed its *fasād*). And in the phrase *aṣlaḥa al-shay' ba'da fasād*,[20] the verb *aṣlaḥa* means *aqāma*[21] (to set right or correct). Thus, the phrase can be translated as "he set right or corrected the thing after *fasād*."

These senses of *aṣlaḥa* clearly show that the act of *iṣlāḥ* is directed only against *fasād*, and this is a crucial limitation of the idea of *iṣlāḥ*. Moreover, they suggest that *iṣlāḥ* is a corrective change of *fasād*. This indication ought to be the core of the definition of *iṣlāḥ*, since it presents the superior category to which *iṣlāḥ* belongs—i.e., that of change—and at the same time it highlights an essential distinguishing characteristic of *iṣlāḥ*, that is, correctness.

By linking this very significant finding with the fact that the outcome of *iṣlāḥ* is *ṣalāḥ*, as stated earlier, *iṣlāḥ* can be basically defined as a corrective change of *fasād* into *ṣalāḥ*. Now, to expand this rather vague definition, the available meanings and usages of both *fasād* and *ṣalāḥ* in the lexicons must be studied.

As to *ṣalāḥ*, it is defined in almost all of the consulted lexicons only by its opposite: *ṭalāḥ* in some lexicons[22] and *fasād* in others.[23] The *Mu'jam al-Waṣīṭ*, however, is an exception, for it gives two senses for *ṣalāḥ*.[24] The first sense is *istiqāmah*. It literally refers to being in a path following a straight line and it is figuratively likened to being in a right path.[25] Obviously, this figurative meaning of *al-istiqāmah* is the one which is applicable to *ṣalāḥ*, rather than the literal meaning. The second sense of *ṣalāḥ* is *al-salāmah min al-ʿayb*[26] (being free from defect), which is a negative sense of the term.

Furthermore, *ṣalāḥ* may also refer to a state of benefit as can be concluded from one of the senses of the intransitive verb *ṣalaḥa*. In the *Muʿjam al-Wasīṭ*,[27] this verb can be used in the sense of *kāna nāfiʿan* (being beneficial).

Another shade of meaning for *ṣalāḥ* is observed by reflecting on a figurative usage of the aoristic verb *yaṣluḥu* stated in some lexicons as in the following sayings: *hādhā al-shayʾ yaṣluḥu lak*[28] (this thing is suitable for you), *hādhā al-adīm yaṣluḥu li al-naʿl*[29] (this leather is suitable for sandals), and *fulān lā yaṣluḥu lisuḥbatik*[30] (such a person is not appropriate to accompany you). According to this usage, *ṣalāḥ* implies suitability or appropriateness.

In the light of the senses of *ṣalāḥ* previously discussed, it can be stated that the outcome of the act of *iṣlāḥ* is a state of benefit, directness in the sense of commitment to a right path, absence of defect and suitability.

Turning to the two opposites of *ṣalāḥ*, a number of meanings and usages of the terms are mentioned in Arabic lexicons and are thus worth studying. With regard to *fasād*, it is used in the following senses, as listed in the *Muʿjam al-Wasīṭ*:[31] *al-talaf wa al-ʿatab* (destruction and ruin), *al-iḍṭirāb wa al-khalal* (disorder and deficiency), *al-jadb wa al-qaḥṭ* (barrenness and drought), and *ilḥāq al-ḍarar*[32] (inflicting detriment). If we examine these senses, the last one appears to be the most general, since the others can be regarded as various forms of detriment.

Additional forms of *fasād* can be concluded from the following usage of its verb *fasada*. In the phrase *fasada al-shayʾ*, *fasada* can mean:[33] *baṭala* (became false, invalid or of no avail). Thus, a further form of *fasād* is a state of falsehood or invalidity.

One more form of *fasād* can be learned from the origins of the name of *ḥarb al-fasād* applied to a war which happened in the pre-Islamic period between two Arab sub-tribes.[34] It was called so, because the first group patched their sandals with the ears of the second, and the second group drank wine in the skulls of the first.[35] Giving this war in particular the name of *ḥarb al-fasād* indicates that these acts deviated unjustifiably from the established moderation of warfare at the time. Consequently, an unjustified deviation from an established moderate norm is a form of *fasād*.

Unlike *fasād*, no direct and explicit meaning is found in the lexicons for the second antonym, *ṭalāḥ*. However, a meaning is given to a related infinitive: *al-ṭalāḥah*, which means *al-i'yā*[36] (fatigue, jadedness, or tiredness) and *al-suqūṭ min al-safar*[37] (travel-weariness).[38] Related to *ṭalāḥ* also, *iṭlāḥ* is given as a *maṣdar* for the transitive verb *aṭlaḥa* as in *aṭlaḥtuhu anā iṭlāḥā*[39] meaning *ḥasartuhu*[40] (I weakened him or I fatigued him). Another similar usage is stated for the related inflection *ṭalīḥ*. It is used as an epithet in the saying *nāqah ṭalīḥu asfār*[41] meaning *jahadahā al-sayr wa hazalahā*[42] (a she-camel exhausted and rendered lean by its journeys). By linking all these similar and related meanings, it can be concluded that *ṭalāḥ* implies lack of ability to function according to one's essential nature, due to overwork or overuse.

In addition, *al-ṭalāḥ* implies lack of goodness or benefit, as is indicated by a usage of the related word *ṭāliḥ*. When it is applied to a man, *ṭāliḥ* means *lā khayra fīh*[43] (in whom there is no goodness or benefit).

The Islamic perspective of *iṣlāḥ*

As with any Islamic term, the definition of *iṣlāḥ* has to include the Islamic dimension of the term, especially when the definition is used within an Islamic context, such as the present topic. This vital dimension is highlighted below by examining the usages of the term in the two essential Islamic resources: the Qur'an and the Ḥadīth.

The Qur'anic usages of iṣlāḥ

The term *iṣlāḥ* and the related derivatives are used in the Qur'an in various contexts.[44] Some of these usages, however, are beyond the scope of the present examination and thus they are excluded right from the beginning. Among these excluded usages are those in the context of *ṣulḥ*,[45] because it is outside the range of this study, as noted above. Also the usages of *iṣlāḥ* as a direct action of Allah[46] are excluded for the same reason.

Thus, the examination here is restricted to the Qur'anic contexts in which the idea of *iṣlāḥ* is referred to as a human task, the outcome of which is a state of *ṣalāḥ*. The approach of this examination is semantic. It attempts to derive the meanings from the text itself. For the purpose of elucidation, two helpful tools are used. The first is to examine each Qur'anic text in the light of its context. The context usually gives helpful hints for the intended meaning of the text.[47] The second useful tool is to link the text under examination with the related Qur'anic texts in other places since very often "the Qur'an explains itself."[48] Within the extent of this approach, a number of the most celebrated Qur'anic exegeses, both early and late, are consulted, with special attention given to exegeses focusing on semantic indications.

A very basic point observed by examining the Qur'anic usages of *iṣlāḥ* meaning a human task is that the term *iṣlāḥ* does not seem to be transferred from its original Arabic meanings to a purely religious or technical meaning as in the usages of some other Qur'anic concepts. Moreover, the idea of *iṣlāḥ* is presented in the Qur'an as meaning the opposite of *ifsād*. This is evident in a number of *āyāt* (Qur'anic verses) which mention the two ideas in conflict with each other. For instance, the Qur'an states "Allah knows the *mufsid* from the *muṣliḥ*" (Qur'an, 2:220).

However, the Qur'anic usages of *iṣlāḥ* and its opposite indicate a number of distinguishing characteristics of the Islamic perspective of *iṣlāḥ*, which add some unique Islamic nuances to the concept. It is important then to consider these characteristics and nuances in defining the concept of *iṣlāḥ* from the Islamic perspective.

One of these distinguishing characteristics concerns the evaluation of *iṣlāḥ*. The Qur'an considers *iṣlāḥ* as an extremely necessary, very honourable and highly praised task. From the Qur'anic prospective, *iṣlāḥ* is a safeguard for society, as the Qur'an clearly states: "Thy Lord would not destroy communities unjustly while their members were *muṣliḥūn*" (Qur'an, 11:117). In addition, the reward of the *muṣliḥūn* is guaranteed in the Qur'an; Allah states: "surely We leave not to waste the reward of the *muṣliḥūn*" (Qur'an, 7:170). At the same time, the *mufsidūn*, totally opposite to the *muṣliḥūn*, are strongly condemned in the Qur'an: "Allah loves not the *mufsidūn*" (Qur'an, 5:64 and 28:77).

Moreover, fulfilling the task of *iṣlāḥ* was the utmost concern of the prophets mentioned in the Qur'an. The Prophet Shu'ayb, for instance, clearly states to his people: "I desire only the *iṣlāḥ*, as far as I am able" (Qur'an, 11:88). Similarly, the Qur'an quotes the Prophet Ṣāliḥ as he forbids his people from *ifsād* (Qur'an, 7:74). Accordingly, those who occupy themselves chiefly with *iṣlāḥ* tread in the steps of the prophets and thus they are appropriately regarded as *muṣliḥūn* from the Islamic perspective. This, then, may rightly be considered an Islamic standard for a *muṣliḥ*, i.e., *iṣlāḥ* should be the top priority of one who ranks among the *muṣliḥūn*.

Comprehensiveness is another characteristic of the Qur'anic perspective of *iṣlāḥ*. The Qur'anic scope of *iṣlāḥ* is very broad; it includes various fields and is not limited within the confines of religion in its strict sense. This appears in the following observations.

First, the usage of the term *iṣlāḥ* denotes generality in the following *āyah*: "They ask thee concerning orphans. Say: *iṣlāḥ* for them (*lahum*) is good" (Qur'an, 2:220). As the term *iṣlāḥ* here is indefinite and followed by *lahum*, it is not restricted to any particular matter to do with orphans but instead is related to all their affairs.[49]

Second, the verb *aṣlaḥa* is linked with *tawbah* (Islamic repentance) for different kinds of sin and crime: (1) theft (*sariqah*) in Qur'an, 5:38-39, (2) fornication (*fāḥishah*) in Qur'an, 4:15-16, (3) evil (*sū'*) in Qur'an, 6:54 & Qur'an, 16:119, (4) concealing what Allah has sent down in clear proofs and guidance (*kitmān mā anzala Allāh min al-bayyināt wa al-hudā*) in Qur'an, 2:159-60, (5) denying belief after believing (*kufr ba'da īmān*) in Qur'an, 3:86-9, (6) hypocrisy (*nifāq*) in Qur'an, 4:145-146, and (7) accusing chaste women of fornication (*qadhf al-muḥṣanāt*) in Qur'an, 24:5. It is worth noting that the idea of *iṣlāḥ* in these contexts is related to the self, as the contexts suggest, although the verb *aṣlaḥa* has no explicit object in any of them.[50]

Finally, the broad variety in the examples of the *mufsidūn*, and similarly the examples of *ifsād* mentioned in the Qur'an, indicate in a contrary way the wide scope of the Qur'anic perspective of *iṣlāḥ*. Some of the clearest examples of the *mufsidūn* given in the Qur'an are as follows. Firstly, hypocrites: in referring to them, Allah says: "Truly, they themselves are the *mufsidūn* but they are not sensible" (Qur'an, 2:11). Secondly, the people of the Prophet Lot: in Qur'an, 29:30, for example, the Prophet Lot prays: "My Lord, give me victory over the people who are *mufsidūn*." Thirdly, Pharaoh and his chiefs: "Then We sent, after them, Moses with Our tokens to Pharaoh and his chiefs, but they acted unjustly towards them. So behold thou how was the end of the *mufsidūn*" (Qur'an, 7:103). Fourthly, the sorcerers of Pharaoh before they believed in the Lord of the Prophet Moses:

> *Then, when the sorcerers came, Moses said to them, 'Cast down whatever you will cast.' And when they had cast, Moses said, 'What you have produced is sorcery; Surely Allah will suppress it. Surely, Allah upholds not the work of the mufsidūn.* (Qur'an, 10:80-81)

Lastly, the transgressors (*al-fāsiqūn*): after mentioning them in Qur'an, 2:26, the Qur'an in the following *āyah* lists some of their attributes. Among these attributes is that they are "causing corruption (*yufsidūn*) in the earth." Among the examples of *ifsād* indicated in the Qur'an are the following:

1. Barring others from the path of Allah, as is suggested by the following *āyah*: "For those who disbelieve and bar [others] from the path of Allah, We shall add chastisement over their chastisement, for that they were causing corruption (*yufsidūn*)" (Qur'an, 16:88). The *āyah* shows that these people deserve two penalties. Since they are disbelievers, it is understood that the first penalty is for their disbelief. The additional penalty therefore has to be for their additional evil deed, that is, barring others from the path of Allah.[51] Thus, their act of *ifsād* refers to this evil deed since it is the cause of their additional penalty, as is understood from the phrase "for that they were causing corruption (*yufsidūn*)."

2. Shedding blood: after being told by the Creator that a successor will be set on the earth, the angels reply in Qur'an, 2:30: "How can Thou set therein one who will cause corruption (*yufsid*) on it and shed blood …" Since the conjunctional style in this reply is in the type of *ʿatf al-khāṣ ʿalā al-ʿām*[52] (joining the particular to the general), then it is understood that shedding blood is *ifsād*.

3. Destroying tillage and stock: with the same conjunctional style as in the above example, the verb *yufsidu* is joined with the phrase "to destroy tillage and stock" in Qur'an, 2:205.

4. Turning away from the truth and following falsehood: this can be derived from Qur'an, 3:62-63. Following an episode from the story of Jesus, the Qur'an comments:

    This certainly is the true narrative. There is none worthy of worship save Allah, and surely Allah is the All-mighty, the All-wise. And if they turn away, surely Allah knows the mufsidūn. (Qur'an, 3:62-63)

    This context shows that turning away from the truth and following falsehood instead is *ifsād*.[53]

The most distinguishing characteristic of the Qur'anic perspective of *iṣlāḥ* is the one concerning its criteria. It is essential to note that, from the Qur'anic perspective, not every claim of *iṣlāḥ* can be justified as a real *iṣlāḥ*. The claim of the hypocrites which is refuted in the Qur'an proves this. When it is said to the hypocrites that they should not cause *ifsād*, they are quoted in the Qur'an as saying: "we are only *muṣliḥūn*" (Qur'an, 2:11), but the Qur'an refutes this claim: "Truly, they themselves are the *mufsidūn* but they are not sensible." (Qur'an, 2:12).

This shows that certain criteria have to be met in order to justify a case of *iṣlāḥ* from the Qur'anic perspective. The Qur'anic usages of *iṣlāḥ* and the related words indicate a number of such essential criteria.

Among these criteria is conforming to the original right order of the earth and its beneficial norms, which have been set by the Creator. This is indicated in Qur'an, 7:56: "Do not cause corruption (*lā tufsidū*) in the earth after the *iṣlāḥ* of which." The phrase "after the *iṣlāḥ* of which" indicates that it is *ifsād* to change the original right order of the earth and its beneficial norms which have been set by the Creator.[54] As a result, conforming to them is a criterion of *iṣlāḥ*.

Another criterion of *iṣlāḥ* indicated in the Qur'an is being committed to truthfulness, since the opposite is a criterion of *ifsād*, as stated in the Qur'an. Following an episode from the story of Jesus, the Qur'an comments:

> *This certainly is the true narrative. There is none worthy of worship save Allah, and surely Allah is the All-mighty, the All-wise. And if they turn away, surely Allah knows the mufsidūn.* (Qur'an, 3:62-63).

This context shows that turning away from the truth and following falsehood instead is a sign of *ifsād*.[55] On the contrary, committing to truthfulness is a criterion of *iṣlāḥ*.

Two further criteria of *iṣlāḥ* are: being firmly committed to the Scripture of Allah and seriously worshipping Him. These criteria can be highlighted in the following examination of the *āyah* Qur'an, 7:170. This *āyah* starts with the relative pronoun "those" and is followed by two descriptions, those "who hold fast to the Scripture and keep up the prayer." It appears from the predicate in the *āyah*, which is "surely we do not waste the wage of the *muṣliḥūn*," that these descriptions are for the *muṣliḥūn*.

Prophetic usages of iṣlāḥ

As the second primary source of Islam after the Qur'an, the Prophetic Ḥadīth need to be consulted in order to gain a complete picture of the original Islamic perspective of the concept of *iṣlāḥ*. What does this primary source add to the Qur'anic semantic and characterizing points concerning *iṣlāḥ*? By searching in a number of the leading collections of Ḥadīth,[56] two groups of Prophetic traditions are found helpful to examine for the sake of the present task: the traditions which related to *iṣlāḥ* and those which related to its opposites.

Several useful semantic and characterizing points which shed more light on the Islamic perspective of *iṣlāḥ* are indicated in some Prophetic traditions, in which *iṣlāḥ* or related derivatives are employed. The most striking Prophetic tradition related to *iṣlāḥ* is the one about the strangers (*al-ghurabā'*). Among the different narrations of this tradition,[57] the extended narration of al-Tirmidhī is of special significance, because it refers explicitly to the idea of *iṣlāḥ*. The last part of this narration reads:

> Surely the *dīn* was strange when it began and it will become strange as in its beginning, so blessedness for the strangers (*al-ghurabā'*) who will set right or correct what people would have corrupted or perverted in my norm (*yuṣliḥūn mā afsada al-nnās min sunnatī*).[58]

By praising the strangers and introducing them as *muṣliḥūn*, this unique narration gives a valuable Prophetic justification for *iṣlāḥ*. In addition, the narration clearly shows that one task of *iṣlāḥ* from the Islamic perspective is to restore the original norm of Islam as exemplified in the life of the Prophet Muḥammad (ṣ).

Another Prophetic tradition related to *iṣlāḥ* is that in which the Prophet (ṣ) used the verb *yuṣliḥu* in the sense of repair. As narrated by Abū Dāwūd, the Prophet (ṣ) said: "When a thong of one of you is cut, then he should not walk in one sandal until he repairs (*yuṣliḥu*) his thong ..."[59] By being directed to the way someone dresses, this Prophetic teaching signifies that among the Islamic dimensions of *iṣlāḥ* is the outward appearance or the exterior and not just the purely inward religious dimensions, a point which assures the comprehensiveness of the Islamic perspective of *iṣlāḥ*.

Although it is true that Islamic *iṣlāḥ* can be directed to the exterior, the priority, however, should be given to the interior. This is another distinguishing characteristic of the Islamic perspective of *iṣlāḥ*. The priority given to looking inward is evident in the very well-known Prophetic tradition in which it is clearly stated that the *ṣalāḥ* and the *fasād* of the whole body depend on the condition of the heart.[60] This shows that the priority in *iṣlāḥ* should be given to the interior state.

Before leaving this tradition, an additional significant indication can be highlighted. The tradition indicates that self-based *iṣlāḥ* can be in the form of purifying the heart. More elucidation on this form of *iṣlāḥ* is found in the following interesting Prophetic tradition: "Truly, *ṣāliḥ* mode (*hadī*), *ṣāliḥ* manner (*samt*), and moderation (*al-iqtiṣād*) are one part of twenty five parts of Prophecy (*al-nubūwh*)."[61] In addition to showing the degree of importance of self-purification from the Islamic perspective, this tradition indicates that self-purification is meant in the religious sense.

One further Prophetic tradition related to *iṣlāḥ*, which is worth noting, is the tradition about the *muṣliḥ* slave. As narrated by the Imam Muslim, the Prophet (ṣ) said: "For the owned slave who is *muṣliḥ* there are two rewards."[62] The sense of *iṣlāḥ* in this narration becomes clear when another narration of the same tradition is linked with it.

In the other narration of the tradition—which is also narrated by the Imam Muslim but from another chain of narrators—the Prophet (ṣ) said: "Surely, if the slave advises his master and perfects his worship to Allah, his reward will be doubled for him."[63] This narration explains that what qualifies the slave to be a *muṣliḥ* and thus to deserve a double reward are his advice and the perfection of his worship. Thus, giving advice and perfecting one's worship are two *iṣlāḥī* works.

Reflecting on the Prophetic usages of the opposites of *iṣlāḥ* leads correspondingly to some additional elucidation of the Islamic perspective of *iṣlāḥ*. One of these usages is in the following Prophetic tradition in which *fasād* is articulated:

> If someone, whose religiousness (*dīn*) and morality (*khuluq*) please you, proposed to marry a girl through you, then you should accept his proposal; unless you do that, there would be *fitnah* (temptation) on earth and wide *fasād*.[64]

This tradition shows that preference should be given to the religiousness (*dīn*) and morality (*khuluq*). Although it is specifically mentioned in the context of marriage, this principle can also be applicable in other matters. Therefore, giving the priority to the *dīn* and *khuluq* can be considered an Islamic criterion of *iṣlāḥ*. Having mentioned the *dīn*, it is worth mentioning another Prophetic tradition which indicates a unique Islamic form of *iṣlāḥ* concerning the *dīn*. In this tradition, the comparative form of the adjective *fāsid* (i.e., *afsad*) is used in an interesting comparison: "Two hungry wolves released in a herd of sheep are not more harmful (*afsada*) to them than one's greed for wealth and fame to his *dīn*."[65] Conversely, to cure spiritual illnesses such as the greed for wealth and fame is an Islamic way of *iṣlāḥ* in the circle of *dīn*.

Phrasing the definition of *iṣlāḥ*

In light of the previous analysis, we may attempt to incorporate all the features of *iṣlāḥ* in the following tentative definition: *iṣlāḥ*, as an Islamic concept, is a human corrective task in which any state of *fasād* is correctively changed into its opposite desired state which meets the Islamic criteria presented in the Qur'an and or exemplified in the Sunnah of the Prophet Muḥammad (ṣ); and by *fasād* it is meant a state of loss of the benefit of a thing, inexcusable detriment, or unjustified deviation from a moderate norm.

Now, if there is any change in the meaning of *iṣlāḥ* over time, as has been recently argued,[66] it would be, in our view, due to the differences on the justification of the criteria of both *fasād* and its opposite state, which are the variables in the definition of *iṣlāḥ*.

Iṣlāḥ and reform: Degree of equivalence

In the literature in English concerning the topic of *iṣlāḥ*, the term is generally translated as reform.[67] To justify this translation, however, the degree of equivalence between the two terms needs to be precisely examined.

According to the Oxford English Dictionary,[68] there are various lexical senses of "reform" when it is used as a transitive verb.[69] By examining these senses and comparing them to those of *iṣlāḥ* discussed above, the following two observations can be made.

First, there are some senses of "reform" which are equivalent or at least very similar to some shades of the meaning of *iṣlāḥ*. These senses are:[70] (1) to make a change for the better in (an arrangement, state of things, practice), (2) to correct, put right (an error or mistake), (3) to bring (a person) to abandon some evil conduct and adopt a right one, (4) to improve one's own character, (5) to bring into a better state or improve, either by some change of form, or by the removal of faults or abuse, and (6) to put an end to (disorder etc.) by introducing a better procedure.[71]

Second, "reform" has some other equivalent or very similar senses to some of those indicated by *iṣlāḥ*, which are now obsolete.[72] These include the following:[73] (1) to restore to the original form, (2) to rebuild after (destruction …), and (3) to repair (damage …). The image associated with these senses of "reform" is crucial to the meaning of *iṣlāḥ*. Being out of date, however, these senses of the term are no longer reflected in its current usage. This considerably reduces the degree of equivalence between *iṣlāḥ* and reform in its current usage.

But even if all the senses of reform are considered, the scope of *iṣlāḥ* is still broader. Thus, some essential dimensions of *iṣlāḥ* will be lost when the term is replaced by "reform". This loss is enough to make the serious researcher avoid the use of "reform" in place of *iṣlāḥ*, at least for the sake of precision. At the very most, "reform" is only a partial equivalent for *iṣlāḥ*.

What really widens the gap between the two terms are their religious overtones. *Iṣlāḥ* is an Islamic concept, whereas "reform" is ecclesiastical: it has been tied to the tradition of the Reformation of the 16th century which led to the establishment of the Protestant churches.[74] Therefore, using the latter to refer to the former may cause considerable misunderstanding.

In short, to avoid any confusion, the term *iṣlāḥ* should not be translated as "reform". Alternatively, it should be used in its transliterated form and explained in detail whenever there is a need. When translation is unavoidable, however, the adjective "Islamic" should be used before "reform" as a rendering for *iṣlāḥ* in order to reduce the gap between the two terms.

The relationship between *iṣlāḥ* and other concepts

This section compares and contrasts the Islamic concept *iṣlāḥ* with the following three concepts: *tajdīd* (renewal or restoration), *taghyīr* (change), and *al-amr bi al-maʿrūf wa al-nahy ʿan al-munkar* (commanding right and forbidding wrong).

The aim of this step is not, however, to fully analyse these concepts, but rather to shed more light on the concept of *iṣlāḥ* itself by highlighting the main similarities and differences between *iṣlāḥ* and these three concepts which are sometimes, justifiably or not, associated with *iṣlāḥ*. This aim alone guides the following examination and controls its points of interest.

Iṣlāḥ vs. tajdīd

The term *tajdīd* is used in some studies[75] to mean the same or similar to the Islamic term *iṣlāḥ*. But the examination below shows that, although there are some similarities between the two terms, there are also some important differences which need particular attention.

Unlike *iṣlāḥ*, the concept of *tajdīd* is not Qur'anic, i.e., the word does not appear in the Qur'an. It originated as an Islamic concept, however, from a unique Prophetic tradition in which the derived verb *yujaddid* is employed: "Verily, Allah will send to this *ummah* (Muslim nation) at the head of each hundred years *man* (the one or those who) *yujaddidu* for it its *dīn*." As a result, the concept *tajdīd*, which is the *maṣdar* (infinitive noun) from the verb "*yujaddidu*," refers in the Islamic sense to the task mentioned in this tradition. The one who fulfils this task is called the *mujaddid*.

In order to precisely compare and contrast *iṣlāḥ* and *tajdīd*, it is essential to fully examine the implications of the task referred to in the above tradition. The starting point in this examination is the indication of *dīn* to which the task of *tajdīd* is directed.

The term *dīn* is a comprehensive Islamic concept. Based on a deep examination of the uses of the term *dīn* and the related derivatives both in classical Arabic and in the Qur'an, a study by Maududi[76] demonstrates that the Qur'an employs the term in one or more of the following four senses or shades of meaning: "(1) Sovereignty and supreme authority, (2) obedience and submission to such authority, (3) the system of thought and action established through the exercise of that authority, and (4) retribution meted out by the authority, in consideration of loyalty and obedience to it, rebellion and transgression against it."[77]

The study also shows that in some Qur'anic contexts, the term is used in a sense of

> a whole way of life in which a person gives his submission and obedience to someone whom he regards as having the ultimate authority [i.e., Allah alone in the case of the *dīn* of Islam]; [he]

shapes his conduct according to the bounds and laws and rules prescribed by that being, looks to him for recognition, honour, and reward for loyal service, and fears the disgrace or punishment that could follow any lack on his part.[78]

These nuances of meaning of *dīn* show how comprehensive this concept is. It is, however, vital to recall that the primary signification of the concept is obedience and submission. This distinguishes *dīn* from other similar Arabic terms referring to a system of religion, such as *millah*. As al-Aṣfahānī states, "*dīn* is similar to *millah* but the former is used as regard to obedience and submission to the Sharī'ah."[79]

Now, what is meant by the task of *tajdīd* when it is directed to the *dīn* of the Muslim *ummah* in the above sense of *dīn*? To answer this question, we should study the meaning of the verb *yujaddidu* mentioned in the tradition about *tajdīd*. Being a transitive verb in the *muḍāri'* (aorist) tense, *yujaddidu* means to make or render *jadīd*. With regard to the meaning of the epithet *jadīd*, there are three possible senses in the lexicons. The primary sense of *jadīd* is derived from *al-jadd* meaning *al-qaṭ*[80] (cut); it is said *thawbun jadīd* meaning a garment newly cut off by the weaver.[81] Based on this primary sense, *jadīd* is used, as al-Aṣfahānī states, for anything which has been newly or recently originated.[82] A second sense of *jadīd* is learned from its *maṣdar* (infinitive), *al-jiddah*, as opposed to *al-bilā* or *al-khaliq*[83] (the state of becoming shabby or worn out). A third sense of *jadīd* presented in some lexicons is *mā lā 'ahda laka bih*[84] (a thing of which you have had no knowledge).

It is obvious, however, that the task of *tajdīd* mentioned in the tradition about the *mujaddid* should not be interpreted—on the basis of the indications of the first and the last senses of *jadīd*—as changing the *dīn* of the *ummah* or making it different in a sense amounting to a loss of original identity, otherwise this tradition would contradict with other Prophetic traditions which proscribe *bid'ah* (innovation in the *dīn*). Therefore, to avoid falling in to this kind of contradiction, the Islamic *tajdīd* should be bound by the original model of the *dīn* which is presented in the Qur'an and the Sunnah and is believed to have been exemplified by the first Muslim Community.

Having considered this, the only possible sense of *jadīd*, in the light of which the task of *tajdīd* can be interpreted correctly, is the third one. Accordingly, the Islamic task of *tajdīd* can be understood as a human corrective activity by which the *dīn* of the Muslim *ummah* is revived and restored in the light of its original model after a state of obliteration, loss or deviation.

Comparing and contrasting this interpretation of *tajdīd* and the previous definition of *iṣlāḥ*, the following similarities and differences can be accepted:

1. Both *tajdīd* and *iṣlāḥ* are Islamic corrective tasks; however, the former was introduced only in the Ḥadīth, while the other was introduced in both the Qur'an and the Ḥadīth.
2. Unlike *iṣlāḥ*, the scope of *tajdīd* is restricted within the field of *dīn*, as is stated in the tradition of *tajdīd*.
3. It is in the field of *dīn* only, where *iṣlāḥ* may overlap with *tajdīd*.
4. Every *mujaddid* is *muṣliḥ* but not every *muṣliḥ* is *mujaddid*.
5. The task of *tajdīd* is bound by more restrictive conditions than those of *iṣlāḥ*.

Iṣlāḥ vs. taghyīr

The term *taghyīr* in Arabic is the *maṣdar* (infinitive noun) of the transitive verb *ghayyara*, as in the phrase *ghayyarahu* which can mean one or more of the following: *ḥawwalhu, baddalhu,* and *j'alahu ghayra mā kān*[85] (he transformed it, converted it and rendered it different). Thus, it is equivalent to the term "change" in English. This shows that *taghyīr* can linguistically be either a change for the better or a change for the worse.

In the Qur'an, however, the aoristic form of verb *ghayyara*—i.e., *yughayyiru*—appears only in contexts where change is for the worse: "Surely I [Satan] will mislead them ... and surely I will command them so they will change (*falayughayyirānna*) Allah's creation ..." (Qur'an, 4:119), "... Allah would never change a grace that he conferred on a people until they change (*yughayyirū*) what is within themselves" (Qur'an, 8:53), "... Surely Allah does not change (*yughayyiru*)[86] the condition of a people until they change (*yughayyirū*)[87] what is within themselves. And whenever Allah wills harm (*sū'*) for a people, nothing turns it back; apart from Him, they have no protector." (Qur'an, 13:11).

It is worth noting that *taghyīr* cannot be considered either an Islamic concept or an Islamic task such as *iṣlāḥ*; it does not seem that there is a direct Qur'anic or Prophetic appeal to change for the sake of change. The only exception to this observation occurs when *taghyīr* is directed against *al-munkar*. It is only then that *taghyīr* becomes part of the Islamic unique duty *al-amr bi al-maʿrūf wa al-nahy ʿan al-munkar*, as will be shown when this duty is compared and contrasted with *iṣlāḥ*.

In addition to the above essential difference between *iṣlāḥ* and *taghyīr*, another major difference between the two terms can be clearly observed from the meaning of the term *taghyīr* itself: *taghyīr* is more general than *iṣlāḥ*. Therefore, not every *taghyīr* is *iṣlāḥ* whereas every *iṣlāḥ* is a particular form of *taghyīr*, since *iṣlāḥ* is a corrective change. The two terms may overlap only when *taghyīr* is directed against *fasād*.

Iṣlāḥ vs. al-amr bi al-maʿrūf wa al-nahy ʿan al-munkar

The phrase *al-amr bi al-maʿrūf wa al-nahy ʿan al-munkar* is a combination of two parts. The first part consists of two terms which are opposite in meaning to those in the second: *amr*, which means "commanding" or "enjoining," stands opposite to *nahy*, which means "forbidding", while *maʿrūf*, which literally means "known," is the opposite of *munkar*, which literally means "unknown."[88]

Similar to *iṣlāḥ*, the duty of *al-amr bi al-maʿrūf wa al-nahy ʿan al-munkar* is firmly rooted and highly valued in the Qur'an and the Ḥadīth. There are numerous favourable references to the doctrine in these two basic sources of Islam. These references clearly establish the obligatory nature of the task and show the need for it. In the Qur'an, for instance, Allah addresses the believer as follows: "Let there be a nation of you, calling to what is good, and commanding what is *maʿrūf*, and forbidding what is *munkar*; those are the prosperers" (Qur'an, 3:104).

The external sense of this doctrine suggests that it denotes merely a verbal duty and thus it may seem far distinct from *iṣlāḥ*, which is a sort of change. However, by fully examining both the Qur'anic and Prophetic references related to this subject, it becomes evident that the duty is not always verbal, but can be in other forms as well, particularly as a response to *munkar*. In a famous Prophetic tradition, which can be conveniently called "the three modes tradition,"[89] the Prophet (ṣ), for instance, states: "Whoever sees a particular *munkar* and is able to change it with his hand, let him do so; if he can't, then with his tongue; if he can't, then with his heart …" It is not within the purpose of the present discussion, however, to examine all the possible "modes" of the duty and the controversial issues which they may raise. What is connected to the present theme, nevertheless, specifically arises when the duty is in the form of changing *munkar* physically. This is mainly because the duty in this form becomes a sort of "human corrective change" and thus it belongs to the same general classification of *iṣlāḥ*.

In order to know precisely the relationship between *iṣlāḥ* and "changing *munkar*," we should analyse the meaning of the term *munkar* as an Islamic concept and compare, or contrast it with *al-fasād*. To start with, *al-munkar*, as its literal sense reveals, indicates disapproval and rejection. Like *fasād*, the term can be generally classified as a categorical negative value term. There is disagreement among the Qur'anic exegeses, however, on what can justifiably be listed under this categorical term; some have restricted it to particular sins, while others have widened it to include every evil.[90] The external sense of the term, nevertheless, suggests, as Abū Ḥayyān points out, *al-ʿumūm* (generality or general character). This general character makes the present task of comparing and contrasting the meaning of *munkar* and *fasād* very difficult.

Yet, within the Islamic discipline of *fiqh* (jurisprudence)—where the rules and conditions of the duty of *al-amr bi al-maʿrūf wa al-nahy ʿan al-munkar* are normally studied—the generality of the term *munkar* has been restricted by certain conditions which have to be present in a particular case, in order to justifiably consider such a case a *munkar* and thus eligible for opposition as a duty. By considering these conditions, the present task becomes easier. According to al-Ghazālī's account, there are four conditions with regard to *munkar*:[91] (1) being forbidden in the Sharīʿah[92] , (2) currently existing, (3) being apparent for the exponent of the duty, and (4) being known without the need of *ijtihād*.[93]

In the light of the above conditions, it becomes apparent that *munkar* overlaps with *fasād* when all these conditions exist in a particular case; however, *fasād* is wider than *munkar* since the former is not necessarily restricted by all these conditions. As a result, *iṣlāḥ* partially overlaps with "changing *munkar*."

Another difference between the two tasks appears in their ultimate goals. The task of changing a particular *munkar*, such as drinking wine publicly, can be fulfilled by simply stopping it. The task of *iṣlāḥ*, in contrast, is not completely fulfilled unless a *fāsid* person—e.g. one who drinks wine—is guided to repent and to become *ṣāliḥ* instead.

Notes

1. There are useful brief discussions of the definition of the term—though not sufficient enough for the need of the present study—in the following sources: A. Merad, *Iṣlāḥ*, in *EI²*, Leiden: E.J. Brill, 1978,

Vol. 4, p. 141; and John O. Voll, "Renewal and Reform in Islamic History: *Tajdid* and *Islah*," in John L. Esposito (ed.), *Voices of Resurgent Islam*, Oxford: Oxford University Press, 1983, pp. 33f.

2. The methods of definition are discussed thoroughly by Richard Robinson in his unique book *Definition*, Oxford: Clarendon Press, 1962, pp. 93-148.

3. Robinson, *Definition*, p. 97.

4. For a scholarly discussion on the advantages and disadvantages of the analytical method of defining, see Robinson, *Definition*, pp. 97f.

5. Toshihiko Izutsu, *The Structure of the Ethical Terms in the Koran: A Study in Semantics*, Tokyo: Keio Institute of Philological Studies, 1959, p. 6.

6. Izutsu, *The Structure*, p. 6.

7. Namely: (1) *Kitāb al-'Ayn* of al-Khalīl b. Aḥmad (d. 170/786); (2) *Jamharah al-Lughah* of Ibn Durayd (d. 321/933); (3) *al-Muḥīṭ fī al-Lughah* of al-Ṣāḥib b. 'Abbād (d. 385/995); (4) *al-Ṣiḥāḥ fī al-Lughah* of al-Jawharī (d. 393/1003); (5) *al-Muḥkam wa al-Muḥīṭ al-A'ẓam fī al-Lughah* of Ibn Sīdah (d. 458/1066); (6) *Asās al-Balāghah* of al-Zamakhsharī (d. 538/1144); (7) *Lisān al-'Arab* of Ibn Manẓūr (d. 711/1311); (8) *Tāj al-'Arūs* of Murtaḍā al-Zabīdī (d. 1205/1791); (9) and finally the late lexicon, *al-Mu'jam al-Wasīṭ* of the Arabic Language Academy in Cairo. For a scholarly and informative English account on the traditional Arabic lexicons, which is drawn chiefly from the unique work of al-Suyūṭī, *al-Muzhir*, see the preface to Lane's *Madd al-Qāmūs*: an Arabic—English Lexicon, London: Williams and Norgate, 1863, pp. xii-xx.

8. A. Merad, *Iṣlāḥ*, *EI²*, Vol. 4, p. 141.

9. See, for example, Merad, *Iṣlāḥ*, Vol. 4, p. 141; and Voll, *Renewal and Reform*, p. 32.

10. John Wilson, *Thinking With Concepts*, Cambridge: The University Press, p. 30.

11. Ibn Sīdah, *al-Muḥkam*, eds. Muṣṭafā al-Saqqā et al., Cairo: Ma'had al-Makhṭūṭāt bi Jāmi'ah al-Duwal al-'Arabiyyah, 1958-1973, under the radical letters *ṣ-l-ḥ*.

12. See al-Khalīl b. Aḥmad, *al-'Ayn*, ed. Mahdī al-Makhzūmī and Ibrāhīm al-Sāmarrā'ī, Baghdad: Wazārah al-Thaqāfah wa al-I'lām, 1980-1985, under the radical letters *ṣ-l-ḥ*.

13. See al-Jawharī, *al-Ṣiḥāḥ*, ed. Aḥmad 'Abd al-Ghafūr 'Aṭṭār, Cairo: Dār al-Kitāb al-'Arabī, 1377 AH, under the radical letters *ṣ-l-ḥ*.

14. See al-Jawharī, *al-Ṣiḥāḥ*, under the radical letters *ṣ-l-ḥ*.

15. All the explanations concerning *iṣlāḥ* and its related derivatives are found in Arabic lexicons under its three basic radical letters: *ṣ-l-ḥ*. In some lexicons, all the words containing these radical letters

are listed under the last letter '*ḥ*' whereas in others they are listed under the first letter '*ṣ*', depending on the method of listing in the respective lexicon.

16. The term is introduced in the Arabic lexicons with the definite article '*al*,' which is of the generic type in this context.

17. See, for instance, al-Jawharī, *al-Ṣiḥāḥ*, under the radical letters *ṣ-l-ḥ*; and Ibn Manẓūr, *Lisān al-'Arab*, Beirut: Dār Ṣādir, 1997, under the radical letters *ṣ-l-ḥ*.

18. Under its radical letters *f-s-d*.

19. Ibrāhīm Muṣṭafā et al. (eds.), *al-Mu'jam al-Waṣīṭ*, Istanbul: Dār al-Da'wah, 1989, p. 520, under the radical letters *ṣ-l-ḥ*.

20. Ibn Sīdah, *al-Muḥkam*, under the radical letters *ṣ-l-ḥ*.

21. Ibid.

22. See al-Khalīl b. Aḥmad, *al-'Ayn*, Cairo: Majma' al-Lughah al-'Arabiyyah, under the radical letters *ṣ-l-ḥ*; Ibn Durayd, *Jamharah*, Hyder Abad: Dāirah al-Ma'ārif, 1344-1345 AH, under the radical letters *ḥ-ṣ-l*; and Ibn Sīdah, *al-Muḥkam*, under the radical letters *ṣ-l-ḥ*.

23. See al-Jawharī, *al-Ṣiḥāḥ*, under the radical letters *ṣ-l-ḥ*; and Ibn Manẓūr, *Lisān al-'Arab*, under the radical letters *ṣ-l-ḥ*.

24. Muṣṭafā et al. (eds.), *al-Mu'jam al-Waṣīṭ*, under the radical letters *ṣ-l-ḥ*.

25. See al-Rāghib al-Aṣfhānī (502/1108), *Mufradāt Alfāẓ al-Qur'ān*, ed. Ṣafwān Dāwūdī, Damascus: Dār al-Qalam and Beirut: al-Dār al-Shāmiyyah, 1997, under the radical letters *q-w-m*.

26. Muṣṭafā et al. (eds.), *al-Mu'jam al-Waṣīṭ*, under the radical letters *ṣ-l-ḥ*.

27. Ibid.

28. See al-Jawharī, *al-Ṣiḥāḥ*, under the radical letters *ṣ-l-ḥ*.

29. Al-Zamakhsharī, *Asās al-Balāghah*, Beirut: Dār Iḥyā' al-Turāth al-'Arabī, 2001, under the radical letters *ṣ-l-ḥ*.

30. Al-Zamakhsharī, *Asās al-Balāghah*, under the radical letters *ṣ-l-ḥ*.

31. Muṣṭafā et al. (eds.), *al-Mu'jam al-Waṣīṭ*, under the radical letters *f-s-d*.

32. Strangely, although *fasād* is a noun, the phrasing of this sense suits an infinitive and not a noun.

33. See Murtaḍā al-Zabīdī, *Tāj al-'Arūs*, ed. 'Abd al-Sattār Aḥmad Farrāj et al., Kuwait: Wazārh al-Irshād wa al-Anbā', 1965-1989, under the radical letters *f-s-d*.

34. See Murtaḍā al-Zabīdī, *Tāj al-'Arūs*, under the radical letters *f-s-d*.

35. Ibid.

36. Ibn Sīdah, *al-Muḥkam*, under the radical letters *ṭ-l-ḥ*.

37. Ibid.

38. In translating the lexicographical quotes, I have benefited much from the unique Arabic-English lexicon of Lane, Cambridge: Islamic Texts Society, 2003.

39. See Ibn Durayd, *Jamharah*, under the radical letters *ḥ-ṭ-l*.

40. Al-Jawharī, *al-Ṣiḥāḥ*, under the radical letters *ṭ-l-ḥ*.

41. Ibid.

42. Ibid.

43. See Ibn Manẓūr, *Lisān al-'Arab*, under the radical letters *ṭ-l-ḥ*.

44. For a comprehensive listing of these usages, see 'Abd al-Bāqī, *al-Mu'jam al-Mufahras li al-Fāẓ al-Qur'ān al-Karīm*, Cairo: Dār al-Ḥadīth, 1991, under the radical letters *ṣ-l-ḥ*, pp. 520-523, and for an electronic search, visit: *http://www.altafsir.com/Quran_Search.asp*.

45. As in Qur'an, 2:224, Qur'an, 4:114, Qur'an, 49:9-10.

46. As in Qur'an, 21:90, Qur'an, 33:71, and Qur'an, 47:2.

47. Calling it the "contextual approach," I applied this tool in my MA dissertation and found it very helpful: see Mohamed al-Musleh, "The Qur'anic Treatment of the Story of Ibrāhīm (Abraham): A 'Contextual' Approach," MA Dissertation, SOAS, University of London, 2000-2001.

48. For the history and the significance of this principle in interpreting the Qur'an, see Muhammad Abdel Haleem, *Understanding the Qur'an: Themes and Style*, London: I.B. Tauris & Co Ltd, 1999, pp. 160-162.

49. See Ibn 'Āshūr, *al-Taḥrīr wa al-Tanwīr*, Qur'an, 2:220.

50. According to some *mufassirūn* (Qur'an exegetes), it is possible that the verb *aṣlaḥa* in some of these contexts, namely in Qur'an, 3:89, is an intransitive verb in the sense of *dakhala fī al-ṣalāḥ* (to come under the state of *ṣalāḥ*), see, for example, Maḥmūd al-Alūsī (d. 1270/1854), *Ruḥ al-Ma'ānī fī Tafsīr al-Qur'ān al-'Aẓīm wa al-Sab' al-Mathānī*, Beirut: Dār al-Fikr, 1997, Vol.

51. See, for example, Ibn Kathīr (d. 774/1373), *Tafsīr al-Qur'ān al-'Aẓīm*, ed. Sāmī b. Muḥammad al-Salāmah, 1999, Vol. 4, p. 593. The same edition available online: *http://www.qurancomplex.com/Quran/tafseer/Tafseer.asp?t=KATHEER&TabID=3&SubItemID=1 &l=arb*.

52. See al-Alūsī, *Ruḥ al-Ma'ānī*, Vol. 1, p. 353.

53. I was led to this point by the inspiring interpretation of the *āyah* by Ibn Kathīr, *Tafsīr*, Vol. 2, p. 55.

54. For a justified argument of this indication, see Ibn 'Āshūr, *al-Taḥrīr wa al-Tanwīr*, Qur'an, 7:56.

55. I was led to this point by the inspiring interpretation of the *āyah* by Ibn Kathīr, *Tafsīr*, Vol. 2, p. 55.

56. These are: (1) the *Ṣaḥīḥ* of al-Bukhārī (d. 256/870); (2) the *Ṣaḥīḥ* of Muslim Ibn al-Ḥajjāj (d. 261/875);(3) the *Sunan* of Abū Dāwūd al-Sijistānī (d. 275/889); (4) the *Musnad* of Aḥmad Ibn Ḥanbal (d. 241/855); (5) the *Sunan* of Ibn Mājah (d. 273/887); (6) the *Ṣaḥīḥ* of al-Tirmidhī (d. 279/892); (7) and the *Sunan* of al-Nasā'ī (d. 303/915).

57. The basic wording of this tradition is narrated in several books of Ḥadīth including Muslim's *Saḥīḥ*, see the edition with the commentary of al-Nawawī (d.676/1277), *al-Minhāj Sharḥ Ṣaḥīḥ Muslim Ibn al-Ḥajjāj*, ed. Khalīl Ma'mūn Shayḥā, Beirut: Dār al-Ma'rifah, 1996, under *Kitāb al-Īmān, Bāb Bada' al-Islām Gharībā*, no. 370, Vol. 2, p. 354.

58. Al-Tirmidhī, *al-Jāmi' al-Ṣaḥīḥ*, ed. Muḥammad Muḥammad Nassār, Beirut: Dār al-Kutub al-'Ilmiyyah, 2000, under *Kitāb al-Īmān, Bāb Majā' ann al-Islām Bada' Gharībā*, no. 2630, Vol. 3, pp. 449f.

59. Abū Dāwūd, *Sunan*, ed. Muḥammad 'Abd al-'Azīz al-Khālidī, Beirut: Dār al-Kutub al-'Ilmiyyah, 1996, under *Kitāb al-Libās, Bāb fī al-Inti'āl*, no. 4137, Vol. 3, p. 72.

60. See al-Bukhārī, *Ṣaḥīḥ*, Riyadh: Dār al-Salām, 1999, under *Kitāb al-Īmān, Bāb Fad'l man Istabra' li Dīnih*, no. 52, p. 12.

61. Abū Dāwūd, *Sunan*, under *Kitāb al-Adab, Bāb fī al-Waqār*, no. 4776, Vol. 3, p. 253.

62. Muslim, *Ṣaḥīḥ*, under *Kitāb al-Aymān, Bāb Thawāb al-'Abd wa Ajruh Idhā Naṣaḥ li Sayidih wa Aḥsan 'Ibādata Allāh*, no. 4296, Vol. 11, p. 138.

63. Ibid.

64. Al-Tirmidhī, *al-Jāmi' al-Ṣaḥīḥ*, under *Kitāb al-Nikāḥ, Bāb mā Jā' Idhā Jā'akum man Tarḍ'awn Dīnah fā Zawijūh*, no. 1085, Vol. 2, pp. 172f.

65. Ibid, *Bāb mā Jā' fī Akhdh al-Māl bi Ḥaqqih*, no. 2376, Vol. 3, p. 319.

66. Voll, for instance, states that "over the centuries the specific meanings of *tajdid* and *islah* [sic] have changed, depending on the evolution of Islamic thought and the changing circumstances of the Islamic community," (Voll, "Renewal and Reform," p. 32).

67. See, for instance, A. Merad, *Iṣlāḥ*, in *EI²*, Vol. 4, p. 141; and John O. Voll, "Renewal and Reform in Islamic History: *Tajdid* and *Islah* [sic]," in John L. Esposito (ed.), *Voices of Resurgent Islam*, pp. 33f.

68. Which is the most comprehensive English dictionary.

69. See *The Oxford English Dictionary*, 2nd ed., Oxford: Oxford University Press, 1989, the entry "reform." Available also online: *http://dictionary.oed.com*.

70. *The Oxford English Dictionary*, the entry "reform."

71. Compare these senses with the lexicographical meanings of *iṣlāḥ* above.

72. *The Oxford English Dictionary*, the entry "reform."

73. Ibid.

74. See Konrad Repgen, *Reform*, translated from German to English by Robert E. Shillenn, in *the Oxford Encyclopaedia of the Reformation*, New York & Oxford: Oxford University Press, 1996, Vol. 3, p. 392,.

75. See, for example, Voll, *Renewal and Reform*, pp. 33f.

76. S. Abul A'la Maududi, *Four Basic Qur'anic Terms*, translated from Urdu to English by Abu Asad, Lahore (Pakistan): Islamic Publications Ltd., 1982.

77. Maududi, *Four Basic Qur'anic Terms*, p. 94.

78. Ibid, pp. 99f.

79. Al-Rāghib al-Aṣfhānī (502/1108), *Mufradāt Alfāẓ al-Qur'ān*, ed. Ṣafwān Dāwūdī, Damascus: Dār al-Qalam and Beirut: al-Dār al-Shāmiyyah, 1997, under the radical letter *d-ī-n*.

80. See Ibn Sīdah, *al-Muḥkam*, under the radical letters *j-d-d*; al-Jawharī, *al-Ṣiḥāḥ*, under the radical letters *j-d-d*; and Murtaḍā al-Zabīdī, *Tāj al-'Arūs*, under the radical letters *j-d-d*.

81. Ibid

82. Al-Rāghib al-Aṣfhānī, under the radical letter *j-d-d*.

83. See Ibn Sīdah, *al-Muḥkam*, under the radical letters *j-d-d*; al-Jawharī, *al-Ṣiḥāḥ*, under the radical letters *j-d-d*; Ibn Manẓūr, *Lisān al-'Arab*, under the radical letters *j-d-d*; and Murtaḍā al-Zabīdī, *Tāj al-'Arūs*, under the radical letters *j-d-d*.

84. See Ibn Sīdah, *al-Muḥkam*, under the radical letters *j-d-d*; Ibn Manẓūr, *Lisān al-'Arab*, under the radical letters *j-d-d*; and Murtaḍā al-Zabīdī, *Tāj al-'Arūs*, under the radical letters *j-d-d*.

85. Murtaḍā al-Zabīdī, *Tāj al-'Arūs*, under the radical letters *gh-y-r*.

86. As the closing of the *āyah* indicates, the change here is for the worse. In addition, there is an agreement among the classical *mufsirūn* (Qur'anic exegeses) on this connotation.

87. See the previous note.

88. The term *ma'rūf* is derived from *'irfān* which means *'lm* (knowledge) whereas *munkar* is derived from its opposite *nakirah*, see Ibn Manẓūr, *Lisān al-'Arab*, under the radical letters *'-r-f*.

89. I have borrowed this name from Michael Cook, *Commanding Right and Forbidding Wrong in Islamic Thought*, Cambridge: Cambridge University Press, 2000, p. 32.

90. See, for instance, Ibn Jarīr al-Ṭabarī (d. 310/923), *Tafsīr*, ed. Aḥmad Muḥammad Shākir, Beirut: Mu'asasah al-Risālah, 2000, Vol. 7, p. 61, the same edition available online: *http://www.qurancomplex. com/Quran/tafseer/Tafseer.asp?t=TABARY&TabID=3&SubItemID =1&l=arb*, Ibn Kathīr, *Tafsīr*, Vol., p. and.

91. Al-Ghazālī, *Iḥyā' 'Ulūm al-Dīn*, Beirut: Dār Iḥyā' al-Turāth al-'Arabī, n.d., Vol. 2, pp. 324f. For an extended English summary of al-Ghazālī's account on the duty, see Cook, *Commanding Right*, pp. 428-446.
92. The comprehensive body of Islamic rules and laws.
93. The scholarly mental activity of deriving a rule of the Sharī'ah from authoritative evidence.

2

Setting the historical context

Introduction

When studying a historical figure like al-Ghazālī, it is essential to consider the historical context in which he lived. Failure to do so may in the first instance lead to serious misunderstanding of his thoughts; essentially, as Samuel Zwemer puts it, "We cannot understand a man unless we know his environment."[1] In the second instance, it could cause extremely incorrect evaluation of his achievement particularly since the criteria of judgment and the circumstances in the time of al-Ghazālī were very different to those in the contemporary age, as ʿAbd al-Maqṣūd has rightly stated.[2]

In order to avoid committing such a serious methodological oversight, it is not enough to simply know al-Ghazālī's biography since, as Zwemer has interestingly pointed out, "biography is only a thread in the vast web of history, in which time is broad as well as long,"[3] but more than that we need, he continues, to "transport ourselves to the time in which he lived."[4] Thus, I ought to present an overview of the age of al-Ghazālī in this chapter, before turning to the main task of the study. The focus of this overview is the historical information which is important to bear in mind at the outset, and at the same time shall establish a necessary foundation and introductory background for the forthcoming discussions.

The overall condition of Islamdom[5]

At the beginning of the age of al-Ghazālī, Islamdom was spread across three continents. The Arab Peninsula, the Levant, Mesopotamia, the Persian Plateau, Northern Africa and al-Andalus (Muslim Spain) formed *Dār al-Islām* at that time. However, the frontiers of Islamdom kept changing slightly over the age. Muslims gained new strategic lands, while losing other valuable ones.[6]

Over this age, Islamdom was noticeably in a complex, diverse and changing condition, to the extent that making any sweeping generalization here may create an unbalanced picture of that age. The classical Muslim society with its dominant purely Arabic-language culture under the uniting umbrella of the magnificent caliphate had changed into a diverse society, both linguistically and culturally,[7] which was ruled by multiple independent "governments" with no single uniting political force. On one hand, there were clear symptoms of decline in Islamdom, and the Muslims, generally speaking, were suffering from fundamental weaknesses; in the words of Hillenbrand, they "were living through exceptionally turbulent times."[8] On the other hand, there were, at the same time, particular elements of prosperity and strengths, and overall the Muslim *Ummah* was still, as Hodgson put it, "certainly the most widely spread and influential on the globe."[9]

To better understand the complex condition of Islamdom in the age under study, and to gain a balanced picture of that age, an extended overview is necessary. Thus, a somewhat detailed outline of the political and religio-intellectual dimensions of that age will be drawn below.

The political setting

Al-Ghazālī lived in a time of totally new political order compared to the earlier classical 'Abbāsid era. By the birth of al-Ghazālī, the 'Abbāsid Caliphate had already been suffering from political disintegration. There was no single political power ruling the whole of Islamdom at that time. Instead, the Islamic *ummah* was ruled by various individual local "governments." Furthermore, the Caliphate had been challenged by the competing Fāṭimid Caliphate in Egypt based on Ismā'īlism and which had been receiving advantageous support from the Ismā'īlī Shiite all around Islamdom, but this opponent Caliphate suffered from symptoms of weakness during the age of al-Ghazālī.

While the early part of the age of al-Ghazālī witnessed the rapid rise of the Seljuk and Almoravid dynasties, towards the end of the same age they had started to decline.

To adequately understand the changing political setting of that age, an overview on the status of the Caliphate and the provincial "governments" of the time is presented under the following sub-headings.

The status of the 'Abbāsid caliphate

Al-Ghazālī lived through the reigns of three successive 'Abbāsid caliphs. During the first seventeen years of al-Ghazālī's life, the 'Abbāsid Caliph of the time was al-Qā'im bi Amrillāh,[10] who was the twenty sixth caliph in the line of the 'Abbāsid dynasty. Then, his grandson, al-Muqtadī bi Amrillāh[11] who was twenty years old,[12] succeeded him and held the Caliphate till he died in 487/1094. In the last eighteen years of al-Ghazālī's life, the Caliph was al-Mustaẓhir Billāh,[13] whose reign ended with his death, seven years after the death of al-Ghazālī.

With regard to their personal characteristics, it is reported that all three caliphs were religious, and were men of Islamic morality and noble personality. The historian Ibn al-Athīr

(d. 630/1233), for example, characterized al-Qā'im as "pious, religious, ascetically-minded, learned, held a strong trust in Allah Almighty, and very patient."[14] With regard to al-Qā'im's attitude to ruling, Ibn al-Athīr reported that "he was devoted to justice and fair treatment, and always wanted to satisfy people's needs,[15] not thinking to deny anything which was requested from him."[16]

Similarly, al-Muqtadī was religious, beneficent, and a man of strong personality and great zealousness.[17] Concerning al-Mustaẓhir, it is reported that he was of good morality, beneficent, charitable, kind, generous, and that he loved *'ulamā'* and pious people.[18] It is worth mentioning that al-Mustaẓhir was highly praised by al-Ghazālī in his book, *Faḍā'iḥ al-Bāṭiniyyah wa Faḍā'l al-Mustaẓhiriyyah*, in which he firmly states that the Caliph al-Mustaẓhir was qualified for the *imāmah* (supreme leadership of the Muslims) since he, as al-Ghazālī passionately argued and desperately attempted, though not very convincingly, to prove from the Sharī'ah perspective, was gifted with the requisite qualities and conditions for that position.[19]

These reported good characters of the three caliphs, however, are not projected in the status of the Caliphate itself which, although it somehow retained its authority, had lost its previous power.[20] During the reign of al-Qā'im, to begin with, the Caliphate suffered from a dramatic decline and its centre experienced a state of disorder for a while. Moreover, the Caliph himself was debased to the extent that he was imprisoned for a period of time! This started in the year 450/1058 when the commander and chief of the army of Baghdad, Arslān al-Basāsīrī, who turned away from al-Qā'im and supported the Fāṭimid Caliph, al-Mustanṣir Billāh, instead, took control of Baghdad and imprisoned the Caliph al-Qā'im.[22] As the populace inclined towards al-Basāsīrī,[22] a rebellion took place during which the harem of the Caliph was entered without permission and the Caliph's palace was plundered.[23]

From the time of al-Basāsīrī's revolutionary movement in Baghdad, the name of the 'Abbāsid Caliph was replaced by the name of the Fāṭimid Caliph in the Friday *khuṭbah* and in the coins struck.[24] This ignominious fall from power of the 'Abbāsid Caliph did not end until al-Basāsīrī fled Baghdad in 451/1059 as the first great Seljuk[25] Sultan Tughril-Beg,[26] responding to an appeal for help from the Caliph al-Qā'im,[27] marched into Iraq, with no other thought but, as Ibn al-Athīr reported,[28] to restore the Caliph to his Court. Consequently, the Caliph returned to his throne in the same year.[29]

To a considerable extent, the Caliph al-Qā'im was rehabilitated by the Sultan Tughril-Beg[30] who initially regarded the Caliph, from whom he had obtained a valuable legitimacy of his rule,[31] as his master and treated him with great respect on various occasions.[32] The Caliph in turn was so pleased with him to the extent that he placed him in control of all the lands that were under the Caliph's authority and addressed him as *Malik al-Mashriq wa al-Magrib* (the King of the East and West).[33] In addition, to cement his relationship with the Sultan, he married his niece.[34]

Nevertheless, great tension developed shortly between the two. Some of Tughril-Beg's actions disturbed and offended the Caliph. Tughril-Beg's daring marriage to the Caliph's daughter is a case in point. The marriage broke the noble tradition of the previous 'Abbāsid caliphs, because it was the first marriage of a non-Arab to a member of the Caliph's own family.[35] In addition, the marriage took place despite the initial opposition of the Caliph who was eventually compelled to accept it.[36] Moreover, the actual control in Iraq, including Baghdad—the hometown of the Caliph and the centre of the Caliphate—passed within a couple of years into the hands of Tughril-Beg and thus the power of the Caliph became very limited, even in the purely Caliphate responsibilities, such as the administration of the revenues of Iraq.[37]

On one hand, the spiritual dominion of the Caliph al-Qā'im became wider[38] during the reign of Tughril-Beg's successor the

Sultan Alp Arslān[39] (455/1063-465/1072) who succeeded in occupying new lands in the name of the 'Abbāsid Caliphate.[40] In return, the Caliph bestowed on the new Sultan the honorific titles *'Aḍud al-Dawlah* (the Strong Arm of the State) and *Ḍiyā' al-Dīn* (the Light of the Religion).[41] Furthermore, the cordial relation between the two was strengthened to a certain extent when the Caliph's son and heir apparent, al-Qā'im, married the Sultan's daughter in 464/1071-1072.[42] On the other hand, the new Sultan gradually interfered in the Caliphate's affairs to the extent that he dared to appoint Caliphate officers without the knowledge of the Caliph and even without paying attention to his annoyance.[43]

Following the death of the Caliph al-Qā'im, the Caliphate in al-Muqtadī's days, as Ibn al-Athīr states, became greater than it had been before.[44] New strategic and valuable lands[45] were occupied by Malik Shāh—the Seljuk Sultan who succeeded Alp Arslān—and came under the spiritual dominion of the Caliph al-Muqtadī. To a certain extent, al-Muqtadī was honoured by the Sultan Malik Shāh,[46] but he also was eventually intensely annoyed by the growing control and interference of the Sultan and his officials in the Caliphate's prerogatives.[47] For example, Malik Shāh made the Caliph unwillingly discharge his vizier, Fakhr al-Dawlah.[48] Although al-Muqtadī, on the advice of Niẓām al-Mulk—the wise and pious vizier of Malik Shāh—married Malik Shāh's daughter seeking his cordiality, the marriage soon ended in separation, and the relation between the two became worst to the extent that Malik Shāh marched from Ispahan to Baghdad aiming to replace the Caliph, but he died before he completed his plan.[49]

During the reign of al-Mustaẓhir, who succeeded his father, al-Muqtadī, the Caliphate experienced very difficult times; yet, as Muir puts it, "whether in the history of the fanatical strife at home, or of the Crusade Christians in the Syrian lands, the Caliph's name is hardly ever noticed."[50] In addition, he, as well, experienced disturbance by the Seljuks[51] similar to that in his father's days, but to a relatively lesser extent, due to the conflicts which occurred among the Seljuks themselves during his reign.[52]

It is important to bear in mind though that these serious tensions between the ʿAbbāsid Caliphs and the Seljuk Sultans did not, as precisely noted by Huart, "have its roots in religious questions but was of a personal nature."[53] The Seljuks always regarded the office of the Caliphate as the highest authority of the whole Islamic *ummah*, and thus, as Sunnī military leaders loyal to the ʿAbbāsid Caliphate, they were religiously responsible for defending it.[54]

Although the ʿAbbāsid Caliphate had lost its classical fame by the time of al-Ghazālī, the Caliph of the time continued to exercise some power and authority, though it was limited, and seems to have been mostly symbolic or prestigious. The Caliph, for instance, was still responsible for appointing the Caliphate officials such as *Qāḍī al-Quḍāh* (the Chief Jurist). Moreover, he continued to be considered a political legitimizer for the independent local rulers. In order for the position of any ruler to be considered legitimate in a particular province, and thus be supported by both the general public and the *ʿulamāʾ*, the ruler had to be accredited by the Caliph of the time. This explains the determination of the rulers of that time to receive such legitimacy. For example, when the Almoravid Emir Yūsuf b. Tāshfīn took control over Granada in 483/1090,[55] which was the beginning of his rule in al-Andalus (Muslim Spain), he wrote to the ʿAbbāsid Caliph al-Muqtadī in Baghdad seeking his accreditation; the Caliph in turn legitimized his rule, and thus the Emir received his letter of investiture from Baghdad.[56]

As an upholder of the Sharīʿah and within his power—regardless of how limited it was—the Caliphs of the time also attempted to combat some aspects of *fasād* that appeared in their reigns. Al-Muqtadī, for example, ordered the expulsion of singing girls and *mufsidāt* from Baghdad, and prohibited boatmen from ferrying men and women together.[57] He also prohibited the outflow of waste water from bath-houses into the Tigris, and made their owners dig pits for the waste water.[58]

The caliph's officials of the time also played certain administrative roles.[59] However, the real players in the whole political scene at that age were not the Caliph or his officials, but rather the Seljuk Sultan and his officials, as we shall further illustrate below.

The Seljuk sultanate

Before spreading their supremacy over Iraq and before starting their noticeable interference in the 'Abbāsid Caliphate office in Baghdad,[60] the Seljuks[61] had already furthered their sway over vast areas of Central and Western Asia,[62] displacing the former Ghaznavid and the Būyid authorities there. In the first three decades of the age of al-Ghazālī, the expansion of the Seljuks continued and reached its zenith at the death of the Sultan Malik Shāh in 485/1092, which was a turning point in the history of the so-called "Great Seljuks."

After establishing his rule in Kirmān, which was almost independent, the Seljuk commander, Qāwurt,[63] succeeded in crossing the Persian Gulf and bringing Oman under his control, putting an end to the Būyid rule there, during the reign of his younger brother, the Seljuk supreme Sultan Alp Arslān (455/1063-465/1072).[64]

Moreover, the Sultan Alp Arslān himself successfully mounted daring raids into the Byzantine Empire. A year after his accession, Alp Arslān campaigned in Armenia, capturing its old capital, Ani, and other key Armenian cities from their Byzantine garrisons.[65] This tremendous achievement, as reported by Ibn al-Athīr,[66] was an occasion for rejoicing in Muslim communities and a victory which attracted special praise of the 'Abbāsid Caliph in whose Court the victory's report was read.

In addition to expanding his Sultanate by conquest, Alp Arslān succeeded in making some rulers of the time give allegiance to him. For example, in 457/1064-1065, as the Sultan crossed the Oxus marching towards Jand, where his ancestor had been buried, the ruler of Jand received him and loaded him with magnificent gifts, and pledged his allegiance.[67]

During the reign of the forceful Sultan Malik Shāh (465/1072-485/1092), the Seljuks further expanded their frontiers by conquering new strategic lands. Being ordered by the Sultan to conquer al-Ḥijāz and Yemen, a number of the Seljuk emirs marched on this campaign in 485/1092-1093 until they reached Yemen and took control of it, treating its inhabitants wickedly.[68] Furthermore, the Sultan personally led successful raids into Transoxiana, bringing under his rule important lands such as Samarqand and Kashghar.[69]

In this reign also, Sulaymān b. Qutalmish, a distant cousin of Malik Shāh, succeeded in making new conquests in Asia Minor, capturing Byzantine cities as far as the shores of the Sea of Marmara, and founding a Seljuk dynasty in Anatolia with its capital at Nicaea in about 470/1077; this was an almost totally independent dynasty which lasted to the early years of the eighth/ fourteenth century and which has become known as the Seljuks of Asia Minor or al-Rūm.[70]

Being Sunnīs and loyal to the 'Abbāsid Caliph, the Seljuks attempted to put an end to the Fāṭimid Shiite rule, as they had successfully done with regard to the Būyid Shiite authority. Concerning their attempt against the Fāṭimids, the Seljuks were partially successful for they liberated some key lands during the age under study; an achievement which may be seen as a victory for all Sunnīs of the time.[71] In addition to al-Ḥijāz and Yemen,[72] Aleppo slipped from the Fāṭimids' hands, and submitted to the Sultan Alp Arslān in 463/1070-1071;[73] Jerusalem and other neighbouring towns were taken from Egyptian garrisons by Atsiz al-Khawārizmī, one of the emirs of the Sultan Malik Shāh, in 463/1071;[74] the same Emir also besieged Damascus, which had been under the suzerainty of the Fāṭimids, in 468/1076;[75] and at Malik Shāh's command, his brother, Tutush, conquered Homs and other Fāṭimid Syrian coastal cities in 485/1092-1093.[76]

Despite their remarkable expansion, the Seljuks had various internal weaknesses, some of which were inherent in their Sultanate system.[77] As Klausner rightly pointed out, "the tendency toward internal quarrels and the division of the imperial territory into petty principalities during the Seljuk period may be considered a basic weakness of the empire and a major cause of its demise."[78] Internal disputes over supremacy among the Seljuk emirs occurred frequently throughout Seljuk history, including the period of the Great Seljuks.

In 456/1063, Shihāb al-Dawlah Qutalmish, a member of the Seljuk family, rebelled against the Sultan Alp Arslān and marched with large forces to Rayy to seize control, but the Sultan despatched a great army to suppress the rebellion, and the two armies joined in a battle which ended in the death of Qutalmish and the overwhelming defeat of his army.[79] In the same year, Fakhr al-Mulk Payghu b. Mīkhā'īl, who had ambitions to take power for himself, rebelled in Herat against his nephew Alp Arslān, who as a result marched against him with large forces and suppressed the rebellion, however he spared his uncle's life and treated him respectfully.[80] Three years later, the Sultan Alp Arslān went into another battle, but this time against his elder brother Qāwurt, the ruler of Kirmān, after he rebelled against the Sultan; yet the Sultan succeeded in suppressing the rebellion, forgiving his elder brother and restoring him to his rule.[81]

The death of the Sultan Alp Arslān in 465/1072 provoked a bloody dispute over the throne of the Sultanate between Malik Shāh, who was named by his father Alp Arslān as his successor, and his uncle Qāwurt who again declared an armed rebellion against the new Sultan and unsuccessfully intended to seize the Sultanate.[82] Similarly, Tekesh rebelled against his brother the Sultan Malik Shāh in 473/1081, seized Tirimidh and other towns, and marched to Nīshāpūr, with the ambition of controlling Khurāsān. However, the Sultan hastened to Khurāsān and arrived before his brother, who withdrew to Tirimidh; peace was then arranged between the two,[83] though it did not last long. Four years later, Tekesh abandoned his allegiance to his brother and declared a new rebellion which again was put down by Malik Shāh, who took his brother prisoner this time.[84]

Beside their internal weaknesses, the Seljuks faced some very serious external threats. One of the biggest threats was the Christian Byzantine counter-attack. This began in 462/1069-1070 when the Byzantine Emperor, Romanus, attacked Manbij in al-Shām with a large army, plundering its territories and killing its inhabitants, but because of the serious lack of provisions he returned to his home lands.[85] In the following year, he marched again with a vast heterogeneous army, but this time eastward, aiming first to reoccupy Armenia,[86] which had been recently conquered by the Seljuks.[87]

The Seljuks, however, responded well, though temporarily, to this external threat. As soon as he received the news of Romanus' march, the awe-inspiring Sultan Alp Arslān announced *jihād* against the Emperor and hurried with relatively small troops to confront this grave threat immediately.[88] At Malazgirt,[89] the two armies clashed in a decisive one-day battle on Friday, 14/11/463-19/8/1071, ending with a bitter defeat for the Byzantine army, and the capture of the Emperor Romanus himself, who was treated honourably and kindly by the Sultan, who freed him for a ransom, the release of all Muslim prisoners in the Byzantine Empire, and a promise of military support whenever needed.[90]

Although this historic victory of the Seljuks, as Runciman put it, "was the most decisive disaster in Byzantine history," it did not put an end to the Byzantine danger. It only provided a temporary protection of the Seljuk frontiers and removed the threat of a possible alliance between the Byzantines and the Fāṭimids.[91]

In addition to the Byzantine threat, the Seljuks suffered terribly from the revolt of the Nizārī Ismāʿīlī Shiites, known also as the Bāṭiniyyah,[92] which seriously attempted to put down the whole Seljuk rule.[93] Towards the end of Malik Shāh's reign, followers of this Shiite schism, under the leadership of Ḥasan al-Ṣabāḥ (d. 518/1124), secured themselves in the fortress of Alamūt in the mountains of Daylam north of Qazvīn.[94] Considering this a growing threat, Malik Shāḥ commanded the Emir Arslān Tāsh to march against this dangerous group in 485/1092, but the Emir was completely defeated.[95] Consequently, these Ismāʿīlī Shiites adopted a policy of open revolt which took the form of dreadful large-scale assassinations of their enemy's effective political, as well as intellectual leaders.[96] The assassination of the Sultanate's renowned vizier Niẓām al-Mulk[97] in 485/1092 is a case in point.[98]

This murder was a severe blow for the Sultanate. In his capacity as the vizier or the chief minister for thirty years, he played a fundamental role in the expansion and the administration of the Seljuk Sultanate. During the reign of Alp Arslān, Niẓām al-Mulk, as Bosworth concisely put it, "had a free hand in directing the administration of the empire; in addition, he spent much time on military duties, accompanying his master and also undertaking expeditions of his own."[99] His authority became greater during the reign of Malik Shāh who handed him all the administrative affairs.[100] Thus, much of the Seljuk achievements in these two reigns resulted from the contribution of Niẓām al-Mulk.

The death of Niẓām al-Mulk was a tremendous loss, not only for the Seljuks, but also for all the subjects of the Sultanate especially the Sunnī *ʿulamāʾ* of the time. Being just and pious, he abolished many types of dues and taxes.[101] He was credited with enhancing the Sunnī educational and intellectual activities by founding—and generously supporting—the Niẓāmiyyah[102] *madrasahs* (institutions of Islamic specialized learning) in several cities of the Sultanate.[103] Being himself a scholar, Shāfiʿī in *madhhab*,[104] he cancelled the cursing of the Ashʿariyyah from the Friday *khuṭbah*[105] and brought the Ashʿarī *ʿulamāʾ*, who had fled the lands in which the cursing applied, to their home towns.[106] It is reported that the Vizier's court was bustling with leading *ʿulamāʾ* and men of letters from whom he received much praise.[107]

Despite his noticeable authority in the Sultanate, Niẓām al-Mulk encountered considerable opposition. Various Sultan's officials and relatives challenged his power and caused him disturbance.[108]

Only a month after the murder of his Vizier, the Sultan Malik Shāh faced his death. Consequently, the Seljuks painfully experienced a relatively long period of internal disorder and violent conflict,[109]in which a visible decline of the Sultanate started. As Bosworth nicely and precisely described, "instead of that sultan's firm rule, a situation immediately arose involving various young, untried princes and their ambitious mothers, with no wise and restraining hand in the state like Niẓām al-Mulk."[110]

When Malik Shāh died, his ambitious widow, Turkān Khātūn, with the help of her vizier Tāj al-Mulk, placed her six-year-old[111] son, Maḥmūd, on the throne of the Sultanate, after securing the backing of the army and emirs, by distributing large sums of money to them,[112] and after getting a conditional agreement of the 'Abbāsid Caliph al-Muqtadī.[113] Fearing that Barkyāruq, Malik Shāh's oldest son and Maḥmūd's thirteen-year-old[114] half-brother, may dispute the Sultanate with her son, Turkān Khātūn duly issued an order for his arrest.[115] Soon after he was arrested in Isfahan, however, the adversary Niẓāmiyyah party, which consisted of Niẓām al-Mulk's relatives and partisans,[116] rioted in the city, freeing Barkyāruq from prison and proclaiming him Sultan. Driven only by their hate of Tāj al-Mulk, who had been a deadly enemy of their murdered master, Niẓām al-Mulk.[117] As a result, Turkān Khātūn and her son marched with the army from Baghdad to Isfahan, but as they approached the city, Barkyāruq and the Niẓāmiyyah party left the city towards al-Rayy, whereupon several emirs with their troops joined Barkyāruq's group, forming a single force.[118] Consequently, Turkān Khātūn sent the army to fight Barkyāruq and the two forces joined in a fierce battle, which resulted in complete defeat of Turkān Khātūn's army and the capture of Tāj al-Mulk, who was then killed by the Niẓāmiyyah men in 486/1093.[119]

This defeat though did not stop that ambitious lady from acting against Barkyāruq until her sudden death in 487/1094, followed shortly by her son's death.[120]

Another serious dispute over succession occurred in these troubled times between Barkyāruq and his uncle Tutush, the governor of Damascus, who attempted to take over the Sultanate following his brother's death. When Tutush with his troops succeeded in taking control of some Syrian and Iraqi territories and set out to Azerbaijan in 486/1093,[121] Barkyāruq took his army and marched against his uncle. At this critical point, two of the chief commanders in Tutush's troops agreed to leave him and join Barkyāruq, whereupon Tutush withdrew to al-Shām, realizing that he had become incapable of meeting Barkyāruq's force.[122] In the following year and after gathering numerous troops, Tutush resumed his activity to usurp the Sultanate by attacking and controlling several cities in al-Shām, Iraq, Armenia and Azerbaijan.[123] This violent attack ended only when he was completely defeated, and then slain in a decisive battle with his nephew Barkyāruq, which took place near Rayy in 488/1095.[124]

At the beginning of the year 487/1094, Barkyāruq gained the recognition of the 'Abbāsid Caliph al-Muqtadī, who bestowed on him the honorific title *Rukn al-Dīn* (Pillar of Religion), and his name started to be mentioned in the Friday *khuṭbah* in Baghdad.[125] Nevertheless, Barkyāruq did not enjoy this recognition long, for a number of his close relatives, other than his uncle Tutush, rebelled against him. His uncle Arslān Arghūn repelled in Khurāsān, before he was murdered by a page in 490/1097; Barkyāruq whereupon controlled Khurāsān without fight and handed it to his brother Sanjar.[126] In the same year, Muḥammad b. Sulaymān, a cousin of Barkyāruq's father, allied with the ruler of Ghazana, who supported him with a large well-equipped army, rose in revolt against Barkyāruq in Khurāsān, but it was suppressed by Sanjar.[127]

The most serious and long-running revolt against Barkyāruq was lead by his half-brother Muḥammad. In a period of eight years, starting from 490/1097, there were ongoing fierce struggles with changing success between these two brothers.[128] This period was characterised by changes of allegiance among the Turkish, Kurdish, and Arab emirs which added to the general confusion of the time.[129] For example, Sanjar inclined towards his full-brother Muḥammad; and the majority of the Niẓāmiyyah party as well as some other emirs left Barkyāruq and took the side of his brother.[130]

This long-standing dispute, which lead to massive destruction and widespread harm, ended only when Barkyāruq, lacking resources, took the initiative and arranged for a permanent peace agreement in 497/1104, consisting of agreed division of the Sultanate between him and his brother Muḥammad so that each one would be an independent sultan in his own lands.[131] In the following year, Barkyāruq died, after appointing his fourteen-year-old son Malik Shāh as his successor,[132] who was shortly dethroned by the Sultan Muḥammad.[133] Thus, Muḥammad became the only supreme Seljuk Sultan for the following thirteen years (498/1105-511/1118).[134]

Similar to the previous Sultans, Muḥammad, in order to secure his reign, had to deal with members of the Seljuk dynasty who rebelled against him.[135] In 499/1105, he suppressed the rebellion of Mankubars,[136] a grandson of Alp Arslān, in Nahāwand.[137] In the following year, Qilij-Arslān,[138] the Seljuk independent ruler of al-Rūm, controlled Mosul, omitted the name of the Sultan Muḥammad from the *khuṭbah* and replaced it with his name; but then he was defeated by the Sultan's commander Jāwlī,[139]and eventually drowned in a river.[140]

The gravely everlasting internal crisis, from the death of Malik Shāh onwards, profited only the lurking enemies of the Seljuks. The Bāṭinīs, the old enemies of the Seljuks, intensified their dreadful activity during this crisis, contributing to the turbulence of the time. Moreover, in the same period, the Crusaders[141] came onto the scene, starting a fierce military campaign and eventually invading valuable Muslim lands in Anatolia and the Levant, which became an awful nightmare for the Seljuks, in particular, and all Muslims of the time, in general.[142]

The Fāṭimid independent caliphate

The existence of the Fāṭimid Caliphate clearly exemplified the serious problem of the political disunity of Muslims during the time of al-Ghazālī. By completely rejecting the authority of the 'Abbāsid Caliph and adopting the name of Caliphate, the Fāṭimid Caliphate broke the symbolic political unity of the Muslim *ummah*. According to the Fāṭimid's ideal, however, the adaptation of the name of Caliphate was a dream to restore the Muslim unity.[143] Although the Fāṭimid Caliphate was an outcome of an Ismā'īlī *da'wah* (religious preaching),[144] it was not meant to be a state representing the Ismā'īlīs only, but all Muslims, a dream which never became real.[145]

Being based on the Ismā'īlī's tradition, the legitimacy of the Fāṭimid Caliphate was always challenged. The Fāṭimid's claim of being descendants of the daughter of the Prophet, Fāṭimah, and her husband 'Alī, the cousin of the Prophet (ṣ), through Ismā'īl son of Ja'far al-Ṣādiq—on which the Fāṭimids relied in legitimizing their authority—was denied by their opponents.[146] Furthermore, the claimed origin of the Fāṭimids is wrapped with uncertainty, for several different genealogies are found in the sources, even those of the Ismā'īlīs.[147] The Sunnī historians, with very few exceptions, refer to the Fāṭimids as 'Ubaydīs, connecting them to 'Ubaydallāh al-Mahdī, the first Fāṭimid Caliph. According to al-Suyūṭī, who did not include the Fāṭimid caliphs in his book on Caliphs and argued that their *imāmah* was not legitimate quoting the views of some distinguished *ulmā*, only the ignorant mass call the 'Ubaydīs Fāṭimids.[148]

Regardless of its legitimacy, the Fāṭimid Caliphate was a real challenge to the 'Abbāsid Caliphate. However, the extent of this challenge was reduced by the rise of the Seljuks who, being ideological and political enemies of the Fāṭimids, displaced the Fāṭimids from a number of their former provinces, as shown above. Similarly, more Fāṭimid provinces came under other different authorities. In 484/1091-1092, Sicily was taken from the Fāṭimids, and came under the control of the Franks.[149] Furthermore, the Fāṭimid's African provinces were gradually losing their connection with the central government in Egypt, and had started to become independent or to restore their allegiance to the 'Abbāsid Caliph of the time. As a result, the dominion of the Fāṭimids became very limited. Other than Egypt itself, and with the exception of temporary recognition in some lands,[150] only Yemen, under the dynasty of the Ṣulayḥīs, remained loyal to the Fāṭimid Caliphs, before it was also conquered by the Seljuks in 485/1092-1093.[151]

In addition to its shrinking threat, the Fāṭimid state suffered from serious challenges during the age of al-Ghazālī. One of these challenges was the shaky loyalty of the leaders of the state. There were incidents of disloyalty of some leaders in the Fāṭimid state even in Egypt itself. In 462/1070, for example, Nāṣir al-Dawlah stopped the *khuṭbah* in the name of the Fāṭimid Caliph al-Mustanṣir in Alexandria and the surrounding areas and replaced it by the name of the 'Abbāsid Caliph of the time.[152]

The most serious challenge for the Fāṭimid state was the disorder in Egypt itself for a period of time. A major cause for this was the very terrible seven years' famine (457/1065-464/1072), which exhausted the resources of the state.[153] The military disturbance contributed much to the disorder. Among the Fāṭimid troops, which consisted of soldiers of different origins, including Berbers, Turks, Daylamīs, and Sudanese slaves, there was always a feeling of jealousy and hatred.[154] This feeling provoked battles between the troops on some occasions, as in 454/1062 and 459/1067.[155]

The insecurity of the *viziers*, which generally speaking characterized the Fāṭimid vizierate,[156] seems to be another cause for the disorder in Fāṭimid Egypt. There was continual coming and going of viziers between 454/1062 and 466/1074.[157]

Another serious challenge faced the Fāṭimid state was its loss of the support of the Ismā'īlī "diaspora" resulting from the Nizārī schism.[158] The death of the Fāṭimid Caliph al-Mustanṣir in 487/1094, who had reigned for fifty-eight years, provoked a deep split between the Ismāʿīlīs over the succession to the *imāmah*.[159] When al-Mustanṣir's youngest son Aḥmad was raised to the throne and given the title of al-Mustaʿlī by the Fāṭimid Vizier al-Afḍal, his eldest brother Nizār, who had been originally nominated by his father as successor, rose in revolt. However, this was suppressed and consequently Nizār was put in prison.[160] As a result, the *imāmah* of al-Mustaʿlī was accepted by the majority of the Egyptian Ismāʿīlīs, many in Syria and all of the Yemeni Ismāʿīlīs, while the Persian and some Syrian Ismāʿīlīs were in favour of Nizār, refusing the *imāmah* of his younger brother.

In spite of the above symptoms of decline, the Fāṭimid state—generally speaking—"enjoyed great prosperity."[161] In addition, the Fāṭimid Caliphs of the time, namely al-Mustanṣir who was the richest among the Egyptian caliphs, lived extreme luxurious life.[162]

With regard to the Fāṭimid administration, the actual power was mainly not in the hands of the caliphs.[163] This was partially because the three consecutive Fāṭimid caliphs of the time were placed on the throne while they were mere children: al-Mustanṣir was seven-years old, al-Mustaʿlī was eight and al-Āmir was only five.[164] As a result, there was usually a regent who acted on behalf of the caliph and maintained great power. This led to the interference of women in government, which was an evident feature of the Fāṭimid state. During the first years of his reign, al-Mustanṣir, for instance, was under the regency of his mother.[165]

Moreover, the actual control was in hands of the viziers or military leaders even when the Caliph became mature.[166] For example, the all-powerful Vizier and *Amīr al-Juyūsh* (head of the troops) Badr al-Jamālī, who was summoned by the Caliph hoping to save the state from downfall upon its serious deterioration, held full control of the civil, judicial and religious affairs.[167] The power of the Fāṭimid viziers and the military leaders was so great to the extent that on some occasions they acted against the will of the caliphs. For instance, al-Mustanṣir was forced by the army to accept al-Afḍal, son of Badr al-Jamālī, as his Vizier after the death of his father in 488/1095.

The Almoravid rule

Shortly before the birth of al-Ghazālī, the Almoravids (al-Murābiṭūn), under the spiritual leadership and the supreme authority of the Mālikī scholar 'Abdullāh b. Yāsīn,[168] had enthusiastically emerged[169] from the Western Sahara spreading his *iṣlāḥī* teaching,[170] abolishing illegal practices and announcing *jihād* against the infidels, the oppressors and the superficial followers of Islam in that desert, which was inhabited by disputing tribes.[171]

In a relatively short time, the Almoravids succeeded in making the Saharan tribes either under their authority or their allies through diplomacy, missionary work and eventually a number of challenging militant campaigns,[172] which had been led, in addition to Ibn Yāsīn, initially by the Emir of the army Yaḥyā b. 'Umar, who was killed in one of the battles in about 448/1056, and then by his brother the Emir Abū Bakr.

As a response to a complaint which had been sent to Ibn Yāsīn from the inhabitants of Sijilimāsah about the oppression of its emirs, the Almoravids army marched to the country, liberated its people and appointed their own governor.[173] This being done, the trans-Saharan trade routes came under the control of the Almoravids.[174]

Following this achievement, the Emir Abū Bakr urged his people to control the Maghrib, which had been divided into pretty tribal principalities. Between 448/1056 to 451/1059, they were able to bring under their control strategic territories, including Wādī Dar'ah, the Sūs region and Aghmāt whereupon Abū Bakr married the widow of its ruler, the redoubtable and intelligent queen Zaynab al-Nafrāwiyyah,[175] who would soon play a noticeable role in the history of the Almoravids before her death in 464/1071.

In about 451/1059, the Almoravids lost the founder of their movement, Ibn Yāsīn, in a raid against the heretic Bargwāṭa Berbers. With this incident a new phase of the Almoravids movement began. It transformed itself into a dynastic rule.[176] Although it is reported that Ibn Yāsīn was succeeded by Sulaymān

b. 'Adū as a religious reference,[177] who in turn faced his death in 452/1060, but he had no significant role in the history of the Almoravids when compared to Abū Bakr b. 'Umar[178] who appeared to be the sole ruler of the Almoravids to the extent that the Almoravids golden *dīnārs* [179] were struck in his name.[180]

Having established himself as a ruler, Ibn 'Umar made another raid against the Bargwāṭa, succeeding this time to subjugate these Berbers whose lands extended to the north as far as the Atlantic Ocean.[181] Before finishing the campaign in the Maghrib and the establishment of the Almoravids new capital of Marrakesh, Ibn 'Umar returned to the Sahara in order to resolve a serious dispute between two branches of the Saharan tribes threatening the unity of the Almoravid state, but before that he appointed his cousin Yūsuf b. Tāshfīn as his lieutenant in the Maghrib, committed to him the task of continuing the conquests in the Maghrib and even abounded his new wife Zaynab, after divorcing her, to him.[182]

Having intensified the Almoravids army and made it composed of heterogeneous soldiers changing its old character of being dependent only on particular Saharan tribesmen,[183] the new leader gradually completed the conquest of the whole Maghrib up to Tilimsān which fell in 476/1083.[184] Meanwhile, he continued the construction of Marrakesh,[185] the new capital and his base.

It is reported that Ibn Tāshfīn was known as a pious, strong-willed and subtle man,[186] who was generous to the *'ulamā'*, whom he was constantly consulting.[187] Though faithful to his desert customs, Ibn Tāshfīn ruled his subjects nicely,[188] avoiding cruel acts.

On the advice of his wife, Zaynab, he subtly showed his cousin Ibn 'Umar that he was not willing at all to give him back the supreme authority in the Maghrib when the latter succeeded in re-establishing peace in the Sahara, and returned to the Maghrib, attempting unsuccessfully to resume his previous supremacy.[189] Avoiding conflict, Ibn 'Umar went back to his original land where he met his death in 480.[190] Upon the death of Ibn 'Umar, the Almoravids unanimously submit to Ibn Tāshfīn, calling him Amīr al-Muslimīn,[191] reserving the title *amīr al-mu'minīn* for the 'Abbāsid Caliph, whose title appeared on the Almoravids *dīnārs*,[192] indicating their symbolic loyalty to him.

Due to the religious vigour of Ibn Tāshfīn and his formidable troops, he was called by the Andalusain Muslims to defend their country from the Spanish Christian invasion.[193] After responding successfully to this external challenge, Ibn Tāshfīn found himself with the great opportunity to unite the Andalusian petty states under his rule. As he did in the Maghrib, he succeeded in uniting al-Andalus. "It was under this union that the Muslim civilization of Spain made its greatest impact on Morocco."[194]

The achievement of Ibn Tāshfīn was acknowledged with pride not only in the Maghrib, but also in the Mashriq to the extent that the 'Abbāsid Caliph in Baghdad legitimized his rule upon his request.[195]

In 500/1106, Ibn Tāshfīn faced his death, passing on to his son 'Alī[196], a vast state extending from the Atlanitic Ocean to Bijāya (Bougie) in the North-East and to the Sudan in the South-East; and from Ghana in the South to the north of the Iberian peninsula.[197] 'Alī b. Tāshfīn was acknowledged as *amīr al-muslimīn* throughout the Almoravid provinces, save in Fez where its governor, 'Alī's cousin Yaḥyā b. Abī, refused to submit to him.[198] Consequently, 'Alī marched against him and removed him from his position.[199]

During the reign of 'Alī, which lasted more than the age of al-Ghazālī,[200] the Almoravids rule was troubled by serious challenges[201] and thus it marked the beginning of its decline. The ensuing dramatic events,[202] however, are beyond the scope of this chapter.

The Muslim mule in al-Andalus

During the first three decades of al-Ghazālī's age, there was a state of political confusion in the Iberian Peninsula, al-Andalus, which had started since the central government of the Ummayyad

Caliphate in Cordoba—the capital and the symbol of unity of al-Andalus throughout its history[203]—had become paralysed and eventually collapsed in 422/1031. The Islamic rule there at the time was nothing but a variety of politically disunited petty kingdoms and states[204], which depended on local resources.[205] Their rulers, who were known as *mulūk al-ṭawā'if* (kings of parties or factions), represented varied ethnic groups, namely Berbers, Slavs and local Arab families.[206] A number of these rulers were mainly driven by their own interests, without much concern for the general benefit of Andalusians as a whole.[207] They tended to seek control of their neighbours[208] and thus grasp more resources.[209] To achieve their interests, they did not refrain from forming depraved alliances with the Christian rulers in the north against their brethren Muslims.[210]

There were at least thirty-eight[211] *ṭā'ifah* kingdoms and states, which were of varied strength and size.[212] The strongest among them was in Seville,[213] which was ruled by Banū 'Abbād. During the reign of al-Mu'tamid [214](461/1068-484/1091), who succeeded his father al-Mu'taḍid (433/1042-461/1068), the boundaries of this small kingdom were expanded in the west and south-west.[215] Moreover, Cordoba itself, which had been ruled—since the collapse of the Caliphate there—by Banū Jahwar [216] who had always adopted a peaceful policy towards their neighbours,[217] was added to the kingdom of Seville in 461/1069.[218]

In the north of al-Andalus, there was the Hūdids kingdom, with its capital in Saragossa, which had been founded by Sulaymān b. Muḥammad b. Hūd who had made his five sons governors along the kingdom: Aḥmad in Saragossa, Yūsuf in Lleida, Muḥammad in Calatayud, Lub in Huesca and al-Mundhir in Tudela.[219] Following the death of their father, every one acquired a firm grip on his territory. However, Aḥmad, who was extremely ambitious, did not refrain from using evil tricks to get rid of his brothers, in order to control what their possessions; in this he largely succeeded.[220]

To the south of this kingdom, there was another *ṭā'ifah* state with its capital in Valencia, which was ruled by al-Manṣūr 'Abd al-'Azīz b. Muḥammad b. 'Āmir, who died in 452/1061 and was succeeded by his son al-Muẓafar 'Abd al-Malik.[221] In 1065, al-Ma'mūn Yaḥyā b. Dhī al-Nūn, the *ṭā'ifah* king of Toledo and the father in law of al-Muẓafar, added Valencia to his *ṭā'ifah* kingdom and replaced his son in law by Abū Bakr Muḥammad b. 'Abd al-'Azīz.[222] When the king of Toledo died in 467/1075, he was succeeded by his grandson al-Qādir, Valencia became independent again, but it continued to be ruled by Abū Bakr.[223]

These selected examples clearly show the dangerous political disunity of al-Andalus during this period regardless of its preserved religious and cultural unity.[224] Although there were still striking Andalusian achievements at the time, noticeably in literary activities and particularly in poetry,[225] the Andalusians of this period experienced regrettable conditions chiefly in political affairs as a result of their disunity. They in short, as Kennedy clearly put it, "were increasingly harassed, both militarily and financially, by the Christian powers to the north, and their rulers seem to have been powerless to respond except by paying large sums of money…to their tormentors."[226]

As they became aware of the weakness of the Andalusians, the Christian rulers in the north made use of this opportunity to force *ṭā'ifah* kingdoms to pay excessive tributes to them.[227] For example, the ruler of Castile and Leon, Alfonso VI (457/1065-502/1109), was able to force al-Mu'taḍid, the king of Seville, to enter into the established tributary system.[228]

More grievous experience for the Andalusians of the time was the Christians' aggressive invasion of valuable parts of their lands. Barbastro, for instance, was catastrophically invaded by Normans and Franks after desperate resistance from its people in 456/1064.[229] In the same year, the Andalusians lost Coimbra.[230] More striking was the fall of Toledo in the hands of Alfonso VI in 478/1085.[231]

In response to this sorrowful and threatening condition, a number of Andalusian sincere *'ulamā'* supported by few rulers, or vice versa, made serious efforts to rescue their lands and to revive their unity.[232] Some of these efforts were fruitful. A good example is the successful mobilization of local volunteers for the *jihād* against the invaders of Barbastro, an effort which led to liberation of the city in 475/1065.[233] The most striking effort was the emergency meeting, following the crisis of Toledo, which was summoned by the *ṭā'ifah* king of Seville, al-Mu'tamid, and was attended by some *'ulamā'* and other *ṭā'ifah* rulers.[234] The result of this was an agreement to seek the support of the Almoravids' Emir, Ibn Tāshfīn, and his strong army.[235]

Responding to this call, Ibn Tāshfīn crossed with his army from the Maghrib to al-Anadalus where he was joined by some of the *ṭā'ifah* rulers and their troops. These joint forces clashed with the Christians army under Alfonso VI at Zallāqah on Friday 12 Rajab 479 (23/10/1086), which lead to a decisive defeat of the army of Alfonso VI and its retreat to Toledo with great loss.[236] Shortly after this, Ibn Tāshfīn and his army, save a garrison unit, returned to the Maghrib for uncertain reasons.[237]

The defeat of Alfonso VI at Zallāqah did not stop the Christians' growing serious threat in al-Andalus, and this threat was by no means enough reason for the *ṭā'ifah* rulers to unite and halt the disputes between them. As a result, a number of letters from the Andalusian notables and *fatāwā* from some *fuqahā'* of the Mashriq, among them al-Ghazālī, were sent to Ibn Tāshfīn urging him to rescue Islam and Muslims in al-Andalus.[238]

In response to this, Ibn Tāshfīn marched to al-Andalus, but this time with two challenging tasks: resisting the Christian threat and dethroning the depraved *ṭā'ifah* kings, a matter in which he was supported by *fatāwā* from some of the Andalusian *fuqahā'*.[239] On both, he performed effectively. Before his death in 500/1106, he could occupy almost all of al-Andalus,[240] establishing the Almoravids rule there which lasted more than the age of al-Ghazālī.

The first crusade and the Muslim response

As shall be examined below, the response of al-Ghazali to the grave challenge of the Crusaders has prompted heavy criticism. Believing it important to bear in mind the chronological sequence of the Crusading campaign and the Muslim response to it before examining Ghazali's position in particular, I therefore devote this section for this purpose.

Through the determined and successful efforts of both Pope Urban II and the Byzantine Emperor Alexius Commenus, large allied western European forces, under various independent princes joined with several priests and assisted militarily and logistically by the Emperor, devotedly launched a military campaign—which has become known as the First Crusade—aiming eventually to capture the sacred city of Jerusalem from Muslims after freeing the way across Asia Minor and the Levant from the Seljuk and any other Muslim rulers; and thus reoccupying the lands which had been recently lost from the Christian Byzantine Empire following its grave defeat by the Seljuks at Malazgirt in 463/1071.[241]

Unwilling to wait for the arrival of the main crusading forces and ignoring the advice of the Byzantine Emperor, over 20,000 initial French, German and Italian Crusader armies, called the People's Crusade in the sources, launched savage raids into western Anatolia, plundered a number of villages—torturing and killing their Greek Christian inhabitants—and drove to the gates of Nicaea, the capital city of the Seljuk Sultan of al-Rūm, Qilij-Arslān. Eventually, however, they were completely defeated by this Sultan towards the end of 489/1096.[242]

Underestimating the actual threat of the coming Crusades, and self-deluded by his dazzling victory, Qilij-Arslān left his capital city at that critical time and marched eastwards to deal with his rival, the Emir Dānishmend, who had controlled north-eastern Anatolia—after the death of Qilij-Arslān's father—and blockaded the Armenian city Melitene.[243] This was the ideal chance for the Crusaders to advance towards Nicaea. When he received the news that the Franks had laid siege to Nicaea, Qilij-Arslān declared a truce with Dānishmend and rushed to save his capital.[244] After a valiant but unsuccessful attempt to break through the firm Crusader siege all around the city, the Sultan helplessly withdrew eastward, leaving the garrison of Nicaea to their own devices. They soon completely surrendered on 29-6-490/18-6-1097; and Byzantine troops entered the city, and thus it came under the mercy of the Emperor, which provoked the bitterness of the European Crusaders.[245]

Soon after his painful withdrawal, the Sultan Qilij-Arslān started to prepare seriously for undertaking *jihād* against the Christian invaders, gathering more Turkish troops and even allying with his opponent the Emir Dānishmend against their common enemies.[246] On 12/7/490-30/6/1097, these joint Turkish troops set up an ambush near Dorylaeum, and waited for the arrival of the Crusaders who had set out from Nicaea in regiments.[247] Shortly after a Crusading army set up camp close to Dorylaeum, it was fully surrounded by the Turks and shot by hail of arrows which killed many Christian soldiers.[248] Unaware that the trapped army was just a group of the Crusaders, the Turks were badly shocked as they saw another Crusading army come to reinforce their fellow Christians.[249] In a while, panic spread through the Turk camp as a third Crusading army appeared suddenly from the rear, whereupon the Turkish troops put to flight in crucial defeat.[250] In his flight, Qilij-Arslān met Syrian troops who came to assist him, but it was too late.[251]

This decisive defeat of the Turkish forces opened the way for the Crusaders to advance up to the frontiers of the Levant in a period which lasted from 15/7/490-3/7/1097 to 6/11/490-20/10/1097, during which they entered several Anatolian cities, ending the Turkish control over them, and these were restored to the Byzantine Empire.[252] This period did not witness Muslim resistance which is worth mentioning, save occasional appearance of limited Turkish troops and garrisons which could not withstand the Crusaders. Nevertheless, in particular parts of their expedition, the Crusaders encountered severe difficulties due to scarcity of water and provisions, as well as bad weather and road conditions, which caused the loss of many lives. However, by having a number of refreshing rests in some relieving fertile lands on their way, they eventually managed to approach to the walls of Antioch,[253] which had slipped from the Byzantines to the Seljuks in 477/1085.[254]

When the Crusaders crossed the frontiers of the Levant, time was on their side. As shown above, the main Seljuk armies in the east, which were supposed to play an effective role in resisting the Crusading invasion, were fully engaged in ongoing internal warfare. Moreover, the Levant itself was a field of internal serious dispute among various emirs, namely between the Seljuk Emir Riḍwān b. Tutush of Aleppo and his brother the Emir Duqāq of Damascus. Not long before the advance of the Crusaders to Antioch, there was a bloody war between the Emir Riḍwān, supported by a large host of Turcomans under Suqmān b. Artuq of Saruj, on one side and the Emir Duqāq with the governor of Antioch, the Turcoman Emir Baghī-Siyān,[255] who had recently abandoned the Emir Riḍwān and inclined towards his brother, and their forces on the other side, which ended with the defeat of Duqāq and his forces.[256]

On 6/11/490-20/10/1097 the Crusading armies arrived at the walls of Antioch, and laid siege to the city, which was strongly fortified against attack and full of supplies.[257] As the blockaders' almost ran out of provisions in about two months, the Prince of Taranto, Bohemond I, and the Count of Flanders, Robert II, with 20,000 men were dispatched to raid the villages in the Orontes valley and to bring more supplies.[258] At the village of Albara, Robert with his men, who were in the vanguard, were suddenly surrounded by Muslim forces, under Duqāq b. Tutush of Damascus, to whom Baghī-Siyān had sent his own son to directly appeal for rescuing his city, and joined with the Emir of Ḥamāh, who were in their way to relieve Antioch. However, a surprising assault commanded by Bohemond on the rear of the Muslim forces, at the last moment, rescued Robert's men and forced the Muslims to withdraw to Ḥamāh with more grievous losses than their enemies.[259] Consequently, Bohemond and Robert returned, with almost nothing but exhaustion caused by this clash, to their camp at Antioch, which they found in an extremely depressing state due to the shock of a night attack by a group of Turks from inside the blockaded city shortly after they had left, followed by bad winter weather condition, in addition to the growing food and health crisis.[260]

Following the withdrawal of Duqāq's relief army, Baghī-Siyān of Antioch was forced to urgently plead for help from the Emir Riḍwān of Damascus, who had remained extremely unresponsive to the threat of the Crusaders in short-sighted revenge for Baghī-Siyān's disloyalty during the previous war with his brother Duqāq. Nevertheless alarmed by the seriousness of the threat, he finally embarked on a campaign to deal with the Crusaders supported by the Emir Suqmān b. Artuq of Diyarbakr and the Emir of Ḥamāh.[261] Learning of their approach to Antioch, 700 knights among the Crusaders set up an ambush for the Riḍwān's joint forces between the river and the lake of Antioch.[262] On 28/2/491-8/2/1098, the knights took these forces by surprise, and a fierce battle took place leading to the retreat of the Riḍwān's forces to Aleppo in total disarray.[263] Meanwhile, Baghī-Siyān suddenly attacked in full-scale the Camp of the blockaders, forcing its defenders to be driven back, but by seeing the victorious knights coming back, he ordered his soldiers to return to the city.[264]

By the sixth month of the siege of Antioch, the Crusaders' condition had been eased, while the situation of their blockaded enemies had become more critical. Provided by workmen and building materials from Constantinople, the blockaders had built fortresses to completely prevent any access to the city.[265] As a result, they had succeeded in capturing large quantities of provisions destined for the people of Antioch.[266]

While the situation in Antioch was getting worse, Karbughā[267] of Mosul, accompanied with other forces from various quarters under different emirs, was on his way to rescue the city.[268] Miscalculation led Karbughā, despite the reservation of other army chiefs, to march first against Edessa, which had come under the rule of Count Baldwin who had separated from the Crusaders to raid into Armenia. Karbughā was unaware that Baldwin was too weak to attack him, yet was wholly secure in his strong fortresses; however, after wasting three critical weeks before the walls of Edessa, he finally turned to Antioch.[269] In the meantime, Bohemond, through top secret communication, concluded an agreement with a senior commander in Antioch's government on selling the city to the Crusaders.[270]

The approach of the Karbughā's forces caused panic among the Crusaders to the extent that many of them started to desert.[271] Shortly before the actual arrival of the relief forces, however, the city had suddenly fallen. Through the plot of the treacherous commander who was in charge of guarding one of the Antioch's towers, the Crusaders stormed into the city at the break of dawn of 25/6/491-3/6/1098, massacring all the Turk population who they found, men and women alike; while Baghī-Siyān with some of his men fled in terror; however, he was eventually killed by a band of Armenians.[272] Unlike Baghī-Siyān, his brave son Shams al-Dawlah managed to gather some soldiers and firmly hold the citadel of the city, repelling the assaults of the invaders against it, but unable to mount any offensive attack.[273]

A few days after the fall of Antioch, Karbughā arrived and laid siege to the invaded city.[274] Shams al-Dawlah sought help from Karbughā and requested that he retain command, but the latter demanded that the citadel should be handed over to his commander Aḥmad b. Marwān.[275] To prevent any attempt to break into the city from this most vulnerable part, the Frankish invaders had fortified it by constructing a separate wall and by intensifying their defence there.[276] These precautionary measures proved successful. Ibn Marwān mounted an attack from the citadel, but was driven back with heavy loss.[277]

As the siege continued, the blockaded city sank into gloom.[278] Provisions were growing scarce to the extent that the poor among the Franks started to eat carrion and the leaves of trees, while the rich were eating their sumpters.[279] The morale of the Crusaders declined dramatically.[280] However, "at this juncture the spirits of the Christians were raised by a series of events which seemed to them to show God's special favour,"[281] namely the finding of a lance which claimed to go back to the time of Christ.[282]

Meanwhile, Karbughā's coalition of forces started to look dangerously shaky. His arrogance and mistreatment alienated the other commanders in the coalition and many of them decided to desert him.[283] Moreover, there was growing discord among Karbughā's own troops.[284] Despite these worrying internal problems, Karbughā refused a proposal for conditional surrender of the Franks and insisted on fighting.[285]

Consequently, the Crusaders marched out on 20/7/491-28/6/1098, prepared for the clash with high courage.[286] While they were emerging in small groups, the Muslims wanted to pick them off straight away but Karbughā forbade them, preferring to attack all of them in one blow; however, when all the Franks came out and stood in a great array, many of Karbughā's troops deserted the battle field due to Karbughā's mistreatment and his order of delaying the attack.[287] Shortly, Karbughā himself fled, following other chief commanders, but a group of true *mujāhids* stood firm, fighting for the sake of God and aiming martyrdom.[288] Thousands of these Muslims were killed by the Franks.[289] When the men in the citadel saw that the Muslims were defeated, they surrendered and thus the Crusaders won unexpectedly a complete victory.[290]

Before the fall of Antioch, the Fāṭimids had come onto the scene of the Muslim-Crusader conflict, but rather shamefully in a bad spot. During the Crusader siege of Antioch, a suspicious embassy was dispatched by the Fāṭimid all-powerful Vizier and actual ruler of Egypt, al-Afḍal, to the Crusaders.[291] The proposal of al-Afḍal, as Runciman points out, "seems to have been that a division should be made of the Seljuk empire; the Franks should take northern Syria and Egypt should take Palestine."[292] The Franks, however, "far from being willing to aid the Egyptians to recover Palestine, had every intention of themselves marching on Jerusalem."[293] Nevertheless, underestimating the actual plans of the Franks[294] and profiting from the weakness of the Turks, their traditional enemies, who had been recently defeated by the Crusaders in Antioch, the Fāṭimid army under al-Afḍal undertook an ill-timed expedition to Jerusalem and after blockading it for more than forty days they eventually recaptured it from the Seljuks,[295] despite the initial resistance of its population.[296] Al-Afḍal, however, would discover too late the real objectives of the Crusaders,[297] as we shall see shortly.

In addition to al-Afḍal, there were other Muslim leaders who had unfortunate contacts and forms of collaboration with the Crusaders against their fellow-Muslim political opponents. For example, after the fall of Antioch, the Emir of A'zāz (Azaz), 'Umar, who rebelled against the Emir Riḍwān of Aleppo, sought the help of the Franks when his old master intended to suppress his rebellion.[298]

Following the Franks' complete victory in Antioch, there was a delay to the Crusade for a couple of months due firstly to a serious disagreement among chief Crusader princes, namely Bohemond I of Taranto and Raymond IV of Saint-Gilles, over the possession of Antioch, and secondly to a major epidemic which broke out in the city.[299] An eminent victim of the epidemic was the Bishop of Le Puy, Adhemar, who, as the Pope's representative in the Crusade, had played a very significant role in its success.[300]

Before the resumption of the march to Jerusalem, a number of successful small but fierce raids into the lands nearby Antioch were conducted by segments of the Crusaders, securing provisions and capturing some Syrian towns including Rugia and Albara.[301] On 26/12/491-28/11/1098, a Frankish attack was launched against the town of Ma'rrah al-Nu'mān but it was strongly resisted by its Arab population, whereupon the city was entirely blockaded.[302]

After thirteen days of blockading the town, the Franks, using a large movable wooden tower, forced their way into the town, massacring thousands of its population[303] and even engaging in cannibalism.[304]

In early 492/1099, Raymond and his army set out from Ma'rrah al-Nu'mān to resume the Crusade independently, helplessly leaving Antioch in the full control of the Prince Bohemond.[305] Shortly, other Crusading leaders, save Baldwin and Bohemond, decided to join Raymond and thus he became unchallenged leader of the Crusade.[306]

As Raymond reached Kafartab, the Emir of Shayzar [307] sent a delegation to him, proposing to provide the Franks with provisions and guides on condition that they would not invade his lands.[308] By accepting the proposal, Raymond followed the Emir's guides and led the Franks across the Orontes River.[309] When they reached the town of Masyaf on 22/2/492-22/1/1099, its head reluctantly entered into a treaty with them.[310] Next, they captured Ḥiṣn al-Akrād, taking considerable booty.[311] At this fortress, the Crusaders received envoys from the independent emirs of Hums and Tripoli, helplessly offering precious gifts and proposing treaties.[312] Despite the initiative of the Emir of Tripoli, the Crusaders raided his territory and laid siege to the city of Arqa on 15/3/492-14/2/1099.[313]

In the meantime, a detachment of the Crusaders, encouraged by Raymond, made a surprise attack on the coastal port of Tortosa, which led to its evacuation and thus it easily fell into the hands of the Crusading army, a key triumph for the Crusade; for "it opened up easy communications by sea with Antioch and Cyprus and with Europe."[314] This accomplishment provoked feelings of jealousy among the Crusaders who had remained in Antioch and consequently groups of them set out to follow Raymond.[315]

The siege of Arqa, however, was not successful, mainly because of its strong fortifications and determined resistance of its garrison.[316] After camping behind the walls of the city for three months, Raymond disappointedly decided to lift the siege and continue his march southwards.[317]

As the Crusaders drew near Tripoli, its Emir provided them with guides, provisions and horses.[318] On 20/6/492-19/5/1099, they entered the Fāṭimid northern lands where they did not meet any resistance.[319] When they approached Beirut, its people offered them gifts and safe passage through, if they would leave their rich gardens undamaged and so the Crusaders did.[320] Unlike the case of Beirut, when the Crusaders reached Sidon, they were daringly attacked by its garrison, but it was repelled by the Crusaders who in return damaged the gardens in the suburbs.[321]

Next, the Crusaders marched along the coast and passed by Tyre, Naqoura, Acre, Haifa, Caesarea and Arsuf without any opposition worth mention.[322] Then they turned inland and by the time they reached the fully Muslim town, Ramleh, its inhabitants had already fled, leaving the city to easily become a Christian prize.[323]

On 10/7/492-7/6/1099 the Crusaders arrived before the walls of Jerusalem and besieged the Sacred City, which was a great fortress and which had been well prepared for long siege by its Fāṭimid governor Iftikhār al-Dawlah.[324] Soon the Franks were in great hardship due to scarcity of water and food, in addition to the rough summer weather.[325] After their initial assault failed, they started to construct wooden siege towers in order to enhance their attack.[326] Meanwhile, the priest Peter Desiderius played a considerable role in boosting the morale of the Crusades, which had been sapped by the disappointing circumstances.[327]

Despite being continuously struck with stones and liquid fire from the defence, the Crusaders succeeded in bringing their wooden towers right up to the walls and forced entry into the city on 23/8/492-15/7/1099.[328] Consequently, showing no mercy to its inhabitants, even those who sought refuge in the mosque of al-Aqṣā, the Crusaders horribly massacred a great number of Muslims and Jews alike.[329]

Similar to what happened after capturing Antioch, the fall of Jerusalem generated tension among the remaining Crusader princes over the issue of the throne, but it was finally released by the election of Godfrey of Bouillon as ruler and the hopeless departure of other chief princes, namely Raymond, from the city.[330] Despite this tension, as the news came to them that a relieving Egyptian army under the Fāṭimid Vizier, al-Afḍal, had approached the Palestinian city of Ascalon, the Frankish princes agreed to join together against this threat.[331] On 22/9/492-12/8/1099, the Franks caught the Egyptian army entirely by surprise as they suddenly attacked their camp near Ascalon, killing many of them and taking a lot of booty.[332] Al-Afḍal and some of his men, however, managed to flee back to Egypt, suffering a bitter defeat.[333]

Following the defeat of al-Afḍal, the Muslims in the city of Ascalon, followed by those in the town of Arsuf, offered to surrender to Raymond in person, because of his reputation of keeping his word to those who had surrendered to him at Jerusalem; however, the deal fell through as a result of the objection of Godfrey to such surrender.[334] Consequently, Raymond and other Frankish chief commanders, with their men, angrily deserted Godfrey and thus he became too weak to attack the garrisons of these two locations.[335]

Subsequently, Tancred, the Crusader leader who remained in Palestine after the Battle of Ascalon, raided with his small army in the Palestinian central plateau, over which there had been recent warfare between the Fāṭimids and the Emir Duqāq of Damascus.[336] Profiting much from the disunity of the Muslims and the ongoing family fights among the Turkish emirs, Tancred easily overran this region and established himself as Prince of Galilee.[337]

By strengthening his armed power with many of the Frankish pilgrims who had arrived at Jerusalem five months after its fall, the ruler of Jerusalem, Godfrey, was able to extend his sway over new Palestinian lands.[338] From April 1100 (5/493), the emirs of Ascalon, Caesarea and Acre ended up paying monthly tributes to him.[339]

Shortly before Godfrey's death on 9/9/493-18/7/1100, he had concluded a treaty of alliance with a strong Venetian fleet at the port of Jaffa, agreeing to arrange a joint expedition against the coastal cities of Acre and Haifa.[340] His death postponed the assault on Acre, but the expedition against Haifa was carried out under a number of Crusader commanders with the support of the Venetian fleet.[341] Despite the determined resistance of its small Fāṭimid garrison and its inhabitants, who were mainly Jews, which initially discouraged the Venetians, the city was finally captured by the Franks, who massacred the majority of its Muslim and Jewish inhabitants.[342]

In the summer of 493/1100, the situation in northern Syria was developing remarkably. Responding to an appeal for help from the ruler of Melitene, Gabriel, against the threat of the Danishmend Emir Gűműshtekin, who had been raiding Gabriel's territory, the Prince Bohemond set out from Antioch with a small army to save Melitene.[343] On his way, Bohemond was caught in ambush which had been set up by the Danishmend Emir; Bohemond's army was routed and he was taken captive.[344]

Regardless of such occasional and limited successful resistance, the Muslims, during the remaining years of al-Ghazālī's age, could not liberate their occupied lands from the Crusaders.

The religio-intellectual life

Despite the political disintegration of the Islamic state in the fifth/ eleventh century, there was striking intellectual productivity in various provinces of Islamdom. As al-Dīb has pointed out, each of the provincial "governments" at the time was eager to have its own *madrasahs*, '*ulamā*', men of letters and poets. Associated with the productivity in the intellectual life, however, there were intellectual disputes among various schools of thought.

The purpose of the present section is to shed some light on the main features of the religio-intellectual life of the time, by outlining the major religious movements and intellectual trends. This in preparation for discussing al-Ghazālī's life and thought. Since it is important to bear in mind the background of these movements and trends, their development prior to the age under study will be briefly mentioned.

The trends of sufism

Before al-Ghazālī's support for Sufism,[345] it had gradually gone through a number of phases. It had started as merely various notable and influential trends of asceticism (*zuhd*), scrupulousness (*wara'*) and devotion to divine worship (*'ibādah*) as represented by a number of ascetic Muslims[346] in the first/seventh and second/eighth centuries. However, it was only during the second/eight century, in which worldly aspirations increased among Muslims, compared to the earlier generation, when the name *mutaṣawwifah* or *ṣūfiyyah*,[347] which stands for the advocates of Sufism, was specially given to those who aspired to divine worship.[348]

With the emergence of purely Sufi works during the third/ninth century,[349] Sufism transformed to "a complex theory of the mystical discipline, and thereafter to a highly developed theosophy."[350] Thus, this marked the formation of Sufism as a distinct Islamic discipline,[351] called *'ilm al-taṣawwuf* (the knowledge of the Islamic Mysticism) or as more precisely sometimes called *'ilm al-bāṭin* (the knowledge of the inner self) as juxtaposed with *'ilm al-ẓāhir* (the perceptible knowledge).[352]

In this phase, two distinct trends appeared within Sufism.[353] The first was a moderate trend, largely ethical in nature, represented by Sufis who attempted to justify their *taṣawwuf* in the light of the Qur'an and the Sunnah.[354] The second trend, which tended to be philosophical,[355] was exemplified by extreme Sufis who gave utterances of their claimed very intimate experiences which became known as *shaṭaḥāt*[356] (ecstatic utterances). This extreme trend is usually linked with[357] both Abū Yazīd al-Bisṭāmī (d. 234/848 or 261/848),[358] who is reported to say *subḥānī, subḥānī*[359] (praise be to me, praise be to me), and al-Ḥusayn b. Manṣūr al-Ḥallāj, who was executed by the authorities in 309/922 due to his *shaṭaḥāt*[360] though their ecstatic utterances, as stated by

Knysh, "varied considerably and represented two distinctive types of mystical experience."[361]

It has been widely argued that during this phase some foreign or un-Islamic elements penetrated into the Islamic *taṣawwuf* as is particularly evident in the sayings of the extreme Sufis. Farrūkh, for example, lists four sources of such elements: Greek philosophy, Indian religions, Christianity and even Chinese philosophy.[362] However, such link between the Islamic *taṣawwuf* and foreign sources has been questioned.[363]

During the late fourth/tenth and early fifth/eleventh centuries, the movement of Sufism entered a third phase in which the Sufi tradition developed considerably with the appearance of various Sufi literature covering all the key aspects of *'ilm al-taṣawwuf*.[364] Notable examples of the Sufi works representing this phase and which became classical and original references for the later Sufis are the following:[365]

- *Kitāb al-Luma' fī al-Taṣawwuf* (The Book of Flashes) by Abū Naṣr al-Sarrāj (d. 378/988);
- *Al-Ta'arruf li Madhhab Ahl al-Taṣawwuf* (An Introduction to the Sufi Doctrine) by Abū Bakr al-Kalābādhī (d. 380/990);
- *Qūt al-Qulūb* (The Nourishment for the Hearts) by Abū Ṭālib al-Makkī (d. 386/996);
- *Ṭabaqāt al-Ṣūfiyyah* (Generations of the Sufis) by Abū 'Abd al-Raḥmān al-Sulamī (d. 412/1021).

Towards the end of this phase, there was a sort of decline in the originality of Sufism, as witnessed by the distinguished Sufi of the fifth/eleventh century, Abū al-Qāsim 'Abd al-Karīm al-Qushayrī (d. 465/1072). In his very famous Sufi book, *al-Risālah* (the Epistle) which was completed in 438/1046 as mentioned in his introduction,[366] he sadly describes this phenomenon by stating that most of the earnest (*al-muḥaqqiqīn*) Sufis had eventually vanished.[367] Moreover, he records his sorrowful observation of the rise of pretend Sufis who "claim that the secrets of the Oneness [of God] have been unveiled to them and that they have been freed from human rules."[368] Worrying that this would be considered as the path of the original *ṣūfiyyah*,[369] he composed his book attempting to revive Sufism in the light of the ideas and practices of the earlier true Sufis, whom he carefully distinguished from pretend Sufis. The book is described as "a carefully designed and admirably complete account of the theoretical structure of Sufism."[370]

The *Risālah* of al-Qushayrī "carries a clear apologetic message, casting Sufism as a legitimate and respectable Islamic science that is in complete harmony with the precepts of the *sharīʿa*."[371] Thus, al-Qushayrī on this regard, al-Tiftazānī argues,[372] paved the way for al-Ghazālī who adopted the same idea.

Al-Ghazālī's famous strong announcement that the method of the *ṣūfiyyah* is the soundest method,[373] after experiencing and examining various branches of knowledge and after receiving outstanding recognition as we shall see below, and his serious effort to prove this in the light of the Sharīʿah[374] can be considered a turning point in the history of the movement of Sufism. No wonder he, as Knysh put it, "is seen by many as Sufism's greatest champion."[375]

Like al-Qushayrī, al-Ghazālī attacked most of the contemporary Sufis, accusing them of pretence and falsehood and revealing their faults.[376] In addition, he criticized and rejected the *shaṭaḥāt* of the extreme Sufis, considering them as harmful innovations.[377] Therefore, he can be classified as one of the moderate Sufis and in fact he has been considered as "the master of moderate medieval mysticism."[378]

Although it is true that the movement of Sufism had succeeded in attracting great champions like al-Ghazālī, it is equally true that there have been a number of very noticeable critics and opponents of Sufis, even those who have been widely classified as moderate, since its early formative period.[379] The distinguished Aḥmad b. Ḥanbal (d. 241/855) is a case in point. He is reported to warn of his contemporary, the renowned Sufi al-Ḥārith b. Asad al-Muḥāsibī (d. 243/857) by stating: "Don't be deceived because he lowers his head.

He is a bad person. You cannot know him unless you have tested him. Don't talk to him, and don't pay respect to him."[380] Similarly, Abū Zar'ah used to warn from the books of al-Muḥāsibī.[381]

The anti-Sufi trend continued to exist during the age of al-Ghazālī. This is especially evident in the Maghrib where the Almoravids appeared to oppose the movement of Sufism, "despite a certain Sufi flavour in the lifestyle of the Saharan men in their early *ribāṭs*."[382]

More striking is the anti-Sufi movement which existed in al-Andalus during the Almoravid rule there. The rulers as well as some of the Andalusian *'ulamā'* were involved in this movement, which lead to the burning of al-Ghazālī's *Iḥyā'*. However, there have been considerable controversies over the reasons behind this extremely hostile reaction.[383]

The school of the falāsifah[384]

By the second half of the fifth/eleventh century, the activity of the *falāsifah* in Islamdom had already taken the shape of an intellectual school. Its foreign seeds had been sown in the productive Islamic soil through Arabic translation[385] of Hellenic philosophical works,[386] a process which was seriously developed[387] during the reign of the 'Abbāsid Caliph al-Manṣūr (137/754-159/775) and then it was systematically progressed during the reign of al-Ma'mūn (198/813-217/833).[388]

The precursor[389] of the school and "the earliest systematic protagonist of Hellenism"[390] was al-Kindī (256/873), who is called the *Faylasūf al-'Arab* (philosopher of the Arabs)[391] and is said to have effectively participated in the translation process.[392] He was followed by a number of adherents of Greek philosophy who participated considerably in the development of *falsafah* in Islamdom, namely al-Fārābī (d. 339/950), who, as Ibn al-Nadīm states, "was one of the leaders in the field of logic and the ancient sciences,"[393] and Ibn Sīnā[394] (d. 428/1037) who, according to Vaux, "placed the sum total of Greek wisdom at the disposal of the educated Muslim world in a readily intelligible fashion with his own ingenious developments of it."[395]

Since the early stages of the emergence of this school, there had been an ongoing conflict between the *falāsifah* and the *mutakalimūn*, particularly the Ash'arīs,[396] who were engaged in refuting various philosophical theories which they found incompatible with Islamic doctrine.[397] Some of the *falāsifah* in their turn had attempted seriously to reconcile between *falsafah* and Islam.[398] This, however, had not resolved the serious disagreement between the two parties, which seems inevitable because, as Bello rightly pointed out, "their sources of authoritative knowledge and their educational background are divergent in essence and nature."[399]

Despite the attack of the *mutakalimūn*, *falsafah* continued to be influential during the age under study, particularly among educated Muslims, to the extent that a group of them, as al-Ghazālī himself sadly observed in his time, abandoned all the Islamic duties as a result of being influenced by the *falāsifah*.[400] What intensified such influence of the *falāsifah*, according to al-Ghazālī, was the weak arguments of those who opposed them.[401] This is why he criticized the approach of the *mutakalimūn*, before him, in refuting *falsafah* by stating that what they had to say in their books "was nothing but obscure scattered remarks, patently inconsistent and false, which could not conceivably hoodwink an ordinary intelligent person, to say nothing of one familiar with the subtleties of the philosophical sciences."[402] At the same time, he criticized those who presumed that the way to defend Islam from the 'evil' of *falāsifah* was to reject all their sciences.[403] Moreover, he argued that none of the *'ulamā'* had directed his endeavour to fully and deeply grasp *falsafah* in order to be eligible to undertake the task of refuting its unsound elements.[404] To fill this gap, al-Ghazālī composed his book *Tahāfuh al-Falāsifah* (The Collapse or Inconsistence of the Philosophers) which is a thoroughgoing refutation of particular metaphysical theories[405] of ancient philosophers, after achieving "a profound knowledge of the doctrine of his opponents,"[406] as is evident in his book *Maqāṣid al-*

Falāsifah, which was written before the *Tahāfut*, as we shall further discuss below.

The movement of the Bāṭiniyyah

The name of the Bāṭiniyyah was very noticeable during the age of al-Ghazālī, not only in the political field, but also in the religious and intellectual circles. Among the various appellations given to the Ismāʿīlī sect[407] over different ages,[408] *al-Bāṭiniyyah*, according to al-Shahristānī (d. 548/1153),[409] was the most popular one, particularly in Iraq. The reason behind this appellation is explained by al-Ghazālī himself as follows:

> They were thus named simply because of their claim that the *ẓawāhir* [pl. of *ẓāhir*: exoteric meaning] of the Qur'an and the Traditions have *bawāṭin* [pl. of *bāṭin*: esoteric meaning] analogous, with respect to the *ẓawāhir*, to kernel with respect to the shell; and the *ẓawāhir* by their forms instil in the ignorant and foolish clear forms, but in the view of the intelligent and discerning they are symbols and indications of specific truths.[410]

In order to educe the *bāṭin* from the *ẓāhir*, the Bāṭinīs developed a distinct type of *taʾwīl* which, as Hodgson correctly and shortly describes, "was symbolical or allegoristic in its method, sectarian in its aims, hierarchically imparted, and secret."[411]

Another name for this sect which is worth mentioning is al-Taʿlīmiyyah, so called because, as al-Ghazālī explains, "the basis of their doctrine is the invalidation of *al-raʾy* (individual reasoning) and the invalidation of the exercise of intellects and the call to men to *al-taʿlīm* (instruction or learning) from the infallible Imam."[412] This name, according to al-Ghazālī,[413] was the most appropriate in his time because the contemporary Bāṭinīs emphasised this idea in their propaganda.

In the age of al-Ghazālī, the movement of the Bāṭiniyyah was greatly stimulated by the activity of Ḥasan al-Ṣabāḥ (d. 518/1124)* who travelled widely in Persian regions, acting as a missionary and thus winning numerous partisans.[414] This activity transformed into a widespread dangerous revolt in al-Ghazālī's age, when the followers of al-Ṣabāḥ carried out assassination missions in various regions, targeting particularly active Sunnī political officials and *'ulamā'* alike.[415]

In addition to its threat to the Sunnī political system, shown above, this movement was a real challenge for the Sunnī *'ulamā'* of the time as well. The seriousness of this challenge is evident in the number of al-Ghazālī's books which were devoted to refute their doctrine, as we shall discuss below.

The status of *'ilm al-kalām*

In this context, *'ilm al-kalām* [416] is used to refer to the discipline which, as defined by Ibn Khaldūn,[417] "involves arguing (*al-ḥijāj*) with rational proofs (*bi al-adillah al-'aqliyyah*) in defence of the articles of faith (*al-'aqā'id al-īmāniyyah*) and refuting innovators (*al-mubtadi'ah*) who deviate in their dogmas from the early Muslims (*al-salaf*) and the *ahl al-sunnah*[418]." Before the contribution of al-Ghazālī in the field, *'ilm al-kalām* in this sense had established itself as a distinct branch of Islamic knowledge.

It is difficult, as correctly noted by Gardet,[419] to precisely know when *'ilm al-kalām* became a distinct discipline. It can be generally stated, however, that it had gradually developed as a result of the disputation on certain details of Islamic faith in the first half of the second/eighth century which led to the rise of the Mu'tazilah and other theological sects as separate entities.[420]

The one who has been regarded as the leader (*imām*)[421] of the *mutakalimūn*[422] among the Sunnīs, is Abū al-Ḥasan al-Ash'arī (260/873-3224/935), the founder of the Ash'ariyyah theological school, for he intensively used *kalām* or rational argument to the defence of Islamic faith and to refute the innovations of the Mu'tazilah and the Imāmiyyah,[423] though he was not the first who adopted this approach.[424] His approach was followed by numerous disciples and followers,[425] mainly adherents of the Shāfi'iyyah School of *fiqh*, who became known as the Ashā'irah.[426]

Al-Ashʿarī's approach in *kalām* was then considerably enhanced by al-Qāḍī Abū Bakr al-Baqilānī (d. 403/1013), who "became the head of the approach"[427] at the time. By al-Baqilānī's important contribution, which included the introduction of rational premises on which arguments and speculation on the subject depend,[428] this approach, according to Ibn Khaldūn's evaluation, "was perfected and became one of the best speculative disciplines and religious sciences."[429]

Despite such perfection, the approach was by no means universally accepted even within Sunnī schools. The use of rational arguments was considered by the Ḥanbalīs as an objectionable innovation.[430] The Mālikī School of *fiqh* which was dominant in the Maghrib did not welcome theological speculation.[431]

In the second half of the fifth/eleventh century, a new approach of *kalām* was adopted and it was called the approach of the later *mutakalimūn* (*ṭarīqah al-mutʾakhkhirīn*).[432] Unlike the earlier *mutakalimūn*, the practitioners of the new approach heavily employed logic in their argumentation, considering it as a norm and yardstick for arguments in general and not restricted to philosophical sciences.[433] With the help of this yardstick, they, as Ibn Khaldūn pointed out,[434] rejected many of the basic premises which the earlier *mutakalimūn* had established. Moreover, to refute the *falāsifah*,[435] who became serious opponents of the later *mutakalimūn*[436] after the tide of the Muʿtazilah had receded,[437] they had to "recourse to the weapons which their rationalist opponents had borrowed from the Greeks."[438]

The forerunner of this new approach was al-Ghazālī's teacher Imām al-Ḥaramayn Abū al-Maʿālī al-Juwaynī (d. 478/1085).[439] Although Ibn Khaldūn states that al-Ghazālī was the first to write in accordance with this new approach, traces of such development, as pointed out by Watt,[440] appear in al-Juwaynī's works. Regardless of whether or not he initiated this approach, al-Ghazālī had a distinguished contribution in this field as we shall discuss below.

During the time of al-Ghazālī, *kalām* attracted a lot of adverse publicity. This is evident in the occurrence of dreadful incidents and trials, particularly in Baghdad, as a result of heated disputes over *kalām* even within the Sunnīs themselves, not to mention opposing sects. Two such incidents, which are reported by Ibn al-Athīr, are extremely striking and thus worth mentioning. The first was in 469/1077 when Abū Naṣr, son of Abū al-Qāsim al-Qushayrī, visted Baghdad and held preaching sessions in the Niẓāmiyyah Madrasah.[441] Because he supported the school of al-Ash‘arī and his followers became numerous, his Ḥanbalī opponents attacked the Market of the Madrasah, killing a number of people.[442]

In 470/1077, the second incident occurred when the preacher al-Sharīf Abū al-Qāsim al-Bakrī al-Maghribī, who was also Ash‘arī, was appointed by Niẓām al-Mulk in the Niẓāmiyyah of Baghdad.[443] In his preaching there, he would insult the Ḥanbalīs by saying "Solomon was no unbeliever, but the devils disbelieved[444]; by Allah Aḥmad [i.e. Ibn Ḥanbal] was no unbeliever, but his followers have disbelieved."[445] Consequently, fights and trials occurred between him and his followers on one side and the Ḥanbalīs in the other.[446]

These and similar incidents clearly show how serious the effect of the publicity of *kalām* was during that time.

The condition of *‘ilm al-fiqh*

By the age of al-Ghazālī, *‘ilm al-fiqh* (the Discipline of Islamic Jurisprudence) had passed through its formative stages and had become mature and distinct Islamic scholarship.[447] Only four *madhāhib*—sing. *madhhab*—of *fiqh* (schools of jurisprudence) had continued to be followed and considered as authoritative by the Sunnīs: the Mālikī, the Ḥanafī, the Shāfi‘ī and the Ḥanbalī schools.[448]

It has been repeatedly stated and commonly accepted that the gate of *ijtihād*[449] had been closed since the fourth/tenth century with the agreement of the *fuqahā’*—sing. *faqīh* —(Muslim jurists) themselves.[450] This, however, has been seriously questioned by Hallaq. By systematically and chronologically examining original works of *fiqh* belonging to the fourth/tenth century onwards, he has definitively proven that the activity of *ijtihād* had continued to be used in developing positive rules by the capable *fuqahā'*, who were known as the *mujtahidūn*,[451] in each *madhhab* throughout the first fourth/tenth and fifth/eleventh centuries.[452]

During the age of al-Ghazālī, there were a number of highly qualified *fuqahā'*, such as—in addition to al-Ghazālī himself[453]— Abū 'Abdullāh Muḥammad b. 'Alī al-Dāmigānī (d. 478 AH), 'Alī b. Muḥammad al-Bazdawī (d. 483 AH), Abū al-Walīd Sulaymān b. Khalaf al-Bājī (d. 494), Abū al-Walīd Muḥammad b. Aḥmad b. Rushd al-Qurṭubī (d. 525 AH), Abū 'Abdullāh Muḥammad b. 'Alī b. 'Umar al-Timīmī al-Māzirī (d. 526 AH), Abū Isḥāq Ibrāhīm b. 'Alī al-Fayrūzabādī al-Shīrāzī (d. 476 AH), Ibn al-Ṣabbāg Abū Naṣr 'Abd al-Sayyid b. Muḥammad (d. 477 AH), Abū al-Ma'ālī 'Abd al-Malik 'Abdullāh al-Juwaynī (d. 487 AH), and Ibn 'Aqīl. Some of them considered themselves as capable *mujtahidūn* within the principles of the schools to which they belonged, and they were regarded by others as such.[454] They produced outstanding extended *fiqh* literature which characterized that period.[455]

This period was also characterised by the prevalence of intense debates among *fuqahā'* of various *madhāhib*, especially between Ḥanafīs and Shāfi'īs,[456] and often in the presence of viziers and nobles, particularly in Iraq and Khurāsān.[457] In these debates, each *faqīh* aimed to prove the correctness of his respective *madhab*, to clarify its methodology, to defend the principles of its rules against refutation and to highlight the pitfalls of his opponent *madhab* in the light of certain rules.[458] This activity, in which al-Ghazālī himself was seriously and skilfully engaged during a particular time of his life,[459] was called the art of *al-khilāf wa al-jadal* (polemics and dialectics).[460]

Although this intellectual activity produced interesting subtle scholarship,[461] it, as al-Ghazālī disapprovingly observed,[462] often resulted in evil consequences such as envy, rancour, backbiting and haughtiness, not to say the engagement of those who lack self-restraint in impatient cursing and fierce quarrels. Thus, generally speaking it was motivated by fanaticism, rather than scholarly purposes.[463]

Notes

1. Samuel M. Zwemer, *A Moslem Seeker after God*, New York: Fleming H. Revell Company, 1920, p. 23.
2. Muḥammad al-Saʿīd ʿAbd al-Maqṣūd, *Tarbiyah al-Ṣafwah ʿind al-Ghazālī: Dirāsah tarbawiyyah li Risālah Ayyuhā al-Walad*, in Muḥammad Kamāl Jaʿfar (ed.), *al-Imām al-Ghazālī: al-dhikrā al-miʾawiyyah al-tāsiʿah li wafātih*, Doha: University of Qatar, 1986, p. 470.
3. Zwemer, *A Moslem Seeker*, p. 24.
4. Ibid, p. 23.
5. I have borrowed this practical term from Hodgson who defines it as "the society in which Muslims and their faith are recognized as prevalent and socially dominant in one sense or another—a society in which, of course, non-Muslims have always formed an integral, if subordinate, element…," Marshall G.S. Hodgson, *The Venture of Islam*, Chicago: The University of Chicago Press, 1974, Vol. 1, p. 58. The term Islamdom, as Hodgson has practically noticed, has the following three advantages over the other alternative term, i.e., "Islamic world": (1) More efficient in compound phrases; (2) "Islamic" is too broad; and (3) the world is one, see *ibid*.
6. See below.
7. Hodgson, *The Venture*, Vol. 2, p. 3.
8. Carole Hillenbrand, *The Crusades: Islamic Perspectives*, Edinburgh: Edinburgh University Press, 1999, p. 36.
9. Hodgson, *The Venture*, Vol. 2, p. 3.
10. Abū Jaʿfar ʿAbdullāh b. Aḥmad al-Qādir, titled al-Qāʾim bi Amrillāh. He became Caliph in 422/1031 and continued to hold the position until his death in 467/1075. At the time of this caliph's death, al-Ghazālī had not moved to Baghdad yet.
11. Abū al-Qāsim ʿAbdullāh b. Muḥammad b. ʿAbdullāh, titled Al-Muqtadī bi Amrillāh.
12. Ibn Kathīr, *al-Bidāyah wa al-Nihāyah*, Beirut: Maktabah al-Maʿārif, 1994, Vol. 12, p. 111.
13. Abū al-ʿAbbās Aḥmad b. ʿAbdullāh b. Muḥammad, known by his title al-Mustaẓhir Billāh. He became Caliph in 487/1094 at the age of sixteen succeeding his father al-Muqtadī. Al-Ghazālī and other *ulmā* are among those who attended the *bayʿah* (pledge of allegiance) of al-

Mustaẓhir and who gave the oath of allegiance to him (Ibn al-Athīr, *al-Kāmil fī al-Tārīkh*, Beirut: Dār al-Kutub al-'Ilmiyyah, 1998, Vol. 8, p. 494).

14. Ibn al-Athīr, *al-Kāmil*, Vol. 8, p. 406.

15. It is worth noting that al-Qā'im considered himself as just a trustee. This appears in the following denoting incident which is recorded by Ibn al-Athīr (*al-Kāmil*, Vol. 8, p. 406-407):
"Muḥammd b. 'Alī b. 'Āmir, the steward, said: One day I entered the Store-house. Every one there handed me a petition. So my sleeves became full of them. I said in my heart, 'if the Caliph were my brother, he would ignore all of these,' so I threw them into a pool, while al-Qā'im was watching but I was not noticing. Then, when I entered into his presence, he ordered his servants to retrieve the petitions from the pool. So they were retrieved and he read them through and signed in them, granting what their writers requested. Then he said to me: 'You, fellow! What made you do that?' I replied: 'Fear of their being found irksome.' 'Do not do anything like that again,' he said, 'for it's none of our own money that we have given them. We are but trustees."

16. Ibn al-Athīr, *al-Kāmil*, Vol. 8, p. 406.

17. Jalāl al-Dīn al-Suyūṭī (d. 911/1505), *Tārīkh al-Khulafā'*, Beirut: Dār al-Kutub al-'Ilmiyyah, 1988, p. 338.

18. Al-Suyūṭī, *Tārīkh al-Khulafā'*, p. 341.

19. See al-Ghazālī, *Faḍā'iḥ al-Bāṭiniyyah*, ed. 'Abd al-Raḥmān Badawī, Cairo: al-Dār al-Qawmiyyah, 1964, pp. 169-194, trans., Richard Joseph McCarthy, *Faḍā'iḥ al-Bāṭiniyya*, in Richard Joseph McCarthy, *Deliverance from Error*, translation of *al-Munqidh min al-Ḍalāl* and other relevant works of al-Ghazālī, Louisville, KY: Fons Vitae, n. d, pp. 234-239.

20. For a discussion on the distinction between "authority" and "power" and the attraction between them as illustrated in the 'Abbāsid Caliphate during the fifth/eleventh century, see George Makdisi, "Authority in the Islamic Community," in George Makdisi, *History and Politics in Eleventh-Century Baghdad*, Hampshire: Variorum, 1990, part VIII, pp. 118-120.

21. See Ẓahīr al-Dīn Nīshāpūrī (579/1184 or 80/1185), *The History of the Seljuq Turks From the Jāmi' al-Tawārīkh: An Ilkhanid Adaption of the Saljūq-Nāma of Ẓahīr al-Dīn Nīshāpūrī*, Translated from Persian by Kenneth Allin Luther, ed. C. Edmund Bosworth, Richmond (Surrey): Curzon Press, 2001, p. 42; see also Ibn al-Athīr, *al-Kāmil*, Vol. 8, pp. 341f.

22. Ibn al-Athīr, *al-Kāmil*, Vol. 8, p. 343.

23. See Bosworth (ed.), *The History of the Seljuq Turks*, p. 42.

24. Ibid.
25. Transformed from the Turkish *Selchük*; also spelled Saljuq which is transformed from the Arabic *Saljūq*, (see Carla L. Klausner, *The Seljuk Vezirate: A Study of Civil Administration*, Massachusetts: Harvard University Press, 1973, p. iv).
26. Abū Ṭālib Tughril-Beg Muḥammad b. Mīkā'īl b. Saljūq.
27. Nīshāpūrī, *The History of the Seljuq*, p. 42.
28. Ibn al-Athīr, *al-Kāmil*, Vol. 8, p. 345.
29. Ibid, p. 346.
30. Although he possessed various excellent qualities, he had some bad traits of character; according to Ibn al-Athīr, he was "wise, tactful, one of the most forbearing of men, and the most able to keep his secrets…He used…to take care of the daily prayers, and to fast in Mondays and Thursdays," at the same time he was "tyrannical, brutal and cruel," (Ibn al-Athīr, *al-Kāmil*, Vol. 8, p. 362).
31. The Caliph al-Qā'im gave orders for the *khuṭabā'* (Muslim pulpits) of Baghdad mosques to give the Friday *khuṭabah* (Islamic ceremony) in the name of Toghril-Beg (see, for instance, Nīshāpūrī, *The History of the Seljuq*, p. 41; and Ibn al-Athīr, *al-Kāmil*, Vol. 8, p. 323).
32. See, for instance, Ibn al-Athīr, *al-Kāmil*, Vol. 8, pp. 337 & 346.
33. See Ibn al-Athīr, *al-Kāmil*, Vol. 8, p. 337.
34. Her name was Arslān Khātūn, also called Khadījah; she was the daughter of Dāud, brother of the Sultan Tughril-Beg. The marriage was in 448/1056, a year after the first arrival of Tughril-Beg in Baghdad. (See Ibn al-Athīr, *al-Kāmil*, Vol. 8, p. 327).
35. See Muḥammad Musfir al-Zahrānī, *Nufūdh al-Salājiqah al-Siyāsī fī al-Dawlah al-'Abbāsiyyah*, Beirut: Mu'assasah al-Risālah, p. 102.
36. See, for example, Ibn al-Athīr, *al-Kāmil*, Vol. 8, pp. 357f and al-Suyūṭī, *Tārīkh al-Khulafā'*, p. 335.
37. See, for example, al-Zahrānī, *Nufūdh al-Salājiqah*, pp. 107f.
38. Cf. Sir William Muir, *The Caliphate: Its Rise, Decline, and Fall*, ed. T.H. Weir, Edinburgh: John Grant, 1924, p. 582.
39. Abū Shujā' Alp Arslān Muḥammad b. Abī Sulaymān Chaghri-Beg Dāwūd b. Mikā'īl.
40. See below.
41. C.E. Bosworth, "The Political and Dynastic History of the Iranian World (AD 1000-1217)," in *The Cambridge History of Iran*, Cambridge: Cambridge University Press, 1968, Vol. 5, p. 55.
42. See Ibn al-Athīr, *al-Kāmil*, Vol. 8, p. 391, trans., see Richards, *The Annals*, p. 174-175.
43. Al-Zahrānī, *Nufūdh al-Salājiqah*, p. 109.
44. Ibn al-Athīr, *al-Kāmil*, Vol. 8, p. 494, for translation of sections related to the history of the Seljuk Turks over the year 420/1029

to the year 490/1096-1097, see D.S. Richards, *The Annals of the Saljuq Turks: Selections from al-Kāmil fī al-Tārīkh of 'Izz al-Dīn Ibn al-Athīr*, London: RoutledgeCurzon, 2002, p. 272. I have chiefly relied on Richard's translation of the parts selected by him, but my translation differs from his sometimes, particularly when I think that there is mistranslation of the original text.

45. See below.

46. Cf. Muir, *The Caliphate*, p. 582.

47. Al-Zahrānī, *Nufūdh al-Salājiqah*, pp. 109-113.

48. Ibid, pp. 109f.

49. Tāj al-Dīn Abū Naṣr 'Abd al-Wahhāb al-Subkī (d. 756/1355), *Ṭabqāt al-Shāfi'iyyah al-Kubrā*, Cairo: al-Maṭba'ah al-Ḥusayniyyah, n.d., Vol. 3, p. 143.

50. Muir, *The Caliphate*, p. 582.

51. See al-Zahrānī, *Nufūdh al-Salājiqah*, pp. 114f.

52. See below.

53. Cf. Huart, "Seldjuḳs," *EI*, Vol. 4, p. 210.

54. Ibid.

55. See al-Ḥijī, *al-Tārīkh al-Andalusī*, Damascus: Dār al-Qalam, 1987, p. 423.

56. See Ibn al-Athīr, *al-Kāmil*, Vol. 8, p. 448.

57. Ibid, Vol. 8, p. 494.

58. Ibid.

59. See A.K.S. Lambton, "The Internal Structure of the Saljuq Empire," in *The Cambridge History of Iran*, Vol. 5, p. 213.

60. As presented above.

61. Their name originated from Saljūq b. Tuqqāq, a leader of Ghuzz (Oghuz) tribal Turks, who—knowing that the ruler of Turks, Bayghu (or Yabghu), was thinking to kill him—migrated with his followers to *Dār al-Islām* near Bukhārā and embraced Islām there towards the end of the fourth/tenth century, see, for instance, Ibn al-Athīr, *al-Kāmil*, Vol. 8, p. 236.

62. This includes the following provinces and territories which had been ruled by a number of Seljuk emirs: Khurāsān, Khwārizm, Jurjān, Ṭabristan, Daylam, Azerbaijan, Arran, Iṣfahān and Kirmān, see, for instance, Ḥasan Ibrāhīm Ḥasan, *Tārīkh al-Islām*, Cairo: Maktabah al-Nahḍah al-Miṣriyyah, 1967, Vol. 4, pp. 4-10; and C.E. Bosworth, "The Political and Dynastic History of the Iranian World (AD 1000-1217)," in *The Cambridge History of Iran*, Vol. 5, pp. 23-53.

63. Also spelled as Qavurt and Qāwurd.

64. See C.E. Bosworth, "The Political and Dynastic History of the Iranian World (AD 1000-1217)," in *The Cambridge History of Iran*, Vol. 5, pp. 59 & 88.

65. See Ibn al-Athīr, *al-Kāmil*, Vol. 8, pp. 368-370, trans., see Richards, *The Annals*, pp. 152-155.

66. Ibid, p. 370, trans., see Richards, *The Annals*, p. 155.

67. Ibid, p. 375, trans., see Richards, *The Annals*, p. 157.

68. Ibid, p. 478, trans., see Richards, *The Annals*, p. 252.

69. Ibid, pp. 457-460, trans., see Richards, *The Annals*, pp. 239-242.

70. See, for instance, Cl. Huart, "Seldjuks," in *EI*, Vol. 4, p. 211; and C.E. Bosworth, "Saldjūḳids," in *EI²*, Vol. 8, p. 948.

71. Cf. Huart, "Seldjuḳs," in *EI*, Vol. 4, pp. 209f.

72. See above.

73. Ibn al-Athīr, *al-Kāmil*, Vol. 8, p. 387, trans., see Richards, *The Annals*, p. 168.

74. Ibid, p. 390, trans., see Richards, *The Annals*, p. 173.

75. Ibid, p. 410, trans., see Richards, *The Annals*, p. 191.

76. Ibid, pp. 47f7, trans., see Richards, *The Annals*, pp. 251f.

77. Klausner, *The Seljuk Vezirate*, p. 9.

78. Ibid, p. 10.

79. See Nīshāpūrī, *The History of the Seljuq*, p. 45; and Ibn al-Athīr, *al-Kāmil*, Vol. 8, p. 367, trans., see Richards, *The Annals*, p. 151-152.

80. See Ibn al-Athīr, *al-Kāmil*, Vol. 8, p. 366, trans., see Richards, *The Annals*, p. 149.

81. Ibid, p. 379, trans., see Richards, *The Annals*, p. 160.

82. See Nīshāpūrī, *The History of the Seljuq*, pp. 57f.

83. See Ibn al-Athīr, *al-Kāmil*, Vol. 8, p. 423, trans., see Richards, *The Annals*, p. 202.

84. Ibid, p. 435, trans., see Richards, *The Annals*, p. 216.

85. Ibid, p. 384, trans., see Richards, *The Annals*, p. 166.

86. See, for example, Steven Runciman, *A History of the Crusades*, Cambridge: Cambridge University Press, 1951, Vol. 1, p. 62.

87. See above.

88. See Ibn al-Athīr, *al-Kāmil*, Vol. 8, pp. 388f, trans., see Richards, *The Annals*, pp. 170-171.

89. Also spelled Malazgird and Mantzkirt.

90. See Nīshāpūrī, *The History of the Seljuq*, p. 52; and Ibn al-Athīr, *al-Kāmil*, Vol. 8, p. 389, trans., Richards, *The Annals*, p. 171.

91. Runciman, *A History of the Crusades*, p. 64.

92. See below.

93. See, for instance, Hodgson, *The Venture of Islam*, Vol. 2, p. 58.

94. See W. Madelung, "Ismāʿīlliyya," *EI²*, Vol. 4, p. 199; and Cl. Hurat, "Ismāʿīlliyya," *EI*, Vol. 2, p. 550.

95. Hurat, "Ismāʿīlliyya," *EI*, Vol. 2, p. 550.

96. See Hodgson, *The Venture of Islam*, Vol. 2, p. 58; and W. Madelung, *Ismāʿīlliyya*, *EI²*, Vol. 4, p. 199.

97. Abū ʿAlī Ḥasan b. ʿAlī al-Ṭūsī, he is mostly known by his honorific title *Niẓām al-Mulk*, meaning Order of the Kingship.

98. According to a widely accepted account, Niẓām al-Mulk was assassinated by a Bāṭinī (see, for instance, Ibn al-Athīr, *al-Kāmil*, Vol. 9, p. 37; ʿAbd al-Raḥamān b. Muḥammad Ibn Khaldūn (d. 808/1406), *Kitāb al-ʿIbar*, Beirut: Dār al-Kutub al-ʿIlmiyyah, 1992, Vol. 5, pp. 14f; and al-Subkī, *Ṭabaqāt*, Vol. 3, pp. 142f), but there is another account holding the Sultan Malik Shāh responsible for his murder because of the growing tension built up between the two over time (see, for example, Ibn Khaldūn, *Kitāb al-ʿIbar*, Vol. 5, pp. 14f; and al-Subkī, *Ṭabaqāt*, Vol. 3, pp. 142f). The first account, as al-Subkī pointed out, appears more likely (al-Subkī, *Ṭabaqāt*, Vol. 3, p. 143). Malik Shāh had great trust and deep respect for Niẓām al-Mulk to the extent that he handed him almost all affairs and regarded him as his father, bestowing on him the honorific title "Atābig" which means the father emir (see Ibn al-Athīr, *al-Kāmil*, Vol. 8, pp. 396f, trans., see Richards, *The Annals*, pp. 181f). In addition, he played a considerable role in stabilizing his rule. All this renders the second account very unlikely.

99. Bosworth, The Political and Dynastic History of the Iranian World (AD 1000-1217), in *The Cambridge History of Iran*, Vol. 5, p. 59.

100. See Ibn al-Athīr, *al-Kāmil*, Vol. 8, p. 396, trans., see Richards, *The Annals*, p. 181.

101. See, for example, Ibn Khaldūn, *Kitāb al-ʿIbar*, Vol. 5, p. 15; and Ibn al-Athīr, *al-Kāmil*, Vol. 8, p. 481, trans., see Richards, *The Annals*, p. 257.

102. Named in his honour.

103. See al-Subkī, *Ṭabaqāt*, Vol. 3, p. 137; and Ibn al-Athīr, *al-Kāmil*, Vol. 8, p. 481, trans., see Richards, *The Annals*, p. 257.

104. See al-Subkī, *Ṭabaqāt*, Vol. 3, p. 135.

105. This cursing started during the reign of the Sultan Tughril-Beg who was persuaded by his Vizier ʿAmīd al-Mulk al-Kunurī to order the cursing of both the Shiites and the Ashʿariyyah. (see, for instance, Ibn Khaldūn, *Kitāb al-ʿIbar*, Vol. 5, p. 15; and Ibn al-Athīr, *al-Kāmil*, Vol. 8, p. 481, trans., see Richards, *The Annals*, p. 257)

106. See, for example, Ibn Khaldūn, *Kitāb al-ʿIbar*, Vol. 5, p. 15; and Ibn al-Athīr, *al-Kāmil*, Vol. 8, p. 481, trans., see Richards, *The Annals*, p. 257.

107. Ibn al-Athīr, *al-Kāmil*, Vol. 8, p. 481, trans., see Richards, *The Annals*, p. 257.

108. For a discussion on his opponents from within the Seljuk administration, see Bosworth, "The Political and Dynastic History of the Iranian World (AD 1000-1217)," in *The Cambridge History of Iran*, Vol. 5, pp. 74-77.

109. Cf. Bosworth, "The Political and Dynastic History of the Iranian World (AD 1000-1217)," in *The Cambridge History of Iran*, Vol. 5, p. 102.

110. Bosworth, "Saldjūḳids," in *EI²*, Vol. 8, p. 942.

111. Nīshāpūrī, *The History of the Seljuq*, p. 65.

112. See Ibn Khaldūn, *Kitāb al-'Ibar*, Vol. 5, p. 16; and Ibn al-Athīr, *al-Kāmil*, Vol. 8, p. 482, trans., see Richards, *The Annals*, p. 258.

113. When Turkān Khātūn sent to the Caliph requesting his agreement concerning the mentioning of her son's name in the *khuṭbah* as the Sultan, he agreed on the condition that the Emir Anz should lead the armies and care for the country on the advice of Tāj al-Mulk who should also be in charge of the regulation of the officials and the collection of revenues. She initially refused this condition, but finally she agreed as she was told, by al-Ghazālī who was the Caliph's messenger to her, that the Sharī'ah does not allow her son to be ruler because of his age (see Ibn Khaldūn, *Kitāb al-'Ibar*, Vol. 5, p. 16; and Ibn al-Athīr, *al-Kāmil*, Vol. 8, pp. 484f, trans., see Richards, *The Annals*, pp. 262f).

114. See Nīshāpūrī, *The History of the Seljuq*, p. 65.

115. See Ibn Khaldūn, *Kitāb al-'Ibar*, Vol. 5, p. 16; and Ibn al-Athīr, *Al-Kāmil*, Vol. 8, p. 484, trans., see Richards, *The Annals*, p. 262.

116. Bosworth, "The Political and Dynastic History of the Iranian World (AD 1000-1217)," in *The Cambridge History of Iran*, Vol. 5, p. 103.

117. See Ibn al-Athīr, *al-Kāmil*, Vol. 8, pp. 484f, trans., see Richards, *The Annals*, pp. 262f.

118. See Ibid, p. 485, trans., see Richards, *The Annals*, p. 263.

119. Ibid.

120. See Bosworth, "The Political and Dynastic History of the Iranian World (AD 1000-1217)," in *The Cambridge History of Iran*, Vol. 5, p. 105.

121. See Ibn al-Athīr, *al-Kāmil*, Vol. 8, pp. 487-489, trans., see Richards, *The Annals*, pp. 265f; and Ibn Khaldūn, *Kitāb al-'Ibar*, Vol. 5, pp. 17f.

122. Ibid, p. 489, trans., see Richards, *The Annals*, p. 267.

123. Ibid, p. 494, trans., see Richards, *The Annals*, p. 273; see also K.V. Zettersteen, "Barkiyārūk,," in *EI*, Vol. 1, p. 662.

124. Ibid, p. 502, trans., see Richards, *The Annals*, pp. 278f; ; and Ibn Khaldūn, *Kitāb al-'Ibar*, Vol. 5, p. 19. See also K.V. Zettersteen, "Barkiyārūk,," in *EI*, Vol. 1, p. 662.

125. Ibid, p. 493, trans., see Richards, *The Annals*, p. 271.

126. See Nīshāpūrī, *The History of the Seljuq*, p. 68; Ibn al-Athīr, *al-Kāmil*, Vol. 9, pp. 7-9, trans., Richards, *The Annals*, pp. 289-291; and Ibn Khaldūn, *Kitāb al-'Ibar*, Vol. 5, pp. 20-22.

127. See Ibn al-Athīr, *al-Kāmil*, Vol. 9, p. 9, trans., see Richards, *The Annals*, p. 291; and Ibn Khaldūn, *Kitāb al-'Ibar*, Vol. 5, p. 22.

128. At least five battles raged between the two (see Nīshāpūrī, *The History of the Seljuq*, p. 71; and Ibn Khaldūn, *Kitāb al-'Ibar*, Vol. 5, pp. 25-380.

129. Bosworth, "The Political and Dynastic History of the Iranian World (AD 1000-1217)," in *The Cambridge History of Iran*, Vol. 5, pp. 108f & 114.

130. Ibid, pp. 108f.

131. See Ibn al-Athīr, *al-Kāmil*, Vol. 9, pp. 70f; and Ibn Khaldūn, *Kitāb al-'Ibar*, Vol. 5, pp. 38f.

132. Ibid, p. 77; and Ibn Khaldūn, *Kitāb al-'Ibar*, Vol. 5, p. 40.

133. Ibid, p. 79-81; and Ibn Khaldūn, *Kitāb al-'Ibar*, Vol. 5, pp. 1f.

134. See Bosworth, "The Political and Dynastic History of the Iranian World (AD 1000-1217)," in *The Cambridge History of Iran*, Vol. 5, p. 113.

135. Cf. Bosworth, "The Political and Dynastic History of the Iranian World (AD 1000-1217)," in *The Cambridge History of Iran*, Vol. 5, p. 114.

136. Also spelled Mengü-Bars.

137. See Ibn al-Athīr, *al-Kāmil*, Vol. 9, p. 88; and Ibn Khaldūn, *Kitāb al-'Ibar*, Vol. 5, pp. 43f.

138. Also spelled Qilich-Arsalan.

139. Also spelled Chavli. He had been appointed by the Sultan as the Emir of Mosul, Diyār Bakr and al-Jazīrah, (see Ibn al-Athīr, *al-Kāmil*, Vol. 9, p. 102).

140. See Ibn al-Athīr, *al-Kāmil*, Vol. 9, pp. 104-107; and Ibn Khaldūn, *Kitāb al-'Ibar*, Vol. 5, p. 45.

141. Called *al-ifranj* (Franks) in the Islamic classical sources. Cf. Hillenbrand, *The Crusades*, p. 31.

142. See below.

143. See Hodgson, *The Venture of Islam*, Vol. 2, p. 21.

144. Cf. E. Grafe, "Fāṭimids," *EI*, Vol. 2, p. 88.

145. See Hodgson, *The Venture of Islam*, Vol. 2, p. 21.

146. See M. Canard, "Fāṭimids," *EI²*, Vol. 2, pp. 850-852.

147. Ibid.

148. Al-Suyūṭī, *Tārīkh al-Khulafā'*, pp. 3-5.

149. See Ibn al-Athīr, *al-Kāmil*, Vol. 8, pp. 471-474.

150. As in Mousl and Baghdad upon the revolutionary of al-Basāsīrī.

151. Ibid.

152. See Canard, "Fāṭimīds," *EI²*, Vol. 2, p. 859.

153. Cf. Grafe, "Fāṭimīds," *EI*, Vol. 2, p. 88.

154. See Canard, "Fāttmīds," *EI²*, Vol. 2, p. 858.

155. Ibid.

156. Ibid.

157. Ibid.

158. Stern, S.M., "al-Āmir bi Aḥkām Allāh," *EI²*, p. 440.

159. See Jamāl al-Dīn Abī al-Maḥāsin Yusūf Ibn Taghrībardī (874/1470), *al-Nunjūm al-Ẓāhirah fī Mulūk Miṣr wa al-Qāhirah*, Cairo: al-Mu'assasah al-Miṣrīyah al-'Āmmah li al-Ta'līf wa al-Tarjamah wa al-Ṭibā'ah wa al-Nashr, 1964, Vol. 5, pp. 1425.

160. See Madelung, *Ismā'īlliyya, EI²*, Vol. 4, p. 200.

161. Canard, *EI²*, Fatimids, p. 860.

162. See Philip K. Hitti, *History of the Arabs*, New York: The Macmillan Company, 1951.

163. See Canard, *EI²*, Fatimids, pp. 857f.

164. Ibid, p. 860.

165. See Grafe, "Fāṭimids," *EI*, Vol. 2, p. 91.

166. Cf. Canard, *EI²*, Fatimids, p. 858.

167. See C.H. Becker, "Badr al-Djamālī," *EI*, Vol. 1, p. 560.

168. This scholar has been introduced as the founder of the Almoravids, (see, for instance, Doutté, E. "'Abd-Allāh b. Yāsīn," *EI*, Vol. 1, p. 32) while Yūsūf b. Tāshufīn has been regarded as the real founder of the Almoravids dynasty (see, for example, Halima Ferhat, "Yūsūf b. Tāshufīn," *EI²*, Vol. 2, p. 356.).

169. There is no agreement on the details about the emergence of this movement, as has been correctly observed by Norris (H.T. Norris, "al-Murābiṭūn," *EI²*, Vol. 2, p. 583), but the outline which follows is based on the broadly accepted account of the development of the movement. For a critical treatment of the diverse reports about the Almoravids, see I. Hrbek, and J. Devisse, "The Almoravids," in M. Elfasi, (ed.) *General History of Africa*, California: University of California Press, 1988, Vol. 3, pp. 337-366.

170. For his religious teaching, see Nehemia Levtzion, "'Abd Allāh b. Yāsīn and the Almoravids," in John Ralph Willis (ed.) *Studies in West African Islamic History*, London: Frank Cass, 1979, Vol. 1, pp. 85-88.

171. On the religious and political situations of these tribes prior to the rise of the Almoravids, see Hrbek, "The Almoravids," *General History of Africa*, Vol. 3, pp. 337-342; and Levtzion, "'Abd Allāh b. Yāsīn," *Studies in West African Islamic History*, Vol. 1, pp. 82-85 & 88-90.

172. See 'Alī Muḥammad al-Ṣallābī, *al-Jawhar al-Thamīn bi Ma'rifah Dawlah al-Murābiṭīn*, Sharjah: Maktabah al-Ṣaḥābah, 2001, pp. 54f.

173. See Ibn Khaldūn, *Kitāb al-'Ibar*, Vol. 6, pp. 216f.

174. See Levtzion, "The Western Maghrib," *Cambridge History of Africa*, Vol. 3, p. 333; and Hrbek, "The Almoravids," *General History of Africa*, Vol. 3, p. 347.

175. See Ibn Khaldūn, *Kitāb al-'Ibar*, Vol. 6, p. 217.

176. Cf. Hrbek, "The Almoravids," *General History of Africa*, Vol. 3, p. 348.
177. See Ibn Khaldūn, *Kitāb al-'Ibar*, Vol. 6, p. 217.
178. Cf. A. Bel, "Almoravids," *EI*, Vol. 1, p. 318.
179. On the Almoravids coinage, see Levtzion, "The Western Maghrib," *Cambridge History of Africa*, Vol. 3, p. 336.
180. See Norris, "al-Murābiṭūn," *EI²*, Vol. 7, p. 585.
181. See Bel, "Almoravids," *EI*, Vol. 1, p. 319.
182. See Ibn Khaldūn, *Kitāb al-'Ibar*, Vol. 6, p. 217.
183. On this new strategy, see Ferhat, "Yūsuf b. Tāshufīn," *EI²*, Vol. 2, p. 356; Levtzion, "The Western Maghrib," *Cambridge History of Africa*, Vol. 3, p. 334; and Hrbek, "The Almoravids," *General History of Africa*, Vol. 3, p. 350.
184. Cf. al-Ṣallābī, *al-Jawhar al-Thamīn*, pp. 69-71.
185. The construction of this capital was completed during the reign of Ibn Tāshfīn's son, 'Alī, see Ibn Khaldūn, *Kitāb al-'Ibar*, Vol. 6, p. 218.
186. Ibn al-Athīr, *al-Kāmil*, Vol. 8, p. 329.
187. Ferhat, "Yūsuf b. Tāshufīn," *EI²*, Vol. 2, p. 356.
188. Ibn al-Athīr, *al-Kāmil*, Vol. 8, p. 329.
189. See Ibn Khaldūn, *Kitāb al-'Ibar*, Vol. 6, p. 218.
190. Ibid.
191. Ibn al-Athīr, *al-Kāmil*, Vol. 8, p. 330.
192. See Levtzion, "'Abd Allāh b. Yāsīn," *Studies in West African Islamic History*, Vol. 1, pp. 87.
193. See Ibn Khaldūn, *Kitāb al-'Ibar*, Vol. 6, p. 220.
194. Levtzion, "The Western Maghrib," *Cambridge History of Africa*, Vol. 3, p. 331.
195. See Ibn al-Athīr, *al-Kāmil*, Vol. 8, p. 448.
196. He was carefully chosen by his father as his successor from four other sons, see Lévi-Provencal, "'Alī b. Yūsuf b. Tāshufīn," *EI²*, Vol. 1, p. 389.
197. Cf. Norris, "al-Murābiṭūn," *EI²*, Vol. 7, p. 585; and Bel, "Almoravids," *EI*, Vol. 1, p. 319.
198. Bel, "'Alī b. Yūsuf b. Tāshafīn," *EI*, Vol. 1, p. 290.
199. Ibid.
200. His reign ended in 537/1143, see E. Lévi-Provencal, "'Alī b. Yūsuf b. Tāshufīn," *EI²*, Vol. 1, p. 389.
201. Namely the rise of the Almohads movement. Cf. Bel, "'Alī b. Yūsuf b. Tāshafīn," *EI*, Vol. 1, pp. 290f.
202. For an outline of these events, see Lévi-Provencal, "'Alī b. Yūsuf b. Tāshufīn," *EI²*, Vol. 1, pp. 389f.
203. Cf. Hugh Kennedy, *Muslim Spain and Portugal: A Political History of al-Andalus*, New York: Addison Wesley Longman Limited, 1996, p. 132.

204. See Ibn ʿIdhārī al-Marrākushī, Abū al-ʿAbbās Aḥmad b. Muḥammad. *Al-Bayān al-Mughrib fī Akhbār Mulūk al-Andalus wa al-Maghrib*, Paris: Paul Eeuthner, 1930, Vol. 3, p. 155.

205. See Hodgson, *The Venture of Islam*, Vol. 2, pp. 29f.

206. See D.J. Wasserstein, "Mulūk al-Ṭawāif: 2. In Muslim Spain," *EI²*, Vol. 7, p. 552; Watt, *A History of Islamic Spain*, Edinburgh University Press, 1965, pp. 91f; and Kennedy, *Muslim Spain*, p. 134.

207. ʿAbd al-Raḥmān ʿAlī al-Ḥijjī, *al-Tārīkh al-Andalusī*, Damascus: Dār al-Qalam, 1987, p. 325.

208. See al-Ḥijjī, *al-Tārīkh al-Andalusī*, p. 324.

209. Kennedy, *Muslim Spain*, p. 144.

210. Cf. al-Ḥijjī, *al-Tārīkh al-Andalusī*, pp. 325f

211. This is according to the list of Wasserstein which is based on data in numerous sources, see David Wasserstein, *The Rise and Fall of the Party-Kings: Politics and Society in Islamic Spain 1002-1068*, Princeton: Princeton University Press, 1985, pp. 83-98.

212. See al-Ḥijjī, *al-Tārīkh al-Andalusī*, pp. 354f.

213. Cf. Watt, *A History of Islamic Spain*, p. 92.

214. His full name is Abū al-Qāsim Muḥammad b. ʿAbbād, but he is mostly known by al-Muʿtamid which is abbreviation of his honorific title al-Muʿtamid ʿalā Allāh.

215. See Watt, *A History of Islamic Spain*, p. 92.

216. See Ibn ʿIdhārī al-Marrākushī, *al-Bayān al-Mughrib*, Vol. 3, pp. 185f.

217. See Kennedy, *Muslim Spain*, p. 137.

218. See al-Ḥijjī, *al-Tārīkh al-Andalusī*, p. 325.

219. Ibn ʿIdhārī al-Marrākushī, *al-Bayān al-Mughrib*, Vol. 3, p. 222.

220. See Ibn ʿIdhārī al-Marrākushī, *al-Bayān al-Mughrib*, Vol. 3, pp. 222-224; and al-Ḥijjī, *al-Tārīkh al-Andalusī*, p. 356.

221. Ibid, pp. 164f; and al-Ḥijjī, *al-Tārīkh al-Andalusī*, pp. 366f.

222. See al-Ḥijjī, *al-Tārīkh al-Andalusī*, p. 367.

223. Ibid.

224. On such unity, see Wasserstein, "Mulūk al-Ṭawāif," *EI²*, Vol. 7, p. 553.

225. Cf. Kennedy, *Muslim Spain*, p. 132; and Watt, *A History of Islamic Spain*, p. 92.

226. Kennedy, *Muslim Spain*, p. 145.

227. Ibid, pp. 145-149; and Watt, *A History of Islamic Spain*, p. 93.

228. Ibid, p. 147; and Watt, *A History of Islamic Spain*, p. 93.

229. See Ibn ʿIdhārī al-Marrākushī, *al-Bayān al-Mughrib*, Vol. 3, pp. 225f; and al-Ḥijjī, *al-Tārīkh al-Andalusī*, pp. 359ff.

230. Wasserstein, *The Rise*, p. 249.

231. See Ibn al-Athīr, *al-Kāmil*, Vol. 8, p. 439.

232. See al-Ḥijjī, *al-Tārīkh al-Andalusī*, pp. 336-354.

233. See Ibn 'Idhārī al-Marrākushī, *al-Bayān al-Mughrib*, Vol. 3, p. 227; Kennedy, *Muslim Spain*, p. 151; and al-Ḥijjī, *al-Tārīkh al-Andalusī*, pp. 362f.

234. Cf. Kennedy, *Muslim Spain*, p. 162; and al-Ḥijjī, *al-Tārīkh al-Andalusī*, p. 392.

235. Ibid.

236. See Kennedy, *Muslim Spain*, p. 163 and al-Ḥijjī, *al-Tārīkh al-Andalusī*, pp. 407f.

237. Cf. Kennedy, *Muslim Spain*, p. 163.

238. See al-Ḥijjī, *al-Tārīkh al-Andalusī*, p. 442.

239. Cf. Kennedy, *Muslim Spain*, p. 164.

240. On this, see al-Ḥijjī, *al-Tārīkh al-Andalusī*, pp. 442-444.

241. See, for instance, Runciman, *A History of the Crusades*, 1951, Vol. 1, pp. 110-118, 169 & 175; and Hodgson, *The Venture of Islam*, Vol. 2, pp. 264f. For a discussion of the motives behind the First Crusade based on Islamic chronicles, see Hillenbrand, *The Crusades*, pp. 50-4.

242. See Runciman, *A History of the Crusades*, 1951, Vol. 1, pp. 121-133; and Amīn Ma'lūf, *al-Ḥurūb al-Ṣalībiyyah kamā Ra'āhā al-'Arab*, trans., from French to Arabic by 'Afīf Dimashqiyyah, Beirut: Dār al-Fārābī, 1989, pp. 21-26.

243. See Ma'lūf, *al-Ḥurūb al-Ṣalībiyyah*, p. 28.

244. See Ma'lūf, *al-Ḥurūb al-Ṣalībiyyah*, p. 28.

245. See Runciman, *A History of the Crusades*, Vol. 1, pp. 179-181; and Ma'lūf, *al-Ḥurūb al-Ṣalībiyyah*, pp. 30-31.

246. See Ma'lūf, *al-Ḥurūb al-Ṣalībiyyah*, p. 33.

247. See Runciman, *A History of the Crusades*, Vol. 1, pp. 184-185; and Ma'lūf, *al-Ḥurūb al-Ṣalībiyyah*, pp. 33f.

248. See Ibid, Vol. 1, p. 185-187; and Ma'lūf, *al-Ḥurūb al-Ṣalībiyyah*, p. 35.

249. See Runciman, *A History of the Crusades*, Vol. 1, p. 185-186; and Ma'lūf, *al-Ḥurūb al-Ṣalībiyyah*, p. 35.

250. Ibid, p. 186; and Ma'lūf, *al-Ḥurūb al-Ṣalībiyyah*, p. 35.

251. See Runciman, *A History of the Crusades*, Vol. 1, p. 187; and Ma'lūf, *al-Ḥurūb al-Ṣalībiyyah*, p. 36.

252. See Runciman, *A History of the Crusades*, Vol. 1, pp. 188-193.

253. Ibid, pp. 188-193.

254. See Ibn al-Athīr, *al-Kāmil*, Vol. 8, p. 435: trans., see Richards, *The Annals*, p. 217.

255. Also spelled Yaghi-Siyan.

256. See Ibn al-Athīr, *al-Kāmil*, Vol. 9, p. 11: trans., see Richards, *The Annals*, pp. 293f.

257. See Runciman, *A History of the Crusades*, Vol. 1, p. 216; and Ma'lūf, *al-Ḥurūb al-Ṣalībiyyah*, p. 40.

258. See Runciman, *A History of the Crusades*, Vol. 1, pp. 219f.
259. Ibid, pp. 220f; and Ma'lūf, *al-Ḥurūb al-Ṣalībiyyah*, pp. 44f.
260. See Runciman, *A History of the Crusades*, Vol. 1, pp. 220f; and Ma'lūf, *al-Ḥurūb al-Ṣalībiyyah*, p. 45.
261. Ibid, Vol. 1, p. 225; and Ma'lūf, *al-Ḥurūb al-Ṣalībiyyah*, p. 46.
262. Runciman, *A History of the Crusades*, Vol. 1, p. 225.
263. Ibid, Vol. 1, p. 226.
264. See Runciman, *A History of the Crusades*, Vol. 1, p. 226; and Ma'lūf, *al-Ḥurūb al-Ṣalībiyyah*, pp. 47f.
265. Runciman, *A History of the Crusades*, Vol. 1, pp. 226-229.
266. Ibid, p. 229.
267. Also spelled Kerbogha and Kirbogha.
268. See Ibn al-Athīr, *al-Kāmil*, Vol. 9, p. 15; Runciman, *A History of the Crusades*, Vol. 1, p. 230; and Ma'lūf, *al-Ḥurūb al-Ṣalībiyyah*, p. 51.
269. See Runciman, *A History of the Crusades*, Vol. 1, p. 231; and Ma'lūf, *al-Ḥurūb al-Ṣalībiyyah*, pp. 52f.
270. Ibid, p. 231; Ma'lūf, *al-Ḥurūb al-Ṣalībiyyah*, p. 54; and Ibn al-Athīr, *al-Kāmil*, Vol. 9, p. 14.
271. Runciman, *A History of the Crusades*, Vol. 1, p. 232.
272. See Runciman, *A History of the Crusades*, Vol. 1, pp. 233f; and Ma'lūf, *al-Ḥurūb al-Ṣalībiyyah*, pp. 54f. The chronicler Ibn al-Athīr narrated the fall of Antioch, mentioning the story of the treachery and the retreat of Baghī-Siyān, but according to his narrative, the march of Karbughā started after the city had fallen and his account does not include any of the previous rescue attempts (see Ibn al-Athīr, *al-Kāmil*, Vol. 9, pp. 14f). In my description of this event, as well as other events mentioned in this section, I have chiefly relied on the detailed account of the distinguished historian Steven Runciman on the First Crusade which is an outcome of an in-depth scholarly research on numerous original Western European, Latin, Greek, Arabic, Persian, Armenian, Syriac and Hebrew sources in addition to many secondary sources, as appears in his rich footnotes and extensive bibliography.
273. See Runciman, *A History of the Crusades*, Vol. 1, p. 234; Ma'lūf, *al-Ḥurūb al-Ṣalībiyyah*, pp. 55f.
274. Ibid, p. 234; Ma'lūf, *al-Ḥurūb al-Ṣalībiyyah*, p. 56.
275. Runciman, *A History of the Crusades*, Vol. 1, p. 237.
276. Ibid, p. 237.
277. Ibid, p. 238.
278. Ibid.
279. See Ibn al-Athīr, *al-Kāmil*, Vol. 9, p. 15.
280. Runciman, *A History of the Crusades*, Vol. 1, p. 238.
281. Ibid.

282. Ibn al-Athīr (*al-Kāmil*, Vol. 9, p. 15) states that the lance was buried by a priest who was among the Crusaders. For a discussion of this story, see Runciman, *A History of the Crusades*, Vol. 1, p. 241-246.

283. See Ibn al-Athīr, *al-Kāmil*, Vol. 9, p. 15; Runciman, *A History of the Crusades*, Vol. 1, p. 246; and Ma'lūf, *al-Ḥurūb al-Ṣalībiyyah*, pp. 56f.

284. Runciman, *A History of the Crusades*, Vol. 1, p. 246.

285. See Ibn al-Athīr, *al-Kāmil*, Vol. 9, p. 15; and Runciman, *A History of the Crusades*, Vol. 1, pp. 246f.

286. Runciman, *A History of the Crusades*, Vol. 1, p. 247.

287. Ibn al-Athīr, *al-Kāmil*, Vol. 9, p. 16. In her discussion of the fall of Antioch, Hillenbrand unfortunately misrepresents Ibn al-Athīr's account particularly on this quote by firstly mistranslating the phrase "*ḍarabū maṣāfan 'azīman*" as "they attacked strongly," when it should be translated as "they stood in a great array," and secondly by omitting the reported reason behind the desertion of the Muslim troops (Cf. Hillenbrand, *The Crusades*, p. 58).

288. Ibn al-Athīr, *al-Kāmil*, Vol. 9, p. 16.

289. Ibid.

290. Runciman, *A History of the Crusades*, Vol. 1, p. 249.

291. This contact is clearly mentioned in the Western Crusader sources, see Runciman, *A History of the Crusades*, Vol. 1, p. 229.

292. Runciman, *A History of the Crusades*, Vol. 1, p. 229.

293. Ibid, p. 265.

294. Cf. Hillenbrand, *The Crusades*, p. 47.

295. The city was in the actual hands of the two Turkman emirs: Suqmān b. Artuq and his borther Ilghāzī, who had vowed homage to the Seljuk Emir of Damascus, Duqāq, see Ibn al-Athīr, *al-Kāmil*, Vol. 9, p. 19; and Runciman, *A History of the Crusades*, Vol. 1, p. 265.

296. See Ibn al-Athīr, *al-Kāmil*, Vol. 9, p. 19.

297. Cf. Hillenbrand, *The Crusades*, p. 47.

298. See Runciman, *A History of the Crusades*, Vol. 1, p. 257.

299. Ibid, pp. 249-256.

300. Ibid, p. 252.

301. Ibid, p. 257.

302. See Ibn al-Athīr, *al-Kāmil*, Vol. 9, p. 16; and Runciman, *A History of the Crusades*, Vol. 1, p. 259.

303. Ibid; and Runciman, *A History of the Crusades*, Vol. 1, p. 260.

304. See Ma'lūf, *al-Ḥurūb al-Ṣalībiyyah*, pp. 63f.

305. See Runciman, *A History of the Crusades*, Vol. 1, p. 261.

306. Ibid.

307. Or Shaizar.

308. See Runciman, *A History of the Crusades*, Vol. 1, p. 267; and Ma'lūf, *al-Ḥurūb al-Ṣalībiyyah*, p. 65.

309. Runciman, *A History of the Crusades*, Vol. 1, p. 267.

310. Ibid.

311. See Runciman, *A History of the Crusades*, Vol. 1, p. 269; and Ma'lūf, *al-Ḥurūb al-Ṣalībiyyah*, p. 66.

312. See Ma'lūf, *al-Ḥurūb al-Ṣalībiyyah*, pp. 66f.

313. See Runciman, *A History of the Crusades*, Vol. 1, p. 270; and Ma'lūf, *al-Ḥurūb al-Ṣalībiyyah*, p. 68.

314. Runciman, *A History of the Crusades*, Vol. 1, p. 270.

315. Ibid, pp. 270f.

316. See Runciman, *A History of the Crusades*, Vol. 1, p. 271; and Ma'lūf, *al-Ḥurūb al-Ṣalībiyyah*, pp. 68f.

317. See Runciman, *A History of the Crusades*, Vol. 1, pp. 274f; and Ma'lūf, *al-Ḥurūb al-Ṣalībiyyah*, p. 69.

318. Ma'lūf, *al-Ḥurūb al-Ṣalībiyyah*, p. 69.

319. Runciman, *A History of the Crusades*, Vol. 1, p. 275.

320. See Runciman, *A History of the Crusades*, Vol. 1, p. 276; and Ma'lūf, *al-Ḥurūb al-Ṣalībiyyah*, p. 73.

321. Ibid; and Ma'lūf, *al-Ḥurūb al-Ṣalībiyyah*, pp. 73f.

322. Ibid; and Ma'lūf, *al-Ḥurūb al-Ṣalībiyyah*, p. 74.

323. Runciman, *A History of the Crusades*, Vol. 1, p. 277.

324. See Runciman, *A History of the Crusades*, Vol. 1, pp. 279-281; and Ma'lūf, *al-Ḥurūb al-Ṣalībiyyah*, p. 74.

325. Ibid, pp. 281 & 283.

326. See Ma'lūf, *al-Ḥurūb al-Ṣalībiyyah*, p. 75; and Runciman, *A History of the Crusades*, Vol. 1, p. 282.

327. See Runciman, *A History of the Crusades*, Vol. 1, p. 284.

328. See Runciman, *A History of the Crusades*, Vol. 1, pp. 285f; Ma'lūf, *al-Ḥurūb al-Ṣalībiyyah*, pp. 75f; and Ibn al-Athīr, *al-Kāmil*, Vol. 9, p. 19.

329. Ibid, pp. 285f; Ma'lūf, *al-Ḥurūb al-Ṣalībiyyah*, pp. 75f; and Ibn al-Athīr, *al-Kāmil*, Vol. 9, p. 19.

330. See Hans Eberhard Mayer, *The Crusades*, translated from German by John Gillingham, Oxford: Oxford University Press, 1988, pp. 56f; and Runciman, *A History of the Crusades*, Vol. 1, pp. 289-295.

331. Ibid, p. 57; and Runciman, *A History of the Crusades*, Vol. 1, pp. 289-295.

332. See Ibn al-Athīr, *al-Kāmil*, Vol. 9, p. 21; Runciman, *A History of the Crusades*, Vol. 1, p. 296; and Ma'lūf, *al-Ḥurūb al-Ṣalībiyyah*, p. 79.

333. Ibid; Runciman, *A History of the Crusades*, Vol. 1, p. 296.

334. Runciman, *A History of the Crusades*, Vol. 1, pp. 297f.

335. Ibid, pp. 297f.

336. Ibid, p. 304.

337. Ibid, pp. 304f.

338. Ibid, pp. 303, & 307-309.

339. Ibid, p. 309.

340. Ibid, pp. 312f.

341. Ibid, p. 316.

342. Ibid, p. 316.

343. See Ibn al-Athīr, *al-Kāmil*, Vol. 9, p. 29; Runciman, *A History of the Crusades*, Vol. 1, pp. 320f; and Ma'lūf, *al-Ḥurūb al-Ṣalībiyyah*, p. 88.

344. Ibid; Runciman, *A History of the Crusades*, Vol. 1, p. 321; and Ma'lūf, *al-Ḥurūb al-Ṣalībiyyah*, p. 88.

345. Transformed from the Arabic term *taṣawwuf*.

346. Namely al-Ḥasan al-Baṣrī (d. 110/728), Mālik b. Dinār (d. 128/745), Ibrāhim b. Adham (d. 160/77), Ibn al-Mubārk (d. 181/797), Rābi'ah al-'Adawiyyah (d. 185/801) and Fuḍayl b. 'Iyād, (d. 188/803). For a recent and intelligible English survey of the devotional trends of theses early ascetic Muslims and their diversity, see Alexander Knysh, *Islamic Mysticism: A Short History*, Leiden: Brill, 2000, pp. 10-35.

347. Commonly appears in the English sources as Sufis.

348. Ibn Khaldūn, *Muqaddimah*, Beirut: Dār Iḥyā' al-Turāth, n.d, p. 467, trans., Franz Rosenthal, *The Muqaddimah: An Introduction to History*, London: Routledge & Kegan Paul, 1958, Vol. 3, p. 76.

349. Such as *Kitāb al-Ri'āyah li Ḥuqūq Allāh* (Book of Observance of What is Due to God) by al-Ḥārith al-Muḥāsibī (d. 243/857), *Kitāb al-Kashf wa al-Bayān* (Book of Unveiling and Elucidation) by Abū Sa'īd al-Kharrāz (286/899) and the various *rasā'il* (epistles) of al-Junayd (d. 298/910).

350. A.J. Arberry, "Mysticism," in P.M. Holt and et al. (eds.) *The Cambridge History of Islam*, Cambridge: The Cambridge University Press, 1970, Vol. 2, p. 606.

351. See Abū al-Wafā al-Ghunaymī al-Tiftazānī, *Madhkal ilā al-Taṣawwuf al-Islāmī*, Cairo: Dār al-Thaqāfah wa al-Nashr wa al-Tawzī', 1989, p. 95.

352. See L. Massignon, "Taṣawwuf," *EI²*, Vol. 10, p. 314.

353. Al-Tiftazānī, *Madhkal*, p. 99.

354. Ibid, p. 99.

355. Ibid, pp. 99 &145.

356. On this phenomenon, see the book of 'Abd al-Raḥmān Badawī, *Shaṭaḥāt al-Ṣūfiyyah*, Kuwait: Wakālah al-Maṭbū'āt, 1978. For al-Ghazālī's explanation of this term, see below.

357. See, for example, al-Tiftazānī, *Madhkal*, p. 126.

358. On the contradicting accounts of his date of death, see Abū 'Abd al-Raḥmān Muḥammad b. al-Ḥusayn al-Sulamī (d. 412/1021), *Ṭabaqāt*

al-Ṣūfiyyah, edited by Muṣṭafā ʿAbd al-Qādir ʿAṭā, *Ṭabaqāt al-Ṣūfiyyah*, Beirut: Dār al-Kutub al-ʿIlmiyyah, 1998, p. 68.

359. See, for instance, al-Ghazālī, *Iḥyā' ʿUlūm al-Dīn*, Beirut: Dār Iḥyā' al-Turāth al-ʿArabī, n.d, Vol. 1, p. 36.

360. Such as his saying *anā al-Ḥaq* (I'm the Truth, as stated by al-Ghazālī (al-Ghazālī, *Iḥyā'*, Vol. 1, p. 36). However, there is no agreement on the reason behind al-Ḥallāj's execution. Some argue that this was due to his challenging political views (see, for example, ʿUmar Farrūkh, *Tārīkh al-Fikr al-ʿArabī ilā Ayyām Ibn Khaldūn*, Beirut: 1981, p. 4742). Ironically, he has been considered by some, particularly by European writers, as a "martyr of mystical love," (see, for example, Annemarie Schimmel, *Mystical Dimensions of Islam*, Chapel Hill: The University of North Carolina Press, 1975, p. 62; and Louis Massignon, *The Passion of al-Hallaj*, trans., Herbert Mason, Princeton: Princeton University Press, 1994, pp. 280f). Knysh, *Islamic Mysticism*, p. 140.

361. Knysh, *Islamic Mysticism*, p. 69.

362. ʿUmar Farrūkh, *Tārīkh al-Fikr al-ʿArabī ilā Ayyām Ibn Khaldūn*, Beirut: 1981, p. 474.

363. See, for instance, Aḥmad Amīn, *Ẓuhr al-Islām*, Cairo: Maktabah al-Nahḍah al-Miṣriyyah, 1955, Vol. 4, p. 157.

364. Knysh, *Islamic Mysticism*, p. 116.

365. For an overview of these works and their authors, see Knysh, *Islamic Mysticism*, pp. 118-127.

366. Abū al-Qāsim ʿAbd al-Karīm al-Qushayrī, *al-Risālah al-Qushayriyyah*, edited by ʿAbd al-Ḥalīm Maḥmūd and Maḥmūd b. al-Sharīf, Cairo: Maṭbaʿah Ḥassān, n.d., Vol. 1, p. 20.

367. Al-Qushayrī, *al-Risālah*, Vol. 1, p. 22.

368. Ibid.

369. Ibid.

370. A.J. Arberry, *Sufism: An Account of the Mystics of Islam*, London: George Allen & Unwin LTD, 1969, p. 71.

371. Knysh, *Islamic Mysticism*, p. 131.

372. Al-Tiftazānī, *Madhkal*, p. 148.

373. Al-Ghazālī, *al-Munqidh min al-Ḍalāl*, eds. Jamīl Ṣulībā and Kāmil ʿAyyād, Beirut: Dār al-Andalus, 1967, p. 106.

374. See, in particular, al-Ghazālī, *Iḥyā'*, Vol. 3, pp. 23-26.

375. Knysh, *Islamic Mysticism*, p. 140.

376. See al-Ghazālī, *Iḥyā'*, Vol. 2, p. 250 & Vol. 3, p. 404.

377. See, for instance, al-Ghazālī, *Iḥyā'*, Vol. 1, p. 36.

378. Annemarie Schimmel, *Mystical Dimensions of Islam*, Chapel Hill: The University of North Carolina Press, 1975, p. 55.

379. For a recent collection of papers on the polemics between Sufis and anti-Sufis throughout the Islamic history, see Frederick De Jong

and Bernd Radtke (eds.), *Islamic Mysticism Contested: Thirteen Centuries of Controversies and Polemics*, Leiden: Brill, 1999.

380. Quoted in Josef Van Ess, "Sufism and its Opponents," in Frederick De Jong and Bernd Radtke (eds.), *Islamic Mysticism Contested: Thirteen Centuries of Controversies and Polemics*, Leiden: Brill, 1999, p. 28.

381. Abū al-Faraj ʿAbd al-Raḥmān Ibn al-Jawzī, *Talbīs Iblīs*, Riyadh: Dār al-Mughnī, 2000, p. 186.

382. Norris, "al-Murābiṭūn," *EI²*, Vol. 7, p. 587.

383. Muṣṭafā Binsibāʿ, *Iḥrāq Kitāb al-Iḥyāʾ li al-Ghazālī wa ʿIlāqatuh bi al-Ṣirāʿ bayn al-Murābiṭīn wa al-Mutaṣawwifah*; and Maribel Fierro, "Opposition to Sufism in al-Andalus," in Frederick De Jong & Bernd Radtke (eds.) *Islamic Mysticism Contested*, Leiden: Brill, 1999, pp. 191-197.

384. This Arabic word—sing. *faylasūf*—refers to the adherents of *falsafah* which is used in this context as a technical term referring to all branches of philosophical sciences of Greek origin as had been established and developed in Islamdom since the second/ eight century. This is usually called Muslim Philosophy in the English modern sources (see B. Carra de Vaux, 'Falsafa,' *EI*, Vol. 2, p. 48) or Islamic philosophy (see, for example, W. Montogomery Watt, *Islamic Philosophy and Theology*, Edinburgh: Edinburgh University Press, 1962) and in the Arabic modern sources it is called *al-falsafah al-Islāmiyyah* (see, for instance, Muḥammad ʿAbd al-Raḥmān Marḥabā, *Min al-Falsafah al-Yūnāniyyah ilā al-Falsafah al-Islāmiyyah*, Beirut: Manshūrāt ʿUwidāt, 1983, pp. 336f). In the Muslim classical sources, however, *falsafah* does not seem to be given an Islamic label (see, for instance, Ibn Khaldūn, *Muqaddimah*, Beirut: Dār Iḥyāʾ al-Turāth, n.d., pp. 480f). Since this labelling has always been controversial, it is avoided here.

385. Mostly done by Syriac-speaking Arab Christian translators (see Majid Fakhry, *A History of Islamic Philosophy*, New York: Columbia University Press, 1970, p. 9).

386. Such as those which are ascribed to Socrates, Aristotle and Plato.

387. According to to Ibn al-Nadīm, the Umayyad prince Khālid b. Yazīd b. Muʿāwiyah, who was called the "Wise Man of the Family of Marwān," initiated the process of translation into Arabic by commanding a group of Greek philosophers to translate books on alchemy from Greek and Coptic into Arabic (See Ibn al-Nadīm, *Kitāb al-Fihrist*, ed. Gustav Flügel, Leipzig (Germany) : Verlag Von F.C.W. Vogel, 1871, p. 242, trans., Bayard Dodge, *The Fihrist of al-Nadīm*, New York: Columbia University Press, 1970, Vol. 2, p. 581). Fakhry, however, states that "it is certain that the process

of translating scientific and philosophical works did not begin in earnest until the 'Abbāsid period, and in particular until the reign of al-Manṣūr..."(see Majid Fakhry, *A History of Islamic Philosophy*, pp. 16-18).

388. See Fakhry, *A History of Islamic Philosophy*, pp. 18-24.

389. Cf. B. Carra de Vaux, "Falsafa," *EI*, Vol. 2, p. 48; and Albert Hourani, *A History of Arab Peoples*, London: Faber and Faber Ltd., 1991.p. 172.

390. Fakhry, *A History of Islamic Philosophy*, p. 113.

391. Ibn al-Nadīm, *Kitāb al-Fihrist*, p. 255, trans., Bayard Dodge, *The Fihrist of al-Nadīm*, p. 615.

392. See Fakhry, *A History of Islamic Philosophy*, pp. 82f.

393. Ibn al-Nadīm, *Kitāb al-Fihrist*, p. 263, trans., Bayard Dodge, *The Fihrist of al-Nadīm*, p. 629.

394. Known in English sources as Avicenna.

395. B. Carra de Vaux, "Falsafa," *EI*, Vol. 2, p. 49.

396. As pointed out by Arnaldez, "since strictly orthodox Sunnī Islam has never welcomed philosophic thought, *falsafah* developed from the first especially among thinkers influenced by the sects, and particularly by the Shī'ā; and this arose from a certain prior sympathy, from such sects having absorbed gnostic ideas, some related to Hellenistic types of gnosis, others to Iranian types..." (R. Arnaldez, "Falsafa," *EI²*, Vol. 2, p. 769).

397. Cf. Bello, *The Medieval Islamic Controversy*, pp. 3f.

398. See Fakhry, *A History of Islamic Philosophy*, p. 228.

399. Bello, *The Medieval Islamic Controversy*, pp. 3f.

400. Al-Ghazālī, *Tahāfuh al-Falāsifah*, ed. Sulaymān Dunyā, Cairo: Dār al-Ma'ārif, 1980, p. 74, trans., see Sabih Ahmad Kamali, *al-Ghazali's Tahafut al-Falasifah*, Lahore: Pakistan Philosophical Congress, 1963, p. 2.

401. Al-Ghazālī, *al-Munqidh*, p. 120, trans., see McCarthy, *Deliverance*, p. 90, & W. Montgomery Watt, *The Faith and Practice of al-Ghazālī*, translation of al-Ghazāli's *al-Munqidh* and *Bidāyah al-Hidāyah*, London: George Allen and Unwin Ltd, 1953, p. 73.

402. Al-Ghazālī, *al-Munqidh*, p. 74, trans., see McCarthy, *Deliverance*, p. 61, & W. Montgomery Watt, *The Faith and Practice of al-Ghazālī*, translation of al-Ghazāli's *al-Munqidh* and *Bidāyah al-Hidāyah*, London: George Allen and Unwin Ltd, 1953, p. 29.

403. Al-Ghazālī, *al-Munqidh*, p. 80, trans., see McCarthy, *Deliverance*, p. 64, & W. Montgomery Watt, *The Faith and Practice of al-Ghazālī*, translation of al-Ghazāli's *al-Munqidh* and *Bidāyah al-Hidāyah*, London: George Allen and Unwin Ltd, 1953, p. 34.

404. Al-Ghazālī, *al-Munqidh*, p. 74, trans., see McCarthy, *Deliverance*, p. 61, & W. Montgomery Watt, *The Faith and Practice of al-Ghazālī*, translation of al-Ghazāli's *al-Munqidh* and *Bidāyah al-Hidāyah*, London: George Allen and Unwin Ltd, 1953, p. 29.

405. His reaction to these as well as his position from other philosophical sciences will be further discussed below.

406. Shlomo Pines, 'Islamic Philosophy,' in Sarah Stroumsa (ed.) *Studies in the History of Arabic Philosophy: The Collected Works of Shlomo Pines*, Jerusalem: The Magnes Press, The Hebrew University, 1996, Vol. 3, p. 36.

407. It branched off from Shiite and differed from other sub-divisions by the belief in the *Imāmah* of Ismā'īl (d. 143/760), the eldest son of Ja'far al-Ṣādiq (see Abū al-Fatḥ Muḥammad b. 'Abd al-Karīm b. Aḥmad al-Shahrastānī (d. 548/1153), *al-Milal wa al-Niḥal*, Beirut: Dār Maktabah al-Mutanabbī, 1992, pp. 81f, trans., A.K. Kazi and J.G. Flynn, *Muslim Sects and Divisions: The section on Muslim Sects in Kitāb al-Milal wa'l-Niḥal*, London: Kegan Paul International, 1984, pp. 164ff).

408. Al-Ghazālī counted ten appellations given to this sect and he gave a particular reason for each one (al-Ghazālī, *Faḍā'iḥ al-Bāṭiniyyah*, pp. 21-25, trans., McCarthy, *Faḍā'iḥ*, pp. 156-158).

409. Al-Shahrastānī, *al-Milal*, p. 82, trans., Kazi and Flynn, *Muslim Sects*, p. 165.

410. Al-Ghazālī, *Faḍā'iḥ*, p. 21, trans., McCarthy, *Faḍā'iḥ*, p. 181.

411. Hodgson, "Baṭiniyya," *EI²*, Vol. 1, p. 1098.

412. Al-Ghazālī, *Faḍā'iḥ*, p. 25, trans., McCarthy, *Faḍā'iḥ*, pp. 182f.

413. Ibid, trans., McCarthy, *Faḍā'iḥ*, pp. 183.

414. See W. Madelung, "Ismā'īlliyya," *EI²*, Vol. 4, p. 199; and Cl. Hurat, "Ismā'īlliyya," *EI*, Vol. 2, p. 550.

415. Cf. Hodgson, *The Venture of Islam*, Vol. 2, p. 58.

416. The Arabic term *'ilm* means "a branch of knowledge" while the term *al-kalām* literally means "word or speech". As an approximate rendering, it, as Gardet pointed out, is often translated as "theology" (L. Gardet, "'Ilm al-Kalām," *EI²*, Vol. 3, p. 1141), but this seems a misleading translation.

417. Ibn Khaldūn, *Muqaddimah*, Beirut: Dār Iḥyā' al-Turāth, n.d, p. 458, trans., Franz Rosenthal, *The Muqaddimah: An Introduction to History*, London: Routledge & Kegan Paul, 1958, p. 34.

418. This term is translated by Rosenthal as 'Muslim orthodoxy' (Rosenthal, *The Muqaddimah*, p. 34) but this is liable to prove misleading. To avoid this, it is better to transliterate it and consider it as a technical term. While the Mu'tazilah called themselves *Ahl al-'Adl wa al-Tawḥīd*, the name *Ahl al-Sunnah* was given to those who opposed them, particularly the Ash'ariyyah and the Māturidiyyah

(See Aḥmad Amīn, *Ẓuhr al-Islām*, Cairo: Maktabah al-Nahḍah al-Miṣriyyah, 1955, Vol. 4, p. 96).

419. Gardet, "'Ilm al-Kalām," *EI²*, Vol. 3, p. 1141.

420. Cf. Shlomo Pines, "Islamic Philosophy," in Sarah Stroumsa (ed.) *Studies in the History of Arabic Philosophy: The Collected Works of Shlomo Pines*, Jerusalem: The Magnes Press, The Hebrew University, 1996, Vol. 3, p. 11.

421. Ibn Khaldūn, *Muqaddimah*, Beirut: Dār Iḥyā' al-Turāth, n.d, p. 464, trans., Franz Rosenthal, *The Muqaddimah: An Introduction to History*, London: Routledge & Kegan Paul, 1958, p. 49.

422. This technical term, sing. *mutakalim*, refers to the practitioners of *kalām*.

423. Ibn Khaldūn, *Muqaddimah*, Beirut: Dār Iḥyā' al-Turāth, n.d, p. 465, trans., Franz Rosenthal, *The Muqaddimah: An Introduction to History*, London: Routledge & Kegan Paul, 1958, p. 50.

424. See Montgomery Watt, "al-Ash'arī, Abu'l-Ḥasn," *EI²*, Vol. 1, p. 694.

425. Ibn Khaldūn, *Muqaddimah*, Beirut: Dār Iḥyā' al-Turāth, n.d, p. 465, trans., Franz Rosenthal, *The Muqaddimah: An Introduction to History*, London: Routledge & Kegan Paul, 1958, p. 50.

426. At the same time, besides the Ash'ariyyah, there was the Māturīdiyyah school, which was named after its founder Abū Manṣūr Muḥammad b. Muḥammad al-Samarqandī al-Māturīdī (d. 333/944) and followed by the Ḥanafīs; both schools represented the Sunnīs at the time (see D.B. Macdonald, "Māturīdī,", *EI*, Vol. 3, p. 414; and W. Madelung, "Māturīdiyya," *EI²*, Vol. 6, pp. 847f).

427. This quote is my translation of Ibn Khaldūn's statement in the *Muqaddimah* (p. 465): *taṣadar li al-imāmah fī ṭarīqatihim*, which strikingly mistranslated by Rosenthal (p. 50) as "he attacked the problem of the immate in accordance with the way they had approached it!"

428. Ibn Khaldūn, *Muqaddimah*, Beirut: Dār Iḥyā' al-Turāth, n.d, p. 465, trans., Franz Rosenthal, *The Muqaddimah: An Introduction to History*, London: Routledge & Kegan Paul, 1958, p. 50.

429. Ibn Khaldūn, *Muqaddimah*, p. 465, trans., Rosenthal, *The Muqaddimah*, p. 51.

430. Watt, "al-Ash'arī, Abu'l-Ḥasn," *EI²*, Vol. 1, p. 696.

431. Albert Hourani, *A History of Arab Peoples*, London: Faber and Faber Ltd., 1991, p. 167.

432. Ibn Khaldūn, *Muqaddimah*, p. 466, trans., Rosenthal, *The Muqaddimah*, p. 52.

433. Ibid, pp. 465f, trans., Rosenthal, *The Muqaddimah*, pp. 51f.

434. Ibid, pp. 465f, trans., Rosenthal, *The Muqaddimah*, p. 52.

435. This technical term is discussed below.

436. Cf. Gardet, "'Ilm al-Kalām," EI2, Vol. 3, p. 1146.
437. Hourani, *A History of Arab Peoples*, London: Faber and Faber Ltd., 1991, p. 166.
438. Majid Fakhry, *A History of Islamic Philosophy*, p. 6.
439. Gardet, "'Ilm al-Kalām," EI2, Vol. 3, p. 1145.
440. See Watt, "al-Ash'arī, Abu'l-Ḥasn," *EI²*, Vol. 1, p. 696.
441. Ibn al-Athīr, *al-Kāmil*, Vol. 8, p. 413, trans., D.S. Richards, *The Annals*, p. 193.
442. Ibid, p. 413, trans., D.S. Richards, *The Annals*, p. 193.
443. Ibid, p. 428, trans., D.S. Richards, *The Annals*, p. 207.
444. Quoting the Qur'anic *āyah* [Q: 2:102].
445. Ibn al-Athīr, *al-Kāmil*, Vol. 8, p. 428, trans., D.S. Richards, *The Annals*, p. 207.
446. Ibid.
447. For the formative stages, see Muṣṭafā Aḥmad al-Zarqā, *al-Madkhal al-Fiqhī al-'Ām*, Damascus: Dār al-Qalam, 1998, Vol. 1, pp. 159-202; and Muḥammad al-Khuḍarī, *Tarīkh al-Tashrī' al-Islāmī*, Beirut: Dār al-Kutub al-'Ilmiyyah, n.d., pp. 5-215.
448. See, for instance, Ibn Khaldūn, *Muqaddimah*, p. 448 & 456, trans., Rosenthal, *The Muqaddimah*, Vol. 3, p. 8 & 31.
449. As Hallaq precisely put it, "*ijtihād* is the exertion of mental energy in the search for a legal opinion to the extent that the faculties of the jurist become incapable of further effort," (Wael B. Hallaq, "Was the Gate of Ijtihad Closed?" in Wael B. Hallaq, *Law and Legal Theory in Classical and Medieval Islam*, Hampshire: Ashgate Publishing Limited, 1994, Part V, p. 3).
450. See, for example, Joseph Schacht, "Law and Justice," in P.M. Holt and et al. (eds.), *The Cambridge Histroy of Islām*, pp. 563f; similarly in his book *An Introduction To Islamic Law*, Oxford: Oxford University Press, 1964, pp. 69f; and al-Zarqā, *al-Madkhal al-Fiqhī*, Vol. 1, p. 203.
451. Sing. *mujtahid*, i.e. practitioner of *ijtihād*.
452. Hallaq, "Was the Gate of Ijtihad Closed?" in Hallaq, *Law*, Part V, pp. 10-20.
453. See below.
454. Hallaq, "Was the Gate of Ijtihad Closed?" in Hallaq, *Law*, Part V, p. 15.
455. Al-Zarqā, *al-Madkhal al-Fiqhī*, Vol. 1, pp. 208-209.
456. See al-Ghazālī, *Iḥyā'*, Vol. 1, p. 42.
457. See, for example, Muḥammad al-Khuḍarī, *Tarīkh al-Tashrī' al-Islāmī*, Beirut: Dār al-Kutub al-'Ilmiyyah, n.d., p. 226; and al-Zarqā, *al-Madkhal*, Vol. 1, p. 209.
458. Ibn Khaldūn, *Muqaddimah*, p. 456, trans., Rosenthal, *The Muqaddimah*, Vol. 3, p. 31.

459. See below.
460. Ibn Khaldūn, *Muqaddimah*, pp. 456-457, trans., Rosenthal, *The Muqaddimah*, Vol. 3, pp. 31-34.
461. Al-Zarqā, *al-Madkhal*, Vol. 1, p. 209.
462. Al-Ghazālī, *Iḥyā'*, Vol. 1, pp. 45-47, trans., Nabih Amin Faris, *The Book of Knowledge*, translation of *Kitāb al-'Ilm* of al-Ghazālī's *Iḥyā'*, New Delhi: Islamic Book Service, n.d., pp. 110-116.
463. Al-Zarqā, *al-Madkhal*, Vol. 1, p. 209.

3

The life-experience of al-Ghazālī

Introduction

*A*l-Ghazālī lived for fifty-five years during which he had a very rich and complex experience. This chapter discusses this life-experience. The principal aim of this discussion is to answer the following key question: in which stage of his multi-stage life did he really seek *iṣlāḥ*, and which of his numerous works represent that stage? Answering this question is of a real significance to the present study as the subsequent discussions will be founded on it. To justifiably answer this question, we will need to rely rather heavily on al-Ghazālī's own honest avowals about his spiritual and intellectual development reported in his undoubtedly authentic book *al-Munqidh min al-Ḍalāl* (Deliverance from Error).

Before we proceed further, however, we shall pause for a while to clear up the specious doubts which have been cast by al-Baqarī on the truthfulness of al-Ghazālī in *al-Munqidh*. In his book entitled *I'tirāfāt al-Ghazālī* (The Confessions of al-Ghazālī), which frustratingly discusses in detail al-Ghazālī's account in *al-Munqidh*, al-Baqarī bluntly concludes that this account is mostly not true and generally does not correspond to the historical reality; it is rather by and large a fictional didactic story which al-Ghazālī wished to be his; a story composed of chiefly idealistic confessions with few truthful ones from al-Ghazālī; thus, the book—al-Baqarī spuriously argues—should no longer be considered as a reliable source neither for his own intellectual history nor for his personal spiritual evolution.[1] In his book, al-Baqarī insistently wants to convince his reader that al-Ghazālī, would have sought, "very consciously and often very judiciously, to leave to posterity a fictional image of his personality and to give an interpretation of his life which give him an unrivalled place in all the domains of thought and of the life of the Muslims of his time."[2]

We will closely deal with al-Baqarī's extremely critical discussions of al-Ghazālī's book throughout this chapter, but we ought to express a number of general reservations right at the outset:

The approach of al-Baqarī is subjectively selective, which seems intentional; accepting as truth al-Ghazālī's confessions, which support his prepossession, while rejecting his other declarations contradicting with his own speculation.

Doubting al-Ghazālī's honesty by relying solely on extremely critical reading of a single book, i.e., the *Munqidh*, as al-Baqarī has done, is far from being a sound approach.

In his discussions, al-Baqarī has totally ignored the biographies of al-Ghazālī, namely the one by his contemporary Abū al-Ḥasan ʿAbd al-Ghāfir b. Ismāʿīl al-Fārisī, and other historical evidences which strongly prove the truthfulness of al-Ghazālī's account, as shall be seen below.

The overall structure of al-Baqarī's argument is harmfully affected by, as Abd-El-Jalil perfectly puts it, "its apriorism, its contrived [systematique] character, its aggressiveness, its "lacunae," its para-logisms, and "the geometric spirit" of its author."[3]

Therefore, I side with McCarthy's comment in totally agreeing with Abd-El-Jalil's conclusion regarding al-Baqarī's doubts that "nothing of that authorizes a doubt about Ghazālī's sincerity. The human, intellectual and spiritual value of the *Munqidh* remains firm, though it cannot *of itself alone* serve as an historical source."[4]

Having said this, I feel confident then to use the *Munqidh* as a primary source in this work and particularly in this chapter. However, since, as McCarthy rightly points out "Ghazālī's primary purpose in writing seems to have been didactic, not to give a detailed and precise historical account of himself," I must not rely solely on the book, but rather I shall consult also the primary available biographies of al-Ghazālī whenever the need arises.

Dependent learning and premature authorship

The first reported learning experience of al-Ghazālī started when his poor and pious father, who—regretting that he himself was illiterate—heartily wished that his only two young sons Muḥammad and Aḥmad become learned and educated, charged—on his death—a Sufi friend[5] to educate and take care of them.[6] Following the death of the father, the Sufi began the task until the little money which had been left by the father for this purpose was exhausted.[7] Consequently, the Sufi sent the two brothers to a *madrasah* where free food and accommodation were provided in addition to teaching.[8] Referring to this incident, al-Ghazālī at a later age used to say "we sought knowledge not for the sake of Allah, but it was unwilling to be for the sake of any other than Allah."[9] The truthfulness of the second part of this frequently cited statement, however, has been extremely doubted by al-Baqarī while he selectively has assured the first part,[10] as we shall discuss below.

No certain details are available about the sort of learning al-Ghazālī received in his early childhood, but it seems that he was taught basic Islamic and Arabic studies.[11] For the later time, however, the biographies of al-Ghazālī mention that he studied, while he was still a child, a portion of *fiqh* under Aḥmad al-Rādhkānī[12] in Ṭūs.[13] Then, he left for Jurjān (Gurgan) where he studied under Abū Naṣr al-Ismāʿīlī with whom he recorded *al-Taʿlīqah*,[14] which is his first reported publication on the Shāfiʿī *fiqh*.[15] The writing of the *taʿlīqah*, which is in this context refers to what al-Maqdisī rightly explains as a "collection of notes taken from the lectures of his master, or from both the master's lectures and works,"[16] at al-Ghazālī's time was an essential method of learning.[17] Such *ta'līqah* used to be "studied, memorised and submitted to the master for examination and quizzing with a view to being promoted to the class of ifta'."[18]

In the case of al-Ghazālī, however, he "neglected to impress on his memory what he had written"[19] in the *Ta'līqah*, as the following denoting story[20] shows. Road robbers fell upon him in his way back to Ṭūs and seized all what he had. When they left, he ran after them, but the robber chief threatened him with death, whereupon al-Ghazālī begged him for the return of his *Ta'līqah* only, explaining that it would be of no use for them and that he had travelled just for the sake of hearing, recording and obtaining the knowledge in it. The robber chief then gave it to him, but after scoffing at al-Ghazālī's claimed knowledge, which could be lost by simply taking away the *Ta'līqah*.

Reflecting on this sardonic comment, al-Ghazālī drew a salutary lesson which marked a major turning point in his intellectual experience. Believing that Allah had made the robber say this in order to guide him, al-Ghazālī returned to Ṭūs and spent three years in memorizing the *Ta'līqah* by heart, so that he would not be stripped of knowledge by simply losing his notes, as he is reported to have said.[21]

The most rewarding learning experience of al-Ghazālī started when he travelled in his youth to Nishapur and attached himself to the renowned Imām al-Ḥaramayn al-Juwaynī. This Imam was one of the most leading scholars of the time, not only as a prominent theologian, as he has rather imprecisely been primarily introduced,[22] but also and in fact in the first place, as al-Dīb justifiably presents him,[23] a brilliant scholar of *fiqh* and *uṣūl* (principles of Islamic jurisprudence).

By being trained under this distinguished scholar, al-Ghazālī entered a distinct stage, which lasted until his teacher passed away in 478/1085; and in which he, through hard work, grew to be a notable person.[24] He became, in a relatively short period, fully proficient in Shāfiʿī *fiqh*,[25] highly skilled in *kalām*[26] and a leading figure in *al-khilāf wa al-jadal* (jurisprudential polemics and dialectics).[27] During this early stage, he proved to be so talented a pupil that his teacher, al-Juwaynī, appraisingly described him as "a sea to draw in."[28] In addition, while his teacher was still alive, he used to teach his fellow-students[29] and composed some books.[30]

According to al-Subkī,[31] al-Ghazālī wrote his book entitled *al-Mankhūl*, which is his earliest known authentic book on the discipline of *uṣūl al-fiqh*,[32] during the lifetime of al-Juwaynī.[33] The ending part of the book is "an exposition of the reason for the preference (*taqdīm*) for al-Shāfiʿī's *madhab*, may Allah be pleased with him, over other *madhāhib*."[34] This part contains extreme prejudice and harsh criticism against Abū Ḥanīfah in particular, accusing him of turning the Sharīʿah upside down, disrupting its course and changing its system.[35] In an earlier part of the book, Abū Ḥanīfah is also denied the status of Mujtahid, because, as it stated, he lacked knowledge of Arabic language rules and Ḥadīth.[36] Most probably it is this book about which Ibn Ḥajar al-Haytamī (d. 973/1565) writes in *al-Khayrāt al-Ḥisān fī Manāqib al-Nuʿmān* the following:

> Some of fanatics…brought to me a book attributed to Imam al-Ghazālī containing extreme prejudice and coarse debasement of Imam al-Muslimīn and the unique among the *mujtahid* imams, Abū Ḥanīfah…as if this al-Ghazālī is the known Imam Muḥammad, the Proof of Islam, while he is not; because in his Iḥyāʾ there is praise for Abū Ḥanīfah…Furthermore, on the copy which I saw it is stated that it is compiled by Maḥmūd al-Ghazālī, who is not the Proof of Islam; and this is why it is written on the margin of this copy: this is a Muʿtazilī man, his name is Maḥmūd and the Proof of Islam.[37]

In the closing paragraph of the *Mankhūl*, al-Ghazālī states that the book has been restricted to what Imām al-Ḥaramayn mentioned in his *taʿālīq*[38] (sing. *taʿlīqah* which in this case could be al-Juwaynī's lectures and works).[39] Thus, in this book al-Ghazālī, as Hītū points out, does not look independent.[40] If there is any element of originality in the *Mankhūl*, it would be in its organisation and sectioning, about which al-Ghazālī was curious as he himself states in it.[41] This, however, does not mean that al-Ghazālī merely copies his master in this book. As a matter of fact, he, as Hītū clearly shows, critically discusses al-Juwaynī's views, rejecting many of them.[42]

Al-Juwaynī's early influence on al-Ghazālī seems to have been dominant. His influence, as al-Dīb has noted,[43] is evident by comparing some of the thoughts and even words of al-Ghazālī with those of al-Juwaynī. Moreover, al-Dīb argues that due to the fact that the fame of al-Ghazālī has exceeded al-Juwaynī's and that his books have been much more widespread than those of his teachers, many of the thoughts, particularly in the field of *fiqh*, which have been credited to al-Ghazālī, originally belong to al-Juwaynī.[44] Although al-Juwaynī's influence on al-Ghazālī cannot be denied as it appears particularly in his early works, the argument of al-Dīb cannot be fully followed without reservation, for it is, unfortunately, not free from overstatement. Being full of admiration for al-Juwaynī and curious to show al-Juwaynī's originality, al-Dīb seems to have exaggeratedly discredited al-Ghazālī in favour of his teacher. It is true that al-Juwaynī was an outstanding original scholar and highly influential, but it is equally true that al-Ghazālī was talented and had considerable degree of independence and uniqueness.

Highly distinguished scholarly career

At the age of twenty eight, al-Ghazālī left Nishapur aiming for the camp-court of the Seljuk Vizier Niẓām al-Mulk,[45] which was a centre of gathering of the *'ulamā'* and the literary men.[46] From contact with established *'ulamā'*, meeting tough adversaries and debating with the distinguished, al-Ghazālī witnessed fine encounters.[47] Due to his excellence in polemics and his flowing expression, al-Ghazālī's name gained a great reputation, which spread to distant lands.[48]

Soon after this, being greatly regarded and highly honoured by the Vizier, al-Ghazālī was appointed by him to the professorship in his renowned Niẓāmiyyah *madrasah* at Baghdad.[49] In 484/1091-1092,[50] he arrived in Baghdad and entered into teaching.[51] His lessons drew crowds of pupils; their number reaching 300 at a time, as he himself recorded in *al-Munqidh*.[52] Among those who joined his lessons and were impressed by his skills and abilities were a number of distinguished *'ulamā'* such as Ibn 'Aqīl and Abū al-Khaṭṭāb, as reported by Ibn al-Jawzī.[53]

Throughout his stay in Baghdad, which lasted for four consecutive years,[54] al-Ghazālī had a conspicuous amount of public success. His lecturing and debating, as al-Fārisī narrated, delighted everyone.[55] Furthermore, after reaching the rank of *imāmah* in Khurāsān, he became the Imam of Iraq.[56] Similarly, he, according to Ibn Khallikān, "filled the people of Iraq with admiration, and they conceived for him a great respect."[57] Moreover, it is reported that he possessed an enormous dignity and that his reverence became so great to the extent that it surpassed the honour of the notables and the princes.[58]

As a *faqīh*, al-Ghazālī composed, at this stage in his life, a number of works on the Shāfi'ī *madhhab*, which he revived (*jaddad*) according to al-Fārisī.[59] The most celebrated *fiqhī* books of al-Ghazālī are *al-Basīṭ*, *al-Wasīṭ*, *al-Wajīz*, and *Khulāṣat al-Mukhtaṣar* which have become primary references in the *madhhab*.[60] Furthermore, he composed some works in the field of *uṣūl al-fiqh* (principles of jurisprudence) namely *Shifā' al-Ghalīl*. He also wrote books in the art of *al-khilāf wa al-jadal* (juridical polemics and dialectics) such as *Ma'ākhidh al-Khilāf*, *Lubāb al-Nazar*, *Taḥsīn al-Ma'ākhidh*, and *al-Mabādi' wa al-Ghāyāt*.[61] In addition to these works, he composed several others in various fields, as shall be mentioned below.

Epistemological crisis

In the *Munqidh*, al-Ghazālī records that due to his instinctive thirst for grasping *ḥaqā'iq al-umūr* (the actual reality of things) right from the prime of his life, he was emancipated from the bonds of *taqlīd* (conformism or acceptance of religious dogmas on authority) as early as the age of adolescence.[62] He reveals that—after observing that children of Christians, Jews and Muslims always grew up adhering only to their respective religion and by reflecting on the saying of the Prophet (ṣ) "every infant is born endowed with the *fiṭrah* (a sound nature); then his parents make him Jew or Christian or Magian"—his inmost being was moved to seek the reality of the original *fiṭrah* and to sift the beliefs arising through initially the inculcation of the parents and teachers, as there are differences of opinions in discerning what is true from that what is false of these *taqlīdāt*.[63] Consequently, he became preoccupied with inner quest for what he calls *'ilm al-yaqīn* (knowledge of certitude) which he defines as:

> That in which the known thing is disclosed in a way that no doubt remains along with it, that no possibility of error or illusion accompanies it, and that the mind cannot even entertain such thing. Not only that but also this security from error is so bound to certainty to the extent that even if it is challenged to be wrong, for example, by someone who turns stones into gold or sticks into snakes, this does not create any doubt or denial.[64]

By scrutinizing all his cognitions in the light of this definition of certain knowledge, al-Ghazālī tells us that he suffered an inner state of *safsaṭah* (sophistry) for nearly two months in which he extremely doubted within his soul the certainty of all of his knowledge including the *maḥsūsāt* (sense-perception) and even the *ḍarūriyyāt* (necessary intellectual facts).[65] He was not cured from this malady until he regained the confidence in the certainty of the necessary intellectual facts by "a divine light being cast into his breast," as he puts it.[66]

This vivid story of al-Ghazālī's epistemological doubt has been radically questioned by al-Baqarī; he totally rejects this account of al-Ghazālī's doubt and presents his own interpretation of it.[67] His extremely odd interpretation is summarized as follows: al-Ghazālī made up this story and narrated it at the beginning of the

Munqidh to show that his forthcoming quest for the actual reality was original and independent since this is the normal approach of free thinkers; he took this idea of doubt, but with modification, from the adherence of sophistry without crediting them in the *Munqidh* unlike the case in his other book, *Faḍā'iḥ al-Bāṭiniyyah*, where he discussed the sophistic doubt and explicitly ascribed it to the adherence of sophistry; he did so in the latter, because in it he is arguing against the Bāṭiniyyah, who, by being equipped with philosophy, would discover the source of the idea if he did not mention it and thus covering it would count against him, whereas in the *Munqidh* he is writing to the general readers, so he wanted to convince them that the idea of doubt is his own.[68]

Unlike al-Baqarī, Watt states that there is no reason to doubt al-Ghazālī's experience of such scepticism; yet he strongly doubts that it occurred during an early stage of his life because, according to Watt, it had a philosophical background which "is shown by the fact that he links it up with a consideration of the nature of knowledge and certainty," and thus, Watt adds, "it must have been preceded by some study of philosophy."[69]

Apparently, both al-Baqarī and Watt presuppose that the reported doubt of al-Ghazālī was solely philosophically oriented, and only on this assumption are their views based. This, however, can be effectively challenged by the justifiably convincing findings of Bakar's detailed and in depth analysis of al-Ghazālī's doubt.[70] To illustrate this well, it is necessary to cite rather heavily from Bakar. Before doing so, it is important to bear in mind that when al-Ghazālī recorded this early doubt in the *Munqidh*, he was over fifty, as he mentioned in the preface of the book,[71] and thus the style of his account is not a spontaneous outcome of that early period, but is a product of his late, well-organized and deep thought, as Abu-Sway rightly points out.[72] This does not seem to be taken into the consideration of al-Baqarī and Watt.

Totally unlike al-Baqarī and Watt, Bakar rightly looks at the doubt of al-Ghazālī "as an integral element of the epistemology of Islamic intellectual tradition to which al-Ghazālī properly belongs."[73] He draws our attention to two important factors in the development of al-Ghazālī's doubt. The first is "the specific intellectual, religious, and spiritual climate prevailing in the Islamic world during the time of al-Ghazālī, which no doubt constitutes the main external contributory factor to the generation of doubt in the early phase of his intellectual life."[74] The second "concerns the whole set of opportunities which Islam ever places at the disposal of man in his quest for certainty, and what we know of al-Ghazzālī's life tells us that he was very much exposed to these opportunities."[75]

Bakar's discussion of al-Ghazālī's methodological criticism of *taqlīd* in the *Munqidh* shows that al-Ghazālī was dissatisfied with *taqlīd* because "it could not quench his intense intellectual thirst."[76] Bakar also shows that it was obvious to al-Ghazālī right from his early age that *taqlīd* is "an avenue to both truth and error, but as to what is true and what is false there was an open sea of debate around him, which disturbed him profoundly."[77] This, according to Bakar, led al-Ghazālī "to contemplate upon one of the most central questions in philosophy, namely, the question of what true knowledge is, and this marked the beginning of an intensification of his intellectual doubt."[78]

In addition to this factor in generating al-Ghazālī's doubt, Bakar points out to "another, and more important, religious and spiritual current which contributed to the genesis of his doubt and which deeply affected his mind."[79] Al-Ghazālī himself, Bakar explains, mentioned this "as the existence of numerous schools of thought (*madhāhib*) and groups (*firaq*) within the community of Islam itself, each with its own methods of understanding and affirming the truth and each claiming that it alone is saved."[80] This religious atmosphere, as Bakar refers to, is described by al-Ghazālī in the opening of the *Munqidh* as "a deep sea in which the majority drown and from which only few are saved."[81]

After briefly presenting the views of a number of scholars on the nature of al-Ghazālī's doubt, Bakar states that he agrees with the common view of these scholars that "at the time of his crisis, al-Ghazzālī was neither a philosophical nor a religious sceptic, and that the crisis was an epistemological or methodological one. The *Munqidh* provides ample evidence to support this view."[82]

To illustrate that al-Ghazālī was not a philosophical doubter, Bakar adds:

> He never contested the value of metaphysical certitude. He was always certain of the *de jure* certitude of truth. Thus,…he never questioned the possibility of knowledge of *ḥaqā'iq al-umūr*. His natural, intellectual disposition toward seeking that knowledge was, in a way, an affirmation of his personal conviction in the *de jure* certitude of truth.[83]

Explaining how al-Ghazālī never fell into the "philosophical temptation of the agnostics and relativists,"[84] Bakar further states that al-Ghazālī's doubt was not of truth itself, yet it was "of modes of knowledge and modes of accepting truth. But, since by truth, he meant here the inner reality of things, his quest for that reality also implied a quest for its corresponding mode of knowledge."[85] This was motivated by "a real theoretical awareness of the possibility of another mode of knowing, which the Sufis claim as theirs"[86] and this possibility, in the view of Bakar, "must have agitated his mind through his direct personal encounter with the way of the Sufis"[87] in his early educational background. Based on al-Ghazālī's early background, which was influenced by a number of Sufis, Bakar is convinced that he:

> Was increasingly attracted to the idea of a direct personal experience of God emphasized by the Sufis. However, he felt a bit disheartened when, in these early attempts at following the Sufi path, he failed to attain that stage where the mystics begin to receive pure inspiration from "high above." In the light of this background, there is a strong reason to believe that Sufism plays a central role in leading al-Ghazzālī to his epistemological crisis.[88]

To show how al-Ghazālī was never a religious sceptic, Bakar quotes al-Ghazālī's declaration in the *Munqidh*:

> From the sciences which I had laboured and the methods which
> I had followed in my inquiry into the two kinds of knowledge,
> revealed and rational, I had already acquired a sure and
> certain faith in God Most High, in the prophetic mediation of
> revelation, and in the Last Day. These three fundamentals of
> faith had become deeply rooted in my soul, not because of any
> specific, precisely formulated proofs, but because of reasons and
> circumstances and experiences too many to list in detail.[89]

Commenting on this statement, Bakar says: "The doubting
mind of al-Ghazzālī was never cut off from revelation and faith.
On the contrary, it was based upon a "sure and certain" faith in the
fundamentals of religion."[90] This "sure and certain" faith has its
roots in the idea of degrees of certainty (*yaqīn*) in Islamic gnosis,
as conclusively demonstrated by Bakar.[91]

Now, it would appear possible to accept the conclusion of
Bakar that "it is therefore in the light of Islamic epistemology and,
especially in the light of the idea of degrees of certainty (*yaqīn*) in
Islamic gnosis that the famous Ghazzalian doubt should be studied
and understood."[92]

Independent examination of the seekers after truth

Al-Ghazālī tells us in the *Munqidh* that after his recovery from the
sickness of doubt he started to investigate the paths of those seeking
the truth whom he categorised into four classes: (I) *al-Mutakallimūn*
(the Muslim Theologians), (2) *al-Bāṭiniyyah*, (3) *al-Falāsifah* (the
Philosophers), (4) *al-Ṣūfiyyah* (The Mystics).[93] Explaining the
reason behind this limitation, he states: "The truth cannot transcend
these four classes, for these are the followers of the paths of the quest
for truth; and if the truth eludes them, there remains no hope of
ever attaining it."[94] Reminding us with his abandonment of *taqlīd*,
which was a result of his inmost quest for grasping *ḥaqā'iq al-umūr*
(the actual reality of things), he adds: "For there is no way to return
to *taqlīd* after leaving it, since a condition of being a *muqallid* (a
conformist or uncritical follower of authority) is that one does not

know himself to be such."[95] Thus, he applied himself to thoroughly examine "firstly *'ilm al-kalām* (Islamic theology), secondly the way of *al-falsafah* (philosophy), thirdly the teachings of the Bāṭiniyyah, and fourthly the way of the Sufis."[96]

Before we continue with al-Ghazālī's account, we ought to first deal with the valid question which has bee raised by al-Baqarī[97] as to why al-Ghazālī restricted his search in these four groups, and assumed that the truth does not exceed them. We share with al-Baqarī this wonder, but we do not agree with his speculation that "this is because he knew in advance that the truth which he would follow was only with the Sufis, or because he wanted to make fictitious premises to conclude this."[98] Opposite to this speculation is the following more convincing view of Bakar:

> There is no doubt that al-Ghazzālī had undertaken this comparative study of all the seekers of the Truth with the view of exhausting all the possibilities and opportunities that were open to him in the pursuit of the highest level of certainty, although by then one could already detect in him a special inclination and sympathy towards Sufism.[99]

We may add to Bakar's view that what appeared to be a prior inclination towards Sufism in al-Ghazālī's account could be due to the fact that it was written long after he concluded his examination, as mentioned earlier. Furthermore, even if we presume that "he knew in advance that the truth which he would follow was only with the Sufis," this does not necessarily lead to al-Baqarī's conclusion that his examination was fictitious. Instead, it can still properly be seen as an attempt by al-Ghazālī to affirm or verify his 'prior opinion' about the ultimate truth by conducting an independent examination of all claimed seekers after truth known to him.

Experience with the discipline of kalām

With regard to his experience with *'ilm al-kalām*, al-Ghazālī states: "I obtained a thorough grasp of it. I consulted the works of the most authoritative *mutakalimūn*, and I wrote on the subject what I wanted to write."[100] Despite that he found this discipline adequate for its own purpose, which is, in his view, protecting the Sunnī creed and defending it against the confusion of the innovators, he realized that it was insufficient for his aim: "So *kalām* was not sufficient enough in my case, nor was it a remedy for the malady of which I was complaining."[101] He further explains the extent to which *kalām* was insufficient for his case:

> It is true that when the discipline of *kalām* developed, the *mutakalimūn* showed an earnest desire for progressing from simply defending the Sunnah (orthodoxy) to search for *ḥaqā'iq al-umūr*,[102] and they plunged into the study of substances and accidents with their principles; however, since that was not the aim of their own discipline, their discussion of the subject did not reach conclusiveness. Therefore, it did not provide an effective means of dispelling completely the darkness of the bewilderment due to the differences dividing men.[103]

In his extremely critical discussion against the *Munqidh*, al-Baqarī noticeably miss-presents al-Ghazālī's evaluation of *'ilm al-kalām*. Following his misleading selective quoting of al-Ghazālī, he erroneously restates the assessment in view, and on the basis of which he criticises al-Ghazālī. I do not wish to further illustrate and discuss al-Baqarī's criticism for it is based on a deceptive restatement of al-Ghazālī's evaluation, but here I shall highlight his misleading way of quoting al-Ghazālī. His selective quoting starts as follow:

> I began studying *'ilm al-kalām* and thus I obtained a thorough grasp of it and I wrote some books on it. Subsequently, I found it a discipline adequate for its own aim, which is conserving the Sunnī creed and guarding it from the confusion of the innovators. But a group of the *mutakalimūn* relied on premises which they took over from their adversaries, being compelled to admit them either by *taqlīd*, or *ijmā'* of the *ummah* (the Muslim Community's consensus), or because merely they are from the Traditions and the Qur'an. "This, however, is of little use in the case of one

who admits nothing at all except the primary and self-evident truths...[104]

In addition to his impreciseness throughout his quoting, al-Baqarī plainly disregards the following sentence, which is mentioned by al-Ghazālī just before the last quoted sentence: "Most of their polemics was devoted to bringing out the inconsistencies of their adversaries and criticizing them for the logically absurd consequences of what they conceded."[105] By this omission, the quote deludingly imposes the meaning that al-Ghazālī was dissatisfied with the *kalām* because the *mutakalimūn* "(1) were men of *taqlīd*, (2) because they follow the *ijmā'* of the Muslim Ummah, (3) because they accept the *āyāt* of the Qur'an just because they are Words of Allah, (4) and because they hold fast to the Traditions of Muḥammad only because they are the sayings of the Messenger of Allah (ṣ)."[106] One cannot but be surprised at such a misleading approach.

Examination of the way of the falāsifah

After finishing his examination of *'ilm al-kalām*, al-Ghazālī says that he turned to the science of *falsafah* (philosophy).[107] At this juncture, he had the following firm conviction:

> One cannot recognize what is unsound in any field of knowledge unless he has a complete grasp of that field to the extent that he reaches the level of the most knowledgeable in the principles of that field; then he must even excel him and attain even greater eminence so that he becomes cognizant of the intricate profundities which have remained beyond the ken of the acknowledged master of the field. Then, and only then, it is possible that the defects he alleges will be seen as really such.[108]

Believing that no one among the Muslim scholars directed his attention and endeavour to that end, he girded his loins for the task of learning the science of *falsafah* by "the mere perusal of their writings without seeking the help of a master and teacher."[109] This was in his spare time in Baghdad, as he states in the *Munqidh*:

"I devoted myself to that in the moments I had free from writing and lecturing on the fields of Sharī'ah; and I was then burdened with the teaching and instruction of three hundred students in Baghdad."[110]

About the duration and the result of this independent study of *falsafah*, al-Ghazālī writes:

> Through mere reading in those embezzled moments, Allah Most High gave me an insight into the farthest reaches of the philosophers' sciences in less than two years. Then, having understood their doctrine, I continued to repeatedly examining its intricate and profundities until I comprehended certainly the measure of its deceit and deception, and its precision and delusion.[111]

This experience made al-Ghazālī realize with certainty that "*al-'aql* (the intellect or reason) alone is incapable of fully grasping all issues or of resolving all problems."[112]

The outcome of al-Ghazālī's examination of *falsafah* can be properly appreciated by referring to two of his books: *Maqāṣid al-Falāsifah* (The Meanings[113] of the Philosophers) and *Tahāfut al-Falāsifah* (The Incoherence of the Philosophers),[114] which both belong to the stage in his life in view.[115]

The purpose of the *Maqāṣid* is to provide a necessary background for his criticism of particular metaphysical and physical views of the philosophers in the *Tahāfut* by objectively representing the doctrine of the philosophers, as he clearly states in the introduction of the book:

> You have asked me,[116] my brother, for a thorough exposition, which would contain a refutation of the philosophers, the contradiction of their opinions and (the disclosure of) their hidden errors and mistakes. But you cannot hope to refute them before you know their doctrines and study their dogmas, for to grasp the falsehood of certain doctrines before having a complete understanding of them is absurd. Such an effort leads only to blindness and error. Therefore, before entering upon a refutation of the philosophers, I deemed it necessary to present an exposition and a full description of their ideas of the logical, physical and metaphysical sciences

without, however, distinguishing between the true and the false...
The purpose of this book is to give an account of "The Meanings of
the Philosopher;" and that is its title.[117]

Then, he adds "only after we have completed the exposition
will we begin, earnestly and with zeal, a separate book, to be called
Tahāfut al-Falāsifah."[118]

With regard to the *Tahāfut*, al-Ghazālī reports the story
behind writing it at the beginning of the introduction of the
book. He starts by describing a group of his contemporaries who
renounced their religion:

> Now, I have observed that there is a class of men who believe in
> their superiority to others because of their greater intelligence
> and insight. They have abandoned all the religious duties
> Islam imposes on its followers. They look down at the positive
> commandments of religions which enjoin the performance
> of acts of devotion, and the abstinence from forbidden things.
> They defy the injunctions of Shar' (Islamic Law). Not only they
> don't abide to the limits prescribed by it, but also they have
> renounced the Religion altogether...[119]

Next, he shows how their heresy was a result of their uncritical
emulation (*taqlīd*) of the philosophers:

> The heresy of these people has its basis only in *taqlīd* (uncritical
> acceptance) of whatever one hears from others or sees all
> around...These heretics have heard the awe-inspiring names of
> people like Socrates, Hippocrates, Plato, Aristotle, etc. They have
> been deceived by the exaggerations made by the followers to these
> philosophers—exaggerations to the effect that the ancient masters
> possessed extraordinary intellectual powers: that the principles
> they have discovered are unquestionable: that the mathematical,
> logical, physical and metaphysical sciences developed by them
> are the most profound: that their excellent intelligence justifies
> their bold attempts to discover the Hidden Things by deductive
> methods; and that with all the subtlety of their intelligence and
> the originality of their accomplishments they repudiated the
> authority of religious laws: denied the validity of the positive
> contents of historical religions, and believed that all such things
> are only sanctimonious lies and trivialities. When such stuff

was dinned into their ears, and struck a responsive chord in their hearts, the heretics in our times thought that it would be an honour to join the company of great thinkers for which the renunciation of their faith would prepare them.[120]

Then, he states that he wrote the book as a response to this phenomenon: "When I saw this vein of folly pulsating among these idiots, I decided to write this book in order to refute the ancient philosophers. It will expose the incoherence of their beliefs and inconsistency of their metaphysical theories."[121] He further explains the purpose of the book by saying: "Let it be known that the purpose is to awaken those who think too highly of the philosophers, and consider them to be infallible."[122]

Related to the *Tahāfut* is al-Ghazālī's book entitled *Mi'yār al-'Ilm* (The Criterion of Knowledge), which is most likely written in this same stage of his life.[123] According to Dunyā, the editor of the book, the *Mi'yār* is part, and specifically the last part, of the *Tahāfut* which is in his view a trilogy discussing three philosophical subjects: Physics, Metaphysics and Logic for which al-Ghazālī gives various names such as *Mi'yār al-'Ilm* and *Madārik al-'Uqūl*; and for this precise finding, Dunyā provides clear internal evidences from the *Tahāfut* itself.[124]

The *Mi'yār*, as Macdonlad puts it, is "a book intended to be a standard and guide in intellectual investigations and especially as to the language and technical expressions of the philosophers."[125]

Investigation of the teachings of the Bāṭiniyyah

After telling us that *falsafah* was also inadequate to satisfy his aim fully, al-Ghazālī starts to reveal his experience with the *Ta'līmiyyah*, i.e., *Bāṭiniyyah*.[126] In addition to his interior motive in investigating their teachings, it happened that he was commanded by the 'Abbāsid Caliph of the time, al-Mustaẓhir, to compose a book revealing the reality of their doctrine.[127] Explaining his approach in fulfilling his task, he states:

I began to seek out their works and to collect their views. I had already been struck by some of their novel utterances which were the brainchildren of our own contemporaries but were not consonant with the methodology of their predecessors. So I collected those utterances, arranging them perfectly and formulating them thoroughly, then I conclusively answered them.[128]

Al-Ghazālī's summarizes his findings from the investigation of the Bāṭiniyyah with the following words:

These also we have examined thoroughly, probing their inside and outside. Their reality comes down to deceiving the common folk and the dim-witted by showing the need for the authoritative teacher, and to disputing men's denial of the need for the authoritative teaching by strong and effective argument. So it goes until someone tries to help them about the need for the authoritative teacher by saying: "Give us some of his lore and acquaint us with some of his teaching!" Then the disputant pauses and says: "Now that you have conceded to me that much, you need to seek him by yourself, because my aim was limited to this much." For he knows that, were he to add anything more, he would be put to shame and would be unable to resolve the simplest problem. Nay, but he would be unable to understand it, let alone give an answer to it! This, then, is the reality of their condition…Thus, when we had had experience of them, we also washed our hands of them![129]

His exploration of the method of the sufis

Passing all the previous stages, al-Ghazālī turned with his firm will to explore the method of al-Ṣūfiyyah, knowing that their method is fully accomplished by the union of knowledge and practice, but since their knowledge was easier for him, he therefore began to gain their knowledge.[130] For this purpose, he—in addition to hearing from contemporary Sufi masters—consulted a number of Sufi writings such as *Qūt al-Qulūb* of Abū Ṭālib al-Makkī, the books of al-Ḥārith al-Muḥāsibī, and various reported teachings of al-Junayd, al-Shiblī, and Abū Yazīd al-Bisṭāmī, as he states in the *Munqidh*.[131] As a result, he grasped the very essence of the Sufi theoretical principles and all of what could be gained theoretically of their teachings.[132] Then, it became clear to him that their most distinctive characteristic could not be gained through theoretical knowledge, but only by experiencing *al-dhawq* (spiritual taste), *al-ḥāl* (the state of real ecstasy) and the moral change.[133] He states:

> I knew with certainty that the Sufis were *arbāb al-aḥwāl* (masters of real ecstatic experiences) and not men of words, and that I had apprehended all what can be gained by theoretical knowledge. There remained, then, only what was attainable, not by hearing and study, but by experiencing *al-dhawq* (spiritual taste) and *al-sulūk* (actual disciplining).[134]

This conviction led al-Ghazālī to a totally new experience and a dramatic change in his life, as will be shown below.

Serious inspection of the inner state

When he acquired thorough knowledge of al-Ṣūfiyyah, as illustrated above, al-Ghazālī lived a period of a very serious self-reflection during which he critically examined his inward conditions. Telling about this period he writes in the *Munqidh*:

> I attentively considered my circumstances, and I saw that I was immersed in *al-ʿalāʾiq* (worldly attachments or involvements) which had encompassed me from all sides. I also considered my activities, the best of which being teaching and lecturing, seeing that in them I was applying myself to branches of knowledge unimportant and fruitless in the pilgrimage to the hereafter.[135]

About his intention behind teaching in this period he honestly declares: "I saw that it was not purely for the sake of Allah Most High, but rather was instigated and motivated by the quest for fame and widespread prestige."[136] Thus, he alarmingly became certain that he was "on the brink of a crumbling bank and already on the verge of falling into the Fire,"[137] unless he would mend his conditions.

As a result, al-Ghazālī seriously thought about migrating from Baghdad and quitting all of his worldly interests, but he kept wavering about it: "I incessantly vacillated between the contending pull of worldly desires and the appeals of the afterlife for nearly six months, starting from Rajab of the year 488 AH (July 1095 AD)."[138] At the end of this period, he became tongue-tied and consequently became severely sick of grief to the extent that the physicians lost hope of treating him.[139] In the *Munqidh*, al-Ghazālī explains how this crisis was over:

> When I perceived my helplessness and when my capacity to make a choice had completely collapsed, I sought refuge with Allah Most High as does a hard pressed man who has no way out of his difficulty. He answered me…and made it easy for my heart to turn away from fame, wealth, children and associates. I openly showed that I had resolved to set out to Mecca, while planning in my mind to travel to al-Shām. This I did as a precaution, lest the Caliph and the group of my associates might learn of my resolve to settle in Damascus.[140]

Consequently, he left Baghdad after he had distributed what wealth he had, save that suffice his essential needs and the sustenance of his children with the excuse that "the money of Iraq was earmarked for the welfare of the people, since it was an endowment for Muslims."[141]

This straightforward story of al-Ghazālī's remarkable leave of Baghdad and the reasons behind it has become a subject of controversy. Opposing views about the reality of this reported event and of al-Ghazālī's condition prior to it have been put forward by a number of writers on al-Ghazālī. Some have strangely dared to make a diagnosis for his described sickness. Ormsby, for instance, thinks that "certain of his symptoms suggest "melancholy" (*sawdā'*), though the temporary loss of speech may point to other conditions."[142] Similarly, Farrūkh confidently, though weirdly, states that "we assert that al-Ghazālī was afflicted with *al-kanz* or *al-ghanz*, which is a psychological disease largely appears among those who are of extreme religious course."[143] At the end of his long description of the disease, which is based on medical sources, Farrūkh states that the patient of *al-kanz* normally inclines towards a religious life.[144]

This awkward approach has been criticised by Abu-Sway.[145] Challenging particularly Farrūkh, he states that "even if Farrūkh were a physician or a clinical psychologist, which he is not, none of al-Ghazālī's statements warrants the decisive terms that he applied in his "diagnosis."[146] Commenting on Farrūkh's last statement, Abu-Sway says: "The latter statement misleads the reader to conceive al-Ghazālī's "conversion" as a symptom of a disease rather than a genuine religious experience."[147] I fully agree with Abu-Sway and add that one cannot but be greatly astonished at such a risky approach in dealing with historical accounts.

About the motive behind al-Ghazālī's departure from Baghdad, there have been various theories which, to variant extent, question his own clear account. Farid Jabre, for example, claims that the migration was because of his fear of assassination by the Bāṭinīs.[148] Attempting to prove this, Jabre quotes al-Ghazālī's associate, al-Fārisī, stating that al-Ghazālī "told us, "the door of fear was opened. It was so dreadful that I could not do any work, and finally lost interest completely in all other things.""[149] This "fear," Jabre argues, is not that of Helfire, but that of assassination of the Bāṭinīs.[150] Less vigorously, Macdonald, though does not doubt the truthfulness of al-Ghazālī's account, suggests that "political complications may have helped to bring on his nervous breakdown,"[151] and more specifically he refers to the fact that "Barkiyārūk became Great Seljuk and killed his uncle Tutush immediately before the flight of al-Ghazzālī, and the khalīfa at whose court al-Ghazzālī held important place declared for Tutush."[152]

These speculations, however, do not stand criticism. This is simply because the evidences claimed to support them are far from convincing. Against Jabre, we side with Nakamura who states that "I simply do not understand why this "fear" cannot be that of Hellfire as Ghazālī himself confessed."[153] Challenging

Jabre, Nakamura convincingly points out that "if he had feared the assassination, he would not have dared to criticize the Bāṭinīs;"[154] and "if it is said that Ghazālī was ordered by the Caliph, al-Mustaẓhirī, to do so, then, I would say, how can it be explained that he kept on criticizing them at Hamadhan and Tus after his retirement?"[155] Adding to Nakamura, Abu-Sway logically argues that if it were true that al-Ghazālī feared assassination, he would not have resided in places under the easy reach of the Bāṭinīs.[156] He further adds: "why would he wait for a total of six months in Baghdad, before embarking on his journey, if there was imminent danger and if he was preoccupied with his personal safety?"[157]

As in the case with Jabre's claim, the view of Macdonald has been criticized. Abu-Sway again has challenged it by stating that if al-Ghazālī's only goal was "to disappear from Baghdad in order to escape political difficulties, he could have done so without the trouble of becoming a Sufi, the hardships associated with the distribution of his wealth and leaving his family behind in Baghdad."[158]

In a much more niggling way, al-Baqarī threw nagging doubts on al-Ghazālī's reported motive behind his departure from Baghdad.[159] Totally opposite to what al-Ghazālī clearly stated that he fled from fame and worldly desires, al-Baqarī claims that he did so to satisfy his longing for more fame and prestige by pretending to be one of the Sufis, who—al-Baqarī argues—were, and always are, respected to the highest degree by the general folk in the Muslim community and taken as close associates by the elites.[160] Attempting to support this sweeping generalization about the esteem for the Sufis, al-Baqarī mentions no more than that al-Ghazālī saw how "Niẓām al-Mulk used to respect only claimers of knowledge (ad'iyā' al-'ilm) and poor Sufis, standing up for them whenever they enter his court, out of respect, and seating them close to him…and when he was once asked about this, he said: "These men, when I bring them close to me, they would appraisingly attribute to me what I don't deserve!"[161]

Before going further with presenting al-Baqarī's speculation, we cannot resist making two quick criticisms against his weird approach so far. Firstly, what he mentions about Niẓām al-Mulk, for which he does not mention any source, is obviously false. It is most likely a fabrication of the following incident reported by Ibn al-Athīr:

> Whenever the Imam Abū al-Qāsim al-Qushayrī or the the Imam Abū al-Maʿālī al-Juwaynī came into the presence of Niẓām al-Mulk, he would stand up for the them (i.e., to greet them) and then resume his seat on his cushion. But whenever Abū ʿAlī al-Fārmadhī came in, he would rise to receive him, seat him where he himself had been, and take his seat before him. This was remarked on to him, and he said: "The first two and their like, when they come in to my presence, say to me: 'you are such and such,' praising me for what is not in me. Thus, their words increase my self-satisfaction and pride. The latter Shaykh tells me of my soul's faults and how wicked I am. My spirit is thereby humbled and I recoil from much of what I am doing."[162]

This incident, however, does not support the claim of al-Baqarī. The incident does not indicate that "Niẓām al-Mulk used to respect only claimers of knowledge (*adʿiyāʾ al-ʿilm*) and poor Sufis," and rather it signifies that he used to have a high regard for this particular Shaykh not simply because he was a Sufi but for his honest advise and daring warning. Surely, not every Sufi has such quality as that Shaykh. Similarly, not every sovereign welcomes such advice and warning like Niẓām al-Mulk who, as Ibn al-Athīr reported, "was a scholar, a man of religion, generous, mild-mannered, very forbearing of miscreants, and given to long silences."[163] In addition, the claim of al-Baqarī about this Vizier totally contradicts the reported fact that "his court was bustling with Qur'an readers, *fuqahāʾ*, leading Muslim Imams (religious scholars), and men of charity and piety."[164]

Secondly, his generalization about the admiration of people for the Sufis is not convincing enough. Thirdly, if al-Ghazālī's aim were to add to his prestige—which had already reached an outstanding level before his withdrawal—by pretending to be a Sufi, then there was no need for him to spend eleven years in seclusion and self-reforming, as will be illustrated below.

Referring to the report of al-Zabīdī that al-Ghazālī appointed his brother of teaching instead of him prior to his leave, al-Baqarī uses this single incident to accuse al-Ghazālī of being untruthful in his declaration that he abandoned teaching because it is unimportant and fruitless in the way to the Hereafter otherwise he would not have exposed his brother to such evil.[165] Al-Baqarī here, however, totally neglects the fact that his brother was a true Sufi by that time and thus al-Ghazālī did not doubt his sincerity in teaching. In addition, al-Ghazālī did not state that all teaching was not worthwhile in the Hereafter, as al-Baqarī apparently claims, but only mentioned that he himself was engaged in teaching such sort of knowledge. Thus, his brother, being a Sufi, would not bother himself with such knowledge. Moreover, the testimony of al-Fārisī, which will be presented below, proves the sincerity of al-Ghazālī and leaves no room for speculated doubts such as that of al-Baqarī, Jabre, Macdonald or any one who would echo them.

Seclusion and self-*iṣlāḥ*

For about eleven lunar years[166] followed his first migration from Baghdad, al-Ghazālī lived in a sort of seclusion for the purpose of self-*iṣlāḥ*. According to his account in the *Munqidh*, this started in Damascus where he lived for nearly two years during which his only occupation was "seclusion and solitude, together with spiritual disciplining and combat, and engaging in self-purification, character reforming and heart cleaning for the constant remembrance of Allah Most High," in the way he had learned from the knowledge of *al-ṣūfiyyah*.[167]

From Damascus, al-Ghazālī states, "I travelled to Bayt al-Maqdis (in Jerusalem), where I used to go daily into the Dome of the Rock and shut myself in."[168] Then, he adds, "I was inwardly moved by an urge to perform the duty of Ḥajj (the Muslim pilgrimage) and to draw succour from the blessings of Mecca and Medina and the visit to the tomb of the Messenger of Allah Most High (ṣ)…"[169] Therefore, he travelled from Jerusalem to Ḥijāz.[170]

Although al-Ghazālī migrated from Baghdad with the intention of not going back, as he states, he was drawn to it by certain concerns and the appeals of his children.[171] After returning to Baghdad in 490/1097, however, he chose to live in seclusion, still longing for solitude and heart purification, though with some occasional disturbances which resulted from the necessities of livelihood, as he declares.[172]

In the course of those periods of seclusion, al-Ghazālī reveals, "things impossible to count or list in detail were disclosed to me."[173] However, for the purpose of profiting his reader, he gives his general evaluation of the Sufis and their way:

> I knew with certainty that the Sufis are those who uniquely follow the way to Allah Most High, their mode of life is the best of all, their way the most direct of ways, their ethic the purest. Indeed, were one to combine the insight of the intellectuals, the wisdom of the wise, and the lore of scholars versed in the mysteries of revelation in order to change a single item of Sufi conduct and ethic and to replace it with something better, no way to do so would be found. For all their motions and quiescences, exterior and interior, are learned from the light of the niche of prophecy. And beyond the light of prophecy there in no light on earth from which illumination can be obtained.[174]

Despite this lavish praise, it should not be taken as representing the exact and only position of al-Ghazālī towards the Sufis and Sufism even after his conversion. As Sherif precisely points out, "the fact that Ghazali identifies himself with the mystics and praises their methods does not mean that he accepts everything they say."[175] We agree with Sherif in stating that "there are many things in which he does not agree with the mystics."[176] As it will come apparent below, serious criticism against *al-ṣūfiyyah* and their *ṭarīqah* (method or way) is voiced in the *Iḥyā'* itself.

Al-Ghazālī's stage of asceticism and self-disciplining has been mentioned in a number of early biographies, though they differ in matter of details, particularly with regard to the places he visited, the duration of his stay in each destination and his activities during these visits. Two of these biographical accounts are well worth quoting: that of al-Fārisī and Ibn Khallikān. According to al-Fārisī's account, al-Ghazālī first performed Ḥajj, and then entered al-Shām where he remained for nearly ten years, visiting *al-mashāhid al-muʿaẓẓamah* (the venerated sanctuaries), disciplining his soul, and regulating his character;[177] subsequently, "he returned to his native land where he kept fast to his house, preoccupied with meditation, tenacious of his time, a godly goal and treasure for hearts to everyone who repaired to him and visited him."[178] While he is in al-Shām, he, as al-Fārisī narrated, "began to compose the renowned works to which no one had preceded him, such as *Iḥyāʾ ʿUlūm al-Dīn* and the books abridged therefrom, such as *al-Arbaʿīn* and others."[179] Ibn Khallikān, however, reported the following:

> He abandoned all the occupations in which he had been hitherto engaged, and entered on the path of asceticism and retirement from the world. He then undertook the pilgrimage to Mecca, and, on his return, he proceeded to al-Shām and stopped for some time at Damascus. During his residence in that city, he gave lessons in the western corner of the Great Mosque. He then set out for Jerusalem, where he applied himself with ardour to the practices of devotion, and visited the holy monuments and venerated spots. He next passed into Egypt and remained for some time at Alexandria, whence, it is said, he intended to sail to Maghrib, in hopes of meeting with the emir Yūsuf b. Tāshafīn, the sovereign of Marrakesh; but, having received intelligence of that prince's death, he abandoned the project... On Leaving Egypt, he returned to Tūs, his native place where he was preoccupied with meditation.[180]

Al-Fārisī's account can be harmonized with that of al-Ghazālī if we would follow the following interpretation suggested by Watt:

> Some of the early biographical notices say that he spent ten years in Syria, having returned there after his pilgrimage to

Mecca. Now it seems probable that he returned to Damascus, and that he regarded his pilgrimage and his visit to Jerusalem as belonging to his Damascus period. This is in accordance with his account, provided that we take his phrase about the "journey to the Ḥijāz" to mean a journey to Mecca and back to Damascus; this seems to be a reasonable interpretation.[181]

On his visit to Egypt and intended plan to visit Ibn Tāshafin, as it is reported by Ibn Khallikān, there have been conflicting views. Watt, for example, states that "it is certainly possible that there was such a visit on the way to or from Mecca. If it took place, however, it can have been little more than an incident of the journey, and the absence of any mention in *Deliverance from Error* indicates that it had no spiritual significance to al-Ghazālī."[182] Abu-Sway, however, totally rejects this report:

> All other accounts confirm that al-Ghazzāliyy [sic.] was in Khurasan…in 500 AH/1106 C.E., the year in which Ibn Tāshafin died. The idea that al-Ghazzāliyy [sic.] was in Egypt may be refuted on two accounts. His student, Ibn al-ʿArabiyy [sic.] saw him, after returning from his journey, in the wilderness of Baghdad in 491 AH/July 1106, is a clear indication of the falsity of such claims.[183]

Leaving aside the controversy surrounding the details of this mysterious period of al-Ghazālī's life, for it seems extremely difficult to resolve completely because of the contradicting reports, we go on to say that this stage, in general, marked a turning point in the whole personality of al-Ghazālī. His contemporary and associate, al-Fārisī, provides us with an eyewitness account of al-Ghazālī's serious *tawbah* (repentance) or fundamental corrective conversion at that stage. Before delivering his account, it is worth noting that al-Fārisī is introduced by al-Subkī as "*thiqah* (trustworthy)"[184] which, as Abu-Sway correctly states, "in this context is a technical term, which considered by many scholars of *ḥadīth* as the highest rank attributed to a Muslim narrator."[185] Thus, his account is highly reliable.

About al-Ghazālī's conversion, al-Fārisī states:

Thus, the devil of frivolity and of seeking leadership and fame and of taking on bad qualities was transformed into serenity of soul and nobility of qualities, having done with [outward] forms and rites. He took on the appeal of the godly and reduced his hope and devoted his time to the guidance of men and summoning them to what concerned them regarding the afterlife...[186]

Al-Fārisī tells us that his witness was based on investigation and examination, and not merely observation:

Indeed, I often visited him, and I did not find in him what I had formerly been familiar with in his regard, viz. maliciousness and making people uneasy and regarding them disdainfully and looking down upon them out of haughtiness and arrogance and being dazzled by his own endowment of skill in speech and thought and expression, and his quest of glory and high status: he had become the exact opposite and had been cleansed of those impurities. I used to think that he was wrapped in the garment of affectation and pretence. Then, I thought, after investigation and examination that, that the matter was not as I thought, and that the man had recovered from madness.[187]

These remarks are of vital importance. They, as Nakamura[188] and Abu-Sway[189] rightly point out, proves the authenticity and the truthfulness of al-Ghazālī's conversion. They also clearly show how al-Ghazālī was before and after his experience of self-*iṣlāḥ*. This leaves no room for doubting the sincerity of al-Ghazālī's corrective transformation and thus renders any further discussion of this matter unnecessary.

Having stated this, it is not intended here to overstate the significance of al-Ghazālī's conversion. Instead, we agree with Nakamura in stating, against Macdonald's dual division of al-Ghazālī's life based on al-Ghazālī's remarks after his conversion,[190] that "I do not take the clear-cut division of Ghazālī's life into two parts: the former is this-worldly, irreligious and the latter other-worldly, religious."[191] However, we do not follow Nakamura in arguing that we cannot take the remarks of al-Ghazālī about his conversion at their face value on the basis that they "were written or uttered when Ghazālī as a veteran Sūfī looked back upon his non-Sūfī way of life long after his conversion,"[192] and thus, Nakamura adds, it is "quite natural that he should tend to be exaggeratingly critical about it."[193] We cannot fully agree with Nakamura because seeking worldly gains such as fame through supposedly religious activities, which was the case of al-Ghazālī during his teaching career as he himself confessed, is a dangerously serious matter not only from Sufi point view, as Nakamura apparently states, but also from Islamic perspective in general, since it is agreed upon that purification of the intention is of a vital importance according to the Islamic teachings.

Our rejection of Macdonald's clear-cut dual division of al-Ghazālī's life, however, is based on another standpoint. It is simply because his view indicates that al-Ghazālī lived almost entirely a secular life before his conversion. This, in our view, is quite extreme. Al-Ghazālī's remarks about his life before his conversion do not necessitate that all his activities in that period were "on purely business basis"[194] or "that he thought only of the reputation and wealth which they were bringing him."[195] Rather, there are clear indications in his remarks that some of his early activities were purely religiously motivated. His examination of various sects at the time is a lucid example. He clearly states in the *Munqidh* that his only motive behind that examination was "to discriminate between the proponent of truth and the advocate of error, and between the faithful follower of the Sunnah and the heterodox innovator,"[196] and that is undoubtedly a purely religious aim. Therefore, al-Ghazālī's avowal regarding his impure intention during his teaching career should not be reflected back on all his previous activities.

Now, it would seem reasonably justified to argue that al-Ghazālī's period of seclusion marked the beginning of his attempt at general *iṣlāḥ*. This is firstly because the outcome of that period, as illustrated above, was his self-*iṣlāḥ*, which is according to his own teaching a prerequisite for general *iṣlāḥ*.[197] Secondly, he, as mentioned above, composed in the same period his celebrated work, the *Iḥyā'*, which is intended to be a major project of *iṣlāḥ*, as will be shown below.

Striving for general *iṣlāḥ*

Following his noticeably long experience of seclusion and self-*iṣlāḥ* illustrated above, al-Ghazālī entered a distinct period which can be properly considered as a stage of striving for general *iṣlāḥ*. This classification of that stage, which lasted till his death, is based firstly on al-Ghazālī's account in the *Munqidh* which clearly shows that his sole desire at that stage was *iṣlāḥ*. After revealing his experience of seclusion in the book, al-Ghazālī immediately informs us about his observation of the widespread of the weakness of men's faith among various classes and of the reasons behind that according to his own investigation.[198] Subsequently, he saw that it was inevitable at such a time to abandon his seclusion and engage in exposing such sophistries, particularly because he considered himself a very skilled practitioner in such activity, but he kept hesitating and making excuses to remain in seclusion:

> Then, I said to myself: "When will you devote yourself completely to laying bare this affliction and to battling against this dreadful darkness? It is a time of tepidity and an era of error. But even if you were to engage in calling men from their evil ways to the truth, all the men of this age would be hostile to you: how, then, would you stand up against them? And how could you put up with them? For that could be done only at favourable time and under a pious and irresistible Sultan."[199]

His hesitation, however, ended when he was strictly summoned by the authority to hasten to Nīshāpūr in order to teach in its Niẓāmiyyah. Thus, al-Ghazālī states, "it occurred to me that the reason for excusing yourself has lost its force. Hence your motive for clinging to seclusion should not be laziness, ease, self-aggrandizement and protecting yourself from the harm caused by men."[200] Shortly, he became more convinced and encouraged to make such move, as he explains:

I consulted on that matter a number of those skilled in discerning hearts and visions. They unanimously advised me to abandon my seclusion and to emerge from my *zāwiyah* (hospice). In addition to that, many recurrent dreams of pious men attested that this move would be a source of goodness and right guidance, and that it had been decreed by Allah—Glorious be He—for the head of this century. For Allah—Glorious be He—has indeed promised to revivify His religion at the beginning of each century. So my hope was strengthened and I became quite optimistic because of these testimonies.[201]

Al-Ghazālī, then, concludes his account about this new move by revealing his intention in returning to teaching and clearly stating his desire for *iṣlāḥ*:

I know well that, even though I have returned to teaching, I have not really returned; for returning means coming back to a previous state. Formerly, I used to convey the knowledge by which fame is gained, and to invite men to it by words and deeds, and that was my aim and my intention. But now I invite men to the knowledge by which fame is renounced and its lowly rank recognized. This is now my intention, my aim, my desire. Allah knows that to be true of me. I now earnestly desire to achieve the *iṣlāḥ* of myself and others.[202]

Secondly, the following biographical notices of al-Fārisī concerning the same stage, which generally agree with al-Ghazālī's account, support the above classification. Explaining how the Vizier Fakhr al-Mulk, son of Niẓām al-Mulk, insistently asked al-Ghazālī to return to teaching, al-Fārisī states:

He [i.e., Fakhr al-Mulk] heard of and verified al-Ghazālī's position and rank and the perfection of his superiority and his standing and the soundness of his belief and the purity of his conduct. So he sought a blessing from him and had him brought and listened to what he had to say. Then he asked al-Ghazālī not to let his breaths and useful lessons remain sterile, with no one profiting from them or learning from their lights, and he went all out in importuning and suggesting until al-Ghazālī agreed to go forth…He could not but yield to the authority.[203]

Distinguishing between al-Ghazālī's motive at this stage and that in his first teaching experience, al-Fārisī explains that "by bringing forth that with which he had busied himself, he aimed at guiding the deviators (*al-shādhah*) and benefiting the seekers of guidance (*al-qāṣidīn*) without going back to what he had been divested of, viz. seeking honour and wrangling with his peers and condemning the headstrong."[204] In addition, al-Fārisī reports that he, and others, wonderingly asked al-Ghazālī about his wish for doing what he was summoned to do, and thus al-Ghazālī in defence of that said: "According to my religion I could not conceivably hold back from the summons and the utility of benefiting *al-ṭālibīn* (the disciples). It was indeed imperative for me to disclose the truth and to speak of it and to call to it—and he was truthful in that."[205] Showing that his desire for benefiting and reforming others continued even after his abandonment of formal teaching, al-Fārisī goes on to say:

> He set up a nearby a *madrasah* for the seekers of knowledge and *khānqāh* (sojourn) for the Sufis. He apportioned his time to the task of those present, such as the recital of the Qur'an and keeping company with the men of hearts and sitting down to teach, so that not a single moment of his time or of those with him was profitless until the eye of the time attained him and the days begrudged him to the men of his age. Then the Merciful translated him to His gracious proximity.[206]

Thirdly, the reported activities of al-Ghazālī at that stage are mostly, if not all, of *islāḥī* nature. He, for example, was teaching the *Iḥyā'*.[207] The book is undoubtedly intended to be a major project of *islāḥ* from al-Ghazālī's point of view. This is clearly indicated in the introduction of the book. To illustrate this well, there seems no better way than literally quoting the words of al-Ghazālī. Addressing his imagined wayward reader, al-Ghazālī states:

> For what has loosened the bond of silence from my tongue and imposed the responsibility of speech and the obligation of utterance on me is your persistent blindness to the essence of reality along with your obstinate aid of what is baseless,

flattering ignorance, and stirring up of evil against anyone who prefers to depart slightly from the ways followed by mankind and who inclines a little from the common practice of men in order to conform to the dictates of knowledge.[208]

Explaining the reason behind such insistence on going astray at the time, he adds:

There is no reason for your persistent disapproval except the malady which has become an epidemic among the multitudes. That malady consists in insufficient observation of the high importance of this matter, the gravity of the problem, and the seriousness of the crisis; in not seeing that the next life is approaching and this world is waning; that death is imminent but the journey is still long; that the provisions are scanty, the danger is great, and the road is blocked; and that whatever learning or work not purely devoted to Allah is rejected.[209]

Clarifying the seriousness of the malady of the time and the difficulties surrounding its treatment, he goes on to say:

With neither guide nor companion the journey on the road to the next life, with its many pitfalls, is toilsomely tiresome. The guides to the road are the *'ulamā'* (religious scholars) who are the heirs of the prophets, but our time is void of them and only the superficial [or those who just apparently resemble them] (*al-mutarassimūn*) remain, most of who have been overcome by Satan and lured by iniquity. Every one of them has become infatuated with his immediate fortune. Thus, they have begun to consider good as evil and evil as good, so that the knowledge of religion has become effaced and the torch of guidance has been extinguished in all over the world. They have made the people imagine that there is no knowledge except the *fatwā* of a government by which judges seek help in settling disputes when the foolish people quarrel; or ability in disputation by which one who seeks glory arrays himself to conquer and silence by argument; or adorned rhymed prose by which the preacher seeks to gradually persuade the common folk, since they do not see anything but these three to trap and snare unlawful vanities (of this world). As to the knowledge of the path to the next life, according to which the pious forefathers trod and which Allah in His Book called *fiqh* (discernment), *ḥikmah* (wisdom), *'ilm* (knowledge), *ḍiyā'* (illumination), *nūr* (light), *hidāyah* (right guidance), and *rushd* (rectitude), it had become folded away and quite forgotten among people.[210]

Then, he clearly states that writing the *Iḥyā'* was an attempt to treat that malady: "Since this is a penetrating breach and an intensely black calamity in religion, I have deemed it important to occupy myself in composing this book in order to revive the knowledge of religion and to reveal the ways of the early Imams, and to clarify the beauties of the beneficial branches of knowledge current among the prophets and the virtuous fathers."[211]

The *iṣlāḥī* nature of the *Iḥyā'* is also apparent throughout the book for therein are corrective treatments for various phenomena of *fasād* diagnosed by al-Ghazālī, as shall be extensively illustrated in the following chapter.

Other than the *Iḥyā'*, al-Ghazālī composed and taught works of *iṣlāḥī* purposes at this stage in view. The following two in particular are worth brief mention. The first is the *Munqidh*; besides his didactic account about his intellectual and spiritual experience, which in itself has an *iṣlāḥī* function, al-Ghazālī includes in the *Munqidh* his diagnosis of the slackness of Īmān (Islamic faith), which was a phenomenon of *fasād* in his time, and directs to his suggested remedies for it, as shall be illustrated in more detail in the following chapter.[212]

The second work of *iṣlāḥī* significance is al-Ghazālī's *Iljām al-'Awām 'an 'Ilm al-Kalām*, which is his last known book. As the title indicates, the book was a corrective response to the phenomenon of the publicity of *kalām* at the time of al-Ghazālī, which had harmful consequences as was shown above.

In addition to composing and teaching such *iṣlāḥī* works, al-Ghazālī sent several letters[213] of *iṣlāḥī* purposes to ruling members as well as *'ulamā'* and other contemporaries, responding correctively to particular wrongdoing and challenges of the time, as shall become apparent in the following chapter.

Notes

1.   ʿAbd al-Dāym Abū al-ʿAtā al-Baqarī, *Iʿtirāfāt al-Ghazālī*, Cairo: Dār al-Nahḍah al-ʿArabiyyh, 1971, pp. 167-169.

2.   The quote is a good summary for the explicit message which al-Baqarī repeatedly puts across his reader; it is originally from an article for J.M. Abd-El-Jalil in *Autor de la Sincérité d' al-Gazzālī*. Vol. I. pp. 57-72, Damascus: Mélanges Louis Massignon, 1956, which is a counter argument of al-Baqarī's book, and it is cited in the introduction of McCarthy to the *Deliverance from Error*, p. 24.

3.   Cited in the introduction of McCarthy to *Deliverance from Error*, p. 26.

4.   Ibid.

5.   Unnamed in the sources.

6.   See al-Subkī, *Ṭabaqāt*, Vol. 4, p. 102.

7.   Ibid.

8.   Ibid.

9.   Ibid.

10.   See, al-Baqarī, *Iʿtirāfāt al-Ghazālī*, p. 28.

11.   Cf. W. Montgomery Watt, *Muslim Intellectual: A Study of al-Ghazali*, Edinburgh: The University Press, 1963, pp. 21f.

12.   Or al-Zādkānī.

13.   See, the earliest biography of al-Ghazālī by Abū al-Ḥasan ʿAbd al-Ghāfir b. Ismāʿīl al-Fārisī, who was his contemporary and associate, which is quoted from his lost book, *al-Siyāq fī Tarīkh Khurāsān*, by Ibn ʿAsākir al-Dimashqī (d. 571/1176), in *Tabyīn Kadhib al-Muftarī*, Damascus: al-Qudsī, 1347 AH, p. 291, trans., McCarthy, *Deliverance*, p. 14; see also, Abū al-ʿAbbās Shams al-Dīn Aḥmad b. Muḥammad b. Khallikān (d. 681/1282), *Wafiyyāt al-Aʿyān wa Anbāʾ Abnāʾ al-Zamān*, ed. Iḥsān ʿAbbās, Beirut: Dār Ṣādir, 1977, Vol. 4, p. 2176, trans., Bn Mac Guckin De Slane, *Ibn Khallikān's Biographical Dictionary*, Paris: Oriental Translation Fund of Great Britain and Ireland, 1868, Vol. 2, p. 621; and al-Subkī, *Ṭabaqāt*, Vol. 4, p. 103.

14.   See, the biography of al-Ghazālī by Muḥammad b. al-Ḥasan al-Ḥusaynī al-Wāsiṭī (d. 776/1374), which is originaly recorded in his unprinted book, *al-Ṭabaqāt al-ʿAliyyah fī Manāqib al-Shāfiʿiyyah*, but a seperate mannscript of the biography itself has been recently edited by ʿAbd al-Amīr al-Aʿsam and printed as an appendix in al-Aʿsam's book, *al-Faylasūf al-Ghazālī*, p. 177; see also, al-Subkī, *Ṭabaqāt*, Vol. 4, p. 103.

15.   See, ʿAbd al-Raḥmān Badawī, *Muʾallafāt al-Ghazālī*, Kuwait: Wakālah al-Maṭbūʿāt, 1977, pp. 3-5.

16.   George Makdisi, *The Rise of Colleges: Institutions of Learning in Islam and the West*, Edinburgh: Edinburgh University Press, 1981, p. 114.

17. See, Makdisi, *The Rise of Colleges*, p. 114.
18. Ibid.
19. D.B. Macdonald, "The Life of al-Ghazzālī with special reference to his religious experiences and opinions," *JAOS*, 1887, p. 76.
20. The story is recorded by al-Subkī on the authority of both Asʿad al-Mayhanī and the Vizier Niẓām al-Mulk who heard it from al-Ghazālī himself, see al-Subkī, *Ṭabaqāt*, Vol. 4, p. 103.
21. Al-Subkī, *Ṭabaqāt*, Vol. 4, p. 103.
22. See, for example, Watt, *Muslim Intellectual*, p. 23.
23. Being specialized in al-Juwaynī and an editor of a number of his books, ʿAbd al-ʿAẓīm al-Dīb is considered an authority in this regard. In light of his deep study of al-Juwaynī, he has concluded that introducing this Imam principally as a theologian and that theology or *kalām* is his first discipline is a false postulate and that his books in *fiqh* and *uṣūl*, which are his first fields, are much more than those on *kalām*, see, for example, his introduction to al-Juwaynī's book, *al-Ghiyāthī*, Doha: al-Shuʾūn al-Dīniyyah, 1400 AH, p. 17ff.
24. See, Ibn Khallikān, *Wafiyyāt al-Aʿyān*, Vol. 4, p. 217, trans., Slane, *Ibn Khallikān's Biographical Dictionary*, Vol. 2, p. 622.
25. For the condition of *fiqh* during the age of al-Ghazālī, see above.
26. For the definition of this branch of knowledge, see above.
27. See, Shams al-Dīn Muḥammad b. Aḥmad al-Dhahabī, *Siyar Aʿlām al-Nubalāʾ*, ed. Muḥ al-Dīn Abū Saʿīd ʿUmar b. Gharāmah al-ʿAmrawī, Beirut: Dār al-Fikr, 1997, Vol. 14, pp. 320-321; and al-Subkī, *Ṭabaqāt*, Vol. 4, p. 103..
28. Al-Subkī, *Ṭabaqāt*, Vol. 4, p. 103.
29. See, al-Ghazālī's biography by al-Fārisī, cited in Ibn ʿAsākir al-Dimashqī, *Tabyīn*, p. 292, trans., McCarthy, *Deliverance*, p. 14; and al-Dhahabī, *Siyar Aʿlām al-Nubalāʾ*, Vol. 14, p. 321.
30. See, al-Ghazālī's biography by al-Fārisī, cited in Ibn ʿAsākir al-Dimashqī, *Tabyīn*, p. 292, trans., McCarthy, *Deliverance*, p. 14; Ibn Khallikān, *Wafiyyāt al-Aʿyān*, Vol. 4, p. 217, trans., Slane, *Ibn Khallikān's Biographical Dictionary*, Vol. 2, p. 622; and al-Dhahabī, *Siyar Aʿlām al-Nubalāʾ*, Vol. 14, p. 321.
31. Al-Subkī, *Ṭabaqāt*, Vol. 4, p. 103. Cf. George F. Hourani, "A Revised Chronology of Ghazālī's Writing," in *JAOS*, Vol. 104, No. 2, Apr.-June 1984, p. 290.
32. The authenticity of the book has been confirmed by ʿAbd al-Raḥmān Badawī (*Muʾallafāt al-Ghazālī*, p. 6-10) and more recently by the editor of the *Mankhūl*, Muḥammad Ḥasan Hītū (in his introduction to al-Ghazālī's *al-Mankhūl min Taʿlīqāt al-Uṣūl*, Muḥammad Ḥasan Hītū (ed.), Damascus, n.p., 1970, pp. 31-33), who has convincingly cleared up the doubts which have been aroused over its authenticity.

33. Al-Subkī's dating of the *Mankhūl* has been recently doubted by the editor of the book, Muḥammad Ḥasan Hītū, because of the occasional appearance of the phrase *raḥimah Allāh* (may Allah have mercy upon him) following the name of Imām al-Ḥaramayn which indicates, in the view of Hītū that the book was written after his death (Hītū's introduction to al-Ghazālī's *al-Mankhūl*, pp. 34f). However, this is not a definite proof since it is possible that such phrase was added in later versions of the book.

34. Al-Ghazālī, a*l-Mankhūl*, pp. 488-504.

35. Ibid, p. 488.

36. Ibid, p. 471.

37. Cited in Badawī, *Mu'allafāt al-Ghazālī*, p. 8.

38. Al-Ghazālī, *al-Mankhūl*, p. 504.

39. See, Makdisi, *The Rise of Colleges*, p. 114.

40. See, Hītū's introduction to al-Ghazālī's *al-Mankhūl*, p. 35.

41. Al-Ghazālī, *al-Mankhūl*, p. 504.

42. Hītū's introduction to al-Ghazālī's *al-Mankhūl*, p. 36.

43. See, al-Dīb's introduction to al-Juwaynī's book, *al-Ghiyāthī*, pp. 146-151.

44. Ibid.

45. See, al-Ghazālī's biography by al-Fārisī, cited in Ibn 'Asākir al-Dimashqī, *Tabyīn*, p. 292, trans., McCarthy, *Deliverance*, p. 14; Ibn Khallikān, *Wafiyyāt al-A'yān*, Vol. 4, p. 217, trans., Slane, *Ibn Khallikān's Biographical Dictionary*, Vol. 2, p. 622; and al-Dhahabī, *Siyar A'lām al-Nubalā'*, Vol. 14, p. 321.

46. See, al-Ghazālī's biography by al-Fārisī, cited in Ibn 'Asākir al-Dimashqī, *Tabyīn*, p. 292, trans., McCarthy, *Deliverance*, p. 15; and al-Subkī, *Ṭabaqāt*, Vol. 4, p. 103.

47. Al-Ghazālī's biography by al-Fārisī, cited in Ibn 'Asākir al-Dimashqī, *Tabyīn*, p. 292, trans., McCarthy, *Deliverance*, p. 15.

48. See, al-Ghazālī's biography by al-Fārisī, cited in Ibn 'Asākir al-Dimashqī, *Tabyīn*, p. 292, trans., McCarthy, *Deliverance*, p. 15; Ibn Khallikān, *Wafiyyāt al-A'yān*, Vol. 4, p. 217, trans., Slane, *Ibn Khallikān's Biographical Dictionary*, Vol. 2, p. 622; and al-Dhahabī, *Siyar A'lām al-Nubalā'*, Vol. 14, p. 321.

49. See, al-Ghazālī's biography by al-Fārisī, cited in Ibn 'Asākir al-Dimashqī, *Tabyīn*, p. 292, trans., McCarthy, *Deliverance*, p. 15; Ibn Khallikān, *Wafiyyāt al-A'yān*, Vol. 4, p. 217, trans., Slane, *Ibn Khallikān's Biographical Dictionary*, Vol. 2, p. 622; al-Dhahabī, *Siyar A'lām al-Nubalā'*, Vol. 14, p. 321; and al-Subkī, *Ṭabaqāt*, Vol. 4, p. 103.

50. See al-Subkī, *Ṭabaqāt*, Vol. 4, pp. 103f. In this year al-Ghazālī reached the age of thirty-four.

51. See, al-Ghazālī's biography by al-Fārisī, cited in Ibn 'Asākir al-Dimashqī, *Tabyīn*, p. 292, trans., Mc Carthy, *Deliverance*, p. 15;

Ibn Khallikān, *Wafiyyāt al-A'yān*, Vol. 4, p. 217, trans., Slane, *Ibn Khallikān's Biographical Dictionary*, Vol. 2, p. 622; al-Dhahabī, *Siyar A'lām al-Nubalā'*, Vol. 14, p. 321; and al-Subkī, *Ṭabaqāt*, Vol. 4, p. 103.

52. Al-Ghazālī, *al-Munqidh*, p. 74, trans., McCarthy, *Deliverance*, p. 61, & Watt, *The Faith*, p. 30.

53. Abū al-Faraj 'Abd al-Raḥmān b. 'Alī b. Muḥammad, known as Ibn al-Jawzī (d. 597/1201), *al-Muntaẓam fī Tārīkh al-Mulūk wa al-Umam*, Hyderabad: Dā'irah al-Ma'ārif al-'Uthmāniyyah, 1359 AH, Vol. 9, p. 169.

54. Tell 488/1095.

55. Al-Ghazālī's biography by al-Fārisī, cited in Ibn 'Asākir al-Dimashqī, *Tabyīn*, p. 292, trans., McCarthy, *Deliverance*, p. 15.

56. Ibid.

57. Ibn Khallikān, *Wafiyyāt al-A'yān*, Vol. 4, p. 217, trans., Slane, *Ibn Khallikān's Biographical Dictionary*, Vol. 2, p. 622.

58. See, al-Ghazālī's biography by al-Fārisī, cited in Ibn 'Asākir al-Dimashqī, *Tabyīn*, p. 292, trans., McCarthy, *Deliverance*, p. 15; and al-Dhahabī, *Siyar A'lām al-Nubalā'*, Vol. 14, p. 321.

59. Ibid.

60. See, al-Qurrah-Dāghī's introduction to al-Ghazālī's *al-Wasīt*, Vol. 1, pp. 250-253.

61. See, Badawī, *Mu'allafāt al-Ghazālī*, pp. 33-37.

62. Al-Ghazālī, *al-Munqidh*, p. 63; trans., see McCarthy, *Deliverance*, pp. 54f, & Watt, *The Faith*, p. 21.

63. Ibid, p. 63; trans., see McCarthy, *Deliverance*, p. 55, & Watt, *The Faith*, p. 21.

64. Ibid, p. 64; trans., see McCarthy, *Deliverance*, p. 55, & Watt, *The Faith*, pp. 21f.

65. Ibid, pp. 65-67; trans., see McCarthy, *Deliverance*, pp. 55-57, & Watt, *The Faith*, pp. 22-25.

66. Ibid, pp. 67f; trans., see McCarthy, *Deliverance*, p. 57, & Watt, *The Faith*, p. 25.

67. See, al-Baqarī, *I'tirāfāt al-Ghazālī*, pp. 40-50.

68. Ibid.

69. Watt, *Muslim Intellectual*, p. 51.

70. Osman Bakar devoted a chapter on "The Place of doubt in Islamic Epistemology: al-Ghazālī's Philosophical Experience" in his book entitled *History and Philosophy of Islamic Science*, Cambridge: The Islamic Texts Society, 1999, pp. 39-60.

71. Al-Ghazālī, *al-Munqidh*, p. 62; trans., see McCarthy, *Deliverance*, p. 54, & Watt, *The Faith*, p. 20.

72. Mustafa Mahmud Abu-Sway, "al-Ghazālī's Spiritual Crisis Reconsidered," *al-Shajarah*, Vol. 1, No. I, 1996, p. 83.

73. Bakar, *History and Philosophy*, p. 40.
74. Ibid, p. 40.
75. Ibid, pp. 40f.
76. Ibid, p. 45.
77. Ibid, p. 45.
78. Ibid, p. 45.
79. Ibid, pp. 45f.
80. Ibid, p. 46.
81. Al-Ghazālī, *al-Munqidh*, p. 61; trans., see McCarthy, *Deliverance*, p. 54, & Watt, *The Faith*, p. 20.
82. Bakar, *History and Philosophy*, p. 52.
83. Ibid, p. 52.
84. Ibid, p. 52.
85. Ibid, p. 52.
86. Ibid, p. 53.
87. Ibid, p. 53.
88. Ibid, pp. 53f.
89. Al-Ghazālī, *al-Munqidh*, p. 102; trans., see McCarthy, *Deliverance*, p. 78, & Watt, *The Faith*, p. 56.
90. Bakar, *History and Philosophy*, p. 54. Although there is no reason to doubt that al-Ghazālī was not a religious sceptic, we may raise the reservation that the quotation to which Bakar refers to does not seem relevant to the doubting period.
91. See, Bakar, *History and Philosophy*, pp. 55-59.
92. Ibid, pp. 53f.
93. Al-Ghazālī, *al-Munqidh*, p. 69; trans., see McCarthy, *Deliverance*, p. 58, & Watt, *The Faith*, p. 26.
94. Ibid, p. 69; trans., see McCarthy, *Deliverance*, p. 58, & Watt, *The Faith*, p. 27.
95. Ibid, p. 69; trans., see McCarthy, *Deliverance*, p. 58, & Watt, *The Faith*, p. 27.
96. Ibid, p. 70; trans., see McCarthy, *Deliverance*, p. 59, & Watt, *The Faith*, p. 27.
97. Al-Baqarī, *I'tirāfāt al-Ghazālī*, p. 65.
98. Ibid, p. 66.
99. Bakar, *History and Philosophy*, p. 58.
100. Al-Ghazālī, *al-Munqidh*, p. 71; trans., see McCarthy, *Deliverance*, p. 59, & Watt, *The Faith*, p. 27.
101. Ibid, p. 72; trans., see McCarthy, *Deliverance*, p. 60, & Watt, *The Faith*, p. 28.
102. I think both McCarthy and Watt missed the point here, so this is according to my understanding of the original.

103. Al-Ghazālī, *al-Munqidh*, p. 72; trans., see McCarthy, *Deliverance*, p. 60, & Watt, *The Faith*, pp. 28f.

104. Al-Baqarī, *I'tirāfāt al-Ghazālī*, pp. 66f.

105. Al-Ghazālī, *al-Munqidh*, p. 72; trans., see McCarthy, *Deliverance*, p. 59, & Watt, *The Faith*, p. 28.

106. Al-Baqarī, *I'tirāfāt al-Ghazālī*, p. 67.

107. Al-Ghazālī, *al-Munqidh*, p. 74; trans., see McCarthy, *Deliverance*, p. 60, & Watt, *The Faith*, p. 29.

108. Ibid, p. 74; trans., see McCarthy, *Deliverance*, p. 60, & Watt, *The Faith*, p. 29.

109. Ibid, p. 74; trans., see McCarthy, *Deliverance*, p. 61, & Watt, *The Faith*, pp. 29f.

110. Ibid, p. 74; trans., see McCarthy, *Deliverance*, p. 61, & Watt, *The Faith*, pp. 29f.

111. Ibid, pp. 74f; trans., see McCarthy, *Deliverance*, p. 61, & Watt, *The Faith*, pp. 30.

112. Ibid, p. 91; trans., see McCarthy, *Deliverance*, p. 71, & Watt, *The Faith*, p. 44.

113. As Macdonald precisely explains, "A *maqṣad* is what is intended or meant. *Maqṣad al-kalām* is "the intended sense of the saying." The word is thus a synonym of *ma'nā* in the sense "meaning" or "idea."" D.B. Macdonald, "The Meanings of the Philosophers by al-Ghazzali," *Isis*, Vol. 25, No. 1, May 1936, p. 9, available online in PDF: *http://www.ghazali.org/articles/dbm1.pdf*.

114. Al-Ghazālī, *Tahāfut al-Falāsifah*, ed. Sulaymān Dunyā, Cairo: Dār al-Maʿārif, 1980.

115. Cf. George F. Hourani, "A Revised Chronolgoy of Ghazālī's Writings," in *JAOS*, Vol. 104, No. 2, Apr.-June 1984, pp. 292f.

116. As Macdonald points out, "following a regular convention in the writing of didactic treatises, al-Ghazzālī begins with an address to a supposed disciple who has asked for instruction," (Macdonald, "The Meanings of the Philosophers," p. 10).

117. Al-Ghazālī, *Maqāṣid al-Falāsifah*, ed. Maḥmūd Bījū, Damascus: Maṭba'at al-Ṣabāḥ,, 2000, p. 10; trans., see, Gershon B. Chertoff, "The Logical Part of al-Ghazālī's Maqāṣid al-Falāsifah: In an anonymous Hebrew translation with the Hebrew commentary of Moses of Narbonee, edited and translated with notes and an introduction and translated into English," a PhD thesis, Columbia Universtiy,1952, part II, pp. 2f, available on line in PDF form on *http://www.ghazali.org/books/chertoff.pdf*.

118. Al-Ghazālī, *Maqāṣid*, p. 11; trans., see, Chertoff, "The Logical Part of al-Ghazālī's Maqāṣid al-Falāsifah,", part II, p. 4.

119. Al-Ghazālī, *Tahāfut al-Falāsifah*, ed. Sulaymān Dunyā, Cairo: Dār al-Maʿārif, 1980, p. 73; trans., see Sabih Ahmad Kamali, *al-Ghazali's Tahafut al-Falasifah*, Lahore: Pakistan Philosophical Congress, 1963, p. 1.
120. Al-Ghazālī, *Tahāfut*, pp. 73f; trans., see Kamali, *al-Ghazali's Tahafut*, pp. 1f.
121. Ibid, p. 75; trans., see Kamali, *al-Ghazali's Tahafut*, p. 3.
122. Ibid, p. 82; trans., see Kamali, *al-Ghazali's Tahafut*, p. 8.
123. See, Hourani, "A Revised Chronolgoy," p. 293.
124. Dunyā's introduction to al-Ghazālī's *Miʿyār al-ʿIlm*, ed. Sulaymān Dunyā, Cairo: Dār al-Maʿārif, 1961, pp. 14-21.
125. Macdonald, "The Meanings of the Philosophers," p. 14.
126. Al-Ghazālī, *al-Munqidh*, p. 91; trans., see McCarthy, *Deliverance*, p. 71, & Watt, *The Faith*, p. 44.
127. Ibid, p. 91; trans., see McCarthy, *Deliverance*, p. 71, & Watt, *The Faith*, p. 44.
128. Ibid, p. 92; trans., see McCarthy, *Deliverance*, p. 71, & Watt, *The Faith*, p. 44.
129. Ibid, p. 99; trans., see McCarthy, *Deliverance*, p. 77, & Watt, *The Faith*, pp. 53f.
130. Ibid, p. 100; trans., see McCarthy, *Deliverance*, p. 77, & Watt, *The Faith*, p. 54.
131. Ibid, pp. 100f; trans., see McCarthy, *Deliverance*, p. 77, & Watt, *The Faith*, p. 54.
132. Ibid, pp. 100f.
133. Ibid, p. 101; trans., see McCarthy, *Deliverance*, p. 78, & Watt, *The Faith*, pp. 54f.
134. Ibid, p. 102; trans., see McCarthy, *Deliverance*, p. 78, & Watt, *The Faith*, p. 55.
135. Ibid, p. 103; trans., see McCarthy, *Deliverance*, pp. 78f, & Watt, *The Faith*, p. 56.
136. Al-Ghazālī, *al-Munqidh*, p. 103; trans., see McCarthy, *Deliverance*, p. 79, & Watt, *The Faith*, p. 56.
137. Ibid, p. 103; trans., see McCarthy, *Deliverance*, p. 79, & Watt, *The Faith*, p. 56.
138. Ibid, p. 104; trans., see McCarthy, *Deliverance*, pp. 79f, & Watt, *The Faith*, pp. 57f.
139. Ibid, p. 104; trans., see McCarthy, *Deliverance*, pp. 79f, & Watt, *The Faith*, p. 57.
140. Ibid, p. 104; trans., see McCarthy, *Deliverance*, p. 80, & Watt, *The Faith*, p. 58.
141. Ibid, p. 104; trans., see McCarthy, *Deliverance*, p. 80, & Watt, *The Faith*, p. 58.

142. Eric L. Ormsby, "The Taste of Truth: The Structure of Experience in al-Ghazali's al-Munqidh," in Wael B. Hallaq & Donald P. Little (eds.) *Islamic Studies Presented to Charles J. Adams*, Leiden: Brill, 1991, pp. 144f, available online in PDF: *http://www.ghazali.org/articles/eo1.pdf.*

143. 'Umar Farrūkh, *Tārīkh al-Fikr al-'Arabī ilā Ayām Ibn Khaldūn*, Beirut: Dār al-'Ilm li al-Malāyīn, 1981, p. 494.

144. Farrūkh, *Tārīkh al-Fikr*, p. 496.

145. Abu-Sway, "al-Ghazālī's Spiritual Crisis Reconsidered," pp. 85-87.

146. Ibid, p. 86.

147. Ibid, p. 87.

148. Cited in Watt, *Muslim Intellectual*, p. 140.

149. Cited in Kojiro Nakamura, "An Approach to Ghazālī's Conversion," *Orient*, Vol. 21, 1985, pp. 49f.

150. Nakamura, "An Approach to Ghazālī's Conversion," p. 50.

151. Macdonald, "al-Ghazālī, " *EI*, Vol. 2, p. 146.

152. Ibid.

153. Nakamura, "An Approach to Ghazālī's Conversion," p. 50.

154. Ibid, p. 50.

155. Ibid, p. 50.

156. Abu-Sway, "al-Ghazālī's Spiritual Crisis," p. 88.

157. Ibid, p. 90.

158. Ibid, p. 88.

159. Al-Baqarī, *I'tirāfāt al-Ghazālī*, pp. 106f.

160. Ibid, p. 106.

161. Ibid, p. 107.

162. See Ibn al-Athīr, *al-Kāmil*, Vol. 8, p. 481, trans., see Richards, *The Annals*, p. 257.

163. Ibid, Vol. 8, p. 480, trans., see Richards, *The Annals*, p. 257.

164. Ibid, Vol. 8, p. 480, trans., see Richards, *The Annals*, p. 257.

165. Al-Baqarī, *I'tirāfāt al-Ghazālī*, pp. 123f.

166. Started in 488/1095 and ended in 499/1106 as al-Ghazālī mentions in the *Munqidh*, p. 122.

167. Al-Ghazālī, *al-Munqidh*, p. 105; trans., see McCarthy, *Deliverance*, p. 80, & Watt, *The Faith*, p. 59.

168. Ibid; trans., McCarthy, *Deliverance*, p. 80f, & Watt, *The Faith*, p. 59.

169. Ibid, pp. 105f; trans., McCarthy, *Deliverance*, p. 81, & Watt, *The Faith*, p. 59.

170. Al-Ghazālī, *al-Munqidh*, p. 106; trans., McCarthy, *Deliverance*, p. 81, & Watt, *The Faith*, p. 59.

171. Ibid; trans., McCarthy, *Deliverance*, p. 81, & Watt, *The Faith*, p. 59f.

172. Ibid, McCarthy, *Deliverance*, p. 81, & Watt, *The Faith*, p. 60.

173. Ibid, McCarthy, *Deliverance*, p. 81, & Watt, *The Faith*, p. 60.

174. Ibid, McCarthy, *Deliverance*, p. 81, & Watt, *The Faith*, p. 60.

175. Mohamed Ahmed Sherif, *Ghazali's Theory of Virtue*, Albany: State University of New York Press, 1975, p. 166.

176. Ibid.

177. Al-Ghazālī's biography by al-Fārisī, cited in Ibn ʿAsākir al-Dimashqī, *Tabyīn*, p. 293, trans., McCarthy, *Deliverance*, p. 15.

178. Ibid, p. 16.

179. Ibid, p. 16.

180. Ibn Khallikān, *Wafiyyāt al-Aʿyān*, Vol. 4, p. 217, trans., Slane, *Ibn Khallikān's Biographical Dictionary*, Vol. 2, p. 622.

181. Watt, *Muslim Intellectual*, p. 145.

182. Ibid, p. 146.

183. Abu-Sway, Mustafa. *Al-Ghazzāliyy* [*sic*]: *A Study in Islamic Epistemology*, Kuala Lumpur: Diwan Bahasa dan Pustaka, 1996, p. 24.

184. Al-Subkī, *Ṭabaqāt*, Vol. 4, p. 106.

185. Abu-Sway, "al-Ghazālī's Spiritual Crisis Reconsidered," p. 85.

186. Al-Ghazālī's biography by al-Fārisī, cited in Ibn ʿAsākir al-Dimashqī, *Tabyīn*, p. 293, trans., McCarthy, *Deliverance*, pp. 15f.

187. Al-Ghazālī's biography by al-Fārisī, cited in Ibn ʿAsākir al-Dimashqī, *Tabyīn*, p. 294, trans., McCarthy, *Deliverance*, pp. 16f.

188. Kojiro Nakamura, "An Approach to Ghazālī's Conversion," *Orient*, Vol. 21, 1985, p. 50.

189. Abu-Sway, "al-Ghazālī's Spiritual Crisis Reconsidered," p. 58.

190. See Macdonald, "The Life of al-Ghazzālī," pp. 75f.

191. Nakamura, "An Approach to Ghazālī's Conversion," p. 50.

192. Ibid, pp. 51f.

193. Ibid, p. 52.

194. See Macdonald, "The Life of al-Ghazzālī," p. 75.

195. Ibid, pp. 75f.

196. Al-Ghazālī, *al-Munqidh*, p. 62; trans., see McCarthy, *Deliverance*, p. 54, & Watt, *The Faith*, p. 20.

197. In the *Iḥyā'*, al-Ghazālī repeatedly warns of being occupied with the *iṣlāḥ* of others, before the *iṣlāḥ* of the self, see, for example, *Iḥyā'*, Vol. 1, p. 39; trans., see William Alexander MaCall, "The Book of Knowledge: Being a Translation, with Introduction and Notes of al-Ghazzālī's Book of the Iḥyā', Kitāb al-ʿIlm," a PhD thesis, Hartford Seminary Foundation, May, 1940, p. 156, available online in PDF: *http://www.ghazali.org/books/McCall-1940.pdf*, *and also Nabih Amin Faris, The Book of Knowledge, translation of Kitāb al-ʿIlm of al-Ghazālī's Iḥyā', New Delhi: Islamic Book Service, n.d., p. 93*, available online in PDF: *http://www.ghazali.org/books/knowledge.pdf.*

198. Al-Ghazālī, *al-Munqidh*, pp. 117-120; trans., see McCarthy, *Deliverance*, pp. 88-90, & Watt, *The Faith*, pp. 71-73.

199. Ibid, p. 121; trans., see McCarthy, *Deliverance*, p. 91, & Watt, *The Faith*, p. 74.

200. Ibid, p. 121; trans., see McCarthy, *Deliverance*, p. 91, & Watt, *The Faith*, p. 74.

201. Ibid, p. 122; trans., see McCarthy, *Deliverance*, p. 92, & Watt, *The Faith*, p. 75.

202. Ibid, p. 123; trans., see McCarthy, *Deliverance*, p. 92, & Watt, *The Faith*, p. 76.

203. Al-Ghazālī's biography by al-Fārisī, cited in Ibn 'Asākir al-Dimashqī, *Tabyīn*, pp. 293f, trans., McCarthy, *Deliverance*, p. 16.

204. Ibid, p. 294, trans., McCarthy, *Deliverance*, p. 16.

205. Ibid, p. 295, trans., McCarthy, *Deliverance*, p. 17.

206. Ibid, pp. 295f, trans., McCarthy, *Deliverance*, p. 18.

207. Al-Zabīdī lists a number of pupils who orally received the book from al-Ghazālī, see Murtaḍā al-Zabīdī (d. 1205/1791), *Itḥāf al-Sādah al-Muttaqīn bi Sharḥ Iḥyā' 'Ulūm al-Dīn*, Beirut: Dār al-Kutub al-'Ilmiyyah, 2005, Vol. 1, pp. 62-65.

208. Al-Ghazālī, *Iḥyā'*, Vol.1, p. 2; trans., see MaCall, "The Book of Knowledge," p. 2, and also Faris, *The Book of Knowledge*, p. ix.

209. Ibid, p. 2f, and also Faris, *The Book of Knowledge*, p. x.

210. Al-Ghazālī, *Iḥyā'*, Vol.1, p. 2; trans., see MaCall, "The Book of Knowledge," p. 3f, and also Faris, *The Book of Knowledge*, p. x.

211. Ibid, p. 4, and Faris, *The Book of Knowledge*, pp. xf.

212. Al-Ghazālī, *al-Munqidh*, pp. 117-131; trans., see McCarthy, *Deliverance*, pp. 88-98, & Watt, *The Faith*, pp. 68-85.

213. His letters in Fārsī composed in al-Ghazālī, *Makātīb*; some have been translated into English by Abdul Qayyum, *Letters of al-Ghazzali*, Lahore: Islamic Publications, 1976.

4

Survey of al-Ghazālī's *iṣlāḥī* efforts

Introduction

The previous chapter has broadly shown how al-Ghazālī became solely concerned with *iṣlāḥ* at a late stage of his life. This leads to the following question being raised: to what extent did al-Ghazālī at that stage correctively respond to the *fasād* of his age? In our view, it is essential to tackle this question in order to fairly justify the classification of al-Ghazālī as a *muṣliḥ*, recalling that *iṣlāḥ*, as has been defined above, is a corrective task in which any state of *fasād* is changed into its opposite Islamically justified state. To objectively answer this question, it is necessary to survey al-Ghazālī's efforts of *iṣlāḥī* nature. This chapter is devoted to this task.

The approach adopted in this chapter is inductive; a number of al-Ghazālī's *iṣlāḥī* works, particularly the *Iḥyāʾ*, have been carefully studied in order to extract sufficient particulars, the selection of which is made in the light of the analysis of the term *iṣlāḥ* revealed in the first chapter. It is not intended though to undertake a critical assessment in the present chapter. This is because, firstly, including such an assessment here would take up disproportionate space. Secondly, we believe that objectivity necessitates that we present al-Ghazālī's *iṣlāḥī* efforts as perceived, before any assessment is made. Therefore, the assessment will be postponed to the following two chapters, which will be devoted to that purpose, though in an overall way. This, however, does not mean that the present survey is merely descriptive but rather analytical, to some extent, as well. The extent of the analysis is directed by the purpose of highlighting the *iṣlāḥī* aspects of al-Ghazālī's selected efforts.

The survey is by no means inclusive, but the best attempt is made to cover all the main *iṣlāḥī* efforts of al-Ghazālī and to objectively incorporate them—it is hoped—in an intelligible and handy account. For the sake of this hoped for intelligibility and handiness, the present chapter is divided into the following three main sections:

- Al-Ghazālī's diagnosis of *fasād*.
- Al-Ghazālī's *iṣlāḥī* attempts to eradicate the roots of *fasād*.
- Al-Ghazālī's *iṣlāḥī* treatments of the phenomena of *fasād*.

Al-Ghazālī's diagnosis of *fasād*

The basis of al-Ghazālī's *iṣlāḥī* efforts is his diagnosis of *fasād*. This includes not only particular phenomena of *fasād* in his time, but also what, in his view, lies at the root of *fasād* in general. Therefore, it is important to start with his analysis of the roots of *fasād*, before dealing with the diagnosed phenomena.

The roots of fasād

Getting at the roots of *fasād*, in general, can be considered the starting point of al-Ghazālī's attempt at *iṣlāḥ*. This is based on his general rule that *iṣlāḥ* cannot be fully achieved without knowing the roots of *fasād* against which *iṣlāḥ* is directed. In the *Iḥyā'*, he repeats "one cannot prescribe a remedy (*al-dawā'*) without diagnosing the malady (*al-dā'*); for remedy means to counteract the causes of the malady."[1] Clarifying this rule, he continues "for every disease results from a cause (*sabab*), the remedy for it consists of dissolving the cause, removing it and cancelling it."[2]

At least four dangerous roots of *fasād* are clearly dealt with in the works of al-Ghazālī under review:

- Ignorance.
- Love of the *dunyā* (purely worldly pleasure).
- Weakness of the impulse or motive of *dīn* (religion).
- The dominion of the innate stimuli of *fasād*.
- These will be explained below in turn.

Ignorance

Ignorance (*jahl*) is seen by al-Ghazālī as the root of all misery (*shaqāwah*) and the source of every loss (*khusrān*).[3] Throughout his life, and particularly in his late years, as is evident in his works, al-Ghazālī was always concerned to find out what causes people to be ignorant, or more specifically not to perceive realities or truth. In the *Iḥyā'*, for example, he highlights a number of main causes of ignorance in this sense, namely:

1. *Taqlīd*: By *taqlīd* al-Ghazālī specifically means "accepting an opinion (*qawl*) without proof (*ḥujjah*)."As a general rule, *taqlīd*, in the view of al-Ghazālī, "is not a way to knowledge (*laysa ṭarīqan ilā al-'ilm*), neither in *al-uṣūl* (the fundamentals of religion) nor in *al-furū'* (the branches of religion)".Moreover, *taqlīd*, he states, can be a veil which obscures the reality of things from the heart, which, according to his teaching, is the seat of knowledge.[4] Al-Ghazālī noticed that it was this veil that prevented most theologians (*mutakalimūn*), fanatical followers (*muta'aṣibūn*) of the schools of jurisprudence (*madhāhib*) and even righteous men (*ṣāliḥūn*) from the perception of realities.[5]

2. Satisfaction with the mere intellectual sciences while dispensing with the religious knowledge, which is gained by learning and understanding the Qur'an and the Sunnah of the Prophet (ṣ),

or the vice versa. On the one hand, al-Ghazālī believes that anyone who relies entirely on the intellect alone, without benefiting from the light of the Qur'an and the Sunnah, is deluded.[18] On the other hand, he is convinced that anyone who entirely sets aside the intellect and is satisfied with mere *taqlīd* in religion is ignorant.[7] For him, "the intellectual sciences are like food and the knowledge of Sharī'ah are like medicines,"[20] and thus, he adds, one cannot do without the other.[9]

3. Lack of knowledge of the reality of man's own heart (*qalb*):[10] According to al-Ghazālī, the lack of knowledge regarding the reality of man's heart (*qalb*) leads man to be ignorant of his Lord, because man, al-Ghazālī explains, is predisposed to know God simply by reason of his heart (*qalb*), not because of any of his other faculties.[11] If a man, he declares, fails to know his heart (*qalb*), he indeed knows not himself and thus he indeed knows not his Lord.[24] And the one, al-Ghazālī further states, "who knows not his heart is even more ignorant of other things."[13] He believes that most people do not know their hearts and therefore they do not really know their own selves.[26] What has intensified man's ignorance about his own reality, in the view of al-Ghazālī, is that he is wrapped up and involved heavily in worldly works, which have initially resulted from the need for food (*qūt*), dress (*kiswah*), and home (*maskan*).[15] Such engagement, in excess, spoils people's minds and causes them to forget or misconceive not only their real nature, but also the purpose of their creation and their final destination, as al-Ghazālī explains.[28]

Love of the dunyā

Another major root of *fasād* diagnosed by al-Ghazālī is love of the *dunyā*.[29] In this context, al-Ghazālī does not use the term *dunyā* in its literal sense, which is this world's life; he uses it rather to refer to any purely worldly pleasure which does not contribute to the joys of the Afterlife.[30]

This root of *fasād* has been given very considerable emphasis by al-Ghazālī because of its extremely harmful effects. As al-Ghazālī warns us, it is "the beginning of all misdeeds" (*ra's kul khaṭī'h*),[31] "the fountain-head of destructive sins" (*ra's al-khaṭāyā al-muhlikah*),[32] "the root of all deficiency," (*asās kul nuqṣān*) and "the source of all *fasād*" (*manba' kul fasād*).[33] This is why al-Ghazālī considers the *dunyā* a very dangerous enemy to man.[22]

Al-Ghazālī relates various sorts of *fasād* and sins to love of the *dunyā*.[23] Examples of these are the following:

- This love is the root of all engrossing mental distractions (*khawāṭir*) which disturb the concentration of a Muslim's devotional prayer (*ṣalāh*).[36]
- This love stops us from fulfilling the duty of "forbidding wrong" (*al-nahy 'an al-munkar*). This is because greed, which is a symptom of this love, leads to cowardice and weakness.[37]
- This love prevents from loving God for these two loves do not gather in one heart, as al-Ghazālī explains.[38]
- This love leads to various afflictions of the heart, such as envy.[39]

According to al-Ghazālī, what makes people greedy for the *dunyā* is their excessive desire for food and sex.[40] In addition, he explains that preferring the *dunyā* over the Afterlife is man's dominant trait, as Allah says, "Yet you prefer the life of this world, while the Afterlife is finer and more lasting"[41] (Qur'an, 87:16-17). Al-Ghazālī reminds us that there are many aspects of this love. [42] Among them are: love of wealth and love of status.[43]

Weakness of the impulse of religion

A further dangerous root of *fasād* in the eyes of al-Ghazālī is the degrading of the impulse or motive of religion (*bā'ith al-dīn*). By this, he means "the will-power (*quwwah al-irādah*) emerging in response to the signals of certainty (*tanba'ith bi ishārah al-yaqīn*), and taming the desire (*al-shahwah*) which emerges at the direction of devils (*ishārah al-shayāṭīn*)."[44] Thus, the impulse of religion, according to the teachings of al-Ghazālī, is a condition of man's heart[45] and it is one of the major distinctions between men and animals, since it is not found in animals. This denotes that when the impulse of religion degrades, it cannot bring desire under control and this leads to *fasād*.

Dominion of the innate stimuli of fasād

Another big root of *fasād*, according to al-Ghazālī, is the dominion of what he calls the inherent qualities of man which stimulate *fasād* or more specifically sins (*mathārāt al-dhunūb*).[34] In the *Iḥyā'* al-Ghazālī specifies that there are four of such qualities: wildness (*bahīmiyyah*), bestiality (*sab'iyyah*), devilry (*shayṭāniyyah*), and superiority (*rabbāniyyah*).[47] He clarifies that all these qualities are collected in the heart of every man from the time of his creation.[48]

When any of these four qualities becomes predominant and are not controlled, it results in various forms of *fasād*.[37] To further explain this, al-Ghazālī goes on to say that the dominion of anger or irascibility (*ghaḍab*), which is a principle quality of bestiality, causes man to commit the fierce and cruel acts of a predatory animal.[50] Similarly the dominion of appetite or desire (*shahwah*) makes man behave like a beast in acts of greed and lust.[51] Like anger, desire is naturally very rebellious; it often tends to exceed its proper rational limits and causes *fasād*. Al-Ghazālī elucidates that what makes appetite very difficult to control by reason or intellect (*al-'aql*) is that it is perfected or completed in man at a much earlier age, than his reason is.[52] Furthermore, by continuously following and satisfying desire, it develops quickly and thus becomes stronger than the power of reason. This is why desire, in the view of al-Ghazālī, is man's worst enemy.[53] "And since man is distinguished from beast by discernment, but at the same time shares with them anger and appetite, there results in him devilishness. So he becomes evil, using discernment to devise varieties of evil and attaining his purpose by cunning and artifice and deception."[42] In addition, based on the divine element in his soul, man claims lordship for himself, and loves mastery and supremacy and such things.[43]

Phenomena of fasād

Besides the roots of *fasād*, al-Ghazālī diagnoses a number of phenomena of *fasād*, which were prevalent in his time. At least eight major phenomena are very evident in the *iṣlāḥī* works of al-Ghazālī and these will be outlined below.

Widespread weakness and laxity of īmān

One of the phenomena of *fasād* diagnosed by al-Ghazālī is the widespread weakness and laxity of *īmān* (Islamic faith). After ascertaining that this was widespread in his time, al-Ghazālī records in the *Munqidh*[44], the method by which he discovered the reasons behind it. He states that "for a time I went after individual men, questioning those who fell short in following the *shar'* (Islamic revealed Law)."[45] From this investigation, he concluded that there were four reasons behind the laxity of people's *īmān*:[46] These are demonstrated below.

1. Deception by those engrossed in the science of philosophy. Al-Ghazālī mentions two forms of such deception in the *Munqidh*.[59] The first may be summarized as follows: being amazed by the precision of the philosophers in some divisions of their sciences, such as mathematics, many people formed what al-Ghazālī finds[48] a high opinion of the philosophers and started to accept everything they said as truth. Consequently, people blindly followed them even as far as heresy, supposing them to be justified. According to al-Ghazālī, what intensified the deception unwittingly caused by the philosophers was the weak counterarguments of those who opposed them.[61] The second form of this deception is evident in the claim that by studying philosophy, they became followers of wisdom, which in their view is the true meaning of prophesy, and were

thereby absolved from following authority and conducting acts of worship which are—as they claimed—intended for common people in order to control their misdeeds.[50]

2. Having strayed through the path of Sufism. Two examples are mentioned in the *Munqidh* for those whose faith is weakened as a result of this. The first is those who claim that they have reached a degree in mysticism which is beyond the need of regular worship.[51] The second is those who offer one of the specious arguments of the Latitudinarians (*ahl al-ibāḥah*) as an excuse for the slackness of their faith.[64] An example of such an argument is, as it appears in the *Iḥyā'*, the assumption that the purpose of spiritual disciplining (*mujāhadah*) is to completely suppress all desires; and since this is impossible, they deny the religion and licentiously follow their desires.[65]

3. Being confused by the specious arguments of the party of Ta'līmiyyah or Bāṭiniyyah. Al-Ghazālī explains in the *Munqidh* that because of the confusion caused by the fallacious arguments of this party, some people become doubtful of every doctrine, declaring that "the truth is doubtful, the way to it blocked, there is much disagreement about it, and no one view is preferable to any other. Moreover, rational proofs contradict one another so that no reliance can be placed on the opinion of independent thinkers..."[54]

4. Being deceived by the bad actions of those popularly regarded as *'ulamā'*. Al-Ghazālī states that by asking those who have fallen short in following the *shar'* about the cause of their failings, some would reply that "if this were a matter one was bound to observe, then the *'ulamā'* would be those most properly bound to it. But among the most renowned among the learned, so-and-so does not perform the prescribed Prayers, and such a one drinks wine, and another devours the assets of religious endowments and the property of orphans, and another feathers his nest with the lavish largesse of the Sultan without being circumspect over what is *ḥarām* (Islamically

unlawful), and another accepts bribes for his judgments and testimony, and so on in many similar instances!"[67]

Widespread sickness of heart and evil character

A vital phenomenon of *fasād* diagnosed by al-Ghazālī is the wide spread of heart[56] sickness (*amrāḍ al-qulūb*) and evil character (*akhlāq khabīthah*), which, according to his teaching, is a reflection of the former, as we shall see below. In different places in the *Iḥyā'*, he warns that the heart's sickness is noticeably more widespread in his time than in the past, and there is a worrying ignorance about how to treat it, to the extent that this type of knowledge—as he sadly and worryingly notes—has quite vanished.[69]

The ignorance about healing sickness of the heart was a real concern of al-Ghazālī at the stage in view. About this ignorance, he states that "people neglect the knowledge of purifying the hearts and are concerned only with ways to treat physical ailments."[58] Al-Ghazālī's concern was based on his observation that the spread of this sickness was more serious than physical illness and mentions three reasons for this:[59]

1. The affected person does not realise that he is sick.
2. Unlike physical illness, its aftermath (*'āqibah*) does not appear in this life.
3. The lack of doctors (*aṭṭibā'*)[60] to treat it and the vanishing of knowledge about it.[61]

Another reason for al-Ghazālī's concern was that, unlike physical illness, the sickness of the heart "abides even after death, and for all eternity."[62]

In the *Iḥyā'*, al-Ghazālī sets forth in detail the symptoms of this sickness, its causes, and its consequences. In a section entitled "An Exposition of the Signs of the Heart Diseases and the Signs of its Return to Health" (*bayān 'alāmāt amrāḍ al-qulūb wa 'alāmāt 'awdahā ilā al-ṣiḥḥah*) al-Ghazālī presents a general symptom of the sickness, as follows:

Know that each member of the body has been created for a particular function, and that it becomes ill when it is no longer able to perform it, or else does so in a disturbed fashion: the hand ails when it can no longer strike…Likewise the heart falls ill when it becomes incapable of performing the activity proper to it and for which it was created, which is the acquisition of knowledge, wisdom, and gnosis (*ma'rifah*), and the love of Allah and of His worship, and taking delight in remembering Him, preferring these things to every other desire, and using all one's other desires and members for the sake of His remembrance… Therefore, whosoever possesses a thing which is more dear to him than Allah is harbouring a sickness in his heart, just as a man who, loving to eat mud, and having lost his desire for bread and water, must needs suffer a sickness in his belly.[75]

Prevalent spurious religiousness

Al-Ghazālī's diagnosis of *fasād* includes forms of spurious religiousness which, as he observed, were prevalent in his time. One form of such religiousness is extravagance (*tanaṭu'*) of devotion. In various places in the *Iḥyā'*, al-Ghazālī warns against religious extravagance, since it often leads to harmful consequences. For example, he warns against excessive scrupulousness (*wara'*) and considers it a form of extravagance in religiousness.[64] Even if it does not harm the scrupulous person himself, it may, as al-Ghazālī precisely observes, suggest to others that such scrupulousness is vital and thus, because they cannot fulfil even what is easier than this, they would totally ignore scrupulousness altogether.[77] According to al-Ghazālī such a conviction made many people of his time give up trying to live a religious life.[78]

Other forms of spurious devotion diagnosed by al-Ghazālī are those which were represented by the following groups.

1. The majority of Sufis: In the *Iḥyā'* al-Ghazālī severely criticizes most of the Sufis of his time for being idle, for relying on charity, and for imitating pious people in their dress and

words, jus for show and the seeking of followers, while their heart is devoid of true piousness.[79]

2. Groups of worshippers (*arbāb al-'ibādah*): al-Ghazālī diagnoses in the *Iḥyā'* various forms of spurious religious activities as practised by the adherents of the following types of Islamic worship or duties: devotional prayer (*ṣalāh*), recitation of the Qur'an, pilgrimage to Makkah (*ḥajj*), asceticism (*zuhd*) and "commanding right and forbidding wrong" (*al-amr bi al-ma'rūf wa al-nahy 'an al-munkar*).[80]

3. Classes of wealthy people (*arbāb al-amwāl*): al-Ghazālī gives selective examples in the *Iḥyā'* of spurious religious activities performed by groups of wealthy people.[81] A case in point is choosing forms of worship in which no expenditure is necessary while hoarding their money out of stinginess.[82]

Popularity of public wrongs

Another phenomenon of *fasād* diagnosed by al-Ghazālī is the popularity of wrongs (*munkarāt*) which are commonly met with in public. In the *Iḥyā'*, he states that there are many examples of such wrongs in his age, to the extent that it is impossible to enumerate all of them.[83] He nevertheless mentions a representative selection of these wrongs in a chapter entitled "Common Wrongs in Customs" (*al-munkarāt al-ma'lūfah fī al-'ādāt*). This selection, which is likely to have been contemporary, includes wrongs in mosques (*al-masājid*), wrongs in markets (*al-aswāq*), wrongs in streets (*al-shawāri'*), wrongs in bath-houses (*al-ḥammāmāt*), wrongs of hospitality (*al-ḍiyāfah*) and general wrongs.[84]

The main cause behind this phenomenon, as explained by al-Ghazālī, was the virtual disappearance of the knowledge and practice of the duty of "commanding right and forbidding wrong" in his age.[73] Consequently there was a great deal of flattery (*mudāhanah*) among people of his time.[86]

Widespread heretical innovations

Another phenomenon of *fasād* with which al-Ghazālī was greatly concerned was widespread heretical thoughts or forms of heretical innovation (*bid'ah*) in his time. He diagnosed many forms of *bid'ah* during his life. I shall, however, focus on those forms which he considered very dangerous. Such forms may fall into three categories: Sufic deviant thoughts, philosophical heresy, and Bāṭinī deviated teachings.

A. Sufic deviant thoughts

In the *Iḥyā'*, al-Ghazālī classifies some of the claims evolved by some of the Sufis of the time as very harmful ecstasy (*shaṭaḥ*). A case in point of such claims is the claim of excessive love (*'ishq*) of Allah which leads to the assertion of having attained "oneness or unity (*itiḥād*) with Allah, the removal of the veil (*ḥijāb*), seeing (*mushahadah*) Him with the naked eye (*ru'yah*) and mouth to mouth conversation."[87]

According to al-Ghazālī such claims do great harm, particularly to the common folk, since it leads to giving up outward deeds and idleness.[88] Satisfying themselves with the self-justification offered by such claims, several farmers, as al-Ghazālī narrates, relinquished their farms.[77]

Another example of Sufic deviance against which al-Ghazālī warns is the claim of some that they are free from religious commandments, giving false excuses for disobeying the Islamic rules.[90]

B. Philosophical heresy

The second type of thinking which al-Ghazālī has classified as heretical includes a number of metaphysical theories, which were originally developed by ancient philosophers, and which were blindly accepted by a group of people in his time.[91] According to him, the thoughts of philosophers—excluding things which are not to be denied at all, because they are not connected to religion—fall under two categories: the first is what must be counted as unbelief (*kufr*) and the second is what must be counted as heretical innovation (*bid'ah*); out of twenty main wrong doctrines of the philosophers connected to metaphysics, three count as unbelief and the rest count as *bid'ah*.[80] The first three are as follows:[93] (1) There is no resurrection for bodies and only spirits are rewarded and punished. (2) God knows universals but not particulars. (3) The world is everlasting, without beginning or end. However, their doctrine on certain further issues in metaphysics— such as their denial of the attributes of God—is close to that of the Mu'tazilites who, al-Ghazālī declares, should not be considered infidels because of such views.[94]

Although geometry and arithmetic, as part of philosophy,[83] are both permissible (*mubāḥ*) according to the teachings of al-Ghazālī, most of those who practise them have, al-Ghazālī noticed, crossed the line to admit innovations (*bid'ah*).[96]

C. Bāṭinī deviated teachings

The third form of dangerous *bid'ah* diagnosed by al-Ghazālī is the esoteric interpretation of the Bāṭinīs, which dismisses the obvious literal meaning of words in favour of esoteric meanings.[97] In the *Iḥyā'*, al-Ghazālī mentions this method as an example of what he calls heresies (*ṭāmāt*); and he considers it unlawful and capable of great harm. He explains the reason behind this judgment as follows:

> When words are changed from their literal meanings, without either holding fast to authoritive tradition from Ṣāḥib al-Shar' [i.e., the Prophet (ṣ)] or a necessity justified by reason, the loss of confidence in words becomes inevitable and the benefits of the words of God and His Apostle are in sequence nullified. For no trust can be placed in whatever is understood therefrom, while esoteric meaning cannot be verified; rather opinions differ therein and it is open to various interpretations.[98]

Relying on this method, the Bāṭinī s, al-Ghazālī states, destroyed all the Sharī'ah by interpreting all its literal meaning to conform to their own views.[99] According to al-Ghazālī the adherents of this widespread and harmful innovation sought nothing but strange things because human nature is fond of the unusual.[100]

Al-Ghazālī states in the *Munqidh* that although such innovation was weakly supported, it was widespread, due to the weak counterarguments of its critics who out of fanaticism contradict the Bāṭinī s in everything they said, even when their arguments were sound.[89] Thus, hearing these sound arguments and the weak counterarguments of their critics, many were seduced into thinking that the doctrine of the Bāṭinīs is sound.[102]

Fasād of the vast majority of the 'ulamā'

A crucial phenomenon of *fasād* according to the diagnosis of al-Ghazālī is the *fasād* of the vast majority of the *'ulamā'* of his time. In the introduction of the *Iḥyā'*, he states that his time is bereft of true *'ulamā'* and only the superficial, or those who just apparently resemble them (*al-mutarassimūn*), remain, "most of whom have been overcome by Satan and lured by iniquity; every one of them was so wrapped with his immediate fortune that he came to see good as evil and evil as good."[91] This seems the most serious phenomenon of *fasād* in his diagnosis. This is mainly because al-Ghazālī held such *'ulamā'* originally responsible for the general *fasād* of the time. He repeatedly states in the *Iḥyā'* that "the *fasād* of the people is due to the *fasād* of the kings and the *fasād* of the kings is due to the *fasād* of the *'ulamā'*."[92] In his view, had it not been evil judges (*qudāh*) and evil *'ulamā'*, the *fasād* of the kings would have been decreased because they would have been fearful from the forbidding of the *'ulamā'* of their wrongdoing.[93]

After al-Ghazālī's self-*iṣlāḥ*, this phenomenon received very considerable attention from him. In the *Iḥyā'*, al-Ghazālī gives emphasis to the *fasād* of the *'ulamā'* and highlights various symptoms of it. He uses the term evil *'ulamā'* (*'ulamā' al-sū'*) for those who suffer from these symptoms. Examples of these symptoms are listed below.

1. Love of the *dunyā*:[94] The most remarkable symptom of this *fasād* diagnosed by al-Ghazālī is that the *'ulamā'* of his time were ill with love of the *dunyā*.[107] Instead of treating people from this source of *fasād*, the *'ulamā'* themselves became its victims.[108]

2. Envy: Another symptom of the *fasād* of the *'ulamā'* highlighted by al-Ghazālī is envy. He diagnosed the cause of it by stating that seeking wealth and status (*jāh*) through their knowledge is what causes envy between them.[97] Following his habitual approach, al-Ghazālī specifies what he means by the term *jāh*: to dominate the hearts (*mulk al-qulūb*).[98] He further explains how seeking of wealth and status causes envy between the *'ulamā'* themselves.[99]

3. Not forbidding wrongs out of cowardice: In the *Iḥyā'*, al-Ghazālī accuses the *'ulamā'* of his time of lack of courage for they were not fulfilling the duty of "commanding right and forbidding wrong," particularly when the wrongdoer is a ruler.[112] According to him such cowardice resulted from their greed for worldly pleasures.[113]

4. Teaching undeserving students: A further symptom of the *fasād* of the *'ulamā'* according to al-Ghazālī is that they did not mind teaching anyone, regardless of his characters and motives. He noticed that some of the *'ulamā'* were teaching foolish (*sufahā'*) and wicked (*ashrār*) people, who were engaged in wickedness and whose ultimate purpose for attaining knowledge was to argue with *'ulamā'*, and to seek prestige and wealth. What encouraged these *'ulamā'* to do so, in the view of al-Ghazālī, was their love of supremacy, seeking many followers, and boasting, though they were claiming that

their intention was to spread knowledge regardless of who would receive it.[114]

5. Relying on the approach of hope (*rajā'*): Similarly al-Ghazālī accused the preachers of his time of preferring the approach of hope (*rajā'*) over the approach of intimidation although the former was not suitable for the people of his time in his view.[115] Nevertheless, since the aim of the preachers was to please people so that they would praise them in return, they relied on the approach of hope for it is easier on the heart and more pleasant than the other approach.[116] As a result, *fasād* increased and the transgressors persisted in their transgression as al-Ghazālī sadly noted.[117]

6. Pride: Pride is another symptom of *fasād* among the *'ulamā'* according to the diagnosis of al-Ghazālī. He generally thinks that it is very rare to find a scholar (*'ālim*) free from pride. Moreover, according to him, it was very unusual to find a scholar in his time who would have felt sorry for losing the quality of being free from pride.[118]

7. Being fully engaged in controversies and debate: al-Ghazālī accused the *'ulamā'* in his age of being fully engaged in juridical controversial issues. In the *Iḥyā'*, he explains that the reason behind this was that there were celebrities who enjoyed listening to debates in jurisprudence, so the *'ulamā'* favoured what these celebrities favoured but they claimed that they were doing this for the sake of Allah.[119]

8. Fanaticism (*ta'aṣṣub*): According to al-Ghazālī, the evil *'ulamā'* in his age adopted fanaticism (*ta'aṣṣub*) as their rule of conduct and their method of approach (*'ādātahum wa ālātahum*).[108] In the context of discussing the causes of fanaticism and the reasons behind its continuation in his time, al-Ghazālī states in the *Iḥyā'*:

> The *madāris* (religious institutions of learning) have been given to people whom fear of Allah has become little, whose insight into religion has grown weak, whose desire of this present world

has become intense, and greed to seek followers has grown strong. They have not been able to have a follower and attain fame (*jāh*) except through fanaticism. So they have veiled this fact within their own breasts, and have not reminded their followers of the wiles of Satan therein, but indeed they have acted as the agents of Satan in carrying out his wiles against them. So men have continued in fanaticism and have forgotten the major principles of their religion (*ummahāt dīnihim*). Thus they have perished and caused others to perish.[109]

Fasād of ruling members

In addition to the '*ulamā*', al-Ghazālī holds the rulers responsible for the spread of *fasād* in the society. In general, the *fasād* of the subjects (*ra'iyyah*), al-Ghazālī believes, is due to the *fasād* of the kings.[122]

Al-Ghazālī on one hand believes that the caliphate after the rightly guided caliphs passed on to men who—generally speaking—undeservedly occupied it.[123] On the other hand, he legitimized the 'Abbāsid Caliph of the time and the sultans who give him their pledge of allegiance.[124] This legitimization, however, does not mean a complete approval of their policies and administrations.

As in the case of the *fasād* of the '*ulamā*', al-Ghazālī in various places of the *Iḥyā'* diagnoses aspects of *fasād* among ruling members in his time. He states that injustice among them was widespread.[125] One of the most crucial aspects of their *fasād* diagnosed in the *Iḥyā'*, besides their general injustice, is that related to their financial policies. In his detail discussion on what is lawful (*ḥalāl*) and unlawful (*ḥarām*) of the income of the sultans of his time, he states that the majority of their wealth (*amwāl*) is *ḥarām*, and that the *ḥalāl* in their hands is nothing or rare.[126] Similarly he states that the majority of the wealth of the militant men is *ḥarām*.[127] This is mainly because of their unlawful financial policies such as taking (*jizyah*) unjustly,[128] applying (*kharāj*) on Muslims, and accepting bribery (*rashwah*).[129]

In addition, other aspects of *fasād* among ruling members were highlighted by al-Ghazālī's in some of his letters to some Seljuk sovereigns, as shall be seen below.

Al-Ghazālī's *iṣlāḥī* attempts to eradicate the roots of *fasād*

Al-Ghazālī did not satisfy himself with simply getting at the roots of *fasād*, but he, as is evident in his *iṣlāḥī* treatises, attempted to eradicate them. His attempts will be illustrated below in the same order as the roots of *fasād* demonstrated above.

Counteracting the causes of ignorance

The main thoughts of al-Ghazālī which can be considered as counteractions of the causes of ignorance listed above are summarized under the following sub-headings.

Distinguishing between acceptable and unacceptable taqlīd

In general, al-Ghazālī strongly condemns *taqlīd* since it can lead to ignorance or lack of perception of realities, as mentioned above. Rejecting the view of the Ta'līmiyyah that the way to get at truth (*ṭarīq ma'rifah al-ḥaq*) is *taqlīd*, he, in the *al-Mustaṣfā min 'Ilm al-Uṣūl*, which is his latest known book in the genre of *uṣūl al-fiqh*, clarifies that "by *taqlīd* we specifically mean accepting an opinion (*qawl*) without proof (*ḥujjah*) so whenever there is a lack of proof, and truth is not known, neither by common sense (*bi ḍarūrah*) nor by evidence (*bi dalīl*), then imitation (*al-ittibā'*) therein would be based on ignorance (*jahl*)."[118] Furthermore, in the course of his refutation of the Ta'līmiyyah's speculations, he quotes a number of *āyāt* (Qur'anic verses) which, he states, forbid *taqlīd* and direct to knowledge,[119] namely: "Pursue not that you have no knowledge..." (Qur'an, 44:36) "Produce your proof, if you speak truly." (Qur'an, 2:111)

He, however, does not completely oppose *taqlīd*, rather he distinguishes between acceptable and unacceptable *taqlīd*. While he strongly supports the prevailing view of the *'ulamā'* that *taqlīd* is *ḥarām* (Islamically unlawful) in the case of those who are capable of *ijtihād*,[120] he totally refuses the odd argument of a group of Qadariyyah that even *al-'awāmm*, i.e., the ordinary people or general folks, must look profoundly into the evidence (*yalzamuhum al-naẓar fī al-dalīl*).[121] He entirely rejects this opinion on the basis of the following two proofs. The first is, "the consensus of the Companions (*ijmā' al-ṣaḥābah*), for they used to give *fatwā* (jurisprudence views) to the *'awāmm* without ordering them to achieve the rank of *ijtihād*."[134] The second is that, "a consensus has been reached (*al-ijmā' mun'aqid*) that *al-'āmī* (an ordinary man) is charged (*mukallaf*) with *al-aḥkām* (Islamic rules), and thus enjoining him to achieve the rank of *al-ijtihād* is impossible, because it would lead to the abandon of crops and live-stock, the quit of the industries and the crafts, and the ruin of the world when all people would have to seek *al-'ilm* ([religious] knowledge)."[135] In short, *al-ittibā'*, i.e., the following of the *'ulamā'* or the *muftīs* in this context, is, for practical reasons, unavoidable in the case of the *'awāmm* according to al-Ghazālī.

In addition, al-Ghazālī sets out some conditions which have to be met in order that *taqlīd* or *ittibā'* in the case of the *'awāmm* proves to be acceptable. With respect to seeking *fatwā*, a *'āmī* must ask only a person who is known for *'ilm*, i.e., religious knowledge, and *'adālah* (righteousness).[136]

In the matter of *īmān* (Islamic faith), however, al-Ghazālī necessitates, as in the *Iḥyā'* for example, that every *mukallaf* firstly learn and understand the *shahādah*, i.e., there is no god but Allah and Muḥammad is the Messenger of Allah (ṣ), and secondly firmly believe in it without any doubt or hesitation.[125] This, however, can, as he assures, be obtained by mere *taqlīd* without necessarily the means of investigation (*baḥth*), penetration (*naẓar*), and formulating evidence (*taḥrīr al-addillah*).[138]

This is why al-Ghazālī seriously attacks in *Fayṣal al-Tafriqah bayn al-Islām wa al-Zandaqah* a group of *mutakallimūn* who charge the *'awāmm* with unbelief (*kufr*) just because they do not acquire Islamic creed through their own way of *kalām*.[127] He accuses them of being extremist, because firstly they restrict the mercy of Allah and the entrance of Paradise to a limited group among the *mutakallimūn*, and secondly they are ignorant of what has been reported, through *tawātur* way, that the Prophet (ṣ) and his Companions accepted the Islam of the illiterate Arabs who did not concern themselves with the science of reasoning (*'ilm al-dalīl*).[128] Similarly, he challenges the speculation that the means to find *īmān* is *kalām* and abstract reasoning, because *īmān*, he declares, "is light (*nūr*) which is cast by Allah on the hearts of His servants as a bestowal and gift from Him."[141] Al-Ghazālī, however, does not deny that the reasoning of the *mutakallimūn* may lead to *īmān*, but this, according to him, is very rare and it is not the only way to *īmān*.[142]

According to al-Ghazālī, *kalām* is not only unnecessary for the *'awāmm* but also extremely risky, because it may lead this group of people to unbelief (*shirk*).[131] To warn against this potential risk, he composed his book *Iljām al-'Awāmm 'an 'Ilm al-Kalām* (Restraining the General Folks from the Science of *kalām*). In the opening of the book, he states that one of the purposes of the book was to distinguish between what is obligatory on general people in matters of faith and that which they should be restrained from.[132] Answering a possible objection that forbidding the *'ammī* from investigation in matters of faith would lead him to be ignorant about the belief in Allah and his divine attributes, which are obligatory, he asserts that firmly rooted belief (*al-taṣdīq al-jāzim*) has six levels and that some of which can be obtained by the *'awāmm* without being involved in *kalām* and that the Qur'anic evidences are enough to secure their faith.[145] Although he states that the most superior belief is that which is supported by sound reasoning, he still believes that the *'ammī*, with such acceptance of faith, is no doubt a believer.[134]

To fully appreciate al-Ghazālī's position from *taqlīd* on matters of faith, we need to be acquainted with his view on the role of the intellect on these matters, which shall become clear below.

Assuring the need for both intellectual knowledge and religious knowledge

Against the two extreme attitudes towards intellectual knowledge and religious knowledge, demonstrated above, al-Ghazālī assures the need for both and calls for unity and harmony between them.[147] To correctly understand his position from both, we need first to be acquainted with what he means by the two types of knowledge.

By intellectual knowledge (*al-'ulūm al-'aqliyyah*), he means that "by which the innate intellect makes its judgments and which does not come into existence through imitation (*taqlīd*) and hearing (*samā'*);"[148] and he divides it into: a) axiomatic (*ḍarūrīyah*) such as man's knowledge that one person cannot be in two places, and b) acquired knowledge (*'ulūm muktasabah*) which is gained by learning and deduction (*istidlāl*).[149] While by religious knowledge, he means that which is gained by way of acceptance on authority (*taqlīd*) from the prophets and it is "acquired by learning the Book of Allah and the Sunnah of the Apostle of Allah, and understanding their meaning after having heard them."[150]

Now regarding the need for these types of knowledge, al-Ghazālī asserts that with religious knowledge, man's soul can be perfected in quality and cured from its diseases.[151] Intellectual knowledge, he adds, is not sufficient to cure man's soul, though it is needed.[152] Explaining how the intellect is needed, while it is insufficient alone, he further states:

> ...just as the intellect is not sufficient to make continuous the causes of physical health, but needs to gain the experiential knowledge of the properties of medicines and herbs by learning them from the physicians (*aṭibbā'*) and not by reading in books, since the intellect alone cannot find this knowledge. But after

it is heard it cannot be understood except by means of the intellect.[153]

Thus, he concludes, "the intellect cannot dispense with hearing (*samāʿ*) [i.e., revelation in this context] nor can hearing (*samāʿ*) dispense with the intellect."[154]

Rejecting the supposition of those who think that intellectual knowledge is opposed to that of religion, and that it is impossible to achieve harmony between them, he declares that such supposition "arises from blindness in the eye of insight (*ʿayn al-baṣīrah*)."[155]

Despite his assertion of the need for intellectual knowledge, al-Ghazālī does not consider all intellectual sciences praiseworthy. In this respect, he divides these sciences into three types:

A. Praiseworthy knowledge (*ʿulūm maḥmūdah*): all the intellectual sciences which are connected with what is beneficial to the present world, as medicine and arithmetic, and they are two divisions: a) *farḍ kifāyah* (Islamically ordained on the Muslim community as a whole): every branch of knowledge which is indispensable to the welfare of this world, such as medicine and arithmetic; but if some members of the community undertake it, the obligation falls away from others; and b) *faḍīlah* (a virtuous knowledge but not obligatory) which is the extra investigation into the details of the above sciences, which, though helpful in reinforcing the efficacy of whatever is absolutely needed, is not necessary.[156]

B. Blameworthy (*madhmūmah*) knowledge: any intellectual knowledge which is blamed for one of the following three reasons:

   1. When it leads either its possessor or someone else into harm, such as magic and talismans which are used for harming people.[157]
   2. When it is harmful to its possessor in the majority of cases, such as astrology, which in itself is not blameworthy, for

it has two parts: (a) one concerned with calculation, and (b) one concerned with the decree of the stars and is inferential.[158] The Prophet (ṣ) has warned against it for three reasons: (a) It is harmful to most people who get the impression that the stars cause effects, as most of man's observation is limited to the subordinate causes.[159] (b) The rules based on it are purely conjecture (*takhmīn maḥḍ*) and prognostication is right only by coincidence; thus, disapproval of it lies in the fact that it is ignorance from this respect.[160] (c) There is no benefit in it and results in a great loss of valuable time; what it decreed is finished, and it is impossible to guard against it.[161]

3. When its practitioner does not gain a real learning advantage because it is beyond his depth, as learning details of sciences before their major principles, or the obscure things before the plainly seen; so such knowledge is blameworthy for this particular practitioner.[162]

C. Permissible (*mubāḥ*) knowledge: such as learning poetry which has nothing unsound in it, history, and the like.[151]

However, with regard to the religious (*shar'iyyah*) branches of knowledge, al-Ghazālī states that they are all praiseworthy (*maḥmudah kulluhā*), but sometimes they are confused with those which are thought to be religious, though really blameworthy (*madhmūmah*),[164] as shall be further explained below.

Revealing aspects of the reality of man

It has been stated earlier that one of the major causes of ignorance according to al-Ghazālī is the lack of knowing the reality of man's own heart (*qalb*), which leads man to be ignorant about his reality and his Lord. As a counter to this, al-Ghazālī reveals in the *Iḥyā'* various aspects of man's reality, which shall be briefly illustrated under the following sub-headings.

A. The essential characteristics of man's heart

One fundamental aspect of the reality of man can be identified, in the view of al-Ghazālī, by exposing the essential characteristics of man's heart (*qalb*). This is based on his belief that if a man knows his heart, he would know himself.[165] This is why al-Ghazālī often stresses the importance of the knowledge of the heart. For him "the knowledge of the heart (*qalb*) and of the true meaning of its qualities is the root of religion."[166]

For the purpose of exposing the characteristics of man's heart as one aspect of his reality, al-Ghazālī devoted the first *kitāb* (book) of the third *rub'* (quarter) of the *Iḥyā'* to this matter. At the beginning of this *kitāb*, he clarifies that the word heart (*qalb*) does not refer to the physical heart; however, it is employed—as in the Qur'an—in the following sense: "a spiritual, divine subtlety (*laṭīfah*)...which is the essence of man...is what perceives, knows, and realizes...is spoken to, punished, blamed and responsible."[167]

For various states of this spiritual essence, al-Ghazālī applies three other terms: spirit (*rūḥ*), self or soul (*nafs*), and intellect (*'aql*).[168] Because he noticed that there was great obscurity about the difference and applications of these terms among the *'ulamā'*, al-Ghazālī explains their meanings and applications right at the beginning of the abovementioned *kitāb*: entitled *Kitāb Sharḥ 'Ajā'ib al-Qalb* (Book of Explanation of the Wonders of the Heart).[169]

Unlike the body, which belongs to the material world, the heart in the teachings of al-Ghazālī is immortal. Thus, it is more precious and essential than any other part of man. In his view, it is considered the sixth unique sense of man, which can also be called *nūr* (light).[170] What is perceived by this sense—he believes—cannot be mistaken, whereas what is perceived by citation can be wrong—e.g. seeing what is far, close and what is small, big.[171]

Only through the heart—al-Ghazālī believes—man is prepared to know Allah, and not by any members of his body.[172] It is the means by which man works for Allah, strives towards Him, and draws near to Him.[173] Allah's acceptance or rejection of man relies on the condition of his heart.[174]

In addition, the good and evil qualities of a man's external aspect are merely reflections of the condition of his heart—al-Ghazālī points out.[175] Moreover, all members of the body are originally under the control of the heart and all follow its instructions.[176]

In order to fully understand the relationship between the heart and the bodily members, al-Ghazālī specifies that the original purpose for which the heart is created is to travel over the spiritual stations (*manāzil*) to the meeting of Allah.[177] In its spiritual journey, the heart is in need of two essential things: the body as a mount and knowledge as provisions.[178] Thus, caring for the body and maintaining it is—al-Ghazālī believes—a necessity for fulfilling the original purpose of the heart.[179] For this purpose, the heart is provided with the following helpers or soldiers (*junūd*) according to al-Ghazālī's terminology: First, for the need of feeding the body, the necessary appetites or desires (*al-shahwāt*) are created in the heart, and the organs are created as their tools.[180] Second, for protecting the body from destructive things, anger (*ghaḍab*) and the hand and foot, which function under the demands of anger, are created.[181] Third, for knowing nourishment, the senses and the sense organs are created.[182]

All these soldiers are originally submissive to the heart, but the soldiers of anger (*ghaḍab*) and desire (*shahwah*) may, as al-Ghazālī explains,[183] oppose it to the extent of dominating and enslaving it and thus becomes a real loser, as it is being cut off from its spiritual journey. However, the heart has other soldiers, namely knowledge (*'ilm*), wisdom (*ḥikmah*), and reflection (*tafakkur*), which are provided—al-Ghazālī further explains—as helpers against anger (*ghaḍab*) and desire (*shahwah*).[184]

Furthermore, the unique characteristics of man's heart are, according to al-Ghazālī, knowledge and will (*irādah*) which are not found in animals.[185] Al-Ghazālī illustrates that this will (*irādah*) is different than that of desire (*shahwah*) and can even be contrary to desire.[186] Without this *irādah*, the judgment of the intellect or reason (*al-'aql*), which perceives the consequences of matters, would be wasted, because this *irādah* is the spur that moves the bodily members according to the judgment of reason.[187]

B. The real purpose of man's life

Another aspect of the reality of man, which is clarified by al-Ghazālī, is the real purpose of man's life. This can be seen as a response to the people's forgetfulness or failure to know the real purpose of their life, which resulted from their full busyness and engagement in worldly works, as mentioned above.

Al-Ghazālī's account on this aspect is based on his rejection of some assumptions about the purpose of man's life. Five of these assumptions are worth mentioning before presenting what is regarded the real purpose of life in the view of al-Ghazālī. The first is of those who think that the purpose of life is just to survive for some time, so they work hard to gain food and then eat to be able to work again and so on.[188] The second assumption which is rejected by al-Ghazālī is of those who claim that the aim of this life is not to be exhausted by hard work, but rather to enjoy life by satisfying the desires for food and sex, which in their view is the ultimate happiness.[189] The third wrong assumption in the view of al-Ghazālī is of those who think that achieving happiness is the purpose of life and it consists in gaining big wealth, so they work day and night for this purpose.[190] The fourth view about the purpose of life, which al-Ghazālī rejects, is of those who assume that widespread fame is what brings happiness in this life, so they exhaust themselves in gaining money not to spend it on food but in getting expensive things in order to attract attention and seen to be wealthy.[191] The fifth rejected assumption is of those who claim that happiness is not about gaining respect and influence, so their efforts are directed towards gaining wide political authorities so that their orders would be followed.[192]

Totally unlike these assumed purposes of life, the real purpose of life according to the teachings of al-Ghazālī is to prepare for being qualified for attaining the otherworldly happiness, which is, he believes, the true ultimate aim of man and is the true blessing as it consists of life without death (*baqā' lā fanā' lah*), joy without sorrow (*surūr lā ghamm fīh*), knowledge without ignorance (*'ilm lā jahl ma'ah*), and wealth without poverty (*ghinā lā faqr ba'dah*).[193]

C. The true perfection of man

A further aspect of the reality of man which is illuminated by al-Ghazālī is the true perfection of man. Although al-Ghazālī admits that evilness is part of human nature,[194] he believes that man can achieve true perfection in this life.[195]

However, as in the case of man's purpose of life, the true perfection of man was—as al-Ghazālī noticed—widely confused with fancied perfection.[196] For the purpose of unveiling the truth on this critical matter, al-Ghazālī devoted a section in the *Iḥyā'* titled: "Exposing real perfection and fancied (*wahmī*) perfection which is not real." In this section he sets criteria for true perfection.

For al-Ghazālī what forms true perfection of man are the qualities that are characterised by both eternality in a sense of accompanying man's soul after death, and usefulness in the Afterlife in a sense of bringing man's soul nearer to Allah.[197] Based on these criteria, al-Ghazālī explains that man's true perfection has three aspects.[198] The first is the perfection of knowledge that consists of knowing Allah, His attributes, His works, and His wisdom in the creations. The second aspect of perfection is power that is needed only as a mean to knowledge. The third aspect of perfection is freedom (*ḥurriyyah*) from enslavement to carnal desires.

In light of this concept of perfection, al-Ghazālī states that most people are concerned with what they mistakenly think is perfection, namely fame, and wealth which are not eternal.[199]

Guiding to the way of being free from love of the dunyā

Since love of the *dunyā* (purely worldly pleasure) is a very dangerous cause of *fasād*, as explained earlier, al-Ghazālī paid considerable attention to attempting to show how to be free from this love. His effort can be divided into two major thrusts: the first is the explication of the reality of the *dunyā* and the second is the illustration of the true nature of death and the Afterlife.

Explicating the reality of the dunyā

In the *Iḥyā'*, al-Ghazālī explicates the dispraise (*dhamm*) of the *dunyā*, its reality, its features, the need of it, and the way by which it deceives people.[188] By this detailed explanation, he aims to warn from the harm of the *dunyā* so that it can be avoided.[189] In his view, to remove its harmful love from the heart it is not enough that its lovers know the dispraise of the *dunyā* but also they should know what is meant by the dispraised *dunyā* and how to distinguish between that which should be avoided in it from that which should not be shunned.[202]

The dispraised *dunyā*, al-Ghazālī explains, is every purely worldly desire that would not have any fruit in the Afterlife at all,[203] and is called *hawā*[204] (base desire). Consequently, he excludes two types of worldly desires from the dispraised *dunyā*: any desire in the worldly life the fruit of which continues into the Afterlife, and every desire that is necessary for survival and health in this life, unless the intention behind it is purely worldly.[205]

Attempting to show to what extent the *dunyā* in this sense is dispraised, al-Ghazālī quotes and comments on numerous influential citations from Prophetic traditions (*akhbār*), non-Prophetic *exempla* (*āthār*), and exhortations (*mawā'iẓ*) which dispraise the *dunyā*.[206] He, however, does not quote from the Qur'an because, as he points out, the *āyāt* on this theme are so many and so obvious to be cited.[207]

In order to explain how the *dunyā* deceives people, al-Ghazālī illustrates some remarkable features of it using imaginary examples.[208] Among these imaginary examples are:

- In its quick and invisible movement, the *dunyā* like shadow appears still, but in reality it is moving continuously, and its movement is not noticed except when it disappears.[209]
- In its unnoticed decisiveness, the *dunyā* is similar to confused dreams in that their decisiveness is not realized except after awakening.[210]
- In its enmity for its people and its dreadful harm, the *dunyā* is like a woman who attracts men to marry her, but kills them after they do.[211]
- In that its appearance does not reflect its evil essence, the *dunyā* is like an elderly woman who puts on adornments to deceive people by her look.[212]

Following these and other imaginary examples of the *dunyā*, al-Ghazālī exposes how people have become fully engaged in the *dunyā* and how they have misunderstood the purposes of this life and have thus gone astray.[213] To fulfil this aim, al-Ghazālī first classifies the substances[202] of the *dunyā* and highlights their main benefits for man.[203] Second, he specifies their relationships with man: a relation with the heart (*al-qalb*), i.e., his love for them, and another relation with the body, i.e., being busy in making them usable.[216] Third, he discusses in detail the causes, the needs, and the consequences of the crafts and careers generated from the second relation of man with the substances of the *dunyā*.[217] Finally, he gives various examples of people whose way of thinking had been spoiled by the full engagement in the works of the *dunyā*, and thus hold false views about how to live in this life.[218]

Al-Ghazālī also clarifies the real purpose of this world by repeated reminder that this world is only the sowing-ground of the next (*al-dunyā mazra'h al-ākhirah*).[207] From this aspect, the world is very essential: it is a venue for the happiness in the Afterlife, which is the only complete or perfect happiness in the teachings of al-Ghazālī, as stated earlier. In order to gain this happiness, however, its necessary means need to be achieved in this life.[208] This is why each breath in this life is considered by al-Ghazālī as "a precious jewel which does not have an equivalent substitute."[221]

Based on this discussion, it is wrong to assume, as al-Ghazālī explains, that hating the *dunyā* is intended in itself.[222] He believes that the perfect position to adopt regarding the *dunyā* is neither to hate nor to love it, as both distract from the love of Allah.[223] He also believes that the way of totally removing the love of the *dunyā* from the heart is by patiently living an abstinent (*zuhd*)[212] life.[213]

The above account, however, is only a general treatment for the malady of love of the *dunyā*, and since the *dunyā* consists, as al-Ghazālī states,[214]of various elements, he also gives a detailed treatment for each primary element which is considered an aspect of the love the *dunyā*. Among these primary elements is, for example, love of wealth (*al-māl*), which al-Ghazālī discusses in a considerable detail.[227]

Illustrating the true nature of death and the afterlife

In addition to explicating the reality of the *dunyā*, al-Ghazālī illustrates the true nature of death and the Afterlife in the concluding *kitāb* (book) of the *Iḥyā'* as an attempt to awaken the heedless lovers of the *dunyā*.

After refuting three false and mistaken notions about the nature of death, al-Ghazālī exposes death as only a change in the state of man in which the spirit (*al-rūḥ*) after leaving the body—i.e., the body is no longer subject to its dictates—is not extinguished but rather it will continue to survive either in a condition of torment or bliss.[216] Between the states of death and life, he continues, there are two differences: The first is that man upon death is deprived of all his bodily parts as he is deprived from all of his belongings and relatives and the second is that certain things which have never been disclosed to man in life are going to be revealed to him after death.[229]

In addition to this exposition of the true nature of death, al-Ghazālī covers, in the same *kitāb*, other topics related to death, its preludes and consequences, and the conditions of the next world, so that, as he states, "this may act as an encouragement to preparedness."[230] This is because, he believes, "preparation for something can never be easy unless its memory is constantly renewed in the heart, and this can only be done through reminding oneself by paying attention to those things which cause it to be recalled and by looking to those matters which tell of it."[231]

Introducing measures to strengthen the impulse of religion

To resolve weakness of the impulse of religion (*bāʿith al-dīn*), al-Ghazālī introduces measures by which this impulse or motive is strengthened. In his view, this can be strengthened in two primary ways: a) Reflecting on the fruits of struggling against (*mujāhadah*) what oppose the impulse of *dīn*, i.e., the desires (*al-shahawāt*); and b) training the will-power (*quwwah al-irādah*) gradually to overcome the desires by acting against them.[232]

In addition to these measures, al-Ghazālī suggests a negative way to strengthen this impulse. That is weakening the motive of passion (*bāʿith al-hawā'*), against which the impulse of *dīn* continuously struggles; the weaker the motive of passion becomes, the stronger the strength of *dīn* would be, and vice versa, as al-Ghazālī teaches us.[233] According to al-Ghazālī's teachings, the motive of passion is weakened by self disciplining, as shall be further explained below.

Withstanding the innate stimuli of fasād

Al-Ghazālī discusses how to withstand the innate stimuli of *fasād*, when he deals with what he calls the disciplining of the soul (*riyāḍah al-nafs*). Since the teachings of al-Ghazālī on this form of disciplining are going to be discussed below under the means of treating sickness of the heart, it seems better to postpone the discussion on this point till then.

Al-Ghazālī's *iṣlāḥī* treatments of the phenomena of *fasād*

In addition to his attempts to eradicate the roots of the *fasād*, al-Ghazālī was predominantly concerned, at this stage in his life under study, with treating the phenomena of *fasād* diagnosed by him. The purpose of this section is to show how al-Ghazālī treated these phenomena. For each phenomenon mentioned above, particular treatments are evident in al-Ghazālī's works of *iṣlāḥī* nature, as will be shown below.

Prescribing remedies for the weakness of īmān

After analysing the four reasons behind the phenomenon of widespread weakness and laxity of *īmān* (Islamic faith) as mentioned above, al-Ghazālī mentions in the *Munqidh* four remedies for this phenomenon.[222]

The first treatment is for those who were perplexed by the teachings of the Taʿlīmites or Bāṭinīs. The treatment for them is, al-Ghazālī says, "what we have mentioned in our book *al-Qisṭās al-Mustaqīm* (The Correct Balance)."[235] In *al-Qisṭās*, al-Ghazālī records an argumentative dialogue between him and a Bāṭinī who questioned him and disputed with him over the true balance by which true knowledge is perceived. The dialogue starts with the following question from the Bāṭinī:

> I see that you claim the perfection of knowledge. By what balance, then, is true knowledge perceived? Is it by the balance of independent reasoning (*al-ra'y*) and analogy (*al-qiyās*)? But that is extremely contradictory and ambiguous and is the cause of disagreement among men. Or is it by the balance of authoritative instruction (*al-taʿlīm*)? In this case you would be obliged to follow the infallible Teacher-Imam-but I do not see you desirous of seeking him out.[224]

After totally rejecting balancing true knowledge by independent reasoning and analogy, al-Ghazālī states that he weighs knowledge by the "correct balance" following the Qur'an[237] [Qur'an, 17:35]. According to him, this balance consists of five Qur'anic scales of knowledge.[238]

By being asked about the way by which he knew the correctness of this balance, al-Ghazālī answers:

> I also know that by authoritative teaching (*al-taʿlīm*) but from the Imam of Imams Muḥammad b. ʿAbdullāh b. ʿAbd al-Muṭṭalib (*ṣ*). For I, though I do not see him, hear his teaching which has come to me through impeccable transmission (*tawātur*) which I cannot doubt. His teaching is simply the Qur'an, and the clearness of the correctness of the Qur'an's scales is known from the Qur'an itself.[239]

Following that, he explains in detail each of the five scales by elucidating its meaning, its standard, and its use in argumentation.[240] Then, he mentions examples of the scales by which Bāṭinīs weighed their arguments and he highlights their falsity.[241] Finally, he discusses the dispension by Prophet Muḥammad (*ṣ*) and the *ʿulamā'* from any other Imam.[242]

The second treatment targets those who offer one of the specious arguments of the Latitudinarians (*ahl al-ibāḥah*) as an excuse for the slackness of their faith. Al-Ghazālī says in the *Munqidh*: "as for the fanciful assertions of the Latitudinarians (*ahl al-ibāḥah*), we have listed their specious arguments under seven categories and resolved them in our book *Kīmyā' al-Saʿādah* (The Alchemy of Happiness)."[231]

The third treatment is directed to those "whose faith has become corrupt through philosophy to the extent of rejecting the very principle of prophesy (*nubuwwah*)."[232] For them, al-Ghazālī discusses in the *Munqidh*[245] the true nature of prophesy and its existence.[234]

This discussion is founded on the main argument of al-Ghazālī that man goes into various stages in perception, and in each stage he perceives particular categories of existents by specific means of perception. Al-Ghazālī lists eight stages of perception:[247]

1. The stage of touching in which certain categories of existents are perceived such as heat and cold, moisture and dryness, smoothness and roughness.
2. The stage of sighting in which colours and shapes are perceived.
3. The stage of hearing of sounds and tones.
4. The stage of tasting.
5. The stage of perceiving the other sensibles.
6. The stage of discernment (*tamyīz*) at nearly the age of seven, in which things additional to the world of sensibles are perceived.
7. The stage of perceiving through the intellect (*al-ʿaql*), in which things necessary, possible, and impossible that do not occur in the previous stages are apprehended.
8. The stage of perceiving through prophecy, in which things beyond the ken of intellect are seen, i.e., the unseen (*al-ghayb*).

Against the doubt of some intellectuals about the existence of things perceptible through prophecy, al-Ghazālī states that they do not have any supporting reason except that they have not attained that stage themselves.[248] Moreover, he presents two further proofs for its existence. The first is that there is an analogous sample of the special character of prophecy; in that which is apprehended in dreaming.[249] "For the sleeper perceives the unknown that will take place in the future, either explicitly or in the guise of an image, the meaning of which is disclosed by interpretation."[250] The second proof is that there is knowledge in the world of the same sort as that perceptible through prophesy; that is knowledge which could not conceivably be obtained by the intellect or observation alone, but can be acquired only by a divine inspiration.[251] "For instance there are some astrological rules (*aḥkām nujūmiyyah*)[240] based on phenomena which occur only once every thousands years; how, then, could knowledge of that be obtained empirically?!"[241]

In addition to the above discussion, al-Ghazālī discusses the claim of those who verbally profess belief in prophecy, but equate the prescriptions of revelation with philosophic wisdom. According to al-Ghazālī, this is in reality a disbelief in prophecy because "faith in prophecy is to acknowledge the affirmation of a stage beyond reason: in it an eye penetrates whereby a special perception of certain perceptibles (*mudrakāt khāṣah*) is apprehended; from the perception of these, the intellect is excluded."[242]

Attempting to convince them of the possibility of the existence of such prophetic perception, al-Ghazālī relies on proofs drawn from arguments which pertain to the philosophers' own science. Setting forth examples of marvellous perceptions acknowledged by natural philosophers and astrologers as 'special perceptions,' al-Ghazālī wonders how those who are influenced by philosophers believe in such perception, while they deny the prophetic special perceptions which are confirmed by miracles![255]

The fourth treatment is devoted to tackling the weakness of faith resulting from scandalous conduct of the *'ulamā'*. This treatment consists of three lines of thought,[256] which are summarized as follows:

1. The *'ālim*[257] who commits forbidden deeds knows that such deeds are prohibited, and yet he does so because his desire overcomes him as in the case of an ordinary man.
2. The ordinary man ought to believe that the *'ālim* can be brought to safety even if he leaves some duties undone because of the merit of his knowledge, though it might be additional evidence against him. But the ordinary man has no intercessor whatsoever if he gives up good works.
3. True knowledge stands between the learned man and commission of sins, except slips from which, in moments of weakness, no man is free. This sort of knowledge, however, is not attained by means of the various types of knowledge with which most people busy themselves.

Teaching how to cure sickness of the heart and refine character

As an *iṣlāḥī* response to the wide spread of sickness of the heart and bad characters, al-Ghazālī taught how to cure sickness of the heart and refine character. In the *Iḥyā'*, al-Ghazālī gives two accounts of how sickness of the heart can be treated and how the traits of character may be refined: the first is general and the second is detailed. These two accounts are briefly presented below. Before this, however, it is worth listing what can be considered as guiding rules in al-Ghazālī's treatment.

Setting out guiding rules for curing sickness of the heart and refining character

Throughout the *Iḥyā'*, one comes across what can be considered as guiding rules or principles for curing sickness of the heart and refining the character. The most striking of such rules are the following:

Whenever the cause of a disease is not known, such disease cannot be cured, because curing it is nothing but treating its causes.[246]

The disease does not vanish unless its origins are suppressed or uprooted and any other way of treating it is only an easement for it, but the disease appears again and again.[259]

There has to be a great deal of seriousness in treating a particular disease after knowing its causes and danger.[260]

The heart diseases should be treated one by one and in order.[261]

Patience is an essential pillar in the treatment of sickness of the heart and refining character.[262]

Awareness of the harm of a disease, without will and strength, is not enough.[263]

Every disease needs a special theoretical knowledge, as well as an empirical action to treat it.[264]

*Providing a general account for curing sickness of the heart and
refining character*

In the *Iḥyā'*, al-Ghazālī gives the second "book" (*kitāb*) of the third
"quarter' (*rub'*) the following title: "The Book of Disciplining the
Soul, Refining the Character, and Curing the Sicknesses of the
Heart" (*Kitāb Riyāḍah al-Nafs wa Tahdhīb al-Akhlāq wa Mu'ālajah
Amrāḍ al-Qulūb*). The purpose of this *kitāb*, as al-Ghazālī himself
clarifies, is not to mention the treatments for particular sickness
of the heart or to give details about refining specific traits of
character, but rather to teach in an overall way how to treat
sickness of the heart and how the traits of character can be refined
as an introduction to a more detailed discussion of this topic.[265]
The main points which show how al-Ghazālī fulfilled this purpose
are presented below under the following sub-headings.

A.   Unveiling the true nature of good and bad character

To unveil the true nature of good and bad character, al-Ghazālī
first examines some previous sayings on what good character is,
and concludes that they only treat the fruit of good character,
not its essence, and they do not even cover all of its fruits.[266]
Then, he defines a trait of character in general as follows: "a
firmly established condition of the soul (*hay'ah rāsikhah fī al-
nafs*), from which actions proceed easily without any need for
thinking or deliberation."[267] Thus, a good character according to
al-Ghazālī is a name given for this condition, if it causes beautiful
and praiseworthy acts, i.e., those which are acknowledged by
the intellect and the Sharī'ah (Islamic Revealed Law), whereas
a bad character trait is a name for the condition which causes
ugly acts.[268]

In the light of this definition, al-Ghazālī states that character
is none of the following: a) the acts themselves, for there may be
a man of generous character, for example, but does not make
donation because of lack of wealth or any other obstacles; b) the

ability to act, since every man has been created to be by disposition (*fiṭrah*) capable of acting ugly or beautifully; and c) one's knowledge of the beautiful and the ugly, for knowledge pertains to both in the same way.[269]

To elucidate more, al-Ghazālī compares and contrasts between "creation" (*khalq*) and "character" (*khuluq*), as the former refers to the external form of man, while the latter refers to the inward or the internal form, but both forms can be either ugly or beautiful. Moreover, as man's external appearance looks perfectly beautiful only when all his features are beautiful, so too in order to achieve beautiful character in all aspects, the following four pillars of man's internal must all be beautiful, i.e., settled, balanced, and in the correct proportion to each other: the faculty of rationalness (*quwwah al-'ilm*), the faculty of irascibleness (*quwwah al-ghaḍab*), the faculty of desire (*quwwah al-shahwah*), and the faculty which makes a just equilibrium between these three things (*quwwah al-'adl bayn hādhih al-quwā al-thalāthah*).[270]

B. Specifying criteria for good character

For each of the four faculties mentioned above, al-Ghazālī specifies the criteria by which its goodness can be recognised:

> The faculty of rationalness (*quwwah al-'ilm*) is sound and good when it is easily able to distinguish honesty from lies in speech, truth from falsehood in beliefs, and beauty from ugliness in actions. When this faculty is sound it bears fruit in the form of wisdom (*ḥikmah*), which is the chief of the good traits of character…Regarding the faculty of anger (*quwwah al-ghaḍab*), this is sound when its movements lie within the bounds required by wisdom. Likewise, the faculty of desire (*quwwah al-shahwah*) is sound and good when it under the command of wisdom, by which I mean the command of the *shar'* (Islamic revealed law) and the intellect (*al-'aql*). As for the faculty of making a just equilibrium (*quwwah al-'adl*), it is this which sets desire and anger under the command of the intellect and the *shar'*.[271]

C. Proving the possibility of changing the traits of character

In this general account, al-Ghazālī also proves that the traits of character are susceptible to change. This is his response to the claim of those who state that "the traits of a man's character cannot conceivably be refined, and that human nature is immutable."[272] He states that their claim, which is due to their deficiency, remissness, foulness, and slothness, may be supported by two things: firstly, as the created outward form (*khalq*) of man cannot be changed, and so is the case with the inward form, i.e., character (*khuluq*), secondly, goodness of character requires suppression of one's desire and anger, which are part of human nature, and thus this, as tested by means of a long inward struggle, is impossible.[261] In order to refute this view and unveil the reality of this matter, al-Ghazālī adduces the following points in support of the possibility of changing the traits of character:[274]

- All commandments, discipline, and teachings would be useless, if the traits of character were unchangeable.
- Since it is possible to change even the character of an animal through training, how could such change be denied with respect to man.
- Although anger and desire cannot be suppressed and dominated completely, yet they can be rendered docile by means of self-discipline.

Al-Ghazālī, however, admits that men's temperaments vary in their susceptibleness.[275] This, al-Ghazālī explains, depends on two factors: the first is the original strength of man's instinct (*gharīzah*) and its existing time length.[276] The second factor for this disparity is the degree to which man acts in accordance with his traits of character—as they are reinforced by acting accordingly—and the degree of his satisfaction with them.[277] Accordingly, al-Ghazālī classifies people into four degrees: a) Those who are simply innocent (*ghufl*), but not indulged into desires and thus their character can be refined in a very short time; b) those who know evilness and know they are not acting righteously as they should, but still follow their desires as they are controlled by them; the refining of the character of such people is possible but it is more intractable than the first; c) those who regard evil character as right; the reforming of such people is almost impossible and very rare; and d) those who, due to their being reared with corrupted way of thinking and work accordingly, believe that merit lies in evilness; they are the most difficult to reform.[278]

D. Demonstrating ways for discovering the faults of the self

Since discovering the faults of the self or the soul, according to al-Ghazālī, is a prerequisite for treating them, he teaches four ways by which a man may discover the faults which acquire his soul (*'uyūb nafsih*):[279]

1. Being a disciple of a *shaykh* who is insightful into the faults of the soul so that the *shaykh* will ascertain his faults.
2. Appointing a truthful, perceptive, and a religious friend to be his overseer so that he draws his attention to his dislikeable traits.
3. Listening to what his enemies say about him, for a hostile eye brings out defects (*'ayn al-sukhṭ tubdī al-masāwiyā*).
4. Mixing with people and attributing to one-self their blameworthy traits, because men's temperaments are very similar.

However, al-Ghazālī admits that the first two ways are hardly accessible in his age: such *shaykh* is hardly to be found, and it is rare to find a friend who is neither a flatterer concealing some of your defects, nor jealous, so considering something a fault when it is not.[280]

E. Offering means for character's refining and the soul's purification

Although al-Ghazālī believes that some people may possess good character naturally through Divine grace, such as being born with good character, he suggests in this general account other means of refining character and purifying the heart. A primary mean suggested by al-Ghazālī is spiritual struggle (*mujāhadah*) and self-training (*riyāḍah*) in a sense of "constraining of the self to perform the actions which necessarily proceed from the required trait."[281] For example, the arrogant man who wishes to possess the quality of modesty should struggle against his self in imitating the behaviour of the modest for a long time, until modesty becomes part of his nature and delightful to him.

Refining character and purifying the soul may also be achieved by renouncing everything one finds blameworthy in others. Al-Ghazālī considers this a very effective way of self-discipline.[282] He tells us that "were all people only to renounce the things they dislike in others, they would not need anyone to discipline them."[283]

The best mean of all in the view of al-Ghazālī is to be a disciple of a qualified *shaykh* in self refinement and to follow his instructions in disciplining (*mujāhadah*).[284] For al-Ghazālī all other means are just alternatives for the one who does not have a *shaykh*, but the one who finds such a qualified *shaykh*, he "should stay with him, for it is he who will deliver him from his sickness."[285]

Giving a detailed account for treating sickness of the heart and blameworthy character

The detailed treatment of al-Ghazālī of sickness of the heart and blameworthy character generally consists of two parts: theoretical and practical. As al-Ghazālī repeatedly states, there is no treatment for any heart disease except through theoretical knowledge (*'ilm*) and empirical action (*'amal*),[286] or in other words a mixture of the two.[287] These two parts are broadly illustrated in the following lines.

Although knowledge in general is a treatment for sickness of the heart, each heart disease or blameworthy character needs a specific type of knowledge according to al-Ghazālī's teaching.[288]

Thus, he teaches in the *Iḥyā'* the detailed knowledge required to cure a number of major heart diseases. His account on such knowledge commonly consists of the following: (1) a collection of numerous passages—selected from the Qur'an, the Ḥadīth, and the dicta of the early Muslim generation—on condemnation of the disease, (2) explanations of the disease and the causes of it, and (3) exposition of its harmful effects.

In addition to the theoretical part, al-Ghazālī gives practical prescriptions for treating each of the heart diseases or blameworthy character discussed in the *Iḥyā'*.[277]

Providing a guiding reference for true religiousness

To treat spurious religiousness, al-Ghazālī provides a guide to true religiousness in the *Iḥyā'*. The introduction of the book indicates that the book is intended to be a comprehensive reference for a true religious life. Moreover, throughout the book al-Ghazālī is very concerned to set standards for a true religious man in almost all aspects of his life, including those which relate to his inward self, those which regard his relation with God, and those which concern his relation with his fellow-men.

Reviving the knowledge of commanding good and forbidding wrong

Responding to the main cause behind the phenomenon of the wide spread of public wrongs (*munkarāt*) mentioned above, al-Ghazālī devotes a whole *kitāb* in the *Iḥyā'* to the duty of commanding right and forbidding wrong (*al-amr bi al-ma'rūf wa al-nahy 'an al-munkar*).[278] Following his announcement of the near-absence of anyone seeking to revive the knowledge and practice of this vital duty, al-Ghazālī states that he shall teach its knowledge in four chapters,[279] indicating a revival of it. The first chapter is on the obligatoriness of the duty, its merits, and the condemnation of ignoring it, as indicated in the Qur'an, the Ḥadīth, and the dicta of early Muslim generation.[292] The second chapter discusses the four pillars (*arkān*) of the duty—which are the performer of the duty, the incident in which the duty shall be performed, the wrongdoer to whom the duty shall be directed, and how to perform the duty— and the conditions (*shurūṭ*) of each pillar.[293] The third chapter lists some representative selection of "common wrongs in customs" (*al-munkarāt al-ma'lūfah fī al-'ādāt*), as was referred to earlier.[294] The fourth chapter focuses on how to perform the duty when the wrongdoer is an emir or a sultan.[295]

In addition to theoretically reviving the knowledge of this duty, al-Ghazālī performed the duty himself, particularly against the wrongs committed by some sultans and viziers of the time, as will be demonstrated below.

Refuting widespread innovations and warning from their drawbacks

As a response to the spread of the three forms of heretic innovations mentioned above, al-Ghazālī occupied himself, particularly at the *iṣlāḥī* point in his career, with refuting them and warning of their drawbacks. Starting with the first form, which is Sufic heretic ecstasy (*shaṭaḥ*), al-Ghazālī strongly attacks in the *Iḥyā'* such form of innovation and warns from its harmful consequences.[296] Moreover, he states in the *Munqidh* that he has explained in his book *al-Maqṣad al-Asnā* (The Noblest Aim) the nature of the error in such Sufic ecstatic utterances, namely oneness or unity (*itiḥād*) with God, and inherence or incarnation (*ḥulūl*).[285] In the *Maqṣad*, al-Ghazālī clearly asserts that the claim of unity between man and God is obviously false, because unification between any two similar essences is impossible and it is more impossible when it applies to different essences such as black colour and knowledge, to say nothing of much greater different essences as those of man and God.[286] Similarly, he asserts that inherence (*ḥulūl*) in the sense that the Lord inheres in man and man inheres in the Lord is also impossible because "anything which is self-subsisting cannot inhere in something else which is self-subsisting save in terms of the proximity that may exist between bodies; if inherence is inconceivable in respect of two men, then how is it conceivable between man and the Lord Most High."[287]

As regard to the second form, which is Philosophic heresy, al-Ghazālī states in *al-Munqidh* that the refutation of this form of innovation is the subject matter of his book *Tahāfut al-Falāsifah* (The Incoherence of the Philosophers),[288] which was composed prior to the stage under study and thus is beyond the focus of this chapter.

What concerns us here, however, is al-Ghazālī's response regarding this innovation in his works belonging to his late career. Generally speaking, al-Ghazālī in these works, particularly in the *Munqidh*, concerns himself much with warning from the drawbacks which may arise from dealing with philosophy. In the *Munqidh*, he records the drawbacks which he believes resulted from or are connected with the six divisions of philosophical sciences at the time, i.e., mathematics, logic, physics or natural science, theology or metaphysics, politics, and ethics.[289]

Although he believes that mathematical sciences deal with demonstrated facts (*umūr burhāniyyah*) which cannot be denied and nothing in them entails denial or affirmation of religious matters, yet he finds two drawbacks connected to them.[302] The first is that by admiring the fine precision of their details and the clarity of their proofs, one may wrongly assume that all sciences of the ancient philosophers have the same degree of preciseness and thus blindly follow them, even in their metaphysical views contradicting religion, refusing to admit that their arguments in mathematical topics are apodictic (*burhānī*), whereas those in metaphysical questions are conjectural (*takhmīnī*).[303] Because of this drawback, al-Ghazālī warns off anyone who would embark upon the study of these mathematical sciences.[304] In the *Iḥyā'*, however, he classifies them as permissible and thus no one should be barred from studying them, except the weak-minded person who by studying them might step over into blameworthy sciences and heretic innovations, like most of those who devoted themselves to these sciences as noted by al-Ghazālī.[293] The second drawback connected to these sciences derives from an ignorant friend of Islam who rejects all sciences ascribed to the philosophers, accusing them of ignorance therein and claiming that all their sciences contradict with the Sharī'ah, even their theory of the eclipses of the sun and the moon.[294] Al-Ghazālī accuses anyone who supposes that Islam is defended by the denial of these sciences of committing a great crime against religion because this denial leads those who have knowledge of such matters to believe that Islam is based on ignorance and the denial of apodeictic proof.[307]

Similarly, while asserting that nothing in the logical sciences should be denied, al-Ghazālī states that those who admire the apodeictic demonstrations therein may think that the infidel doctrines of the philosophers are backed up by similar demonstrations and thus hasten into unbelief.[308]

With regard to physical sciences, he concludes that nothing therein should be rejected except certain points which he mentioned in the *Tahāfut*.[309]

Turning to metaphysical sciences, al-Ghazālī argues that they include most of the errors of the philosophers, because they could not satisfy the conditions of proof they lay down in logic.[310]

As regard to political sciences, he argues that the philosophers "took them from the Divine scriptures revealed to the prophets and from the maxims handed down by the predecessors of the prophets."[311] Similarly, he argues that the philosophers took the ethical sciences from the teachings of the mystics, and mixed them with their own doctrines in order to promote the circulation of their own false doctrines using the lustre afforded by these mystic teachings.[312] According to al-Ghazālī, from this practice of incorporating prophetic and mystic teachings in the philosophers' books, two wrong tendencies arise.[313] The first is in the case of those who totally eschew these teachings and even blame anyone who cites from them, assuming that they are erroneous since they are recorded in the philosophers' books and mixed with their false doctrines.[314] Al-Ghazālī strongly criticizes this tendency, and accuses its adherents of being weak-minded who measure the truth by men and not vice versa.[315] The second wrong tendency is in the case of those who through approving and accepting the prophetic and mystic teachings, which are mixed with the philosophers own doctrines, form a high opinion of the philosophers and thus may readily accept their false doctrines.[316]

Concerning the third form of heretic innovation, which is esoteric interpretation of Bāṭinīs, al-Ghazālī summarizes his refutation to this innovation in the *Munqidh*.[317]

The starting point in his refutation is his acknowledgment of the Bāṭinīs' argument on the need for an authoritative infallible teacher.[318] Opposing their claim of the hidden Imam, al-Ghazālī asserts that this infallible teacher must be the Prophet (ṣ).[319] Following that, he answers all of their possible objections. Next, he explains how they deceive common folk and weak-minded people by effectively proving the need for an authoritative teacher and his teaching, until such people concede to them that much and ask them for some of his teaching, then they pause and say go and search for it yourself, knowing that if they were to say anything more, they would be put to shame as they would be unable to resolve even the least problematic matters.[320]

Renewing the mission of true 'ulamā'

Al-Ghazālī made every effort to renew the mission of true 'ulamā', as an *iṣlāḥī* reaction to the *fasād* of the vast majority of the 'ulamā', which he considered a crucial phenomenon of *fasād* in his time as shown above. The foundation of his effort in this regard is his determined attempt to set standards for true 'ulamā' or those whom he calls 'ulamā' al-ākhirah (otherworldly scholars), and to distinguish between them and those who only apparently resemble them. He clearly states in the *Iḥyā'* that "one of the great tasks is to know the signs which distinguish between 'ulamā' al-dunyā (worldly scholars) and 'ulamā' al-ākhirah (otherworldly scholars)."[321]

By *'ulamā' al-dunyā*, he means those "whose sole purpose in pursuing knowledge is enjoying the pleasure of this life and gaining fame (*jāh*) and status (*manzilah*) among its people."[322] Following this definition, he quotes a number of traditions condemning such *'ulamā'* and concludes that they "will occupy a more inferior position and will receive a more severe punishment than the ignorant person."[323] Conversely, the true *'ulamā'*, or *'ulamā' al-ākhirah* (otherworldly learned men), "will be the winners and will be brought close to God."[312]

To distinguish them from the *'ulamā'* of the *dunyā*, al-Ghazālī mentions twelve signs or characteristics of the *'ulamā'* of the *ākhirah*.[313] Al-Ghazālī's reference in specifying these signs are the qualities of the true *'ulamā'* of the early blessed generation (*al-salaf*). He states that each one of these signs "represents several qualities of the *'ulamā'* of the early blessed generation (*al-salaf*)."[314]

These signs are summarised as follows:

1. They do not seek the worldly desires by their knowledge, rather they give the Hereafter the priority over the present world.
2. Their deeds do not contradict their words; they do not enjoin what they would not be the first to do.
3. Their concern is to obtain knowledge which is useful for the Hereafter and they avoid knowledge which is of little benefit or which leads to disputation.
4. They are not interested in luxurious life, but prefer moderation and are satisfied with the least of the necessary worldly things.
5. They try to distance themselves from sultans, avoid visiting them and being their associates as long as they can do so, for the present world is attractive and one who visits sultans may not help being smitten with it. "On the whole, mingling with them is the key to evils, while the way of the otherworldly *'ulamā'* is circumspection."[315]

6. They do not to hasten to give *fatwā* (jurisprudence opinions), but rather avoid it whenever possible.

7. Most of their attention is directed toward knowledge of the inward (*'ilm al-bāṭin*) and spiritual development.

8. Greatly concerned with strengthening their certitude (*yaqīn*).

9. They reflect signs of awe towards God in all aspects of their life.

10. They direct most of their study towards knowledge of practical religion (*'ilm al-a'māl*) and what may corrupt the deeds as well as knowledge of the condition of the heart (*qalb*).

11. Their learning should depend on their insight and understanding with purity of heart, not books or *taqlīd*, for only the Prophet (ṣ) and his Companions are the ones who should be followed.

12. They strictly guard themselves from religious innovations, and not being deceived by people's agreement on innovations contradicting with the norms of the time of the Companions.

The *'ulamā'* of such qualities occupy a very important position in the *iṣlāḥī* teachings of al-Ghazālī. He believes that their degree in religious dignity is second after the prophets.[316] Thus, following the prophets, their real role is to be guides to the right path.[317] And the extent in which they occupy themselves with *iṣlāḥ* of their selves and others reflects the degree of their dignity.[318]

In addition, true *'ulamā'* are regarded by al-Ghazālī as the doctors of religion (*aṭṭibā' al-dīn*) for they deal with the knowledge of treating sickness of the heart (*amrāḍ al-qulūb*).[319] Accordingly, al-Ghazālī says that it is a must (*farḍ 'ayn*) on all *'ulamā'* not only to treat the transgressors who seek treatment from them, but also to enlighten those who are unaware of their transgression, and those who are ignorant in religion since those sick in the heart (*marḍā al-qulūb*) do not know about their illness.[320] For this reason, al-Ghazālī necessitates that each *'ālim* should become responsible for a particular area, instructing its inhabitants in their religion and distinguishing that which may harm them and make them miserable, from that which may benefit them and lead them to true happiness.[333] The *'ālim*, he states, must not wait to be approached and rather he "must devote himself to call the people, as the *'ulamā'* are the heirs of the prophets and the prophets did not abandon the people to their ignorance, but instead, they called upon the people in their assemblies,…seeking them one by one in order to give them guidance."[322]

Al-Ghazālī considers the true *'ulamā'* to be safeguards from wrong religious practices. On various occasions, al-Ghazālī necessitates the supervision of a qualified *'ālim* in order guarantee true religiousness. For instance, to be safe from extravagance in scrupulousness (*wara'*), al-Ghazālī warns from engaging in details of *wara'* without the consultation of an experienced *'ālim*.[335]

In addition to his substantial theoretical effort to renew the mission of true *'ulamā'*, al-Ghazālī tried seriously to be a good example of such *'ulamā'* himself. In light of the discussion in the previous chapter about his life-experience, it can be stated that from the period of his self-*iṣlāḥ* onwards, he was very concerned to meet the standards of true *'ulamā'* which he specified. The testimony of his associate, al-Fārisī, about him, which has been quoted above, shows that his attempt in this regard was highly successful.

After being successful with his self, al-Ghazālī occupied himself with bringing up and training a new generation of *'ulamā'*, who fulfil the mission of true *'ulamā'*. This was initially through his experience of teaching in the Niẓāmiyyah of Nīshāpūr and then by setting up a private *madrasah* and *khānqāh* (sojourn), as has been shown in the previous chapter.

Besides all this effort, he concerned himself with advising and urging the *'ulamā'*, with whom he was contemporary, to undertake their supposed responsibilities and possess the attributes of true *'ulamā'*. This is clearly evident in a number of his letters directed to some *'ulamā'* of his time. In his letter to a judge (*qaḍī*) in al-Maghrib al-Aqṣā, he writes "I would like to employ a rich counsel which I offer you as a gift from the learned,"[324] and he goes on to advising him by saying:

> You should open your eyes and look into the future and find
> out what good deeds you have done for tomorrow. Remember
> none is more sympathetically inclined towards you than your
> own heart. Think deeply for a minute or two and decide what it
> is that you run after.[337]

He warns him from being attracted to worldly temptations
by stating:

> If you want to dig up wells or canals, think how many of them
> have fallen into ruins with time. If you intend to build a grand
> house, remember how fast the magnificent buildings, already
> erected have disappeared and if you want to lay out a beautiful
> garden read: "How many were the gardens and the water springs
> that they left behind. And the corn lands and the good sites and
> pleasant things wherein they took delight! Even so (it was) and
> we made it an inheritance for other folk: And the heaven and
> the earth wept not for them, nor were they reprieved."(Qur'an,
> 44:22-25)…[338]

He further warns him from being associated with the ruler:
"God forbid, if you want to serve the king, you should read this
Ḥadīth: "On the Day of Resurrection the Kings and the viziers
would rise like ants from earth and the common folk would tread
them roughly under their feet."[327]

Counselling ruling members and forbidding their wrongdoing

The ruling members are given a considerable amount of attention
in al-Ghazālī's *iṣlāḥī* teaching. To adequately understand his
iṣlāḥī attitudes towards them, we need to be acquainted with the
following two starting points. The first is his idea about their
supposed role. According to him, "the state (*al-mulk*) and religion
are twins; religion is a foundation while the sultan is a guard, and
whatever has no foundation is destroyed, and whatever has no
guard is lost."[328] Moreover, he believes that the degree of religious
dignity of just sultans or rulers comes immediately after the degree
of the *'ulamā'*, because they put right the life of people, while the
'ulamā' put right their religion.[341] In addition, he considers that

being a just and sincere caliph or emir is one of the best types of worship (*min afḍal al-'ibādāt*).[342] Furthermore, he makes the rulers responsible for vital *iṣlāḥī* tasks. He, for example, demands that "all sultans must appoint, in each village and quarter, a devout *faqīh* to instruct the people in their religion."[331]

The second point, with which we need to be acquainted, is his opinion on the association with them. In general, al-Ghazālī at his late age used to warn from associating with the rulers or sultans, though, before his experience of self-*iṣlāḥ*, he used to frequently associate with them and even served as an ambassador between the Seljuk Sultanate and the 'Abbāsid Caliphate.[332] He clarifies in the *Iḥyā'* the risk of associating with them by stating the following:

> One who associates with them is not free from undertaking to seek their approval and to incline their hearts towards him, although they are unjust. Every religious person (*kul mutadayyin*) ought to disprove of them and straiten their bosoms by making their injustice obvious and by showing the foulness of their deeds. One who visits them either shows regard for their luxury and despises the grace of Allah or he refrains from disapproving them. Then he becomes a dissimulator to them, or in his speech he pretends to please them and approve their condition, and that is clear calumny; or he longs to obtain some of their worldly goods, which is downright unlawful (*suḥt*).[333]

This explains why he vowed, while he was in Jerusalem, that he shall neither attend the court of a ruler, nor take any form of governmental emoluments.[334]

Bearing in mind these two points, we turn now to al-Ghazālī's *iṣlāḥī* response to the *fasād* among contemporary ruling members. His response to that phenomenon of *fasād* can be classified into direct response and indirect response. The latter took the form of daring *fatāwā* against the contemporary unjust sovereigns in general. A number of such *fatāwā* appear in the *Iḥyā'*. One of these, is his *fatwā* that the majority of the wealth (*amwāl*) of the sultans and militant men of the time is *ḥarām*, as stated earlier.

Accordingly he forbids taking gifts from sultans except under strict conditions.[335] Similarly, he devotes a section of the book to discuss in detail what is lawful and unlawful with respect to mingling with unjust sultans.[348]

The direct response of al-Ghazālī to the *fasād* among contemporary ruling members is reflected in his letters to a number of Seljuk sovereigns, counselling them, urging them to fulfil their duties, warning them of injustice, soliciting them to care for their subjects and forbidding their wrongdoing. To vividly illustrate the *iṣlāḥī* nature of his letters to those sovereigns, we shall quote selective extracts from three of his letters in the following lines.

In one of his letters to Fakhr al-Mulk, the son of Niẓām al-Mulk, he blames him of using flattering titles: "Be it known that the flattering titles conferred on men are a devilish invention and as such are improper for a pious Muslim to accept."[337] Urging him to control his lusts and passions, he continues: "According to the strict letter of Islam, the *amīr* is the one who rules with absolute authority over his lusts and passions."[338] He further advises him to be a practicing Muslim: "I, therefore, exhort you to live the ascetic life and fear God and lay upon a store of good works against the day of Reckoning."[339]

In another letter to the same vizier, he brings to his attention how bad the condition in Ṭūs was, due to famine and savage actions of the administrators, urging him to look after the welfare of the residents: "Let me tell you that this city was a howling wilderness due to famine and cruelty meted out to the inhabitants by all government officials...You should be merciful to your subjects and God would be merciful to you."[352] After continuing his daring advice, he concludes his letter by stating: "Meditate on possibilities for an hour or two and think deeply upon the poor people, whose blood and sweat is being consumed by the Government officials..."[353]

To another Seljuk vizier, Mujīr al-Dīn, al-Ghazālī writes a letter of strong words, warning him from oppression and injustice: "Refrain from torturing the innocent masses or else great will be your disgrace from Allah. If you want to escape this punishment, fight the forces of cruelty and injustice like a spiritual here and do not yield to their behests."[354]

Notes

1. See, for instance, al-Ghazālī, *Iḥyā'*, Vol. 4, p. 49, trans., M.S. Stern, *al-Ghazzali on Repentance*, New Delhi: Sterling Publishers Private Limited, 1990, p. 114, available online in PDF form on *http://www. ghazali.org/books/gz-repent.pdf.*
2. Al-Ghazālī, *Iḥyā'*, Vol. 4, p. 49, trans., Stern, *al-Ghazzali on Repentance*, p. 114.
3. Al-Ghazālī, *Iḥyā'*, Vol. 4, p. 401.
4. Al-Ghazālī, *Iḥyā'*, Vol. 3, p. 14, trans., W.J. Skellie, "The Religious Psychology of al-Gahzzālī: A Translation of his Book of the *Iḥyā'* on the Explanation of the Wonders of the Heart."
5. Al-Ghazālī, *Iḥyā'*, Vol. 3, p. 14, trans., Skellie, "The Religious Psychology," p. 51.
6. Ibid, Vol. 3, p. 17, trans., Skellie, "The Religious Psychology," p. 65.
7. Ibid, Vol. 3, p. 17, trans., Skellie, "The Religious Psychology," p. 65.
8. Ibid, Vol. 3, p. 17, trans., Skellie, "The Religious Psychology," p. 65.
9. Ibid, Vol. 3, p. 17, trans., Skellie, "The Religious Psychology," p. 65.
10. It is worth noting that al-Ghazālī's usage of the term heart in this context is not in its material meaning, but rather it is in its spiritual sense denoting the essence of man, as shall be explained below.
11. Al-Ghazālī, *Iḥyā'*, Vol. 3, p. 2, trans., McCarthy, "*Kitāb Sharḥ 'Ajā'ib al-Qalb*," in McCarthy, *Deliverance*, p. 309.
12. Ibid, Vol. 3, p. 2, trans., McCarthy, "*Kitāb Sharḥ 'Ajā'ib al-Qalb*," in McCarthy, *Deliverance*, p. 310.
13. Ibid, Vol. 3, p. 2, trans., McCarthy, "*Kitāb Sharḥ 'Ajā'ib al-Qalb*," p. 310.
14. Ibid, Vol. 3, p. 2, trans., McCarthy, "*Kitāb Sharḥ 'Ajā'ib al-Qalb*," p. 310.
15. Ibid, Vol. 3, p. 225 & 228.
16. Ibid, Vol. 3, p. 228.
17. Ibid, Vol. 3, p. 63.

18. Ibid, Vol. 3, p. 219. For more elaboration on what al-Ghazālī means by love of the *dunyā*, see below.

19. Ibid, Vol. 1, p. 165 & Vol. 4, p. 36.

20. Ibid, Vol. 4, p. 130.

21. Ibid, Vol. 1, p. 165.

22. Ibid, Vol. 3, p. 201.

23. For a further discussion of the teachings of al-Ghazālī on love of the world as the vice from which all other vices come, see Muḥammad Abul Quasem, *The Ethics of al-Ghazālī: A Composite Ethics in Islam*, Selangor (Malaysia): Central Printing Sendirian Berhad, 1976, pp. 124-126.

24. Ibid, Vol. 1, p. 165, trans., Edwin Elliot Calverly, *The Mysteries of Worship in Islam*, trans. of *Kitāb Asrār al-Ṣalāh* of al-Ghazālī's *Iḥyā'*, New Delhi: Kitab Bhavan Exporters & Importers, 1992, p. 53.

25. Ibid, Vol. 2, p. 357.

26. Ibid, Vol. 4, p. 202.

27. Ibid, Vol. 3, p. 196.

28. Ibid, Vol. 3, p. 88, trans., T.J. Winter, *al-Ghazālī on Disciplining the Soul and on Breaking the Two Desires*, trans. of *Kitāb Riyāḍah al-Nafs* and *Kitāb Kasr al-Shahwatayn* of al-Ghazālī's *Iḥyā'*, Cambridge: The Islamic Texts Society, 2001, p. 129.

29. Ibid, Vol. 3, p. 79, trans., see T.J. Winter, *Disciplining*, p. 100.

30. Ibid, Vol. 3, p. 231.

31. Ibid, Vol. 3, p. 231.

32. See al-Ghazālī, *Iḥyā'*, Vol. 4, p. 41, trans., Stern, *al-Ghazzali on Repentance*, p. 99.

33. Ibid, Vol. 4, p. 140.

34. Ibid, Vol. 4, p. 16 & Vol. 3, p. 10.

35. Ibid, Vol. 4, p. 16 & Vol. 3, p. 10.

36. Ibid, Vol. 3, p. 11, trans., McCarthy, "Kitāb Sharḥ 'Ajā'ib al-Qalb," p. 321.

37. In his classification of sins (*dhunūb*) in the *Iḥyā'*, al-Ghazālī lists various examples of sins that are caused by each of these qualities, al-Ghazālī, *Iḥyā'*, Vol. 4, p. 16, trans., Stern, *al-Ghazzali on Repentance*, p. 55.

38. Ibid, Vol. 3, p. 10, trans., McCarthy, "Kitāb Sharḥ 'Ajā'ib al-Qalb," p. 321.

39. Ibid, Vol. 3, p. 10, trans., McCarthy, "Kitāb Sharḥ 'Ajā'ib al-Qalb," p. 321.

40. Ibid, Vol. 4, p. 9.

41. Ibid, Vol. 4, p. 75.

42. Al-Ghazālī, *Iḥyā'*, Vol. 3, pp. 10f, trans., McCarthy, "Kitāb Sharḥ 'Ajā'ib al-Qalb," p. 321.

43. Al-Ghazālī, *Iḥyāʾ*, Vol. 3, p. 10, trans., McCarthy, "Kitāb Sharḥ ʿAjāʾib al-Qalb," p. 321.
44. Al-Ghazālī, *al-Munqidh*, p. 118, trans., McCarthy, *Deliverance*, p. 89, and also Watt, *The Faith*, pp. 70f.
45. Ibid, p. 118, trans., McCarthy, *Deliverance*, p. 89, and also Watt, *The Faith*, p. 71.
46. Ibid, p. 117, trans., McCarthy, *Deliverance*, p. 88-89, and also Watt, *The Faith*, p. 71.
47. Ibid, pp. 79-119, trans., McCarthy, *Deliverance*, pp. 63-89, and also Watt, *The Faith*, pp. 33-72. As an earlier response, al-Ghazālī's observation of this deception was recorded in the *Tahāfut*, as he states in the introduction, (*Tahāfut*, pp. 72-74, trans., Kamali, *al-Ghazali's Tahafut*, pp. 1-2).
48. Ibid, p. 79, trans., McCarthy, *Deliverance*, p. 63, and also Watt, *The Faith*, p. 33.
49. Ibid, p. 120, trans., McCarthy, *Deliverance*, p. 90, and also Watt, *The Faith*, p. 73.
50. Ibid, p. 119, trans., McCarthy, *Deliverance*, p. 89, and also Watt, *The Faith*, p. 72.
51. Ibid, p. 118, trans., McCarthy, *Deliverance*, p. 89, and also Watt, *The Faith*, p. 72.
52. Ibid, p. 118, trans., McCarthy, *Deliverance*, p. 89, and also Watt, *The Faith*, p. 72.
53. Ibid, Vol. 4, p. 42.
54. Ibid, p. 119, trans., McCarthy, *Deliverance*, p. 89, and also Watt, *The Faith*, p. 72.
55. Ibid, p. 118, trans., McCarthy, *Deliverance*, p. 89, and also Watt, *The Faith*, p. 71-72.
56. Heart in this context is in its spiritual sense, as has explained earlier.
57. See al-Ghazālī, *Iḥyāʾ*, Vol. 3, p. 63.
58. Ibid, Vol. 3, p. 368.
59. Ibid, Vol. 4, p. 101.
60. The view of al-Ghazālī on this blackness will be elaborated on more below.
61. Ibid, *Iḥyāʾ*, Vol. 4, p. 401.
62. Ibid, Vol. 3, p. 61, trans., see T.J. Winter, *On Disciplining*, p. 40.
63. Ibid, Vol. 3, p. 62-63, trans., see Winter, *On Disciplining*, pp. 46f.
64. Ibid, Vol. 2, p. 111.
65. Ibid, Vol. 2, p. 111.
66. Ibid, Vol. 2, p. 111.
67. Ibid, Vol. 2, p. 250 & Vol. 3, p. 404.
68. Ibid, Vol. 3, p. 400-404.
69. Ibid, Vol. 3, p. 407-409.

70. Ibid, Vol. 3, p. 409.

71. Ibid, Vol. 2, p. 342.

72. Ibid, Vol. 2, p. 335-342. For an extended summary of these wrongs in English, see Michael Cook, *Commanding Right and Forbidding Wrong in Islamic Thought*, Cambridge: Cambridge University Press, 2000, pp. 442-446.

73. Ibid, Vol. 2, p. 306.

74. Ibid, Vol. 2, p. 306.

75. Ibid, Vol. 1, p. 36, trans., see MaCall, "The Book of Knowledge," p. 144, and also Faris, *The Book of Knowledge*, p. 86.

76. Ibid, Vol. 1, p. 36, trans., see MaCall, "The Book of Knowledge," p. 145, and also Faris, *The Book of Knowledge*, p. 86.

77. Ibid, Vol. 1, p. 36, trans., see MaCall, "The Book of Knowledge," p. 145, and also Faris, *The Book of Knowledge*, p. 86.

78. Ibid, Vol. 3, p. 405.

79. See al-Ghazālī, *al-Munqidh*, pp. 79f. Earlier than the *Munqidh* and in more detail, al-Ghazālī dealt with this type of innovation in *Tahāfut al-Falāsifah*, as mentioned above, but this book is beyond the scope of the present chapter.

80. Ibid, p. 83, trans., McCarthy, *Deliverance*, p. 66, and also Watt, *The Faith*, p. 37.

81. Ibid, p. 84, trans., McCarthy, *Deliverance*, p. 66, and also Watt, *The Faith*, p. 37-38.

82. Ibid, p. 84, trans., McCarthy, *Deliverance*, p. 67, and also Watt, *The Faith*, p. 38.

83. See al-Ghazālī, *Iḥyā'*, Vol. 1, p. 22, trans., see MaCall, "The Book of Knowledge," p. 87, and also Faris, *The Book of Knowledge*, p. 46.

84. Ibid, Vol. 1, p. 22, trans., see MaCall, "The Book of Knowledge," p. 87, and also Faris, *The Book of Knowledge*, p. 46.

85. Ibid, Vol. 1, p. 37, trans., see MaCall, "The Book of Knowledge," p. 144, and also Faris, *The Book of Knowledge*, p. 87.

86. Ibid, Vol. 1, p. 37, trans., see MaCall, "The Book of Knowledge," pp. 147f, and also Faris, *The Book of Knowledge*, p. 88.

87. Ibid, Vol. 1, p. 37, trans., see MaCall, "The Book of Knowledge," p. 148, and also Faris, *The Book of Knowledge*, p. 88.

88. Ibid, Vol. 1, p. 37, trans., see MaCall, "The Book of Knowledge," p. 148, and also Faris, *The Book of Knowledge*, p. 88.

89. Al-Ghazālī, *al-Munqidh*, p. 93, trans., McCarthy, *Deliverance*, p. 72, and also Watt, *The Faith*, p. 45.

90. Ibid, p. 93, trans., McCarthy, *Deliverance*, p. 72, and also Watt, *The Faith*, p. 46.

91. Al-Ghazālī, *Iḥyā'*, Vol. 1, p. 2, trans., see MaCall, "The Book of Knowledge," p. 3, and also Faris, *The Book of Knowledge*, p. x.

92.　See for example, al-Ghazālī, *Iḥyā'*, Vol. 2, p. 357.

93.　Al-Ghazālī, *Iḥyā'*, Vol. 2, p. 150.

94.　Ibid, Vol. 4, p. 51.

95.　Ibid, Vol. 4, p. 51.

96.　Ibid, Vol. 3, p. 63.

97.　Ibid, Vol. 3, p. 195.

98.　Ibid, Vol. 3, p. 195.

99.　Ibid, Vol. 3, p. 195.

100. Ibid, Vol. 2, p. 357.

101. Ibid, Vol. 2, p. 357.

102. Ibid, Vol. 4, p. 369.

103. Ibid, Vol. 4, p. 146.

104. Ibid, Vol. 4, p. 146.

105. Ibid, Vol. 4, p. 146.

106. Ibid, Vol. 3, p. 349.

107. Ibid, Vol. 1, p. 42, trans., MaCall, "The Book of Knowledge," p. 170, and also Faris, *The Book of Knowledge*, pp. 102f.

108. Ibid, Vol. 1, p. 40, trans., MaCall, "The Book of Knowledge," p. 136.

109. Ibid, Vol. 3, p. 35, *trans.*, Skellie *"The Religious Psychology,"* pp. 138-139.

110. Ibid, Vol. 2, p. 150.

111. Ibid, Vol. 1, pp. 42f, trans., see Faris, *The Book of Knowledge*, p. 101.

112. Ibid, Vol. 2, pp. 141f.

113. Ibid, Vol. 2, p. 105.

114. Ibid, Vol. 2, p. 136.

115. Ibid, Vol. 2, p. 65.

116. Ibid, Vol. 2, p. 139.

117. Ibid, Vol. 2, p. 135.

118. Al-Ghazālī, *al-Mustaṣfā min 'Ilm al-Uṣūl*, ed., Ḥamzah Zuhayr Ḥāfiẓ, Jeddah: Sharikat al-Madīnah al-Munawwarah li al-Ṭibā'ah, n.d., Vol. 4, p. 140.

119. Al-Ghazālī, *al-Mustaṣfā*, Vol. 4, p. 144.

120. The scholarly mental activity of deriving a rule of the Sharī'ah from authoritative evidence.

121. Al-Ghazālī, *al-Mustaṣfā*, Vol. 4, p. 147.

122. Ibid, Vol. 4, p. 147.

123. Ibid, Vol. 4, p. 148.

124. Ibid, Vol. 4, p. 150.

125. Al-Ghazālī, *Iḥyā'*, Vol. 1, p. 149, trans., MaCall, "The Book of Knowledge," p. 53, and also Faris, *The Book of Knowledge*, p. 24.

126. Ibid, Vol. 1, p. 149, trans., MaCall, "The Book of Knowledge," p. 53, and also Faris, *The Book of Knowledge*, p. 24.

127. Al-Ghazālī, *Fayṣal al-Tafriqah bayn al-Islām wa al-Zanādiqah*, compacted with other works of al-Ghazālī in *Majmūʿah Rasāʾil al-Imām al-Ghazālī*, Beirut: Dār al-Kutub al-ʿIlmiyyah, n.d. Part 3, p. 93.

128. Al-Ghazālī, *Fayṣal al-Tafriqah*, p. 93.

129. Ibid, p. 93.

130. Ibid, p. 94.

131. Al-Ghazālī, *Iljām al-ʿAwāmm*, p. 57.

132. Ibid, p. 41.

133. Ibid, pp. 79-81.

134. Al-Ghazālī, *Iljām al-ʿAwāmm ʿan ʿIlm al-Kalām*, compacted with other works of al-Ghazālī in *Majmūʿah Rasāʾil al-Imām al-Ghazālī*, Beirut: Dār al-Kutub al-ʿIlmiyyah, n.d. Part 4, p. 81.

135. See, for example, al-Ghazālī, *Iḥyāʾ*, Vol. 3, p. 16f, trans., Skellie, "The Religious Psychology," p. 61-66.

136. Ibid, Vol. 3, p. 16, trans., Skellie, "The Religious Psychology," p. 61.

137. Ibid, Vol. 3, p. 16, trans., Skellie, "The Religious Psychology," p. 65.

138. Ibid, Vol. 3, p. 17, trans., Skellie, "The Religious Psychology," p. 65.

139. Ibid, Vol. 3, p. 17, trans., Skellie, "The Religious Psychology," p. 65.

140. Ibid, Vol. 3, p. 17, trans., Skellie, "The Religious Psychology," p. 65.

141. Ibid, Vol. 3, p. 17, trans., Skellie, "The Religious Psychology," p. 65.

142. Ibid, Vol. 3, p. 17, trans., Skellie, "The Religious Psychology," p. 65.

143. Ibid, Vol. 3, p. 17, trans., Skellie, "The Religious Psychology," p. 66.

144. Ibid, Vol. 1, p. 16, trans., MaCall, "The Book of Knowledge," pp. 60-62, and also Faris, *The Book of Knowledge*, p. 30.

145. Ibid, Vol. 1, p. 29, trans., MaCall, "The Book of Knowledge," p. 116f, and also Faris, *The Book of Knowledge*, p. 67.

146. Ibid, Vol. 1, p. 29, trans., MaCall, "The Book of Knowledge," p. 118, and also Faris, *The Book of Knowledge*, p. 68.

147. Ibid, Vol. 1, pp. 29f, trans., MaCall, "The Book of Knowledge," p. 119, and also Faris, *The Book of Knowledge*, p. 69.

148. Ibid, Vol. 1, p. 30, trans., MaCall, "The Book of Knowledge," p. 120, and also Faris, *The Book of Knowledge*, pp. 69f.

149. Ibid, Vol. 1, p. 30, trans., MaCall, "The Book of Knowledge," p. 122, and also Faris, *The Book of Knowledge*, p. 70.

150. Ibid, Vol. 1, p. 30, trans., MaCall, "The Book of Knowledge," pp. 122f, and also Faris, *The Book of Knowledge*, p. 71.

151. Ibid, Vol. 1, p. 16, trans., MaCall, "The Book of Knowledge," p. 62, and also Faris, *The Book of Knowledge*, p. 30.

152. Ibid, Vol. 1, p. 16, trans., MaCall, "The Book of Knowledge," p. 62, and also Faris, *The Book of Knowledge*, p. 31.

153. Ibid, Vol. 3, p. 2, trans., McCarthy, *Deliverance*, p. 310.

154. Ibid, Vol. 3, pp. 2f, trans., McCarthy, *Deliverance*, p. 310.

155. Ibid, Vol. 3, p. 3, trans., McCarthy, *Deliverance*, p. 311.
156. Ibid, Vol. 3, p. 3-4, trans., McCarthy, *Deliverance*, p. 311.
157. Ibid, Vol. 3, p. 3-5, trans., McCarthy, *Deliverance*, pp. 310-313.
158. Ibid, Vol. 4, p. 297.
159. Ibid, Vol. 4, p. 30.
160. Ibid, Vol. 3, p. 2, trans., McCarthy, *Deliverance*, p. 309.
161. Ibid, Vol. 3, p. 2, trans., McCarthy, *Deliverance*, p. 309.
162. Ibid, Vol. 3, p. 2, trans., McCarthy, *Deliverance*, p. 310.
163. Ibid, Vol. 3, p. 2, trans., McCarthy, *Deliverance*, p. 310.
164. Ibid, Vol. 3, p. 5, trans., McCarthy, *Deliverance*, p. 313.
165. Ibid, Vol. 3, p. 5, trans., McCarthy, *Deliverance*, p. 314.
166. Ibid, Vol. 3, p. 5, trans., McCarthy, *Deliverance*, p. 314.
167. Ibid, Vol. 3, p. 5., trans., McCarthy, *Deliverance*, p. 314.
168. Ibid, Vol. 3, p. 5., trans., McCarthy, *Deliverance*, p. 314.
169. Ibid, Vol. 3, pp. 5f, trans., McCarthy, *Deliverance*, p. 314.
170. Ibid, Vol. 3, p. 6, trans., McCarthy, *Deliverance*, p. 314.
171. Ibid, Vol. 3, p. 6, trans., McCarthy, *Deliverance*, p. 315.
172. Ibid, Vol. 3, p. 6, trans., McCarthy, *Deliverance*, p. 315.
173. Ibid, Vol. 3, p. 6, trans., McCarthy, *Deliverance*, p. 315.
174. Ibid, Vol. 3, p. 8, trans., McCarthy, *Deliverance*, p. 317.
175. Ibid, Vol. 3, p. 8, trans., McCarthy, *Deliverance*, p. 317.
176. Ibid, Vol. 3, p. 228.
177. Ibid, Vol. 3, p. 229.
178. Ibid, Vol. 3, p. 229.
179. Ibid, Vol. 3, p. 229.
180. Ibid, Vol. 3, p. 229.
181. Ibid, Vol. 4, p. 103.
182. Ibid, Vol. 4, pp. 3 & 44.
183. Ibid, Vol. 3, p. 282.
184. Ibid, Vol. 3, p. 282.
185. Ibid, Vol. 3, p. 284.
186. Ibid, Vol. 3, p. 284.
187. Ibid, Vol. 3, p. 282.
188. For this purpose, he devoted a whole *kitāb* in the *Iḥyā'* under the following title: *Kitāb Dham al-Dunyā* (The Book of Condemnation of the World), see al-Ghazālī, *Iḥyā'*, Vol. 3, p. 201-230.
189. Al-Ghazālī, *Iḥyā'*, Vol. 3, p. 201.
190. Ibid, Vol. 3, p. 21.
191. Ibid, Vol. 3, p. 219.
192. Ibid, Vol. 3, p. 222.
193. Ibid, Vol. 3, p. 220.
194. Ibid, Vol. 3, pp. 202-214.
195. Ibid, Vol. 3, p. 202.

196. Ibid, Vol. 3, pp. 214-219.

197. Ibid, Vol. 3, p. 214.

198. Ibid, Vol. 3, p. 214.

199. Ibid, Vol. 3, p. 214.

200. Ibid, Vol. 3, p. 215.

201. Ibid, Vol. 3, pp. 224-230.

202. According to al-Ghazālī, "all what is on earth can be classified into three sections: mineral, plants, and animals," al-Ghazālī, *Iḥyā'*, Vol. 3, p. 224.

203. Al-Ghazālī, *Iḥyā'*, Vol. 3, p. 224.

204. Ibid, Vol. 3, p. 224.

205. Ibid, Vol. 3, pp. 225-228.

206. Ibid, Vol. 3, pp. 228f.

207. See for example, al-Ghazālī, *Iḥyā'*, Vol. 3, p. 58.

208. Al-Ghazālī, *Iḥyā'*, Vol. 4, p. 103. For a detailed discussion of these means, see Abul Quasem, *The Ethics of al-Ghazālī: A Composite Ethics in Islam*, Selangor (Malaysia): Central Printing Sendirian Berhad, 1976, pp. 58-64.

209. Ibid, Vol. 4, p. 394.

210. Ibid, Vol. 4, p. 192.

211. Ibid, Vol. 4, pp. 191f.

212. Al-Ghazālī defines *zuhd* as a state in which man controls his desires (*shahawāt*) and anger (*ghaḍab*) so that they follow the motive (*bā'ith*) of *dīn* and the signal (*ishārah*) of faith (*īmān*), see al-Ghazālī, *Iḥyā'*, Vol. 4, p. 79.

213. Al-Ghazālī, *Iḥyā'*, Vol. 4, p. 316.

214. Ibid, Vol. 3, p. 231.

215. Ibid, Vol. 3, pp. 231-252. For an extended discussion of this aspect, though in an ethical context, see Abul Quasem, *The Ethics*, pp. 127-129.

216. Ibid, Vol. 4, pp. 493f, trans., T.J. Winter, *The Remembrance of Death and the Afterlife*, trans. of *Kitāb Dhikr al-Mawt wa mā Ba'dah* of al-Ghazālī 's *Iḥyā'*, Cambridge: The Islamic Texts Society, 1989, p. 122.

217. Ibid, Vol. 4, p. 494, trans., see Winter, *The Remembrance*, pp. 123f.

218. Ibid, Vol. 4, p. 494, trans., see Winter, *The Remembrance*, p. 2.

219. Ibid, Vol. 4, p. 494, trans., see Winter, *The Remembrance*, p. 2.

220. Ibid, Vol. 4, p. 76.

221. Ibid, Vol. 4, p. 63.

222. Al-Ghazālī, *al-Munqidh*, pp. 124-131, trans., McCarthy, *Deliverance*, pp. 93-98, and also Watt, *The Faith*, p. 77-85.

223. Ibid, p. 124, trans., McCarthy, *Deliverance*, p. 93, and also Watt, *The Faith*, p. 77.

224. Al-Ghazālī, *al-Qisṭās al-Mustaqīm*, ed. Maḥmūd Bījū, Damascus: al-Maṭbaʿah al-ʿIlmiyyah, 1983, pp. 11-12, trans., McCarthy, "The Correct Balance," in McCarthy, *Deliverance*, p. 245.

225. Ibid, p. 14, trans., McCarthy, "The Correct Balance," p. 246.

226. Ibid, p. 14, trans., McCarthy, "The Correct Balance," p. 246.

227. Ibid, p. 15, trans., McCarthy, "The Correct Balance," p. 247.

228. Ibid, pp. 19-41, trans., McCarthy, "The Correct Balance," pp. 249-261.

229. Ibid, pp. 48f, trans., McCarthy, "The Correct Balance," pp. 264f.

230. Ibid, pp. 55-61, trans., McCarthy, "The Correct Balance," p. 268f.

231. Al-Ghazālī, *al-Munqidh*, p. 124, trans., McCarthy, *Deliverance*, p. 93, and also Watt, *The Faith*, p. 77.

232. Ibid, p. 124, trans., McCarthy, *Deliverance*, p. 93, and also Watt, *The Faith*, p. 77.

233. Ibid, p. 110-114, trans., McCarthy, *Deliverance*, pp. 83-87, and also Watt, *The Faith*, pp. 63-68.

234. This can be considered as al-Ghazālī's positive solution for the phenomenon in view whereas his earlier attempt in the *Tahāfut* to disillusion those who think too highly of the philosophers by exposing the incoherence and contradiction involved in their metaphysical thought was a negative solution.

235. Ibid, pp. 110f, trans., McCarthy, *Deliverance*, pp. 83f, and also Watt, *The Faith*, pp. 63f.

236. Ibid, p. 111, trans., McCarthy, *Deliverance*, p. 84, and also Watt, *The Faith*, p. 64.

237. Ibid, pp. 111f, trans., McCarthy, *Deliverance*, p. 84-85, and also Watt, *The Faith*, p. 64-66.

238. Ibid, p. 111, trans., McCarthy, *Deliverance*, p. 84, and also Watt, *The Faith*, p. 64.

239. Ibid, p. 112, trans., McCarthy, *Deliverance*, pp. 84f, and also Watt, *The Faith*, pp. 65f.

240. This term has been mistranslated as 'astronomical' by both McCarthy (*Deliverance*, p. 85) and Watt (Watt, p. 65).

241. Al-Ghazālī, *al-Munqidh*, p. 112, trans., McCarthy, *Deliverance*, p. 85, and also Watt, *The Faith*, p. 65.

242. Ibid, p. 124, trans., McCarthy, *Deliverance*, p. 93, and also Watt, *The Faith*, p. 78.

243. Ibid, p. 125-129, trans., McCarthy, *Deliverance*, p. 94-97, and also Watt, *The Faith*, pp. 78-83.

244. Ibid, p. 130f, trans., McCarthy, *Deliverance*, pp. 97f, and also Watt, *The Faith*, p. 84f.

245. Singular of *'ulamā'*.

246. Al-Ghazālī, *Iḥyā'*, Vol. 3, p. 287, & Vol. 4, p. 49.

247. Ibid, Vol. 3, p. 199.
248. Ibid, Vol. 3, p. 49.
249. Ibid, Vol. 3, p. 64.
250. Ibid, Vol. 4, pp. 49f.
251. Ibid, Vol. 4, p. 63.
252. Ibid, Vol. 4, p. 75.
253. Ibid, Vol. 3, p. 49, trans., see Winter, *On Disciplining*, p. 5.
254. Ibid, Vol. 3, pp. 52f, trans., see Winter, *On Disciplining*, pp. 15f.
255. Ibid, Vol. 3, p. 53, trans., see Winter, *On Disciplining*, p. 17.
256. Ibid, Vol. 3, p. 53, trans., see Winter, *On Disciplining*, p. 17.
257. Ibid, Vol. 3, p. 53, trans., see Winter, *On Disciplining*, p. 18.
258. Ibid, Vol. 3, p. 53, trans., see Winter, *On Disciplining*, p. 19.
259. Ibid, Vol. 3, p. 54, trans., see Winter, *On Disciplining*, p. 19.
260. Ibid, Vol. 3, p. 55, trans., see Winter, *On Disciplining*, p. 24.
261. Ibid, Vol. 3, p. 55, trans., see Winter, *On Disciplining*, p. 24.
262. Ibid, Vol. 3, pp. 55f, trans., see Winter, *On Disciplining*, pp. 24f.
263. Ibid, Vol. 3, p. 56, trans., see Winter, *On Disciplining*, p. 25.
264. Ibid, Vol. 3, p. 56, trans., see Winter, *On Disciplining*, pp. 25f.
265. Ibid, Vol. 3, p. 56, trans., see Winter, *On Disciplining*, p. 26.
266. Ibid, Vol. 3, p. 56, trans., see Winter, *On Disciplining*, pp. 26f.
267. Ibid, Vol. 3, pp. 64f, trans., see Winter, *On Disciplining*, pp. 51-54.
268. Ibid, Vol. 3, p. 64, trans., see Winter, *On Disciplining*, pp. 51f.
269. Ibid, Vol. 3, p. 58, trans., see Winter, *On Disciplining*, p. 32.
270. Ibid, Vol. 3, p. 65, trans., see Winter, *On Disciplining*, p. 54.
271. Ibid, Vol. 3, p. 65, trans., see Winter, *On Disciplining*, p. 54.
272. Ibid, Vol. 3, p. 64, trans., see Winter, *On Disciplining*, p. 51.
273. Ibid, Vol. 3, p. 65, trans., see Winter, *On Disciplining*, p. 54.
274. Ibid, Vol. 3, pp. 196 & 358.
275. Ibid, Vol. 4, p. 75.
276. Ibid, Vol. 4, p. 50.
277. See, for example, al-Ghazālī, *Iḥyā'*, Vol. 3, p. 199.
278. Al-Ghazālī, *Iḥyā'*, Vol. 2, p. 306-357. For an extended summary of this chapter in English, see Cook, Michael. *Commanding Right and Forbidding Wrong in Islamic Thought*, Cambridge: Cambridge University Press, 2000, pp. 428-446.
279. Al-Ghazālī, *Iḥyā'*, Vol. 2, p. 306.
280. Ibid, Vol. 2, pp. 306-312.
281. Ibid, Vol. 2, pp. 312-335.
282. Ibid, Vol. 2, pp. 335-342.
283. Ibid, Vol. 2, pp. 343-357.
284. Ibid, Vol. 1, p. 36 & Vol. 3, p. 405.
285. Al-Ghazālī, *al-Munqidh*, p. 107, trans., McCarthy, *Deliverance*, p. 82, and also Watt, *The Faith*, p. 61.

286. Al-Ghazālī, *al-Maqṣad al-Asnā fī Sharḥ Ma'ānī Asmā' Allāh al-Ḥusnā*, ed. Faḍlah Shaḥādah, Beirut: Dār al-Mashriq, 1971, p. 165, trans., See Robert Stade, *Ninty-Nine Names of God in Islam*, trans. of the major portion of al-Ghazālī's *al-Maqṣad al-Asnā*, Ibadan (Nigeria): Daystar Press, 1970, pp. 132-133.

287. Al-Ghazālī, *al-Maqṣad*, p. 169, trans., see Stade, *Ninty-Nine Names*, p. 136.

288. Al-Ghazālī, *al-Munqidh*, pp. 83-84, trans., McCarthy, *Deliverance*, p. 66, and also Watt, *The Faith*, p. 37.

289. Ibid, pp. 79-90, trans., McCarthy, *Deliverance*, pp. 63-70, and also Watt, *The Faith*, pp. 32-43.

290. Ibid, p. 79, trans., McCarthy, *Deliverance*, p. 63, and also Watt, *The Faith*, p. 33.

291. Ibid, pp. 79-80, trans., McCarthy, *Deliverance*, pp. 63-64, and also Watt, *The Faith*, pp. 33-34.

292. Ibid, p. 80, trans., McCarthy, *Deliverance*, p. 64, and also Watt, *The Faith*, p. 34.

293. Al-Ghazālī, *Iḥyā'*, Vol. 1, p. 22, trans., MaCall, "The Book of Knowledge," p. 87, and also Faris, *The Book of Knowledge*, p. 46.

294. Al-Ghazālī, *al-Munqidh*, p. 80, trans., McCarthy, *Deliverance*, p. 64, and also Watt, *The Faith*, p. 34.

295. Ibid, p. 81, trans., McCarthy, *Deliverance*, p. 64, and also Watt, *The Faith*, p. 34-35.

296. Ibid, p. 80, trans., McCarthy, *Deliverance*, p. 65, and also Watt, *The Faith*, p. 36.

297. Ibid, p. 83, trans., McCarthy, *Deliverance*, p. 66, and also Watt, *The Faith*, p. 36-37.

298. Ibid, p. 83, trans., McCarthy, *Deliverance*, p. 66, and also Watt, *The Faith*, p. 37.

299. Ibid, p. 85, trans., McCarthy, *Deliverance*, p. 67, and also Watt, *The Faith*, p. 38.

300. Ibid, p. 86, trans., McCarthy, *Deliverance*, p. 67, and also Watt, *The Faith*, p. 38.

301. Ibid, p. 86, trans., McCarthy, *Deliverance*, p. 67, and also Watt, *The Faith*, p. 39.

302. Ibid, p. 86, trans., McCarthy, *Deliverance*, pp. 67-68, and also Watt, *The Faith*, p. 39.

303. Ibid, p. 87, trans., McCarthy, *Deliverance*, p. 68, and also Watt, *The Faith*, p. 39.

304. Ibid, p. 89, trans., McCarthy, *Deliverance*, p. 70, and also Watt, *The Faith*, p. 42.

305. Ibid, pp. 93-99, trans., McCarthy, *Deliverance*, pp. 72-77, and also Watt, *The Faith*, pp. 45-54.

306. Ibid, p. 93, trans., McCarthy, *Deliverance*, p. 72, and also Watt, *The Faith*, p. 46.

307. Ibid, p. 93, trans., McCarthy, *Deliverance*, p. 72, and also Watt, *The Faith*, p. 46.

308. Ibid, p. 99, trans., McCarthy, *Deliverance*, p. 77, and also Watt, *The Faith*, pp. 53-54.

309. Al-Ghazālī, *Iḥyā'*, Vol. 1, p. 58, trans., MaCall, "The Book of Knowledge," p. 242, and also Faris, *The Book of Knowledge*, p. 147.

310. Ibid, Vol. 1, p. 59, trans., MaCall, "The Book of Knowledge," p. 242, and also Faris, *The Book of Knowledge*, p. 147.

311. Ibid, Vol. 1, p. 60, trans., MaCall, "The Book of Knowledge," p. 248, and also Faris, *The Book of Knowledge*, p. 150.

312. Ibid, Vol. 1, p. 60, trans., MaCall, "The Book of Knowledge," p. 248, and also Faris, *The Book of Knowledge*, p. 150.

313. Ibid, Vol. 1, pp. 60-82, trans., MaCall, "The Book of Knowledge," pp. 248-345, and also Faris, *The Book of Knowledge*, pp. 150-212.

314. Ibid, Vol. 1, p. 82, trans., MaCall, "The Book of Knowledge," p. 345, and also Faris, *The Book of Knowledge*, p. 212.

315. Ibid, Vol. 1, p. 68, trans., MaCall, "The Book of Knowledge," p. 283, and also Faris, *The Book of Knowledge*, p. 172.

316. Ibid, Vol. 4, p. 98.

317. Ibid, Vol. 1, p. 2, trans., MaCall, "The Book of Knowledge," p. 3, and also Faris, *The Book of Knowledge*, p. x.

318. Ibid, Vol. 4, p. 98.

319. See, for example, al-Ghazālī, *Iḥyā'*, Vol. 4, p. 50, trans., Stern, *al-Ghazzali on Repentance*, p. 115.

320. Ibid, Vol. 4, p. 50, trans., Stern, *al-Ghazzali on Repentance*, p. 115.

321. Ibid, Vol. 4, p. 50, trans., Stern, *al-Ghazzali on Repentance*, p. 115.

322. Ibid, Vol. 4, p. 50, trans., Stern, *al-Ghazzali on Repentance*, p. 115.

323. Ibid, Vol. 1, p. 112.

324. Abdul Qayyum, *Letters of al-Ghazzali*, p. 116.

325. Ibid, p. 118.

326. Ibid, p. 119.

327. Ibid, p. 119.

328. Al-Ghazālī, *Iḥyā'*, Vol. 1, p. 17, trans., MaCall, "The Book of Knowledge," p. 68, and also Faris, *The Book of Knowledge*, pp. 33-34.

329. Ibid, Vol. 4, p. 98.

330. Ibid, Vol. 3, p. 324.

331. Al-Ghazālī, *Iḥyā'*, Vol. 4, p. 51, trans., Stern, *al-Ghazzali on Repentance*, p. 116.

332. In one of his letters to the Sultan Sanjar, al-Ghazālī writes: "on several occasions I served as an ambassador on behalf of your father to the court of the 'Abbāsid caliph al-Muqtadar Billāh and did all that

was possible to remove certain misconceptions between the Seljūq Empire and the ʿAbbāsid Caliphate," (Abdul Qayyum, *Letters of al-Ghazzali*, p. 28).

333. Al-Ghazālī, *Iḥyā'*, Vol. 1, p. 68, trans., MaCall, "The Book of Knowledge," p. 283, and also Faris, *The Book of Knowledge*, p. 172.

334. Abdul Qayyum, *Letters of al-Ghazzali*, p. 28.

335. Al-Ghazālī, *Iḥyā'*, Vol. 2, pp. 135-142.

336. Ibid, Vol. 2, pp. 142-152.

337. Abdul Qayyum, *Letters of al-Ghazzali*, p. 30.

338. Ibid, p. 30.

339. Ibid, p. 37.

340. Ibid, p. 45.

341. Ibid, p. 48.

342. Ibid, p. 87.

5

Assessment of al-Ghazālī's *iṣlāḥī* teachings

Introduction

$\mathscr{H}$aving shown the extent of al-Ghazālī's *iṣlāḥī* efforts in the previous chapter as objectively as I am able, now it is proper that I carry out a general assessment of his *iṣlāḥī* teachings, attempting to firstly discover the main strengths and weaknesses therein, and secondly to show how far they stand against main criticisms. By doing so, hopefully I will make a further key step towards the verification of the hypothesis of the present study.

Hoping to achieve this aim, the present chapter judges al-Ghazālī's *iṣlāḥī* teachings in general, according to the following major criteria: (1) originality, (2) clarity, (3) deepness, (4) balance between individualism and collectivism, (5) realism and practicality, and (6) Islamic-justification.

With this selection of criteria, I certainly do not claim that I will conduct a full or detailed examination of al-Ghazālī's *iṣlāḥī* teachings. This range of criteria, however, shall fulfil the purpose of the present chapter.

Originality

It can be generally stated that originality characterizes al-Ghazālī's *iṣlāḥī* teachings in the main. This is clearly reflected in his diagnosis of *fasād* above, which is mainly based on his own observation and reflection, as is evident in the many fresh and contemporary examples provided in his examination of the roots and phenomena of *fasād* in his time. His lengthy list of the various deluded groups and his detailed explanation of how they were deluded, in the *Iḥyā'*,[1] reflects his own wide observation and fresh reflection. His selection of the "Common Wrongs in Customs," mentioned above, which includes various contemporary examples also shows his continuing dependence on his observation and reflection.

Another aspect of al-Ghazālī's originality which is reflected in his diagnosis is his reliance on his own investigation. This is particularly visible in his approach to discovering the reasons behind the phenomenon of the widespread weakness and laxity of *īmān* (Islamic faith). As has been mentioned above, he questioned for a period of time those who fell short in following the Islamic Revealed Law (*al*-Sharī'ah) and came out with his own conclusion.

The originality of al-Ghazālī is also reflected, to a great extent, in his treatments of the phenomena of *fasād*, which are supported by his fresh insights and unique reasoning. In fact it is typical of al-Ghazālī that he does not simply represent previous thoughts in the topics he discusses, rather he often highlights their shortcomings before he presents his own treatment. This makes his treatments very far from being blindly imitative to any previous ones. A good illustration of this is his discussion of the true nature of good and bad character, which is based on his critical examination of the views of his predecessors and on his highlighting of their shortcomings, as has been stated above.

Al-Ghazālī's originality has greatly impressed a number of distinguished scholars in the East and West, to the extent that he has been considered by some as "the most original thinker that Islām has produced."[2] This, however, may be challenged by the following. As is commonly known among the students of al-Ghazālī, his teachings contain various elements which are identical, in one way or another, to their counterparts in other earlier works, namely Sufi, philosophical, and religious sources. This has led some to accuse al-Ghazālī of plagiarism in a sense of copying from these sources without crediting them. In his book on al-Ghazālī's critics and admirers, al-Qaradawi[3] lists this attitude,[4] which he himself has noticed also, as one of the criticisms which have been raised by some of the contemporary Arab critics of al-Ghazālī.

This criticism is also popular among the orientalists; Arberry, for instance, criticizes al-Ghazālī of extensively plagiarising from *Kitāb al-Tawahhum* of al-Muḥāsibī in the concluding *Kitāb* of the *Iḥyā'*.[5] Likewise, in the brief entry on al-Makkī in the Encyclopaedia of Islam, Massignon writes that whole pages of his *Qūt al-Qulūb* have been copied by al-Ghazālī in the *Iḥyā'*.[6] In a similar way, but without taking it as a judgment on al-Ghazālī's ethical attitude, Lazurus-Yafeh states that "al-Ghazālī evidently copied not only ideas, images, proverbs, quotations and such like; he copied whole parts of books without mentioning the authors' names."[7] Similarly, Margaret Smith, in her article entitled "The Forerunner of al-Ghazālī," asserts that to al-Muḥāsibī "al-Ghazālī owes much more of his teaching than has been generally realized, and much that has been attributed to al-Ghazālī as representing his original ideas, are in fact based upon the earlier teaching of al-Muḥāsibī and, in many instances, is directly borrowed from him."[8]

All this apparently contradicts what have been stated about al-Ghazālī's originality. For various reasons, however, it is difficult to follow those who make such accusations, and it cannot be taken as a postulate and without considerable reservation. The accusation, firstly, does not seem to consider the fact that the concept of plagiarism and the attitude towards it have changed over time; the criteria of this act in the current age is considerably different than that in al-Ghazālī's time.[9] Therefore, it is not a fair approach to use criteria which have been comparatively recently developed in judging works that belong to an age heavily relying on memorisation of knowledge by heart, and on oral transmission of it, as that of al-Ghazālī.

Secondly, in some places of his books, al-Ghazālī does indeed credit the sources from which he directly quotes.[10] In his general account of condemning richness (*al-ghinā*) and praising poverty (*al-faqr*) in the *Iḥyā'*, for instance, he acknowledges borrowing al-Muḥāsibī's teaching on this topic and clearly states that it deserves to be quoted literally.[11]

Thirdly, the approach of selecting particular passages from al-Ghazālī's works and accusing him of copying them from other sources without looking to each work as a whole, leads, I argue, to misleading conclusions. However, by considering each of his works as a whole and then comparing it with the earlier sources which he consulted, one may come to entirely different conclusions. The *Iḥyā'*, for example, is evidently a unique book of its kind, compared to all the sources from which al-Ghazālī borrowed some material here and there. None of al-Ghazālī's critics dares to argue that the *Iḥyā'*, as a whole, is similar to any earlier work of al-Ghazālī's predecessors such as al-Makkī's *Qūt al-Qulūb* or Miskawayh's *Tahdhīb al-Akhlāq*. Thus, by viewing al-Ghazālī's works from this angle, his originality proves itself.

As a matter of fact, achieving such a sort of originality was intended by al-Ghazālī when he composed the *Iḥyā'*, as he clearly states in the introduction of the book:

> Indeed people have composed books concerning some of these ideas, but the present book differs from them in five ways: First, by clarifying what they have obscured and elucidating what they have treated causally; second, by arranging what they have scattered and organizing what they have separated; third, by condensing what they have made lengthy and proving what they have reported; fourth, by omitting what they have repeated and affirming what they have written correctly; fifth, by determining ambiguous matters which have been difficult to be understood and which have not been dealt with in books at all.[12]

Fourthly, it is partial and simplistic approach to accuse al-Ghazālī of plagiarism by merely highlighting materials which al-Ghazālī borrowed from other sources and isolating them from their wider respective contexts. What really matters is not whether al-Ghazālī borrowed particular ideas from other sources, but rather how he uses them in his works. This question seems to be ignored by those who have accused al-Ghazālī of plagiarism.

To scholarly deal with this critical question, it is essential, as Sherif puts it, "to reconstruct and obtain a comprehensive view of al-Ghazālī's thought and understand the way he synthesizes the different traditions…"[13] By attempting to tackle this question in this way, Sherif has proven that al-Ghazālī's deployment of these various and diverse elements serves particular functions in his own teachings, which are very different from their functions in their original sources. By deeply studying al-Ghazālī's ethical teaching—as presented in his principal works—which is, as he observes, a central theme in al-Ghazālī's writings and a good representative of all the diverse fields to which he contributed,[14] Sherif has explored in detail the nature of this aspect of al-Ghazālī's originality, though he has called it "the unity in al-Ghazālī's thought."[15] He has thoroughly examined the treatment of al-Ghazālī of three different and apparently contradictory elements which are present in his ethical writings, namely virtues in philosophical, religious-legal, and mystic traditions, and has intelligently shown how al-Ghazālī was able to synthesize his unique composite theory of virtue—which is in his view a key aspect of his ethical theory—[16]by bringing all of these elements together in a special way in which they complement each other and makes a whole "which is not merely the sum of the parts, but has its own characteristics as an ethical theory."[17] Thus, he assures that al-Ghazālī "never merely copies or combines diverse ideas in a random way, but selects, transforms, and weaves certain aspects of them together with a view to a particular end, ultimate happiness."[18] Sherif concludes by stating that al-Ghazālī freely moves "from one tradition to another, filling in the gaps in the one with the complementary element of the other, and modifying those aspects which cannot, in their original form, be incorporated into his new framework."[19]

In a wider scope, Abul Quasem in his lengthy account of the ethical theory of al-Ghazālī has discussed this composite nature of al-Ghazālī's teaching and has asserted that "with his extraordinary genius, al-Ghazālī was able to mingle the various elements and systemize them into a well-ordered and consistent whole."[20]

Another testimony to the originality of al-Ghazālī, but in another subject area, is delivered by Michael Cook in his book, which surveys the accounts of the duty of "commanding good and forbidding wrong" appearing in literature of the major Islamic sects and schools. Although al-Ghazālī belongs to the Shāfi'ī law-school, Cook is convinced that a distinction should be made between al-Ghazālī's account on the duty and that of all other Shāfi'īs.[21] Therefore, he devotes a whole chapter to al-Ghazālī's account. A major reason behind this, as he points out, is the high distinctiveness of al-Ghazālī's account.[22] Recording his observation of the originality of al-Ghazālī's account of this duty as presented in the *Iḥyā'*, Cook states: "to the best of my knowledge it is almost entirely his own."[23] He further states that even when al-Ghazālī employs earlier thoughts, he presents them in clearly different wordings.[24] In addition, he has observed two further aspects of al-Ghazālī's originality in his account: its striking structure with its unique divisions and its innovative terminologies, and its uncommon perspective which includes the practicalities of the duty.[25]

All these scholarly testimonies effectively acknowledge al-Ghazālī's originality and thus render any further discussion of the accusation of plagiarism unnecessary.

Clarity

Besides originality, admirable clarity is a striking strength of al-Ghazālī's *iṣlāḥī* teachings. By this quality, I mean that his teachings are highly readable and remarkably coherent. As a matter of fact, this characterizes al-Ghazālī's style in general. To illustrate this characteristic, I shall highlight below a number of aspects of the clarity of al-Ghazālī's style supported by representative examples.

Presenting overviews before detailed discussions

In his discussion of a particular topic, al-Ghazālī often presents a vivid overview of the topic under study first, then he follows it with detailed discussion. This attitude is very evident, for example, in his treatment of curing heart sicknesses in the *Iḥyā'*. Before discussing the cures for specific heart sicknesses in detail, he gives a general account of the topic in "The Book of Disciplining the Soul, Refining the Character, and Curing the Sicknesses of the Heart" (*Kitāb Riyāḍah al-Nafs wa Tahdhīb al-Akhlāq wa Mu'ālajah Amrāḍ al-Qulūb*). In the introduction of this *Kitāb*, he explains the purpose of this general account as follows:

> In this Book we shall indicate a number of sicknesses of the heart, and provide a general discourse on how these are to be treated, without giving details of cures for specific ailments, since these will be set forth in the remaining Books (*kutub*) of this Quarter (*rub'*). Our present purpose is to review in an overall fashion how the traits of character may be refined, and to provide a preparatory method for this.[26]

In addition to being important in preparing the reader for the detailed discussion to come, al-Ghazālī is convinced that this method is essential for attaining a comprehensive understanding. Commenting on the interesting organization of his book *al-Mustaṣfā*, al-Ghazālī explicitly mentions this additional significance:

> I have composed it and brought to it an admirable, delicate organization. The reader shall at first look become aware of all the aims of this science and shall grasp all the dimensions of thoughts within it. For every science where the student cannot get at the outset its foundations and structure, leaves him no chance of attaining its inner secrets and goals.[27]

Précising after detailing

What adds to the clarity of al-Ghazālī's writing is his habitual stylistic attitude of making concise précis after his extended discussions. This is very visible in al-Ghazālī's works in general and in the *Iḥyā'* in particular, where précising phrases, such as "in short" (*bi al-jumlah*),[28] appear quite often.[29] A good representative example for this stylistic habit in the *Iḥyā'* is the précis given at the end of the exposition of the reasons of arrogance (*al-kibr*). Al-Ghazālī summarizes his detailed discussion of these reasons in the following very well thought out and precise sentence: "In short, every a blessing (*ni'mah*) which may be regarded as a perfection (*kamāl*), even if it is not really perfection in itself (*bi nafsih*), can become a matter of arrogance."[30]

Giving diferent names to distinguish distinct ideas

For the purpose of clarity, al-Ghazālī usually distinguishes between the ideas or the thoughts which he discusses by giving a name to each distinct one. This point becomes clearer by considering the following example from the *Iḥyā'*. In discussing the involuntary suggestions (*khawāṭir*) which take place in the heart (*al-qalb*) and stir up the desire (*al-shahwah*), he divides them into two categories: "that which provokes evil (*al-sharr*), I mean that leading to a harmful aftermath; and that which motivates to good (*al-khayr*), I mean that which is profitable in the next world."[31] Explaining the need for giving each type a different name, he says that "these are two different suggestions and thus need two different names."[32] Then, he distinguishes between them by name: "The praiseworthy suggestion (*khāṭir*) is called *ilhām* (inspiration) and the blameworthy suggestion, I mean that which leads to evil is called *wiswās* (whispering)."[33] This attitude is based on the general rule, which al-Ghazālī mentions in several places in the *Iḥyā'* that "there is no restraint in terminologies when the meanings are understood" (*lā ḥajr fī al-asāmī baʿd fahm al-maʿānī*).[34] This explains why al-Ghazālī focuses on meanings or contents rather than expressions.[35]

Defining the meanings of the technical terms

Normally al-Ghazālī does not leave the key terms which he uses in technical or special usage without a clear definition, and thus his reader would not become uncertain about what he really means by them. This habitual practice adds to the clarity of al-Ghazālī's teachings, as is very noticeable in his works in general and the *Iḥyāʾ* in particular. It has been shown in the above survey of al-Ghazālī's *iṣlāḥī* efforts that a number of key terms used in al-Ghazālī's diagnosis and treatments in special meanings are fully defined by him, such as *al-taqlīd, al-qalb, al-dunyā, bāʿith al-dīn,* and *al-khuluq.*

Using apt metaphors

Another aspect of the clarity of al-Ghazālī's style is that he frequently uses apt metaphors to illustrate his teachings, particularly when he wants to clarify subtle ideas. Many of such metaphors are given in the *Iḥyāʾ*. A striking example is his use of a pig, a dog, a devil, and a sage to represent the four inherent qualities of man's heart (*qalb*) in order to elucidate the harm of these qualities, when any of them becomes predominant, and to show how to bring them under control. After specifying these four qualities, which are wildness (*al-bahīmiyyah*), bestiality (*al-sabʿiyyah*), devilry (*al-shayṭāniyyah*), and superiority (*al-rabbāniyyah*), and the forms of *fasād* resulting from each one of them when it becomes predominant, he uses these four metaphors as follows:

> "Every man has within him a mixture of these four qualities—I mean superiority (*al-rabbāniyyah*), devilry (*al-shayṭāniyyah*), bestiality (*al-sabʿiyyah*), and wildness (*al-bahīmiyyah*)—and all of these are collected in the heart (*al-qalb*), as though the total in a man's skin is a pig, a dog, a devil, and a sage. The pig is appetite (*al-shahwah*), for a pig is not reproached because of its

colour or shape or form, but because of its greed, covetousness, and avidity. The dog is anger, for the carnivorous beast and the mordacious dog are not dog and beast from the standpoint of their appearance or colour or shape, but rather the essence of the meaning of bestial quality is voracity and hostility and mordacity. Now in man's interior are the voracity and rage of the beast, and the greed and lust of the pig. Thus, the pig through greed invites to the vile and the abomination, and the wild beast by anger calls to injustice and harmful acts. The devil continuously stirs up the appetite of the pig and the wrath of the wild beast, and seduces one by the other and presents to them in a favourable light that for which they have a natural propensity. The sage, who represents the intellect (*al-ʿaql*), is in duty to repel the craftiness and cunning of the devil by revealing his deception through its piercing insight and radiant and clear light; and to break the greed of this pig by making the dog its master. For by means of anger he breaks the vigour of appetite. He wards off the voracity of the dog by making the pig its master and bringing the dog in subjection under its rule. If he does that and is capable of it, the matter is in equilibrium (*iʿtidāl al-amr*) and justice is manifest in the kingdom of the body, and all proceeds on the straight path; but if he is unable to overcome them, they dominate him and bring him into servitude, and so that he is continually seeking out stratagems and carefully thinking to satisfy the pig and please the dog, and thus he will always be in servitude to a dog and a pig."[36]

Giving identical similes

In addition to parables, al-Ghazālī's writings are full of similes which clarify abstract notions. He has a striking ability of giving similes which are highly identical to the ideas which he wants to explain. A good example is the simile in which he compares the disciplining of the soul (*riyāḍah al-nafs*) to the weaning of young children and the training of riding beasts. After stating that the soul (*al-nafs*) "doe not become tame before its Lord or enjoy His remembrance until it is weaned from its habits...,"[37] and that "this is a heavy burden for the aspirant at the outset, but ultimately becomes a source of pleasure,"[38] he gives the following two similes:

> Like a small boy who finds being weaned from the breast a hardship, and cries bitterly and with anguish, and is repelled by the food which is set before him as a substitute for his milk. However, if he is then denied any milk at all, he finds his abstinence from food extremely exhausting, and when hunger overmasters him, he eats. Although this is an effort at first, in due course it becomes second nature to him, so that were he to be returned to the breast he would leave it alone and dislike its milk, having acquired a familiarity with food. Similarly, a riding-beast initially shies away from saddle and bridle, and will not be ridden, and has to be forced to endure these things, and must be restrained with chains and ropes from the roaming at will which had been its custom. Later it becomes so familiar with these things that when it is left untethered it stands quite still.[39]

Making helpful cross-references

Al-Ghazālī's habit of cross-referring to relevant information in his works contributes to the clarity of his style. Throughout his principal books, rich cross-references are often made, an impressive skill prior to the invention of the press particularly in works in the size of the *Iḥyā'*.

There are three forms of cross-references that appear in al-Ghazālī's works. The first is that directing to pertinent discussion to come in the same work.[40] The second is that referring to relevant information mentioned earlier in the same source.[41] The third is that pointing to other books of al-Ghazālī.[42] All this make tracing the related discussions easy and thus helps in attaining a comprehensive understanding of al-Ghazālī's views.

Arranging and structuring his thoughts in a logical way

The writings of al-Ghazālī are easy to follow because they, in general, are arranged and structured in a logical way. In addition, it is one of his stylistic habits that he explains the logic behind the arrangement and the structure of the topics he intends to discuss right at the introduction of his works and also at the beginning of almost every chapter of his books. A case in point is the logic behind the structure of the whole *Iḥyā'* which is explained by al-Ghazālī in the introduction of the book as follows:

> What have made me to arrange this book in four parts is two things: The first, which is the fundamental motive, is that this arrangement in establishing what is true and in exposition is imperative; because the branch of knowledge by which one approaches the next world is divided into the knowledge of the Praxis (*'ilm al-mu'āmalah*) and the knowledge of the Unveiling (*'ilm al-mukāshafah*)…This book only concerns with the knowledge of the Praxis and not with the knowledge of the Unveiling, which is not permitted to be recorded in books… The knowledge of the Praxis is divided into outward knowledge (*'ilm ẓāhir*), I mean the knowledge of actions done by bodily members (*'ilm a'māl al-jawāriḥ*), and inward knowledge (*'ilm bāṭin*), I mean the knowledge dealing with the activities of the hearts (*a'māl al-qulūb*)…The outward part, which is connected with the physical members, is subdivided into acts of worship (*'ibādah*) and habitual acts (*'ādah*). The inward part, which is connected with the states of the heart and the characteristics of the soul, is subdivided into blameworthy and praiseworthy states. So the total makes four divisions…The second motive is that I have noticed that the eager interest of students is in *fiqh* (Islamic jurisprudence) …which is set fourth in four divisions, and he who follows the style of one who is beloved becomes beloved.[43]

Adopting consistent style

The considerable consistency in al-Ghazālī's style is another factor of his clarity. This is also typical of al-Ghazālī. The analysis of Lazarus-Yafeh of the expressions and idioms which very frequently appear in al-Ghazālī's basic and authentic works and thus can be considered, according to her,[44] typical of al-Ghazālī's style shows that there is a remarkable consistency in his style throughout his life.[45]

Using lucid and unsophisticated language

A further element of al-Ghazālī's clarity is that the language of his writing is lucid and free from sophisticated expressions. Thus, it is highly readable. This would be very appreciated if al-Ghazālī's language is compared to, for example, that of his teacher, al-Juwaynī, which has been considered as mysterious even by early established scholars such as al-Subkī.[46]

Deepness

Deepness is another strength of the *iṣlāḥī* teachings of al-Ghazālī. I have particularly noticed this in his diagnosis of *fasād*, which reflects a deep scrutiny of the nature of the *fasād* in his time. As has been shown in the preceding chapter, he deeply diagnosed not only various phenomena of *fasād* in his time, but also the roots of *fasād* in general.

This aspect of al-Ghazālī's deepness has been highlighted in other studies on al-Ghazālī. With reference to the *Iḥyā'*, al-Nadwī, for instance, points out that al-Ghazālī examined therein the whole of the Muslim society at the time.[47] Following his outline of al-Ghazālī's wide and thorough examination of the society and its various classes, al-Nadwī assures that the *Iḥyā'* shows that al-Ghazālī's observation is deep and that he was expert in people's ways of life.[48]

The deepness of al-Ghazālī is also reflected on his scholarly approach in both his diagnosis of *fasād* and his *iṣlāḥī* treatments. It is typical of al-Ghazālī that when tackling a particular issue, he does not satisfy himself with partial treatment of it, but rather he amazingly gives careful attention to almost all the related aspects. In his discussion of the main roots of *fasād*, for example, we have seen how he pays close attention to various aspects of these roots, explaining in detail what causes them and what their consequences are.

Likewise, al-Ghazālī's deepness is evident in the scholarly methods, which he adopted in his diagnosis of the phenomena of *fasād*. A good illustration of this is his investigation of the reasons behind the phenomenon of widespread laxity of *īmān*. He did not rely on his mere impression or quick observation, but rather he questioned for a period of time a number of those who were affected by this phenomenon, as was mentioned above.

What adds to al-Ghazālī's deepness is his insightful analysis. This is also typical of his teachings, which are full of deep insights. A good illustration for this is his profound psychological analysis of man's reality, as has been outlined above.

Balance between individualism and collectivism

The question of whether al-Ghazālī in his *iṣlāḥī* teachings balances between individualism and collectivism, as a test of quality, is problematic and thus requires careful examination.

To begin with, al-Ghazālī has been seriously accused of failing to meet this criterion. Commenting on al-Ghazālī's ethics, Muḥammad Mūsā, for instance, has strongly attacked al-Ghazālī for not being concerned with the interest of the collective in his school of ethics, and that he was solely concerned with the interest of the individual, for he specifies as the ultimate goal of ethics, achieving the individual's happiness and not the happiness of the community as a whole.[49] Similarly, Su'ād al-Ḥakīm has condemned al-Ghazālī for overemphasizing the salvation of the individual whereas Islam, as she has described, commingled between the salvation of the individual and that of the collective.[50]

It is true that what may be called "individual-orientedness" characterizes al-Ghazālī's *iṣlāḥī* teachings in general, and by this it is meant that the utmost goal of his teachings is the individual spiritual salvation of man and his attainment of the ultimate happiness in the next world.[51] It is also true that al-Ghazālī's emphasis on the individual may create a sort of selfish spirit among his followers; by literally following specific instructions in the *Iḥyā'*, in particular, one may end up living a selfish life in the meaning of being exclusively, and probably excessively, concerned with the spiritual development of the self. For example, after warning from being concerned with *iṣlāḥ* of others before finishing the task of *iṣlāḥ* of the self, al-Ghazālī explains in the *Iḥyā'* what he means by finishing from the self-*iṣlāḥ*: "When you have finished purifying yourself and you have become able to forsake the outer and the inner sins and that has become a habit and a second nature..."[52] Now, since it is very difficult, if not impossible, to reach that level of purification, the ardent follower of this advice most likely will never become concerned with *iṣlāḥ* of others.

Although such instruction of explicitly individualistic nature strongly supports the above criticism against al-Ghazālī, it is difficult to form a definitive judgment on the question in view. This is simply because there are several other instructions from al-Ghazālī which clearly show that caring for the collective and taking on responsibilities towards them are two essential elements in his teachings. A good representative example for this is his teachings on the duties of brotherhood, companionship, neighbourhood, relatives, and Muslims in general for which he devoted a whole *kitāb* in the *Iḥyā'*.[53] A more self-evident example is his account on the duty of "commanding right and forbidding wrong" (*al-amr bi al-maʿrūf wa al-nahy ʿan al-munkar*).[54] This account as a whole, and particularly his strong argumentation against the view that uprightness (*al-ʿadālah*) is one of the conditions for performing the duty and that a transgressor (*fāsiq*) cannot perform it,[55] clearly shows apparently opposite position on the issue of *iṣlāḥ* of others before the completeness of *iṣlāḥ* of the self, in contrast with the above view.

Now, the difficult problem is how to resolve the apparent contradiction between al-Ghazālī's teachings of individualistic spirit and those of collective nature. This, in our view, is a very challenging problem and really deserves a separate study, but meanwhile one cannot but affirm such contradiction and consider it a serious weakness in his *iṣlāḥī* teachings. As a provisional attempt to interpret this apparent contradiction, I may suggest that it is a partial contradiction between al-Ghazālī's *fiqhī* views and his teachings, which are based on Sufi tradition or legacy.

I would now like to discuss another criticism levelled against al-Ghazālī, which is not unrelated to the criterion in view. That is the accusation of being passive toward the challenge of the Crusaders facing the Muslim *ummah* in his time. It is a popular criticism among contemporary critics of al-Ghazālī that he kept silent on this external crisis, as there is no reference to it in his works or *fatāwā*, although he witnessed the Frankish invasion of some Muslim lands, namely Jerusalem in 492/1098.[56]

There have been various theories on this unexpected silence. Al-Qaradawi, for example, while admitting that al-Ghazālī's position on this regard is "puzzling," for a man of his status knows what should have been said and done in such condition,[57] he offers two interpretations which can be paraphrased as follows. The first is that when that external threat started and developed al-Ghazālī was in seclusion during which his main concern was self-purification and his own salvation; but even after his abandonment of seclusion, there was no indication of being concerned with that issue, which was related to the future of the whole Muslim *ummah*.[58] This, al-Qaradawi continues, has led some to say that Sufis, including al-Ghazālī, believed that the Crusader invasion was a Divine Punishment for Muslims as a result of their sins; and thus, they were negative towards it.[59] The second interpretation offered by al-Qaradawi, which is more apologetic, is that al-Ghazālī was primarily preoccupied with *iṣlāḥ* from within, for internal *fasād* paves the way for external invasion, as the Qur'an indicates.[60]

Similar to this second interpretation is the view of Abu-Sway who says:

> In my opinion, Al-Ghazzāliyy [sic.] realized that the Islamic Caliphate at the time was corrupt and filled with social and ideological trends that ran against Islamic *shari'ah*. I think he was convinced that the disease was within the state, and that the Crusaders were nothing but the symptoms. Al-Ghazzāliyy understood that the core of the issue was moral. To solve this problem, he wanted to educate people and to revive the role of the Shari'ah and its aims (*maqāṣid*).[61]

What really matters to the present study is whether this criticism disproves the classification of al-Ghazālī as a *muṣliḥ*. In order to fairly answer this question, it is important to consider the following points:

1. The real position of al-Ghazālī on the challenge of the crusaders is not known for certain. This is simply because it is difficult to claim that everything about him was reported, especially during his seclusion period, about which only little is known for sure, as stated above. The fact that nothing was reported as a direct response from him to that challenge does not seem a sound proof to base on it a positive view about his real position or to put in his mouth words that he had not uttered. Silence alone is open to interpretation.

2. By recalling the historical context of the First Crusade and the overall Muslim response, which have been purposely illustrated above, it can be stated that one of the major reasons behind the defeat of Muslims by the Crusaders was the internal conflicts among Muslim leaders in particular, and lack of unity among Muslims in general. As Hillenbrand puts it in short: "It is a familiar tenet of Crusader history that the warriors of the First Crusade succeeded because of Muslim disunity and weakness. Had the First Crusade arrived even

ten years earlier, it would have met strong, unified resistance from the state then ruled by Malikshah, the last of the three so-called Great Seljuq sultans."[62]

3. These internal conflicts mainly resulted from the struggle over worldly interests, or according to al-Ghazālī's terminology in his *iṣlāḥī* teachings "love of the *dunyā*." So, by treating this particular reason behind the internal conflicts, which was one of the major concerns of al-Ghazālī as was shown previously, one can say that he was indirectly responding to the major cause of the defeat of Muslims. In other words al-Ghazālī was concerned with treating what has been called by al-Kīlānī "becoming disposed to defeat" (*qābiliyyah al-hazīmah*).[63]

4. As was shown in the previous chapter, al-Ghazālī's attempts at *iṣlāḥ* focused on several internal challenges of the Muslim *ummah*, which were no less serious than the external ones, not to mention the challenge of the Bāṭinīs, which contributed to the general weakness of Muslims. Now, even if he did not directly respond to the challenge of the Crusader invasion, despite its seriousness, this alone is not enough to discredit him as a *muṣliḥ*. It is not necessary that one has to deal with all the challenges of one's time in order to be considered as a *muṣliḥ* from the Islamic perspective, for not even every prophet did so.

Realism and practicality

For the sake of convenience, realism and practicality are considered here as a dual criterion because they are somehow related.

Making a general judgment on whether al-Ghazālī's *iṣlāḥī* teachings meet this dual criterion is problematic. On one hand, there are various aspects of realism and practicality clearly appearing in his teachings. To start with, it is very evident that al-Ghazālī in his *iṣlāḥī* teachings focuses on practical issues. This can be considered as a characteristic of his religious and spiritual teachings in general. As Timothy Gianotti has recently emphasised, "when it comes to spiritual and religious direction, al-Ghazālī is a most practical man."[64] This, he further states, "is nowhere more clearly seen than in the *Iḥyā'* itself, which is designed to be a step-by-step manual for religious and spiritual formation."[65] Gianotti has concluded his study on what he calls "al-Ghazālī's unspeakable doctrine of the soul" by the following statement: "In the end, I argue that he was, above all else, a practical man, even in his mysticism."[66]

This characteristic appears right at the Introduction to the *Iḥyā'* in which al-Ghazālī states that "the book only concerns with the knowledge of the Praxis (*'ilm al-mu'āmalah*) and not with the knowledge of the Unveiling (*'ilm al-mukāshafah*), which is not permitted to be recorded in books."[67] Commenting on this, Gianotti says:

> So, even though he touches on the knowledge of the Unveiling in this and many other parts of the *Iḥyā'*, he tells us in no uncertain terms that the work itself is about the knowledge of Right Practice—which is for everyone—and not about the disclosure of the contents of mystical noesis—which is beyond most people's ability to bear and is no way a requirement for salvation.[68]

Al-Ghazālī's practicality is also reflected in his continuous warning in the *Iḥyā'* from wasting time on issues that do not lead to actions, or issues for which there is no actual need. For example, he blames the *'ulamā'*, who rather than occupying themselves with problems of their day and those of frequent occurrence, pursue the unusual issues and exhaust themselves in dealing with problems which most likely never occur.[69]

In addition to being focused on practical issues, al-Ghazālī's *iṣlāḥī* teachings are based on existing facts rather than visionary. All the problems which are mentioned in the survey above existed in his time, and none of them can be classified as imaginary.

Furthermore, al-Ghazālī often explicitly rejects impracticable thoughts and ideal solutions. For instance, as has been shown previously, he does not necessitate a complete suppression of desires in order to achieve goodness in character;[70] and he rejects the assumption of a group of Sufis that the purpose of spiritual struggling (*mujāhadah*) is to completely suppress all desires.[71]

On the other hand, there are elements of apparent idealism or extremeness voiced in al-Ghazālī's *iṣlāḥī* teachings, and this has led students of Islamic thought to evaluate some of al-Ghazālī's teachings as being impractical, and even harmful, in the case of many people, if not the majority. Al-Ḥakīm, for example, has condemned al-Ghazālī's division in the *Iḥyā'* of a twenty-four-hour Muslim day into specified parts (*awrād*) and his arrangement of obligatory and voluntarily Islamic worship accordingly,[72] reserving that such an "ideal" pattern of Muslim day cannot be followed except by very few Muslims, and blaming him of addressing himself to a restricted group of Muslims, i.e., devoted worshipers (*al-'ibād*). In reference to the *Iḥyā'* also, al-Nadwī, though he appraises the book in general, states that many of those who restrict their reading to this book, or very often and avidly read in it, would adopt an extreme attitude of asceticism, renouncement of permissible worldly pleasure, and excessive disciplining to the extent that it would affect their health and mind.[73]

To fairly deal with this problematic issue, it is important to consider the following clarifying points about al-Ghazālī's teachings. First, his teachings are based on his differentiation between the strong in religiousness (*al-aqwiyā' fī al-dīn*) or the select few (*al-khawāṣ*), who have high religious and spiritual qualities, and the weak (*al-ḍu'afā'*).[74] In fact, he explicitly states in the *Iḥyā'* that "the aim of such a book as this is that it be helpful to the *aqwiyā'* and established *'ulamā'*," though he says that "we shall strive to make the *ḍu'afā'* understand by means of giving examples so that it may be close to their understandings."[75] Thus, it is crucial to distinguish his teachings which are merely directed to the *aqwiyā'* or the *khawāṣ* from those which are intended for the others. Failing to do this may lead to imprecise judgment.

Second, al-Ghazālī usually takes into consideration the differences in the circumstances of people in his teachings. He, for example, states that "the method of struggle (*mujāhadah*) and discipline (*riyāḍah*) varies from one person to the next, in accordance with their circumstances."[76] Therefore, applying his teachings without considering the different circumstances of people may lead to unfavourable effects.

Third, he considers gradualness a condition for success in religious disciplining and soul purification; and thus he continuously warns from ignoring gradualness for it may lead to reversing results. For example, in his direction of breaking the greed of the stomach, he highlights the harm of not applying gradualness by stating that "the constitution of a man who is accustomed to eating much, and who then changes all at once to eating only a little, will not be able to sustain this, and will be weakened, resulting in considerable hardship and distress."[77]

Fourth, moderation is an essential general guiding principle in al-Ghazālī's teachings for he clearly states that "the most exalted desideratum in all matters and morals is the mean (*al-wasaṭ*), for the best of affairs is the middle course, and both extremes in any matter are blameworthy,"[78] and that "the mean is required in all traits of character which have opposite,"[79] quoting the saying of the Prophet (ṣ), "the best of affairs is the middle course (*khayr al-umūr awāṣituhā*)."[80]

Fifth, although al-Ghazālī teaches that moderation should be aimed for, he at the same time believes that following the middle course should be only after one's nature has been set in equilibrium. A good illustration for this precise point is particularly found in al-Ghazālī's "Exposition of the Variance in the Rule and Merit of Hunger in Accordance with Circumstances of Men" (*bayān ikhtilāf ḥkum al-jūʿ wa faḍīlatih wa ikhtilāf aḥwal al-nās fīh*).[81] After his general statement about the mean (*al-wasaṭ*) quoted above, he goes on to say:

Our discourse concerning the merits which attach to hunger may have suggested that extremeness is required in this regard, but this is certainly not the case. For it is one of the secret wisdom of the Sharī'ah that whenever man's nature demands that he go to an unsound extreme, the Sharī'ah also goes to extreme in forbidding this, in a fashion which to an uninformed man might suggest that it requires the complete opposite of what human nature (*ṭab'*) demands. The *'ālim* (the learned), however, realises that it is the mean that is required. This is because human nature, demanding as it does the maximum of satiety, must be countered by the Sharī'ah with praise of extreme hunger, so that the instincts of man's nature and the prohibitions of the Sharī'ah stand opposite one another, thereby bringing about an equilibrium. For it is unlikely thing that a man might suppress his nature entirely, rather he will realise that he shall never reach this goal. Even were he to go to the greatest extreme in countering his nature, the Sharī'ah would indicate that he had erred.[82]

Explaining the mean in eating for a man of moderate nature, he continues:

You should also know that the best course for a man of moderate nature is to eat so that his stomach is not heavy, but without feeling the pangs of hunger. One should forget one's belly, and not harbour any preference for hunger. For the purpose of eating is the preservation of life and the gaining of strength for worship: a heavy stomach is an obstruction to worship, and so are the pangs of hunger, for they distract the heart.[83]

Al-Ghazālī, however, makes the following exception for this general principle:

This, however, comes about after one's nature has been set in equilibrium. At the outset, should the soul have a tendency to bolt, crave the satisfaction of its desire, and incline to excess, the mean (*al-wasaṭ*) will yield it no advantage; instead one must go to extreme lengths to hurt it with hunger, in the way that one must employ hunger, blows and other things to hurt a riding beast that is not broken in until it becomes moderate in its temperament. When it is broken in, becomes balanced, and reverts to the equilibrium, one may cease training and hurting it.[84]

Although this extreme disciplining is exception to the rule, the following explanation from al-Ghazālī indicates that he believes that it is the best way of disciplining in most cases:

> Since the dominant condition of the soul is one of greed, desire, rebellion, and refusal to worship, the most profitable thing for it is hunger, the pain of which it feels under most circumstances, and which leads to its subjugation. The intention is that the soul should be broken in this way until it becomes balanced, which condition will abide even after it returns to its food.[85]

In his closing of this "Exposition," al-Ghazālī directly addresses those who are in charge of disciplining "wayfarers on the Path of the next world" (*sālikī ṭarīq al-ākhirah*) by stating:

> These secrets should not be unveiled by a *shaykh* of the Path to his aspirants. Instead he should confine himself to praising hunger, and not summon them to moderation (*al-iʿtidāl*), for if he did so they would certainly fall short of it: he should rather summon them towards the very extremes of hunger, in order that such moderation might become easy for them. He should not tell them that the prefect gnostic (*al-ʿārif*) may dispense with self-discipline, for this would furnish the devil with a pathway to their hearts, so that he would constantly be whispering to each of them, "You are a perfect gnostic; what more gnosis and perfection could you need?"…The strong (i.e., in religiousness: *al-qawī*), when he devotes himself to disciplining and *iṣlāḥ* of others, must descend to the level of the weak in order that he might resemble them and be gentle when driving them towards their saving felicity…[86]

In the light of all the discussion above, I conclude that al-Ghazālī's *iṣlāḥī* teachings are considerably realistic and practical, particularly his general principles, but when it comes to matter of details, especially with regard to Soul disciplining, there appear unrealistic and impractical aspects. This is mainly because he necessitates extreme disciplining in most cases, though he believes in moderation as a general rule. In our view, such extreme disciplining can easily lead to alienation from the outset in the case of many people. Thus, I consider it a major weakness in al-Ghazālī's *iṣlāḥī* teachings, regardless of his attempt to justify it, simply because his way of justifying this particular point does not stand criticism, as shall be further discussed below.

Islamic-justification

In the main, al-Ghazālī's *iṣlāḥī* teachings are supported by proofs from the Islamic fundamental sources, namely the Qur'an and the Sunnah. This typifies the works of al-Ghazālī under study. Even in presenting his own insights and reflections in these works, al-Ghazālī almost always justifies them by quoting evidences from the Islamic primary sources. As a general rule, "any insight (*istibṣār*)," he explicitly states, "which can't be justified by (*lā yashhad lah*) the Qur'an and the Sunnah is not reliable."[87] Thus, there is no wonder that his works are full of citation from these two sources.

Al-Ghazālī's justification of his teachings, however, has been seriously challenged by a number of distinguished Muslim scholars over the centuries. This will be further discussed under the following three sub-headings: (1) the "foreign elements" in al-Ghazālī's teachings, (2) al-Ghazālī and the unjustified Sufi tradition, and (3) al-Ghazālī's reliance on unsound *aḥādīth*.

The "foreign elements" in al-Ghazālī's teachings

This section focuses on the question of justification of what have been called "foreign elements" presented in al-Ghazālī's works and which may be traced back directly or indirectly to un-Islamic sources, namely the works of ancient philosophers. Because of such elements, al-Ghazālī has been criticized since his time. His contemporary al-Māzirī[88] (d. 536/1141), the celebrated Malkī scholar, is a good representative early example of those who raised such criticism. In the course of his reply to a question about his view on the *Iḥyā'*, he accused al-Ghazālī of (a) relying much on Ibn Sīnā (Avicenna) in his philosophical thought, (b) engaging in reading *Ikhwān al-Ṣafā* which, as he pointed out, a mixture of philosophy and knowledge of Sharī'ah, and (c) mingling between the knowledge of Sufis and the views of philosophers.[89]

Al-Māzirī was undoubtedly a distinguished Muslim scholar, but one cannot regard his accusation as serious, though it has been continually repeated by the critics of al-Ghazālī, because of the following reasons. First, strangely enough, his view was based on what he heard from al-Ghazālī's students and companions and not on his own reading of the *Iḥyā'*, as he admitted.[90]

Second, his accusation has been effectively challenged by other established Muslim scholars, namely al-Subkī (d. 771/1370).[91] Deprecating the claim that the *Iḥyā'* includes un-Islamic philosophical thoughts, al-Subkī, who unlike al-Māzirī was a close reader of al-Ghazālī's works, refuted the view of al-Māzirī and stated that al-Ghazālī charged Ibn Sinā and the philosophers with disbelief, so how can it be said that he followed them and based his work on their teaching.[92] In his view, the difference in the school of jurisprudence (*fiqhī madhhab*), the approach (*ṭarīqah*), and the disposition (*mazāj*) of al-Māzirī in contrast with al-Ghazālī necessitated repulsion between the two.[93]

Third, the criticism of al-Māzirī is far from being as convincing as al-Ghazālī's own detailed reply to some of his contemporaries who accused him of recording in some of his books thoughts from the works of the ancient philosophers. He states in the *Munqidh*, "as a matter of fact, some of them [i.e., the claimed philosophical thoughts] are the product of my own reflections and it is not improbable that ideas should coincide, just as a horse's hoof may fall on the print of another hoof."[94] In addition to the possibility of coincidence, al-Ghazālī further clarifies that some of the thoughts under question "are found in the *shar'ī* (religious) books and the sense of most is found in the writings of the Sufis."[95] Even with the assumption that a thought is found only in the writings of the philosophers, al-Ghazālī further states that "if what is said is reasonable in itself and corroborated by apodictic proof and not contrary to the Qur'an and the Sunnah, then why should it be shunned and rejected?"[96]

This last statement reflects, to begin with, al-Ghazālī's open-mindness; as a principle he did not totally reject a thought just because it was mentioned by the philosophers. Thus, he, in the words of Winter, "was not a crude 'fundamentalist', opposed on principle to any possibility of learning from abroad."[97] In fact one of al-Ghazālī's concerns was to highlight the harm which may result from such tendency. He states in the *Munqidh* that "if we were to open this door and aim at forgoing every truth which had been first formulated by the mind of one in error, we would have to forgo much of what is true."[98] He further says that such tendency "would be an invitation to those in error to wrest the truth from our hands by putting it into their own books."[99] This principle position of al-Ghazālī agrees with the well-known teaching of the Prophet of Islam who says: "Wisdom is the lost animal of the believer; wherever he finds it, it is he that has the most right to it."

The above statement of al-Ghazālī also shows his criteria for accepting "foreign elements". The first is that they have to be supported by justified proofs. The second is that they do not contradict the Qur'an and the Sunnah.

It is far beyond the limitation of the present study and the limitation of my own knowledge too, however, to fully verify whether al-Ghazālī complied with these criteria in all his *iṣlāḥī* teachings which may be traced back to the works of philosophers. Nevertheless, this can be partially proved by the finding of the previously mentioned study of Sherif with regard to the compliance of al-Ghazālī with these criteria in his theory of virtue, which is very relevant to the present study. Sherif has interestingly demonstrated how al-Ghazālī justifies his employment of some philosophic analysis, which he finds useful in synthesising his own theory of virtue either by drawing upon direct related Islamic argument or at least by showing that they do not contradict with Islamic teaching.[100] Eliminating any possible wrong assumption that al-Ghazālī's attitude is a superficial way of "Islamization," Sherif has concluded that, unlike some other Muslim thinkers who welcome any device which can be used to reconcile philosophic ethics with Islamic moral teachings, al-Ghazālī does not consider the partial modifications he introduces into philosophic virtues sufficient to justify synthesizing those virtues with their Islamic counterparts; a more comprehensive approach, transforming these virtues into an integral part of a new, wider framework, is necessary. [101]

Al-Ghazālī and the unjustified sufi tradition

Another criticism which has been raised since a very early time against al-Ghazālī's justification of his teachings is that he often relies on Sufi traditions which contradict with Islamic principles found in Islamic primary sources, or at least cannot be supported by Islamic evidence. One of the earliest holders of this criticism and a well-known representative of it is Ibn al-Jawzī (d. 597/1201) who strongly attacked al-Ghazālī in a number of his books, namely *Talbīs Iblīs*, and whose attack has been noticeably repeated since his time. Because his criticism has been widely followed and because it has been considered a very serious criticism, it deserves a detailed discussion.

In *Talbīs Iblīs*, Ibn al-Jawzī criticizes al-Ghazālī in the context of his extreme lengthy criticism against the approaches of the Sufis and his polemic against a number of their teachings which in his view completely contradict with the Sharī'ah.[102] Concerning al-Ghazālī, the starting point of his criticism is that he accused him of composing the *Iḥyā'* in the same approach of earlier Sufis chiefly al-Muḥāsabī and that he acknowledged their wrong teachings and strongly supported them.[103] Ibn al-Jawzī mentions three reasons behind al-Ghazālī's support of such teachings:

- Dispensing with *fiqh* and ignoring its law for the sake of Sufism.[104]
- Becoming Sufi himself made him in fully support of the Sufi teachings.[105]

- Relying on fabricated and unsound traditions attributed to the Prophet (ṣ) without knowing that they are spurious.[106]

By examining the criticism of Ibn al-Jawzī, the following comments regarding the validity of his criticism can be made, excluding the point concerning al-Ghazālī's reliance on fabricated prophetic traditions, which will be discussed in the following sub-heading.

First, there is a considerable misquoting of al-Ghazālī by Ibn al-Jawzi; he quite often omits some of al-Ghazālī's words which have crucial effect in understanding the true position of al-Ghazālī on the issues under question. For example, he denounces al-Ghazālī for writing the following statement in the *Iḥyā'*: "The disciple should not concern himself with marriage,"[107] whereas the original text of the *Iḥyā'* reads: "The disciple, in his beginning,[108] should not concern himself with marriage."[109] Noticeably and very strangely the phrase "in his beginning" is omitted in Ibn al-Jawzī's quoting, indicating that al-Ghazālī discourages marriage in general and not in a particular situation and for particular reasons as the original words as well as the context clearly reveal.

Second, Ibn al-Jawzī often disconnects al-Ghazālī's quotes from their respective contexts and does not seem to consider these contexts in his criticism.[110] This leads to great misrepresentation of al-Ghazālī's views. Ibn al-Jawzī, for example, attacks al-Ghazālī's saying in the *Iḥyā'* that "some say: The Lordship has a secret if it was unveiled, the Prophecy would become null...,"[111] while unexpectedly he totally ignores al-Ghazālī's comment immediately following this quote which says: "The one who says this if he did not mean by it that nullity of the Prophecy is with reference to weak people due to their shortcoming in their understanding, then what he said is not true and the reality is that there is no controversy on it [i.e., the Sharī'ah]."[112]

Third, similarly, the approach of Ibn al-Jawzī in presenting the view of al-Ghazālī which he criticizes is very selective; he selects specific quotes from particular places in the *Iḥyā'* and ignores some related discussions either in the same context or elsewhere in the same book, which are important in understanding the true position of al-Ghazālī regarding the problems in view. This shortcoming of Ibn al-Jawzī can be perfectly illustrated in the following example.

In the context of his refutation of the wrong assumption of groups of Sufis who think that having trust (*tawakkul*) in God necessitates giving up means (*al-asbāb*), Ibn al-Jawzī accused al-Ghazālī of being apologist to such groups by accepting the idea of travelling in a desert without food with the intention of relying on God, though with some conditions.[113] This, however, does not precisely reflect the true view of al-Ghazālī on giving up means in the name of having trust in God or *tawakkul*. This is because al-Ghazālī in this particular context is just discussing the conditions that should be met in order to make such travel lawful, as it obviously appears from the context.[114] Nevertheless, his true position from this issue is clearly stated after couple of lines from the above quote where he clearly states that "being away from all means is in defiance of (*murāghamah*) wisdom and an act of ignorant of the Norm (*sunnah*) of Allah Almighty; for acting according to the Norm of Allah Almighty with having trust in Him..., and not the means, does not contradict with *tawakkul*."[115] He further states that if one decides to live in a mountain where there is no water nor grass and where no one normally passes by, then one would be sinful and leading one's self to destruction.[116]

Furthermore, in another context in which al-Ghazālī gives examples for self-delusion (*ghurūr*) among Sufis, he mentions the following example, which Ibn al-Jawzī entirely ignores:

> Among them [i.e., Sufis] one who travels in desert without food in order to justify his claim of *tawakkul*, but he does not realize that this is innovation in religion (*bid'ah*) and it has not been reported from the righteous previous generations (*al-salaf*) nor the companions of the Prophet (*ṣ*), who were more knowledgeable in *tawkkul* than him, yet they did not understand *tawkkul* as an act of risking life and giving up food....[117]

Fourth, it is difficult to follow Ibn al-Jawzī without any reservation on fully equating the approach of al-Ghazālī in the *Iḥyā'* with that of the previous Sufis on the basis of al-Ghazālī's support for their views. In addition to what has been already mentioned with regard to the originality of al-Ghazālī with reference to his use of Sufi works, the following reservation can be expressed over Ibn al-Jawzī's opinion. Although al-Ghazālī in various places in the *Iḥyā'* relies on the literature of earlier distinguished Sufis, he does not restrict himself to their views, and does not simply follow their teachings without critically examining them. In fact, he often highlights the shortcomings of their views and adds essential remarks to their thoughts.[118] Moreover, as a general evaluation, al-Ghazālī characterizes the views of the Sufis as deficient (*qāṣir*) because every one of them, he clarifies, habitually talks on the basis of his own experience or condition (*ḥāl*) only.[119] This is why in various issues, especially those which were debatable among the Sufis, al-Ghazālī did not satisfy himself with what had been said by the earlier Sufis, and thus made his independent examination and came up with his own views on those issues.[120]

Fifth, Ibn al-Jawzī's argument that al-Ghazālī dispensed with the law of *fiqh* in the *Iḥyā'* in favour of Sufism is an unfair generalized judgment. Throughout the book, the *fiqh* of al-Ghazālī is distinctively voiced. In fact, even when he agrees with particular views of earlier Sufis, including those which are quoted by Ibn al-Jawzī, he normally justifies his choice using the reasoning of *fiqh*, in addition to other sorts of reasoning, regardless of whether we agree or disagree with his justification. A case in point is his agreement with al-Muḥāsibī's view that poverty is better than richness.[121] Following his long quote of al-Muḥāsibī's argument on this issue, al-Ghazālī states that this view can be supported by all the traditions which he mentioned in the "Book of Condemnation of the *Dunyā*" and the "Book of Poverty and Abstinence" of the *Iḥyā'*, in addition to other evidences, which he would further mention.[122] Thus, he did not follow the view of al-Muḥāsibī just because al-Muḥāsibī was a Sufi, but because al-Ghazālī was convinced that it could be justified by evidences from the Qur'an and the Sunnah, notwithstanding how sound his evidences were. It is worth noting that al-Ghazālī quotes al-Muḥāsibī in this specific context because he wanted to show that poverty is better than richness in general, but his detailed view on the issue is presented in the "Book of Poverty and Abstinence" in which he discusses the controversy on the issue and deeply examines it,[123] which itself shows his deepness in *fiqh*.

This, however, does not mean at all that the *Iḥyā'* is free from Sufi tradition which clearly contradict with *fiqhī* rules. In fact, al-Ghazālī himself does not deny this, as shall be seen in a moment. This poses the challenging question about al-Ghazālī's true position on such tradition. To adequately tackle this problem, there is a need for a separate detailed study, but, meanwhile, I ought to sum up the controversy surrounding this problem and then give a provisional assessment.

A good representative example of the Sufi tradition contradicting *fiqhī* rules quoted in the *Iḥyā'* is the following story. In his discussion of the practical part of treating love of status (*jāh*), and specifically in the course of describing how some Sufis may treat their soul diseases by some methods which can be seen as unlawful from a *fiqh* perspective, al-Ghazālī recounts the incident of a Sufi whose well-known abstinence had brought him high status and many followers; thus, he entered a bath-house and intentionally wore the clothes of someone else, then, he stood outside on the road; consequently, he was caught, and beaten, and the clothes were taken from him, and as a result, people renounced him.[124]

Referring to this incident, but again not giving any attention to the related discussion in the same context, Ibn al-Jawzī severely condemns al-Ghazālī's telling of such incidents and states:

> Glorious is He who moved Abū Ḥāmid from the circle of *fiqh* by his composition of the book of the *Iḥyā'*, I wish that he had not mentioned in it such things which are unlawful. Strange enough from him to say them, praise them, and call their people *arbāb al-aḥwāl* (People of Spiritual States).[125]

Defending al-Ghazālī, with reference to the same story, Murtaḍā al-Zabīdī (1205/1791) argues that Sufis are *mujtahidūn* in the way of soul purification, so, what they find most beneficial for their hearts they go for it; and that particular incident is inconsistent with the Islamic principle which states that when two potential harms are in dilemma, the less harmful should be committed.[126]

More convincing apologia for al-Ghazālī and a recent strong counter-argument against Ibn al-Jawzī is that of al-Shāmī:

> We side with Ibn al-Jawzī on wishing that al-Ghazālī had not mentioned that story, but we don't side with him in disconnecting it from its immediately preceding context in which al-Ghazālī gives his fiqhī opinion: al-Ghazālī asserts that "the action of the Malāmatiyyah—that is committing apparently disgraceful deeds (*al-fawāḥish*) in order to lower their status in the eyes of people—is unlawful for every individual...Bu what is lawful is doing permissible acts (*fiʿl al-mubāḥāt*) which lower the status among people..." That is what al-Ghazālī has asserted and that is a clear legal opinion, free from ambiguity...[127]

After emphasising that the story under question is mentioned in that particular context and that al-Ghazālī points out that such an act is questionable from a *fiqh* point view, i.e., there is no agreement that it is lawful or unlawful, al-Shāmī states "al-Ghazālī, then, mentions a fact that Sufi *mashāyikh* sometimes treat their personal conditions with different methods than that of *faqīh*. So, what is wrong in al-Ghazālī's position, and where did that cross him out from the circle of *fiqh*?"[128]

Now, I agree with al-Shāmī on the total importance of considering the context in which al-Ghazālī mentions such Sufi tradition, and I side with him on that al-Ghazālī's telling of such incidents in such contexts does not bring him out of the circle of *fiqh*, but I cannot agree with him that there is nothing wrong in al-Ghazālī's approach. Instead, I may argue that al-Ghazālī's reporting of such deviant acts, of which nothing similar seems to have been reported from the early Muslim generations, which is one of al-Ghazālī's own criteria of justification, as has been quoted above, despite his true position on them, is an unfortunate mistake. Such acts are potentially harmful, for they may direct, though unintentionally, to excessive religiousness among the eager readers of al-Ghazālī. In addition, they can easily lead to misunderstanding of the actual position of al-Ghazālī, particularly because not every reader of the *Iḥyā'* has the ability to perform close and comprehensive reading, bearing in mind the large size of the work. Lastly, these odd stories, as I have personally experienced, often sidetrack the reader from the major principles of al-Ghazālī's teachings.

Al-Ghazālī's reliance on unsound aḥādīth

A very popular criticism against al-Ghazālī's justification of his teachings, namely in the *Iḥyā'*, is that he heavily relies on weak and fabricated *aḥādīth* (traditions attributed to the Prophet of Islam). On this, in the words of al-Shāmī, "there is a consensus among the critics."[129] In his harsh criticism of the *Iḥyā'*, Ibn al-Jawzī, for example, frankly accused al-Ghazālī of filling the *Iḥyā'* with spurious (*bāṭilah*) *aḥādīth* without knowing their spuriousness.[130]

Although no one can deny al-Ghazālī's reliance on such *aḥādīth*, this fact has been greatly overstated, and thus it deserves a careful reassessment. As a humble attempt to do so, I would like to highlight the following points.

First of all, it is a gross exaggeration and even a false accusation to say, as al-Ṭarṭūshī reported claiming, that al-Ghazālī filled the *Iḥyā'* "with lying upon the Messenger of Allah (ṣ), for I do not know a book over the face of the Earth which is more lying than it."[131] To totally reject such a puzzling claim, it is important to emphasise that al-Ghazālī quoted the traditions under question from earlier works without being aware of their falsity. Al-Subkī asserts that al-Ghazālī in the *Iḥyā'* "did not report a single *ḥadīth* on his own authority."[132] This means that al-Ghazālī did not commit the crime of *ḥadīth* fabrication, and this can be supported by al-Ghazālī's strict view about that major sin:

> Some presupposed that it is permissible to fabricate *aḥādīth*, encouraging virtuous deeds and warning from sins, and they claim that such a purpose is right; but it is an absolute wrong, for the Messenger of Allah (ṣ), said: (Whoever lies upon me, deliberately, should reserve his seat in Hill-fire) and that must not be committed except when there is an absolute necessity; but there is no absolute necessity, for truthfulness is an alternative to lying and the revealed *āyāt* and the reported traditions are enough. Now, the word of that who says, "those have been repeated and have become ineffective, while what is new is more influential," is a mania (*hawas*) because that is not a justified purpose in contrast with the harmful consequences of lying upon the Prophet (ṣ), and upon Allah Almighty, and that will open the door for things which confuse (*tushawwish*) the Sharī'ah, so, the intended good purpose does not resist the evilness of its consequences. Moreover, lying upon the Messenger of Allah (ṣ), is one of the major sins (*min al-kabā'ir*)…[133]

Secondly, there is a real need to revise what has been considered as a postulate among the students of al-Ghazālī that he ignored the study of the discipline of Ḥadīth.[134] It is true that this has been supported by al-Ghazālī's utterance in his book *Qānūn al-Ta'wīl* that his knowledge in *'ilm al-Ḥadīth* is little (*biṭā'atī fī 'ilm al-ḥadīth muzjāh*),[135] but this should not be taken at its face value. The fresh and unique study of al-Mahdalī about al-Ghazālī's knowledge in the field of Ḥadīth has interestingly shown that he had a considerable interest in this discipline, and that he had a wide study of it.[136] By carefully studying al-Ghazālī's books, the *Mankhūl*, the *Iḥyā'*, and the *Mustaṣfā*, al-Mahdalī has found thereupon expositions and allusions, which clearly show that al-Ghazālī had a knowledge of Ḥadīth.[137]

Thirdly, the accusation of Ibn al-Jawzī, and those who follow him, that al-Ghazālī filled the *Iḥyā'* with such traditions[138] is only an exaggeration,[139] for it indicates that the majority of the traditions in the *Iḥyā'* are false, and that is incorrect, as has been statistically proven in the study of al-Mahdalī employing the following steps.[140] As a starting point, he counted the number of all the traditions in the *Iḥyā'* for which al-Subkī could not find *isnād*[141] (chain of narrators), and thus he found that they are about a quarter of the total number of the quoted traditions in the *Iḥyā'*.[142] This, al-Mahdalī states, "shows that most of the traditions of the *Iḥyā'* have *isnād*, but not finding *isnād* for the rest of the traditions does not necessarily mean that the rest do not have *isnād* because al-Subkī's verification (*takhrīj*) is not final."[143] Next, based on Mamdūḥ's index of the *aḥādīth* of the *Iḥyā'*,[144] al-Mahdalī has added up the total number of these *aḥādīth*, which becomes four thousand eight hundred and forty eight (4,848) traditions, excluding the repeated ones which are not included in the index.[145] It is worth mentioning, as al-Mahdalī clarifies, that there are other traditions in the *Iḥyā'* which are not included in the index, though they are few.[146] Now, this total number, al-Mahdalī has concluded, shows the following:[147]

1. Al-Ghazālī quoted the *aḥādīth* of the *Iḥyā'* from many sources, books of Ḥadīth in particular and other sources in general, because this number is not found in the works of Sufis and *fuqahā'*, nor even half of it.
2. Al-Ghazālī used to consult books of Ḥadīth.
3. He had knowledge of Ḥadīth and this is what led him to consult books of Ḥadīth, before and after the *Iḥyā'*.

Finally, the important question which should be raised here is to what extent were al-Ghazālī's teachings influenced by unsound or weak traditions? This is another critical question which deserves a detailed study, but for the time being, I can offer the following provisional answer.

I have noticed that at least a number of al-Ghazālī's teachings were influenced to a considerable extent by such traditions and that is a serious weakness in his teachings. To representatively illustrate this, I shall go back to the above discussion of his "Exposition of the Variance in the Rule and Merit of Hunger in Accordance with Circumstances of Men" (*bayān ikhtilāf ḥkum al-jū' wa faḍīlatih wa ikhtilāf aḥwāl al-nās fīh*).[148] The starting point of his exposition, as has been quoted above, is the following:

> Our discourse concerning the merits which attach to hunger may have suggested that extremeness is required in this regard, but this is certainly not the case. For it is one of the secret wisdom of the Sharī'ah that whenever man's nature demands that he go to an unsound extreme, the Sharī'ah also goes to extreme in forbidding this...[149]

Now, what is the basis of al-Ghazālī's argument that "whenever man's nature demands that he go to an unsound extreme, the Sharī'ah also goes to extreme in forbidding this"? It seems that it is those traditions quoted by him at the beginning of "The Book of Breaking the Two Desires" (*Bāb Kasr al-Shahwatayn*) which encourage hunger.[150] Based on the verification (*takhrīj*) of al-'Irāqī[151] and that of al-Zabīdī as well,[152] all these traditions are unsound.[153] Thus, al-Ghazālī was influenced here by these unsound traditions. This renders his point on extreme disciplining, discussed above, which is based on this argument, unjustified Islamically and that proves our point.

Notes

1. See al-Ghazālī, *Iḥyā'*, Vol. 3, pp. 88-410.
2. Macdonald, "al-Ghazālī, " *EI*, Vol. 2, p. 146.
3. Al-Qaradawi, *al-Imām al-Ghazālī*, pp. 165-167.
4. For an apology for al-Ghazālī on this attitude, see al-Shāmī, *al-Imām al-Ghazālī*, pp. 169-173.

5. A.J. Arberry, *Revelation and Reason in Islam*, London: George Allen & Unwin LTD., 1956, p. 64.
6. Massignon, *EI*, Vol. 3, p. 174, "al-Makkī." Cf. Mohamed Ahmed Sherif, *Ghazali's Theory of Virtue*, Albany: State University of New York Press, 1975, p. 106, who states "al-Ghazali's originality can be seen in his selection, arrangement, and synthesis of the material he extracted from al-Makkī."
7. Lazarus-Yafeh, *Studies in al-Ghazzali*, p. 20.
8. Margaret Smith, "The Forerunner of al-Ghazālī," *Journal of the Royal Asiatic Soceity*, 1936, p. 65, available online in PDF form on *http://www.ghazali.org/articles/smth-frnr.pdf.*
9. Cf. Gustave E. Von Grunebaum, "The Concept of Plagiarism in Arabic Theory," in *Journal of Near Eastern Studies*, Vol. 3 (4), pp. 234-253.
10. Cf. al-Shāmī, *al-Imām al-Ghazālī*, p. 170.
11. Al-Ghazālī, *Iḥyā'*, Vol. 3, pp. 264-271.
12. Ibid, Vol. 1, p. 3, trans., see MaCall, "The Book of Knowledge," p. 144, and also Faris, *The Book of Knowledge*, p. xiv.
13. Sherif, *Ghazali's Theory of Virtue*, p. 108.
14. Ibid, p. 2.
15. Ibid, p. 1.
16. Ibid, pp. 22f.
17. Ibid, p. 22.
18. Ibid, p. 164.
19. Ibid, p. 163.
20. Abul Quasem, *The Ethics of al-Ghazālī*, p. 35.
21. Cook, *Commanding Right*, p. 340.
22. Ibid, pp. 340 & 446.
23. Ibid, p. 446.
24. Ibid, p. 446.
25. Ibid, pp. 447-450.
26. Al-Ghazālī, *Iḥyā'*, Vol. 3, p. 49, trans., see Winter, *Disciplining*, p. 5.
27. Al-Ghazālī, *al-Mustasfā*, Vol. 1, p. 6, trans., see Ḥammād, "Abū Ḥāmid al-Ghazālī's Jurist Doctrine, p. 305.
28. In some contexts, al-Ghazālī uses the same expression for generalisation.
29. See, for instance, al-Ghazālī, *Iḥyā'*, Vol. 1, pp. 58 & 188, Vol. 2, pp. 78 & 103, and Vol. 3, pp. 328, 353, & 356.
30. Al-Ghazālī, *Iḥyā'*, Vol. 3, p. 353.
31. Ibid, *Iḥyā'*, Vol. 3, p. 27, trans., Skellie "The Religious Psychology," p. 104.
32. Ibid, Vol. 3, p. 27, trans., Skellie "The Religious Psychology," p. 104.
33. Ibid, Vol. 3, p. 27, trans., Skellie "The Religious Psychology," p. 104.

34. Ibid, Vol. 3, p. 189.
35. See Lazarus-Yafeh, *Studies in al-Ghazzali*, p. 253.
36. Al-Ghazālī, *Iḥyā'*, Vol. 3, p. 11, trans., see McCarthy, "*Kitāb Sharḥ 'Ajā'ib al-Qalb*," p. 321, and also Skellie, "The Religious Psychology," p. 38f.
37. Ibid, Vol. 3, p. 68, trans., see Winter, *On Disciplining*, p. 64.
38. Ibid, Vol. 3, p. 68, trans., see Winter, *On Disciplining*, p. 64.
39. Ibid, Vol. 3, p. 68, trans., see Winter, *On Disciplining*, p. 64.
40. See, for example, al-Ghazālī, *Iḥyā'*, Vol. 1, pp. 24, 36, 47, 82, Vol. 2, p. 287, Vol. 3, pp. 09, 118, 171, & Vol. 4, p. 15.
41. See, for example, al-Ghazālī, *Iḥyā'*, Vol. 1, p. 284, Vol. 2, pp. 238, 245, Vol. 3, p. 62, & Vol. 4, p. 316.
42. See, for example, al-Ghazālī, *Iḥyā'*, Vol. 1, p. 37, where he refers to his book *al-Mustaẓhirī*, see also Vol. 1, p. 40, where he refers to his book *Qawā'id al-I'tiqād* and his three books of *fiqh*, *al-Basīṭ*, *al-Wasīṭ*, and *al-Wajīz*, and also Vol. 1, p. 50, where he refers to his book *Mi'yār al-'Ilm*.
43. Al-Ghazālī, *Iḥyā'*, Vol. 1, pp. 3f, trans., MaCall, "The Book of Knowledge," pp. 10-12, and also Faris, *The Book of Knowledge*, p. xv.
44. Lazarus-Yafeh, *Studies in al-Ghazzali*, p. 16.
45. Ibid, p. 50.
46. Al-Subkī, *Ṭabaqāt al-Shāfi'iyyh*, Vol. 6, p. 243.
47. Al-Nadwī, *Rijāl*, Vol. 1, p. 309.
48. Ibid, pp. 309-310.
49. Muḥammad Y. Mūsā, *Falsafah al-Akhlāq fī al-Islām*, cited in al-Qaradawi, *al-Imām al-Ghazālī*, pp. 160-163.
50. Su'ād al-Ḥakīm, "*Makānah al-Ghazālī min al-'Ulūm al-Ṣūfiyyah*," in *Majalah al-Turāth al-'Arabī*, Damasqus: Itiḥḥād al-Kuttāb al-'Arab, Issue 22, year 6, Jan. 1996, cited online: *http://www.awu-dam.org/trath/22/turath22-009.htm, visited on 22/12/2006*, no pagination.
51. Sherif has noticed this in his study on al-Ghazālī's theory of virtue; he states that his theory "is oriented towards the well-being of the individual. It concerns itself primarily with man's individual spiritual salvation, the attainment of ultimate happiness in the Hereafter," (Sherif, *al-Ghazali's Theory of Virtue*, p. 169).
52. Al-Ghazālī, *Iḥyā'*, Vol. 1, p. 39, trans., MaCall, "The Book of Knowledge," p. 159, and also Faris, *The Book of Knowledge*, p. 95.
53. Ibid, Vol. 2, pp. 157-220.
54. Ibid, Vol. 2, pp. 306-357.
55. Ibid, Vol. 2, pp. 312-314.
56. See, for example, al-Qaradawi, *al-Imām al-Ghazālī*, pp. 172f.
57. Al-Qaradawi, *al-Imām al-Ghazālī*, p. 172.

58. Ibid, p. 173.

59. Ibid, pp. 173f.

60. Ibid, p. 174, referring to the opening of Qur'an, 17.

61. Mustafa Abu-Sway, *al-Ghazzāliyy* [*sic*]: *A Study in Islamic Epistemology*, Kuala Lumpur: Dewan Bahasa dan Pustaka, 1996, p. 14.

62. Hillenbrand, *The Crusades*, p. 33.

63. Al-Kīlānī, *Hākadhā Ẓahr Jīl Ṣalāḥ al-Dīn*, p. 106.

64. Timothy J. Gianotti, *al-Ghazālī's Unspeakable Doctrine of the Soul: Unveiling the Esoteric Psychology and Eschatology of the Iḥyā'*, Leiden: Koninklijke Brill Nv, 2001, p. 28.

65. Gianotti, *al-Ghazālī's Unspeakable Doctrine*, p. 28.

66. Ibid, p. 176.

67. Al-Ghazālī, *Iḥyā'*, Vol. 1, pp. 3f, trans., MaCall, "The Book of Knowledge," pp. 10-12, and also Faris, *The Book of Knowledge*, p. xv.

68. Gianotti, *al-Ghazālī's Unspeakable Doctrine*, p. 51.

69. Al-Ghazālī, *Iḥyā'*, Vol. 1, p. 77.

70. Ibid, Vol. 3, p. 44.

71. Ibid, Vol. 4, p. 42.

72. Ibid, Vol. 4, p. 42.

73. Al-Nadwī, *Rijāl*, Vol. 1, p. 314.

74. See, for example, al-Ghazālī, *Iḥyā'*, Vol. 3, pp. 98, 318, 323 & 325.

75. Al-Ghazālī, *Iḥyā'*, Vol. 3, p. 6, trans., McCarthy, "*Kitāb Sharḥ 'Ajā'ib al-Qalb*," p. 315, and also Skellie, "The Religious Psychology," p. 18.

76. Ibid, Vol. 3, p. 69, trans., see Winter, *Disciplining*, p. 65.

77. Ibid, Vol. 3, p. 89, trans., see Winter, *Disciplining*, p. 134.

78. Ibid, Vol. 3, p. 96, trans., see Winter, *Disciplining*, p. 154.

79. Ibid, Vol. 3, p. 96, trans., see Winter, *Disciplining*, pp. 155f.

80. Ibid, Vol. 3, p. 96, trans., see Winter, *Disciplining*, pp. 155f.

81. Ibid, Vol. 3, pp. 96-98, trans., see Winter, *Disciplining*, pp. 154-160.

82. Ibid, Vol. 3, p. 96, trans., see Winter, *Disciplining*, p. 154.

83. Ibid, Vol. 3, p. 96, trans., see Winter, *Disciplining*, p. 155.

84. Ibid, Vol. 3, p. 96, trans., see Winter, *Disciplining*, p. 155.

85. Ibid, Vol. 3, p. 96, trans., see Winter, *Disciplining*, p. 156.

86. Ibid, Vol. 3, p. 98, trans., see Winter, *Disciplining*, p. 160.

87. Ibid, Vol. 4, p. 13.

88. Abū 'Abdullāh Muḥammad b. 'Alī al-Māzirī.

89. Cited in al-Subkī, *Ṭabaqāt*, Vol. 4, p. 123.

90. Cited in al-Subkī, *Ṭabaqāt*, Vol. 4, p. 122.

91. Cited in al-Subkī, *Ṭabaqāt*, Vol. 4, pp. 124-126.

92. Cited in al-Subkī, *Ṭabaqāt*, Vol. 4, pp. 126f.

93. Cited in al-Subkī, *Ṭabaqāt*, Vol. 4, pp. 124f.

94. Al-Ghazālī, *al-Munqidh*, p. 88, trans., McCarthy, *Deliverance*, p. 69, and also Watt, *The Faith*, p. 40-41.

95. Ibid, p. 88, trans., McCarthy, *Deliverance*, p. 69, and also Watt, *The Faith*, p. 41.

96. Ibid, p. 88, trans., McCarthy, *Deliverance*, p. 69, and also Watt, *The Faith*, p. 41.

97. Winter, *Disciplining*, p. XLVII.

98. Al-Ghazālī, *al-Munqidh*, p. 88, trans., McCarthy, *Deliverance*, p. 69, and also Watt, *The Faith*, p. 41.

99. Ibid, p. 88, trans., McCarthy, *Deliverance*, p. 69, and also Watt, *The Faith*, p. 41.

100. Sherif, *Ghazali's Theory of Virtue*, pp. 24-76.

101. Ibid, p. 162.

102. Ibn al-Jawzī, *Talbīs Iblīs*, Riyadh: Dār al-Mughnī, 2000, pp. 181-424.

103. Ibid, p. 181.

104. Ibid, pp. 397 & 399.

105. Ibid, p. 197.

106. Ibid, p. 186.

107. Ibid, p. 336.

108. The emphasis here, and in the following quotes as well, is mine.

109. Al-Ghazālī, *Iḥyā'*, Vol. 3, p. 101.

110. This attitude of Ibn al-Jawzī has been noticed also by al-Shāmī, *al-Imām al-Ghazālī*, pp. 175-179.

111. Ibn al-Jawzī, *Talbīs Iblīs*, p. 384.

112. Al-Ghazālī, *Iḥyā'*, Vol. 1, p. 100.

113. Ibn al-Jawzī, *Talbīs Iblīs*, p. 343.

114. See al-Ghazālī, *Iḥyā'*, Vol. 4, p. 266.

115. Ibid, Vol. 4, p. 266.

116. Ibid, Vol. 4, p. 266.

117. Ibid, Vol. 3, p. 406.

118. See, for example, his remark on the classification of Abū Ṭālib al-Makkī of the major sins where he states that it is not sufficient, al-Ghazālī, *Iḥyā'*, Vol. 4, p. 18.

119. See al-Ghazālī, *Iḥyā'*, Vol. 4, p. 42.

120. See, for example, his examination in the *Iḥyā'* of what is better: patience or thankfulness, Vol. 4, pp. 135-141.

121. Al-Ghazālī, *Iḥyā'*, Vol. 3, pp. 264-274.

122. Ibid, Vol. 3, pp. 264-274.

123. Ibid, Vol. 4, pp. 201-205.

124. Ibid, Vol. 3, p. 288.

125. Ibn al-Jawzī, *Talbīs Iblīs*, p. 399.

126. Murtaḍā al-Zabīdī, *Itḥāf*, Vol. 1, p. 52.

127. Al-Shāmī, *al-Imām al-Ghazālī*, pp. 177f.

128. Ibid, p. 178.

129. Ibid, p. 166.

130. Ibn al-Jawzī, *Talbīs Iblīs*, p. 186.

131. Al-Dhahabī, *Siyar A'lām al-Nubalā'*, Vol. 14, p. 321.

132. Al-Subkī, *Ṭabaqāt al-Shāfi'iyyh*, Vol. 6, p. 127.

133. Al-Ghazālī, *Iḥyā'*, Vol. 3, p. 139.

134. Al-Mahdalī, *al-Imām al-Ghazālī wa 'Ilm al-Ḥadīth*, Cairo: Dār al-Ḥadīth, 1998, p. 28.

135. Al-Ghazālī, *Qānūn al-Ta'wīl*, ed. Maḥmūd Bījū, Damascus: n.p. 1993, p. 30.

136. Al-Mahdalī, *al-Imām al-Ghazālī wa 'Ilm al-Ḥadīth*, p. 14.

137. Ibid, p. 14.

138. Ibn al-Jawzī, *Talbīs Iblīs*, p. 186.

139. Al-Mahdalī, *al-Imām al-Ghazālī wa 'Ilm al-Ḥadīth*, pp. 89f.

140. Ibid, pp. 91-116.

141. Ibid, p. 91.

142. Ibid, p. 91.

143. Ibid, p. 91.

144. See Sa'īd Mamdūḥ, *Is'āf al-Muliḥḥīn bi Tartīb Iḥyā' 'Ulūm al-Dīn*, Beirut: Dār al-Ma'arifah, n.d., pp. 3-75.

145. Al-Mahdalī, *al-Imām al-Ghazā ī wa 'Ilm al-Ḥadīth*, p. 116.

146. Ibid, p. 116.

147. Ibid, p. 116.

148. Al-Ghazālī, *Iḥyā'*, Vol. 3, pp. 96-98, trans., Winter, *Disciplining*, pp. 154-160.

149. Ibid, Vol. 3, p. 96, trans., Winter, *Disciplining*, p. 154.

150. Ibid, Vol. 3, p. 96, trans., Winter, *Disciplining*, p. 154.

151. See al-Irāqī's examination of these traditions in the footnotes of the *Iḥyā'*, Vol. 4, pp. 80-82.

152. Murtaḍā al-Zabīdī, *Itḥāf*, Vol. 9, pp. 8-17.

153. There are few sound traditions condemning satiety, but they are irrelevant to the present point.

6

The effects of al-Ghazālī's attempts at *iṣlāḥ*

The analytical definition of *iṣlāḥ* in the first chapter suggests that in order to fully judge an effort from the *iṣlāḥ* perspective, one needs to know to what extent it has led to the desired corrective change. Based on this, the present chapter attempts to study the main effects of al-Ghazālī's *iṣlāḥī* efforts, in order to complete the task of verifying the hypothesis of the present study.

Achieving this purpose in full, however, is almost an impossible dream. As Knysh has pointed out "a balanced account of the influence of al-Ghazālī will probably not be possible until there has been much more study of various religious movements during the subsequent centuries."[1] What intensifies the difficulty of such a balanced evaluation is the nature of the historical sources. As al-Kīlānī has correctly noticed,[2] the mainly biographical nature of the historical sources has shattered the thematic unity of many historical social phenomena, and thus it has become difficult to reconstruct the whole pictures of these phenomena. In the words of Cook, speaking about the limitation of the sources, "it is notorious that we tend to know too much about scholars in the pre-modern Islamic world and too little about anyone else—apart from rulers."[3]

Despite the limitation of the sources, various phenomena have been considered as effects of al-Ghazālī's efforts, but the evaluation of these effects has been very controversial. I shall discuss below a number of such effects, and assess the main controversial evaluations of them.

The impact of al-Ghazālī's *iṣlāḥī* teachings on his pupils

A central aim of al-Ghazālī's *iṣlāḥī* efforts was to bring up and train a generation of true *'ulamā'*, as a major part of his attempt to renew the mission of true *'ulamā'*, as was shown above. I seek here to discuss the extent to which he achieved in this aim.

In his discussion of al-Ghazālī's effect, as a founder of an *iṣlāḥī* movement, al-Kīlānī stresses that he, through organized and independent teaching, was able to lend his personality together with his line of thought to a large number of pupils, who undertook his message and started to propagate it among all classes of society, and in the schools and the mosques in which they held guiding positions.[4] This argument, however, has been insufficiently supported.[5] In fact it seems almost impossible to fully evaluate such an effect, because we neither know exactly all the pupils of al-Ghazālī, particularly in his *iṣlāḥī* stage, nor do we know to what extent his pupils were influenced by his *iṣlāḥī* teachings, and what their exact role in the claimed *iṣlāḥī* movement was. Therefore, it is difficult to fully and confidently accept al-Kīlānī's overstated argument. Nevertheless, it may at least be partially supported by the following historical data.

To begin with, we recall here that al-Ghazālī returned to teaching in the Niẓāmiyyah of Nishapur for some time, and in his private school in Ṭūs afterwards, until his death, as has been illustrated in chapter three. In that period, it is most likely that many pupils were eager to be taught by al-Ghazālī because of his previous great reputation as an impressive teacher[6] in addition to the reputation of his books, particularly the *Iḥyā'*, as has already been mentioned. As a matter of fact, al-Ghazālī mentioned in one of his late letters that there were one hundred and fifty students who were studying under him at Ṭūs.[7]

Some relevant information about at least a number of al-Ghazālī's pupils can be highlighted by studying the biographical sources which mention some of them by name. In his introduction to the *Itḥāf*, al-Zabīdī[8] lists twenty three of al-Ghazālī's pupils. At least four of them were taught by him in Ṭūs,[9] in which he spent his last years teaching in his private school, one was taught in Nishapur,[10] where he returned to official teaching, and two accompanied him in al-Shām,[11] where he started his self-*iṣlāḥ*. Thus, they were certainly belonging to al-Ghazālī's *iṣlāḥī* stage, and as a result they were most likely influenced highly by his *iṣlāḥī* teachings.

Even some of the pupils who were taught by al-Ghazālī in the period earlier to his *iṣlāḥī* stage became highly interested in his late works, including those of *iṣlāḥī* nature, and consequently played a considerable role in popularizing them. Among these were Abū 'Abdullāh Muḥammad b. 'Alī b. 'Abdullāh al-'Irāqī al-Baghdādī (d. 540f./1145) and Abū Sa'īd Muḥammad b. 'Alī b. 'Abdullāh al-Jāwānī (560/1164) who both narrated al-Ghazālī's book *Iljām al-'Awām*.[12] Among them was also Abū Ṭālib 'Abd al-Karīm b. 'Alī al-Rāzī (522/1128) who memorized the *Iḥyā'* by heart.[13] In addition to al-Qād'ī Abū Bakr Muḥammad b. al-'Arabī (d. 543/1148) and Abū Sa'd Muḥammad b. As'ad b. Muḥammad al-Nawaqānī (d. 556/1161) who were both among those who orally received the *Iḥyā'* from al-Ghazālī, and they in turn narrated it to others.[14]

Other than these, al-Zabīdī[15] lists seven names of those who orally received the *Iḥyā'* from al-Ghazālī and transmitted it to others. These names contributed to the phenomenon of the continuous and wide narration of the book down the centuries, as will be demonstrated in the following section.

By referring to the biographies of all these names,[16] two further remarks are worth making in this context. Firstly, some of these had certain qualities of high righteousness, which shows that those who carried al-Ghazālī's teachings, particularly in his *iṣlāḥī* stage, were in general of righteous qualities. Since the biographies do not clearly state whether this was a result of al-Ghazālī's influence on them, we cannot be certain on this particular point, but it is most likely that he played an essential role in this. Secondly, a number of the above names became very distinguished scholars and impressive intellectuals. This tentatively indicates that they played an effective role in propagating the *iṣlāḥī* teachings of al-Ghazālī.

Appendix 1 summarizes the biographical notes about the standing and the qualities of some of the above names.

The claimed studentship of Ibn Tūmārt under al-Ghazālī

Having discussed al-Ghazālī's influence on his pupils, it is relevant to investigate the conflicting claims about the effect of al-Ghazali on Ibn Tūmārt who succeeded in establishing a reformist movement in the Maghrib which resulted in the rise of the dynasty of al-Muwaḥḥidūn (Almohads).

Within his outline of al-Ghazālī's positive effects as a founder of an *iṣlāḥī* movement, al-Kīlānī[17] includes the claimed influence on Ibn Tūmārt. Relying solely on Ibn Khaldūn's account about the claimed studentship of Ibn Tūmārt under al-Ghazālī in Baghdad, al-Kīlānī plainly states that after being influenced by his teachings, Ibn Tūmārt returned to the Maghrib in order to put these teachings into practice.[18]

This positive claimed effect, on the contrary, has been negatively evaluated by others. Al-Ṣallābī in his book on al-Muwaḥḥidūn, for instance, presents Ibn Tūmārt's movement as a deviated and oppressive school of preaching; and thus he criticizes those who positively evaluate his studentship under al-Ghazālī, arguing that al-Ghazālī was unsettled in his theological teachings.[19]

In both of these opposing evaluations, however, no attention at all has been given to the doubtfulness connected with the story about Ibn Tūmārt's studentship under al-Ghazālī. Although the claimed meeting between the two appears in a number of historical sources, it is still a very doubtful story. For example, Ibn Khaldūn, on whose account al-Kīlānī based his argument, reported the story, but his report denotes uncertainty for he uses the phrase *fī mā zaʿimū*[20] (as they have claimed). Moreover, some other early Muslim historians, such as Ibn al-Athīr,[21] asserted that Ibn Tūmārt never met al-Ghazālī.[22] This assertion can be supported by some historical evidences. Historical sources agree that Ibn Tūmārt's trip to the Mashriq did not start before the year 500 AH, but by this time al-Ghazālī had already permanently left Baghdad, where the meeting between the two was claimed to have occurred.[23]

This strong doubt, nevertheless, may be questioned by the clear reference to Ibn Tūmārt appearing in the introduction to *Sirr al-ʿĀlamīn*, a book which has been attributed to al-Ghazālī. This reference, it has been argued, removes the doubts which have been raised on the meeting between the two.[24] Based on this, Ḥanashī argues that the book is considered the manifesto of Ibn Tūmārt's movement against the state of al-Murābiṭūn (Almoravids).[25]

However, this argument can be strongly challenged by the questionable authenticity of the book under question. Several studies, which have discussed the authenticity of the works attributed to al-Ghazālī, have agreed that the book is almost certainly not authentic.[26] This is based on eternal evidences which may be summarized in the following points:

1. The connection between al-Ghazālī and Ibn Tūmārt mentioned in the introduction is spurious.[27]

2. The book includes materials of superstition, which are almost impossible to be written by a Muslim scholar in the weight of al-Ghazālī.[28]

3. Contrary to al-Ghazālī's distinguished stylistic characteristic, which appears in his genuine works, the materials' distribution in this book is not that systematic.[29]

4. The author makes references to some of his works, such as *Nasīm al-Tasnīm*, which neither appears in any other authentic

book of al-Ghazālī, nor in the sources listing his genuine works.[30]

5.   The book in general is biased against Umawīs and this, as al-'Allāf states, suggests that it was written by a Bāṭinī.[31]

In addition to these remarks, I may add that the purpose of the book which is to provide a guide for kings to support them in their worldly purposes, as frankly stated in the introduction,[32] entirely conflicts with the interests and the teachings of al-Ghazālī at the time in which the book supposed to be written.

This strong doubt on the direct connection between al-Ghazālī and Ibn Tūmārt from the outset renders any judgment of direct effect of the former on the latter very shakily founded. This of course does not eliminate the possibility of indirect influence on Ibn Tūmārt by al-Ghazālī, i.e., through the works of the latter, but that is another issue which is beyond our present concern.

The influence of the *Iḥyā'*

As has been previously illustrated, the *Iḥyā'* of al-Ghazālī is his major project of *iṣlāḥ*, and it includes most of his main *iṣlāḥī* teachings. Therefore, assessing the influence of the book as a whole serves principally the purpose of the present chapter. This is hoped to be achieved firstly by highlighting the great interest in the *Iḥyā'* over the centuries, and then by generally evaluating this interest.

The great interest in the Iḥyā'

Since al-Ghazālī's time and down the centuries, there has been exceptionally great interest in the *Iḥyā'*. This phenomenon can be supported by plentiful evidences. The following are striking selective pieces of these evidences.

Firstly, there has been considerable eagerness with which the book was studied and taught to others over centuries. A denoting early story illustrating this is that of Abū al-Fatḥ, Aḥmad b. 'Alī b. Barhān

(d. 518/1124), who was one of al-Ghazālī's pupils for some time, and who then became a distinguished and hard-working teacher to the extent that he had teaching circles from early dawn to after dark; when he was once asked by a group of students to teach them the *Iḥyā'*, he initially declined due to lack of time, but at their insistence, he devoted a teaching circle on the book at midnight.[33]

Secondly, down the generations, the *Iḥyā'* has been transmitted by various chains of narrators which go back to al-Ghazālī himself. Murtaḍā al-Zabīdī (d. 1205/1791) was one of those who received the book via various *asānīd* (chains of narrators by whom the book was transmitted) which go back to the author. In the lengthy introduction of his extensive commentary on the *Iḥyā'*, al-Zabīdī lists a number of these *asānīd* starting from the ones who orally received the book from al-Ghazālī all the way down to him: several ones were through Jamāl al-Islām 'Alī b. al-Muslim al-Salamī (d. 533/1139), another was through 'Abd al-Khāliq b. Aḥmad b. 'Abd al-Qādir al-Baghdādī (d. 548/1153), two others were through Muḥammad b. Thābit b. al-Ḥasan al-Khūjandī (d. 483/1090f.), several others were through al-Qāḍ'ī Abū Bakr Muḥammad b. al-'Arabī (d. 543/1148), another was through Abū Ṭāhir Aḥmad b. Muḥammad al-Salafī (d. 576/1180), and several more.[34]

Thirdly, there has been incredible attitude of people who learned the book by heart. One of those who memorized the entire *Iḥyā'* is Abū Ṭālib 'Abd al-Karīm b. 'Alī al-Rāzī (522/1128) who was one of al-Ghazālī's pupils.[35] In later centuries there were people who had similar attitude towards the *Iḥyā'*, indicating a continuous remarkable interest in the book. At the beginning of the sixth/seventh century, the Tunsian Sufi 'Abd al-Salām al-Tunisī (d. 486/1093) succeeded in convincing the intellectual circle in Tilimsen of the importance of the *Iḥyā'* and consequently the book began to be transcribed and memorised by the people of Tilimsen.[36] In the seventh/thirteen century, there was, for example, Sharaf al-Dīn Abū al-Faḍl Aḥmad b. al-Shaykh al-Maūṣilī (d. 622/1225) who was teaching the *Iḥyā'* from memory.[37] Similarly, in the nine/fifteenth century there was Shams al-Dīn Muḥammad b. ʿAlī al-Bilālī (d. 820/1417), who was continuously reading from the *Iḥyāʾ* until he developed a special ability in it and almost memorized it all.[38]

These particular reported examples, however, do not seem in any way enough to say, as al-Kīlānī puzzlingly claims, that all of al-Ghazālī's pupils down the centuries had this attitude.[39] They can, however, be used as additional examples for the exceptional interest in the *Iḥyāʾ* down the centuries.

Fourthly, the book has been very widely disseminated. This, as Cook has rightly observed, "is documented by a mass of evidence that remains largely unstudied."[40] A good representative of these is the multiple transcripts of the book available around the globe. There are at least one hundred and nine manuscripts of the *Iḥyāʾ*, which have been written at different dates since the time of the author, available in various cities around the world; they are listed and briefly described in Badawī's work on al-Ghazālī's books.[41]

Lastly, a vast number of summaries and customised versions of the *Iḥyāʾ* have been written over the centuries by people from different origins, sects, schools of thought, and even different religions. To obtain a good idea of the multiplicity, as well as the variety of the summaries and customised versions of the *Iḥyāʾ* and the diversity of their authors as well, it is worth listing in Appendix 2, a number of these in chronological order and highlight the sect, religion or school to which the authors belong, in addition to their origins and places of residence.[42]

Evaluation of the great interest in the Iḥyāʾ

Although the above mass of evidence for the considerable interest in the *Iḥyāʾ* needs intense study in order to come out with a thorough assessment, the following quick observations can be recorded as a provisional evaluation.

The first observation is that the *Iḥyāʾ* has proven to be very successful across different generations, different schools of thought, different sects and even different religions.[43] This can be used as a sufficient proof for Lazarus-Yafeh's general evaluation of al-Ghazālī's thoughts that they "are expressed so convincingly that they crossed the barriers of time and religion."[44]

This extraordinary success of the *Iḥyā'* proves that the book, and consequently al-Ghazālī's *iṣlāḥī* teachings, has been continuously very influential. It is interesting to note that even the critics of al-Ghazālī have been influenced by him to some extent. This is clearly evident in the works of some of his critics, which are based on the *Iḥyā'*, and their admiration for the book in general, or at least in part, as shown in Appendix 2. It is possible to argue, though, that these works could be seen as attempts from these critics to reduce or to stop the harm, which may result from what they considered as faulty elements in the *Iḥyā'*.

In fact the noticeable interest in the book may be used as evidence for accusing al-Ghazālī of being responsible for unfortunate phenomena, such as the wide publicity of fabricated traditions quoted in it among Muslims. As al-Qaradawi states, "because of the dignity of al-Ghazālī among Muslims and the value of the *Iḥyā'*, these weak and fabricated traditions have spread among the Muslim masses."[45]

Another evaluative observation about the great interest in the *Iḥyā'* is that the reproduction of the *Iḥyā'* in various forms over centuries signifies that the book, in general, has proven generally usable up to our present time. The imitations of al-Ghazālī's *Iḥyā'*, as Fierro points out, "indicates that the work itself was considered as catering for certain religious needs."[46]

However, it is important to bear in mind that the customized versions and critically modified summaries, such as al-Ṭarṭūshī's and Ibn al-Jawzī's, indicate partial agreement only. Moreover, the omission and the partial modification of the original materials in most of the above customised versions and reworked summaries may indicate that there is an agreement among their authors that the teachings of al-Ghazālī cannot be taken in full and that they need partial modification or correction. At the same time, nevertheless, it may be stated that they seem to admire the *Iḥyā'* in general since they considered the book as a model for their works.

In short, such continuing interest in the *Iḥyā'* clearly shows that the book has proven to be very influential, but on this alone we cannot confidently judge whether the influence has been positive or negative and this is open to debate.

Al-Ghazālī's effect on sufism

It seems pointless to show how relevant to the purpose of the present chapter is the question of al-Ghazālī's effect on Sufism. So, without being detained by such unnecessary activity, let us turn to the real business and say that al-Ghazālī's announcement of being a champion of Sufism has been considered the greatest victory which the movement has ever made.[47] The rapid spread of Sufism in the successive centuries has been linked with his influence. In addition, after being limited to particular distinguished scholars before al-Ghazālī, Sufism, al-Anṣārī argues, became popular also among general folks after al-Ghazālī.[48]

The evaluation of al-Ghazālī's effect on Sufism, however, has been controversial. On one hand, it has been evaluated as a great achievement by a number of students of Islamic thought. Arberry, for example, states that al-Ghazālī perfected the work of earlier distinguished Sufis, and thus Sufism started to be "accepted as a Muslim science, as a reasonable and laudable way of life."[49] In addition, a reconciliation and assimilation of Sufism with Sunnī theology and *fiqh*, Arberry further states, was achieved by al-Ghazālī.[50] Similarly, Nicholson assures that "through his work and example the Sufistic interpretation of Islam has in no small measure been harmonised with the rival claims of reasons and tradition."[51]

In addition, it has been positively argued that al-Ghazālī largely succeeded in making corrective changes to the movement of Sufism, namely the following:

Trying to set right some Sufi words and actions, so that they agree with the Sharīʿah.[52]

Transferring Sufism "from being concerned solely with *dhawq* (mystical intuition), *taḥlīq* (spiritual flying), *shaṭaḥ* (ecstasy) and *tahwīl* (exaggeration) into a practical ethical science."[53]

Treating the causes of deviation through Sufism, such as ignorance and being concerned with self-discipline before mastering knowledge.[54]

On the other hand, al-Ghazālī's effect on Sufism has been negatively evaluated in some studies; the emergence of "deviated" Sufi trends and thoughts has been traced back, by some writers, to al-Ghazālī's influence to certain degree. Farīd al-Anṣārī is a good representative for this viewpoint. In the course of his criticism of what he calls Sufi spiritual mediating (*wasāṭah rūḥiyyah*), i.e., religiousness through a Sufi mediator (*wasīṭ*), which in his view is a serious deviation from the original path of Islam, al-Anṣārī seriously accuses al-Ghazālī of being responsible for the publicity of such a way of religiousness in the Muslim *ummah*.[55] Although al-Anṣārī states that "al-Ghazālī did not explicitly necessitate the adherence to a mediator (*wasīṭ*) or paying homage (*mubāyaʿah*) to a Shaykh and rather he asserted that it is wrong,"[56] he still holds al-Ghazālī responsible for implanting the idea of *wasāṭah* through the following:

1. legitimizing the Sufi approach in general by considering Sufism as the essence of Islam and the best of all methods, which was an extreme reaction that resulted from his spiritual conversion; that was enough for people to adopt Sufism in that age which was known for blind imitation (*taqlīd maḥḍ*); and thus, Sufism, with its pitfalls namely the *wasāṭah*, became widespread;[57]

2. giving *fiqh* the name of *ʿilm al-dunyā* (worldly knowledge) while naming Sufism *ʿilm al-ākhirah* (knowledge of the next world); and that is the beginning of implanting the Sufi *wasāṭah*, for naturally the followers would have inclined

towards Sufism and would have become disinterested in *fiqh* and even the *fuqahā'* themselves would have sought Sufi mediators;[58]

3. highly praising Sufism and Sufis, with exaggeration, which led to a negative effect in the *ummah*, for religiousness would have to be sought only through Sufis;[59]

4. mentioning the spiritual importance and the high value of a Sufi *shaykh* in the *Iḥyā'*.[60]

Having summarized the major controversy over the evaluation of al-Ghazālī's effect on Sufism, I would like to make the following concluding remarks:

It is an overstatement to say that al-Ghazālī succeeded in reconciling Sufism and Sunnī theology and *fiqh*, because firstly this argued reconciliation between Sharī'ah and Sufism, as Arthur has pointed out, could not put an end to the debate on the authenticity of Sufism.[61] Secondly, as Knysh points out, "the extent to which his teachings were responsible for "reconciling" Sunnīsm with Sufi piety is difficult to ascertain."[62] This is particularly because the tendency "to bring Sufism into the fold of Sunnī Islam by demonstrating its consistency with the ideas and practices of the "pious ancestors"..."[63] had started before al-Ghazālī.

It is difficult to positively hold al-Ghazālī responsible for the emergence of "deviated" Sufi trends, for Sufism had been already established by his time, as illustrated in chapter two above. In addition, Sufi deviated thoughts started before al-Ghazālī, who himself attacked some of them and attempted to correct them, as illustrated in chapter four. It is equally difficult to deny that some of his teachings, particularly those which can be regarded as an extreme reaction resulting from his personal experience, can potentially lead to, or justify, extreme Sufi trends.

The influence of al-Ghazālī on the movement of Sufism cannot be denied since his books of Sufi nature, namely the *Iḥyā'*, have become main references in the field. To make a balanced judgment, this influence, in our view, is two sided, good and bad;

the first is the result of the strengths of his teachings, while the second is due to the pitfalls therein.

The effect on the movement of philosophy

"Al-Ghazālī's study of philosophy undoubtedly had far-reaching results."[64] What concern us here, though, are the following two questions: the first is to what extent al-Ghazālī's criticism affected the movement of philosophy in Islamdom and the second is what the value of his effort in this regard is.

There have been noticeable controversies over these two questions. Although there is some measure of agreement among the researchers that there was a sort of decline in the movement of philosophy in Islamdom for some time after al-Ghazālī, there is a considerable dispute over whether this phenomenon can be linked to al-Ghazālī's criticism of philosophy. This link, on one hand, has been asserted by a number of researchers. According to Nakamura, "philosophy declined in the Sunnī world after al-Ghazālī, and his criticism of philosophy certainly accelerated this decline."[65] Even with the serious efforts of Ibn Rushd (Averroes) to resist this decline by his refutation of al-Ghazālī's *Tahāfut* he, Nakamura further states, could not stop the trend.[66] Similarly, Mclean asserts that "despite Averroes's reply in *Tahāfut al-Tahāfut* some decades later, al-Ghazālī succeeded in quite marginalizing philosophy, especially in Sunnite Islam, and thereby terminating the tradition of Islamic work in Greek philosophy."[67] In a stronger expression al-Ghazālī's criticism has been widely described as the fatal blow to philosophy.[68]

On the contrary, this claimed strong effect has been rejected by others. Badawī,[69] for instance, argues that it is the most serious illusion about al-Ghazālī, and he gives two reasons for this. One is that al-Ghazālī's *Tahāfut* as Badawī has investigated, does not appear in the works of those who dealt with philosophy in the Mashriq during the four successive centuries after al-Ghazālī, such as those of the killed al-Suhrawardī (d. 587/1191), al-Fakhr al-Razī (d. 606/1209), al-Shahristānī (d. 548/1153), ʿUmar al-Kātibī (d. 675/276), ʿAḍud al-Dīn al-Ījī (d. 675/1276), indicating, Badawī argues, that they did not pay attention to the book and that it did not have the claimed effect in turning people away from philosophy.[70] The second reason is that it "is very naive to think that a single book or a criticism of a single author—regardless of how great he was—could put an end to an established branch of knowledge such as philosophy."[71]

Likewise, Watt states that the claim that philosophy was killed off by the effort of al-Ghazālī may be supported by the fact that there were no pure philosophical works in the Islamic East after al-Ghazālī's time,[72] but how far this decline of philosophy was due to his critique or other factors is not evident.[73] Since the distinguished philosopher, Avicenna, had died twenty years before al-Ghazālī, the decline of philosophy, Watt concludes, may have started much earlier than the *Tahāfut*.[74] In addition, since "the traveller Ibn Jubayr (d. 1217) could still find people who professed to follow al-Fārābī and Avicenna," then al-Ghazālī's critique, Watt argues, did not put an end to philosophizing, but it may have contributed to the transformation of its study into two new trends: the first was that philosophical conceptions and methods became part of rational theology and *kalām*, and the second was the fusion of philosophy with Shiite views."[75]

The arguments of both sides of this dispute, however, do not seem that satisfactory, and thus a conclusive study of the question under review is largely needed in order to provide a definite conclusion. Provisionally, one may conclude that no one can deny the effect of al-Ghazālī's criticism on the weakening of the movement of philosophy to some extent, but it is hardly convincing that this criticism put an end to philosophising in Islamdom.

This brings us to the second question regarding the value of this effect which is also disputable. On the one hand, it has been seen as a great achievement by some. According to al-Nadwī,[76] for example, al-Ghazālī provided outstanding support for the religion by putting down the scientific value of philosophy, which had been very influential and prestigious, since the philosophy circle could not present a strong refutation of his *Tahāfut* till the time of Ibn Rushed. Similarly, al-Qaradawi[77] argues that al-Ghazālī had won the battle against philosophy, and that his attack on it succeeded in removing its past halo. In the same way, al-Shāmī[78] considers al-Ghazālī's attack as a victory for Islam, and that he succeeded at least to put philosophy in a state of defence, after it had been in a state of attack.

On the other hand, the same effect has been negatively valued by others. Nasr, for example, has accused al-Ghazālī of being responsible to a large extent for the destruction of rationalism as a major force in the Islamdom,[79] which resulted from his attack against "rationalistic" philosophers.[80] Similarly, El-Ehwany argues that al-Ghazālī unintentionally shut the door on science by his enthusiastic defence of religion, his attack on the doctrines of philosophers, and by his adaptation of the Sufis method, which, in the view of El-Ehwany, is incompatible with rational methods of science.[81] Consequently, since he was considered the Proof of Islam (*Ḥujjah al-Islām*), the Muslims, El-Ehway further argues, followed him and gradually neglected the study of the sciences.[82]

It seems that this dispute is mainly due to the difference of the reference of judgment. The reference of the negative evaluation seems to be the intellectual movement, in general, regardless of whether it is incompatible with Islamic justification. In contrast, the positive evaluation is judged by whether the effect was in favour of Islamic religiousness. In our view, based on the Islamic criteria of *iṣlāḥ* discussed in chapter one, this effect is obviously an *iṣlāḥī* outcome.

The effect of al-Ghazālī's quarrel with the Bāṭinīs

Unlike the case with his effect on philosophy, it does not seem that al-Ghazālī's quarrel with the Bāṭinīs has significantly attracted the attention of the researchers. In my search for relevant literature,

I have not been able to find sufficient discussions of this effect. Therefore, only a few tentative remarks can be made here:

Al-Ghazālī's refutation of the Bāṭiniyyah doctrine seems to be successful, since there is no mention of noticeable counter-argument of al-Ghazālī's refutation appears in the relevant sources.

The decline of the Bāṭiniyyah movement is evident in the sources, but how far al-Ghazālī's efforts contributed to it is not evident. However, by being noticeably influential as shown above, it could be assumed that al-Ghazālī's effort had a considerable effect on the trend.

Watt seems to be correct in the following provisional assessment of the influence of al-Ghazālī's criticism of the Bāṭiniyyah: "[it] may have helped to reduce the intellectual attractiveness of the movement, but its comparative failure, after its success in capturing Alamūt, is due to many other factors."[83]

The influence of al-Ghazālī on the successive *iṣlāḥī* movement

The most striking claimed outcome of al-Ghazālī's *iṣlāḥī* effort has been enthusiastically argued by al-Kīlānī; the main point in this argument is that the reformed generation of Salāḥ al-Dīn, who succeeded in restoring Jerusalem to Muslims, was an outcome of a reforming process started by al-Ghazālī's *iṣlāḥī* efforts.[84] As support for this claim, al-Kīlānī has linked al-Ghazālī to the rise of many reforming *madrasahs*, mainly Sunnī-Sufi, in the successive years which, in the view of al-Kīlānī, reflect a Sufi *iṣlāḥī* movement, the fruit of which was the rise of that generation.[85] He further argues that these *madrasahs* were largely inspired by al-Ghazālī's approach to *iṣlāḥ*.[86] Foremost among these is the Qādiriyyah *madrasah* in Baghdad, which was founded by ʿAbd al-Qādir al-Jīlānī who, as al-Kīlānī states, was largely influenced by al-Ghazālī as appears in his works.[87] Al-Ghazālī's influence on al-Jīlānī, al-Kīlānī further argues, appears also in his approach to self-*iṣlāḥ* which was an adaptation of al-Ghazālī's attitude of "withdrawal and return" (*al-insiḥāb wa al-ʿawdah*).[88]

Although the argument has been interestingly presented, it has some grave pitfalls. The most crucial of which is that it includes some assumptions which lack sufficient supports or proofs. A case in point is al-Kīlānī's central argument that all the *madrasahs* mentioned by him had a unified curriculum, which is virtually identical to that of al-Ghazāliyyah and al-Qādiriyyah *madrasahs*, an argument for which no evidence has been given at all.[89] Thus, the argued link cannot be regarded as a postulate, because it has not been convincingly verified.

Notes

1. Knysh, *Islamic Mysticism*, p. 147.
2. Al-Kīlānī, *Hākadhā Ẓahr Jīl Ṣalāḥ al-Dīn*, p. 101.
3. Cook, *Commanding Good*, p. xiii
4. Al-Kīlānī, *Hākadhā Ẓahr Jīl Ṣalāḥ al-Dīn*, p. 172
5. As a support for this generalized argument, al-Kīlānī strangely gives only three examples of al-Ghazālī's pupils and mentions too little information about them, see al-Kīlānī, *Hākadhā Ẓahr Jīl Ṣalāḥ al-Dīn*, pp. 172f.
6. In Baghdad, the number of students attending al-Ghazālī's lessons reached three hundred, as has been mentioned above.
7. Abdul Qayyum, *Letters of al-Ghazzali*, p. 65.
8. Murtaḍā al-Zabīdī, *Itḥāf*, Vol., 1, pp. 60-62. By checking some biographical sources, namely al-Subkī's *Ṭabaqāt al-Shāfiʿiyyah al-Kubrā*, some of these names appear to be inaccurate or misspelled in the *Itḥāf*, at least in the edition which I have used. Thus, the spelling which is given here is what I think is more accurate.
9. These are Abū Naṣr Aḥmad b. ʿAbd-Allah b. ʿAbd al-Raḥmān al-Khamqarī (d. 544/1149), Abū Manṣūr Muḥammad b. Asaʿad b. Muḥammad al-ʿAṭārī al-Ṭūsī (d. 573/1177-1178), ʿAbd al-Raḥmān b. ʿAlī b. Abī al-ʿAbbās al-Naʿīmī al-Muwaffaqī (d. 542/1147) and Abū al-Ḥasan ʿAlī b. Muḥammad b. Ḥamawayh al-Juwaynī (d. 539/1147), see Murtaḍā al-Zabīdī, *Itḥāf*, Vol. 1, pp. 60-62.
10. His name is Abū Saʿīd Muḥammad b. Yaḥyā b. Manṣūr al-Nīsābūrī (d. 548/1153), see Murtaḍā al-Zabīdī, *Itḥāf*, Vol. 1, p. 61.
11. These are Abū Ṭāhir Ibrāhim b. al-Muṭṭahir al-Jurjānī (d. 513/1119) and Abū al-Ḥasan ʿAlī b. Muslim b. Muḥammad al-Silmī, titled

Jamāl al-Islām (d. 533/1139), see Murtaḍā al-Zabīdī, *Itḥāf*, Vol. 1, pp. 61f.

12. Al-Subkī, *Ṭabaqāt*.

13. Al-Subkī, *Ṭabaqāt* Vol. 7, pp. 179-180, and Murtaḍā al-Zabīdī, *Itḥāf*, Vol. 1, p. 62.

14. See Murtaḍā al-Zabīdī, *Itḥāf*, Vol. 1, pp. 64-65.

15. Ibid, Vol. 1, pp. 62-65.

16. For this purpose, I have consulted a number of biographical sources, see Appendix 1.

17. Al-Kīlānī, *Hākadhā Ẓahr Jīl Ṣalāḥ al-Dīn*, pp. 108 & 174.

18. Ibid, p. 108.

19. ʿAlī Muḥammad al-Ṣallābī, *Iʿlām Ahl al-ʿILm wa al-Dīn bi Aḥwāl Dawlah al-Muwaḥḥidīn*, Sharjah: Maktabah al-Ṣaḥābah, 2001, pp. 5 & 16.

20. Ibn Khaldūn, *al-ʿIbar*, Vol. 6, p. 267.

21. Ibn al-Athīr, *al-Kāmil*, Vol. 9, p. 195.

22. Cf. Rene' Basset, "Ibn Tūmārt" in *EI*, Vol. 2, p. 426.

23. Cf. J.F. Hopkins, "Ibn Tūmārt" in *EI²*, Vol. 3, p. 458.

24. See, for example, Muḥammad ʿUmrānī Ḥanashī, *Shaṭaḥāt Lifuqahāʾ*, electronic book: *http://www.alhiwar.org/ar/content/view/208/29/, no pagination, visited on 1/2/2007.*

25. Ḥanashī, *Shaṭaḥāt Lifuqahāʾ*, electronic book: *http://www.alhiwar.org/ar/content/view/208/29/, visited on 1/2/2007, no pagination,.*

26. See, for example, M.Bouyges, *Essai de chronologie des ouvres d'al-Ghazālī*, Beirut: Librairie Catholique, 1959, p. 75 (I am indebted to my friend, Mokhtar Ben Fredj, for translating the relevant part of the cited work from French); W. Montogomery Watt, "The Authenticity of the Works Attributed to al-Ghazālī," in *JRAS* (Journal of Royal Asietic Society), 1952, pp. 34f; Badawī, *Mullafāt*, pp. 271-272; and Mashad al-ʿAllāf, *Taṣānīf al-Imām Ḥujjah al-Islām*, 2002, electronic book: *http://www.ghazali.org/articles/ma2.htm#d*, visited on 1/2/2007, p. 40.

27. Watt, The Authenticity," p. 34.

28. Al-ʿAllāf, *Taṣānīf*, electronic book: *http://www.ghazali.org/articles/ma2.htm#d, visited on 1/2/2007, p. 40*, and Watt, "The Authenticity," p. 34.

29. Watt, "The Authenticity," p. 34, quoting Asin.

30. Badawī, *Muʾallafāt al-Ghazālī*, p. 273; al-ʿAllāf, *Taṣānīf*, electronic book: *http://www.ghazali.org/articles/ma2.htm#d, visited on 1/2/2007, p. 40*; and Watt, "The Authenticity," pp. 34f.

31. Al-ʿAllāf, *Taṣānīf*, electronic book: *http://www.ghazali.org/articles/ma2.htm#d, visited on 1/2/2007*, p. 40.

32. Al-Ghazālī?, *Sir al-'Ālamīn*, compacted with other works of al-Ghazālī in *Majmū'ah Rasā'il al-Imām al-Ghazālī*, Beirut: Dār al-Kutub al-'Ilmiyyah, n.d., Part 6, p. 3.

33. Al-Subkī, *Ṭabaqāt*, Vol. 6, p. 30.

34. See Murtaḍā al-Zabīdī, *Itḥāf*, Vol. 1, pp. 60-65.

35. See al-Subkī, *Ṭabaqāt*, Vol. 7, pp. 179f; and Murtaḍā al-Zabīdī, *Itḥāf*, Vol. 1, p. 62.

36. Al-Ṭāhir Būnābī, "*Nash'ah wa Taṭwwur al-Adab al-Ṣūfī fī al-Maghrib al-Awsaṭ*," in *Ḥawliyyat al-Turāth*, Algeria: Mistiganim Univesity, Issue #2, Sept. 2004, electronic version: *http://annales.univ-mosta.dz/texte/ap02/15bounabi.htm, visited on 17/11/2006, citing Ibn al-Zayyāṭ al-Tashawwuf ilā Rijāl al-Taṣawwuf, al-Ribat, 1958*, p. 158.

37. Ibn Khallikān, *Wafayāt al-A'yān*, Vol. 1, p. 23.

38. Al-Sakhāwī (d. 902/1497), *al-Ḍaw' al-Lāmi'*, Cairo: 1354 AH, 8:178, cited in Cook, *Commanding Good*, p. 457, n. 211.

39. Although al-Kīlānī strangely claims that all al-Ghazālī's pupils down the centuries had learned his books by heart, he only mentions two examples, see al-Kīlānī, *Hākadhā Ẓahr Jīl Ṣalāḥ al-Dīn*, p. 173.

40. Cook, *Commanding Good*, pp. 450f

41. 'Abd al-Raḥmān Badawī, *Mu'allafāt al-Ghazālī*, Kuwait: Wakālat al-Maṭbū'āt, 1977, pp. 98-112.

42. In Appendix 2 I have benefited much from Cook's well-referenced outline of a number of the summaries of the *Iḥyā*, both published and unpublished (Cook, *Commanding Good*, pp. 451-455). However, I have not restricted myself with this outline for I have consulted other sources as well, and I have mentioned more summaries than those mentioned by Cook.

43. Cf. Cook, *Commanding Good*, p. 450.

44. Lazarus-Yafeh, *Studies in al-Ghazzali*, p. 3.

45. Al-Qaradawi, *al-Imām al-Ghazālī*, p. 157.

46. Maribel Fierro, "Opposition to Sufism in al-Andalus," in Frederick De Jong & Bernd Radtke (eds.) *Islamic Mysticism Contested*, Leiden: Brill, 1999, p. 196.

47. See Arberry, *Sufism*, p. 74.

48. Farīd al-Anṣārī, *al-Tawḥīd wa al-Wasāṭah fī al-Tarbiyah al-Da'awiyyah*, Doha: Wazārah al-Awqāf, 1995, Vol. 2, p. 63.

49. Arberry, *Sufism*, p. 83.

50. Arberry, *Sufism*, p. 74.

51. Reynold A. Nicholson, *The Mystics of Islam*, London: Routledge and Kegan Paul LTD, 1963, p. 25.

52. Al-Qaradawi, *al-Imām al-Ghazālī*, p. 136.

53. Ibid, p. 135.

54. Al-Shāmī, *al-Imām al-Ghazālī*, pp. 132f.
55. Al-Anṣārī, *al-Tawḥīd wa al-Wasāṭah*, Vol. 2, p. 63.
56. Ibid, Vol. 2, p. 71.
57. Ibid, Vol. 2, pp. 68, & 71f.
58. Ibid, Vol. 2, p. 69.
59. Ibid, Vol. 2, p. 69.
60. Ibid, Vol. 2, p. 72.
61. Buehler, Arthur F. "Charismatic Versus Scriptual Authority: Naqshbadī Response to Deniers of Mediational Sufism in British India," in Frederick De Jong & Bernd Radtke (eds.) *Islamic Mysticism Contested*, Leiden: Brill, 1999, p. 491.
62. Knysh, *Islamic Mysticism*, p. 148.
63. Ibid, p. 140.
64. Watt, *Islamic Philosophy and Theology*, Edinburgh: The University Press, 1985, p. 90.
65. Kojiro Nakamura, "al-Ghazālī," in *Concise Routledge Encyclopaedia of Philosophy*, London & New York: Routledge, 2000, p. 314.
66. Ibid, p. 314.
67. George F. McLean, in his introduction to the *Deliverance From Error: A Translation of al-Munqidh min al-Ḍalāl*, translated by Muḥammed Abulaylah, Council of Research in Values and Philosophy, March 2002.
68. See, for example, al-Shāmī, *al-Imām al-Ghazālī*, p. 82; al-Nadwī, *Rijāl*, Vol. 1, p. 287; and al-Qaradawi, *al-Imām al-Ghazālī*, p. 38.
69. Badawī *Awhām Ḥawl al-Ghazālī*, a paper presented in a conference on al-Ghazālī in the University of Muḥammad al-Khāmis, Rabat, 1988, cited online: *http://www.ghazali.org/articles/bd-whm.pdf*, visitied on 1/2/2007.
70. Badawī *Awhām*, cited online: *http://www.ghazali.org/articles/bd-whm.pdf*, visited on 1/2/2007.
71. Id., cited online: *http://www.ghazali.org/articles/bd-whm.pdf*, visited on 1/2/2007.
72. Watt, *Islamic Philosophy*, p. 91.
73. Watt, "al-Ghazālī," in *El²*, Vol. 2, p. 1041.
74. Watt, *Islamic Philosophy*, p. 91.
75. Ibid.
76. Al-Nadwī, *Rijāl*, Vol. 1, p. 287.
77. Al-Qaradawi, *al-Imām al-Ghazālī*, p. 38.
78. Al-Shāmī, *al-Imām al-Ghazālī*, p. 88.
79. Seyyed Hossein Nasr, *Science and Civilization in Islam*, Cambridge: The Islamic Texts Society, 1987, pp. 307f.
80. Nasr, *Science and Civilization*, p. 27.

81. Ahmed Fouad El-Ehwany, "Ibn Rushd," in *History of Muslim Philosophy*, Wiesbaden: Otto Harrassowitz, 1963, p. 556.
82. El-Ehwany, "Ibn Rushd," p. 556.
83. Watt, "al-Ghazālī ," in *El²*, Vol. 2, p. 1041.
84. Al-Kīlānī, *Hākadhā Ẓahr Jīl Ṣalāḥ al-Dīn*, pp. 26f & 101.
85. Ibid, p. 177.
86. Ibid, p. 177.
87. Ibid, p. 184.
88. By this expression, al-Kīlānī refers to al-Ghazālī's retirement from formal teaching in the Niẓāmiyyah for the purpose of self-*iṣlāḥ* and his return to formal teaching afterwards, see Ibid, p. 184.
89. Al-Kīlānī, *Hākadhā Ẓahr Jīl Ṣalāḥ al-Dīn*, p. 238.

Conclusion

The significant findings of all the six chapters above, despite their limitations, are positive enough to make us quite confidently say that our suggested hypothesis is reasonably verified and that the intended purposes of the study are considerably accomplished. To illustrate this in short, I shall conclude this challenging and time-consuming, though worthwhile, study by summing up the key findings of all the discussion above and add few fresh clarifying points, which have not found a proper place in the previous chapters.

1. Based on the interesting results of the semantic analysis of the lexical, Qur'anic, and Prophetic usages of the term *iṣlāḥ* (page 3 and page 5), *iṣlāḥ*, as an Islamic concept, has been provisionally defined (page 15) as a human corrective task in which any state of *fasād* is correctively changed into its opposite Islamically justified state, where *fasād* means a state of loss of the benefit of a thing, inexcusable detriment, or unjustified deviation from a moderate norm. This has provided us with a very useful objective measure of classifying al-Ghazālī as a *muṣliḥ*; to attain a basic level of justifying such a classification, one needs to know the extent of which he correctively responded to the states of *fasād* at his time,

and also the extent to which his response led to the intended corrective change. This important finding has largely shaped the entire study.

2. The examination of the degree of equivalence between this Islamic concept and the meaning and usage of the English term "reform," which is usually considered as a rendering of *iṣlāḥ*, has shown that the gap between the two is considerably wide; therefore, for the sake of preciseness and to avoid confusion, I have concluded (page 16) that the term *iṣlāḥ* should not be replaced by "reform" and instead needs to be transliterated and defined whenever it is necessary, but when translation is unavoidable, then "Islamic reform" seems a more precise and less confusing rendering.

3. By comparing and contrasting between the Islamic concept *iṣlāḥ* with the following three concepts: *tajdīd* (renewal or restoration), *taghyīr* (change), and *al-amr bi al-maʿrūf wa al-nahy ʿan al-munkar* (commanding right and forbidding wrong), it has become very evident that although there are some similarities and partial overlapping between *iṣlāḥ* and these concepts, there are considerably major differences between them. This confirms that *iṣlāḥ* is a distinctive Islamic duty and thus it deserves to be studied as a separate topic, without confusing it with other Islamic concepts.

4. The extended, and hopefully balanced, overview of the historical context at the time of al-Ghazālī (page 30) has clearly demonstrated that he lived in an exceptionally complex, diverse, changeable, and challenging age. Considering that context throughout the study has proven to be crucially important, and has really helped in dealing with the controversy surrounding al-Ghazālī's life and thought.

5. The relatively lengthy discussion of al-Ghazālī's life-experience (page 98) has led to the following two main findings. The first is that his period of seclusion, which was a dramatic turning point in his entire life, marked the starting

point of his determined *iṣlāḥī* efforts (page 122). This has been readily justified by the following two successful *iṣlāḥī* outcomes of that period (page 122): (a) he went through a fundamental self-*iṣlāḥ* or corrective conversion, which is a necessary condition for desiring general *iṣlāḥ*, according to his teachings, and (b) he formulated his main *iṣlāḥī* teachings in his most famous book, the *Iḥyā'* which is aimed to be a major *iṣlāḥī* project. These outcomes, as has been shown (page 122), were asserted by al-Ghazālī's contemporary and associate, al-Fārisī, whose eyewitness testimony renders the doubts which have been cast on the truthfulness of al-Ghazālī's account in the *Munqidh* about his conversion totally unreasonable. The second main finding is that the entire period following al-Ghazālī's successful self-*iṣlāḥ* can be properly considered as a stage in which he strived for general *iṣlāḥ* (page 128). This has been supported by the following proofs (page 128): (a) al-Ghazālī's assertion in the *Munqidh* that his sole desire at that stage was *iṣlāḥ*, (b) al-Fārisī's biographical notices concerning the same stage which back up the above classification, (c) and almost all of al-Ghazālī's reported activities during that stage are of *iṣlāḥī* nature. Based on these two very significant findings, the proceeding survey of al-Ghazālī's *iṣlāḥī* efforts has been justifiably limited to that stage.

6. By surveying al-Ghazālī's main *iṣlāḥī* efforts during the stage in which he devoted himself to *iṣlāḥ* (page 143), it has become quite clear that the extent of such efforts is remarkable. In light of the analysis of the concept of *iṣlāḥ* performed in Chapter One, the extended, and hopefully objective, survey has amply illustrated firstly al-Ghazālī's analysis of the major roots of *fasād* (page 144), secondly his diagnosis of a number of widespread phenomena of *fasād* at his time (page 149), thirdly his *iṣlāḥī* attempts to eradicate the roots of *fasād* analysed by him (page 160), and lastly his *iṣlāḥī* treatments of the phenomena of *fasād* diagnosed by him (page 174). Considering these enormous efforts, which all appear to

be of *iṣlāḥī* nature, is of crucial importance in verifying the suggested hypothesis, but before giving our final judgment the following findings need to be taken into account.

7. The focused assessment of al-Ghazālī's overall *iṣlāḥī* teachings, namely those in the *Iḥyā'*, has revealed that his teachings, generally speaking, are highly original (page 208), abundantly clear and easy to follow (page 213), noticeably deep (page 220), and considerably realistic and practical, particularly his general principles (page 221). Besides these striking strengths, the assessment has shown that his teachings have some serious weaknesses as well, namely: (a) the apparent contradiction between his teachings of individualistic spirit and those of collective nature (page 221), which is really problematic and thus deserves a separate detailed study, (b) there are some elements of extremeness in his teachings, though he believes in moderation as a general rule (page 225), (c) his reporting of some Sufi practices which clearly contradict *fiqhī* rules, regardless of his true position which is problematic and thus deserves a separate detailed study (page 234), (d) and a number of his views were considerably influenced by unsound or weak traditions attributed to the Prophet (ṣ) (page 240). Such weaknesses, in our view, can be easily singled out for valid criticism.

8. By discussing a number of criticisms, which have been directed against al-Ghazālī's teachings (page 208), it has been found that they are not convincingly justifiable and thus they cannot be considered as postulates, though they have been continuously repeated and widely accepted. These are: (a) the accusation of copying from earlier sources without crediting them; for various reasons (page 208), it is difficult to follow such accusation, (b) the accusation of implementing in his teachings un-Islamic or "foreign elements," which may be traced back directly or indirectly to the works of ancient philosophers; but again for a number of reasons (page 231), this criticism cannot be regarded as serious or convincing,

(c) the criticism that he fully supported Sufi tradition even those which contradict Islamic principles found in the Islamic primary sources; yet various reservations can be raised against such a criticism (page 234), (d) and the commonly repeated criticism that he relied heavily on weak and fabricated *aḥādīth*, namely in the *Iḥyāʾ*; but there is an element of exaggeration on this criticism (page 240).

9. By discussing a number of phenomena which have been considered as effects of al-Ghazālī's efforts and assessing the main controversial evaluations of these, the following results have been reached.

    i. Because of the limitations in the sources, it is almost impossible to fully assess the effects of al-Ghazālī's *iṣlāḥī* attempts or his efforts in general (page 249).

    ii. Al-Ghazālī's *iṣlāḥī* teachings most likely influenced many pupils, but the extent of this influence, the whole number of these pupils, and their exact role in passing on his teachings cannot be known for certain (page 250).

    iii. The direct connection between al-Ghazālī and Ibn Tūmārt, the founder of Almohad dynasty, is extremely doubtful, if not a myth, and thus the available evaluations of al-Ghazālī's direct effect on him are shakily founded (page 252)

    iv. The exceptionally great interest in the *Iḥyāʾ* can be supported by ample evidences (page 254). This clearly shows that the book, and thus its *iṣlāḥī* teachings, has proven to be very successful, highly influential, and largely useable over the centuries and across different generations, despite their different schools of thought, sects, and even religions (page 256). However, whether its influence has been positive or negative remains debatable.

    v. Al-Ghazālī's effect on Sufism cannot be denied, but it has been overstated by those who positively evaluated it as well as those who negatively looked at it (page 258). In our view, this effect has both a positive side and a negative one.

vi. It is difficult to totally reject that al-Ghazālī's criticism of philosophy weakened its subsequent movement to some extent, but to claim that it put an end to philosophising in Islamdom is far from convincing (page 261). The debate over the value of this effect is mainly because of the difference on the reference of judgment; the negative evaluation seems to disregard the Islamic justification, while the positive evaluation is based on whether the effect was in favour of Islamic religiousness, but looking at it from the *iṣlāḥ* perspective, it becomes evident that it is an *iṣlāḥī* effect (page 261).

vii. The effort of al-Ghazālī with regard to the challenge of the *Bāṭiniyyah* movement seems to be fruitful, but how far it contributed to its decline is not clear (page 263).

viii. The theory which links al-Ghazālī to the emergence of the Muslim generation which succeeded in freeing Muslim lands from the Crusaders has not been convincingly supported, and thus this cannot be positively regarded as one of al-Gahazālī's *iṣlāḥī* effects (page 264).

By weighing up all these findings, and considering in a balanced way all the points for and against al-Ghazālī, I can quite confidently assert that classifying al-Ghazālī as a *muṣliḥ* is fairly justified and that he significantly contributed to the rich "legacy of the *muṣliḥūn*". His remarkable *iṣlāḥī* efforts and the great strengths of his *iṣlāḥī* teachings considerably outweigh his weaknesses, regardless of how serious they are. I believe that it is gravely unfair to overstate his weaknesses, and disregard his impressive achievement. In fact, it sounds very unreasonable to expect from a single person like al-Ghazālī to accomplish more than what he achieved in order to consider him as a *muṣliḥ*, particularly in his extremely challenging and complex time.

Appendix 1

Al-Ghazālī's pupils: Selected list

Abū 'Abdullāh Muḥammad b. 'Alī b. 'Abdullāh al-'Irāqī al-Baghdādī (d. 540f./1145)

- Became one of the most distinguished *Shāfi* scholars.
  (al-Dhahabī, *Tārīkh al-Islām*, Vol. of ys. 541-550, p. 85)

Abū al-Fatḥ Aḥmad b. 'Alī b. Barhān (d. 518/1124)
- Became a "model of knowledge."
- One to whom crowds of pupils were bound.
- Taught in the Niẓāmiyyah for some time.
  (al-Subkī, *Ṭabaqāt*)

Abū al-Ḥasan 'Alī b. Muslim b. Muḥammad al-Silmī, titled Jamāl al-Islām (d. 533/1139)
- Became an authoritative scholar.
- Became in charge of teaching in the *Āmīniyyah* school in Damascus
  (al-Subkī, *Ṭabaqāt*)

'Abd al-Khāliq b. Aḥmad b. 'Abd al-Qādir al-Baghdādī (d. 548/1153)
- A man of Ḥadīth.
- A religious, virtuous, humble, and beneficial man.
  (al-Dhahabī, *al-'Ibar fī Khabar man Ghabar*, Beirut: Dār al-Kutub al-'Ilmiyyah, n.d., Vol. 3, p. 6)

Abū Naṣr Aḥmad b. 'Abdullāh b. 'Abd al-Raḥmān al-Khamqarī (d. 544/1149)
- Became a well-known *faqīh*.

- His preaching attracted many people.
- A virtuous man.
  (al-Subkī, *Ṭabaqāt*)

'Abd al-Raḥmān b. 'Alī b. Abī al-'Abbās al-Na'īmī al-Muwaffaqī (d. 542/1147)
- Became an established *faqīh*.
- A pious and virtuous man.
  (al-Subkī, *Ṭabaqāt*)

Abū Sa'd Muḥammad b. Yaḥyā b. Manṣūr al-Nīsābūrī (d. 548/1153)
- Became "the head of the *fuqahā'*" in Nīsābūr and taught in its Niẓāmiyyah.
- His name became widely recognized.
- Unique in knowledge and asceticism at the time.
- Even scholars used to travel to him, seeking knowledge.
  (al-Dhahabī, *Tārīkh al-Islām*, Vol. of ys 541-550, p. 337)

Abū al-Ṭāhir Aḥmad b. Muḥammad al-Salafi (d. 576/1180)
- For whom pupils travel in long journeys.
- Was in charge of a school in Alexandria.
  (Ibn Khallikān, *Wafayāt al-A'yān*, Vol. 1, p. 121)

Abū Ṭāhir Ibrāhim b. al-Muṭṭahir al-Jurjānī (d. 513/1119)
- Became one of the distinguished scholars.
- His teaching and preaching were widely welcomed because of his virtuousness.
  (Ibn Manẓūr, *Mukhtaṣar Tarīkh Dimashq*)

Muḥammad b. Thābit b. al-Ḥasan al-Khūjandī (d. 483/1090f.)
- Became in charge of the Niẓāmiyyah of Aṣbahān.
- Was among the most well-known scholars at the time.
- A well-mannered man
  (al-Subkī, *Ṭabaqāt*)

Al-Qāḍ'ī Abū Bakr Muḥammad b. 'Abdullāh b. al-'Arabī (d. 543/1148)
- Was very well-established in various sorts of knowledge.
- A well-mannered man.
  (al-Dhahabī, *Tārīkh al-Islām*, Vol. of ys 541-550, p. 159)

Appendix 2

Summaries and customised versions of the *Iḥyā'*

Lubāb al-Iḥyā'

> Aḥmad b. Muḥammd al-Ghazālī (d. c.520/1126), Sufi-Shāfi'ī from Ṭūs resided in Baghdad.
>
> He is al-Ghazālī's brother who, according to al-Zabīdī, was the first who composed a summary of the *Iḥyā'*. (Murtaḍā al-Zabīdī, *Itḥāf*, 1:56).

Unknown title

> Muḥammad b. al-Walīd al-Fihrī al-Ṭarṭūshī (d. 520/1126), Andalusian Mālikī resided in Alexandria.
>
> In this work, the renowned author "is described as emulating (*yu'ārid' bihi*)" the *Iḥyā'*. (Cook, *Commanding Good*, p. 373 citing Manūnī, '*Iḥyā*',' pp. 135-137, and others).
>
> He states in the introduction that "of the countless works on piety (*taqwā*), the *Revival* is the best, but that it suffers from a number of faults which he proceeds to list." (Cook, *Commanding Good*, pp. 453f, citing Manūnī, "*Iḥyā'*,"p. 135.10).

Mukhataṣar al-Iḥyā'

> Yaḥyā b. Abī al-Khayr al-'Imrānī (d. 558/1163), Yemeni Shāfi'ī.
>
> A second summary of the *Iḥyā'*.(al-Subkī, *Ṭabaqāt*, 7:338.6.).

Unknown title

> Ibn al-Rammāmah (d. 567/1172), Mālikī who was the judge of Fez.

A third summary of the *Iḥyā'*. (Cook, *Commanding Good*, p. 373 citing Manūnī, '*Iḥyā*',' pp. 132f.).

Mukhataṣar al-Iḥyā'

Muḥammad b. Saʿīd al-Qurayẓī (d. 575/1179), Shāfiʿī who was the judge of Laḥj (Yemen).

A fourth summary of the *Iḥyā'*. (Cook, *Commanding Good*, 451-452).

Al-Tafakkur fīmā Tashtamil ʿAlayh al-Suwar wa al-Āyāt min al-Mabādi' wa al-Ghāyāt

Abū ʿAlī al-Hasan b. ʿAlī al-Masīlī (d. late sixth/twelfth century), Malikī lived in Bijāyā (which is now in Algeria).

It is reported that this book was written on the model of the *Iḥyā'* and it became more popular than the *Iḥyā'* particularly in Bijāyā. (Būnābī, "*Nash'aṭ*" opcit, citing Aḥmad Bābā al-Timbiktī, *Nayl*, p. 104; and al-Ghubrīnī (d. 704/1304f.), "'*Unwān*," p. 67).

Unknown title

Muḥammad b. Saʿīd al-Yamanī (d. 595 AH), Yemeni.

A fifth summary. (al-Zabīdī, *Itḥāf*, Vol. 1, p. 56).

Minhāj al-Qāṣidīn

Abū al-Faraj ʿAbd al-Raḥmān b. ʿAlī, widely known as Ibn al-Jawzī (d. 597/1201), Ḥanbalī from Baghdad.

As stated in his introduction, Ibn al-Jawzī noticed that the true disciple resolving to live in spiritual seclusion and wanting a guiding book would prefer the *Iḥyā'*, claiming it to be unique of its type and valuable by itself (*infirāduh fī jinsih wa nafāsatuh fī nafsih*), but since it has faults known only to the scholars, he decided to compose for such a person this work which, as he states, is free from the faults of the *Iḥyā'* but it preserves its sound elements. So this is a reworked summary of the *Iḥyā'*. (See the abridged version of this work made by Aḥmad b. ʿAbd al-Raḥamān b. Qudāmah al-Maqdisī (d. 689/1290), *Mukhtaṣar Minhāj al-Qāṣidīn*, Beirut and Damascus: Dār al-Khayr, 1998, p. 14).

Rūḥ al-Iḥyā' wa Rawḥ al-Aḥyā'

Sharaf al-Dīn Abū al-Fadl Aḥmad b. al-Shaykh al-Mawṣilī (d. 622/1225), Shāfiʿī from Iraq.

A seventh summary of the *Iḥyā'*. (Ibn Khallikān, *Wafayyāt al-Aʿyān*, 1: 24. For a brief description of the manuscript of this summary, see Cook, *Commanding Good*, p. 452 n. 162.).

Unknown title
An eighth summary by the previous author but a bigger size than *Rūḥ*. (See Ibn Khallikān, *Wafayyāt al-Aʿyān*, 1:108.8.).

Dhukhr al-Muntahī fī al-ʿIlm al-Jālī wa al-Khāfī
Jamāl al-Dīn Muḥammad b. ʿAbdullāh al-Khwārazmī al-Shāfiʿī (d. 679/1280f?), Sufi-Shāfiʿī from Makkah.
A ninth summary. (See Cook, *Commanding Good*, 452 n. 163, including a description of the manuscript of this summary and some additional information about the author.).

Ethicon
Gregory Barhebraeus (d. 684/1286), Syrian Christian.
Cook describes this book as a Christian recension of the *Iḥyā'* and he states that "a characteristic feature of this book is its extensive dependence on the *Iḥyā'*..." (Cook, *Commanding Good*, pp. 455 & 601).

Taṣfiyah al-Qulūb min Daran al-Awzār wa al-Dhunūb
al-Muʾayyad Yaḥyā b. Ḥamzah (d. 749/1348f), Yemeni Zaydī.
This book, as Cook noticed, can fairly be considered as a Zaydī recension of the *Iḥyā'*. (Cook, *Commanding Good*, 246).

Qanāṭir al-Khayrāt
Abū Ṭāhir Ismāʿīl b. Mūsā al-Jayṭālī (d. 750/1349f), Ibāḍī from Jīṭāl (now in Libya).
This Ibāḍī book was written on the model of the *Iḥyā'*. (Cook, *Commanding Good*, p. 401).

Janah al-Maʿārif or Iḥyā' al-Iḥyā' fī al-Taṣawwuf
Shams al-Dīn Muḥammad b. ʿAlī al-Bilālī (d. 820/1417), Sufi-Shāfiʿī lived in Cairo.
A tenth summary which was written in 807/1405. (See Cook, *Commanding Good*, p. 457 n. 211) The summary was widely beneficial especially for Maghribīs. (al-Sakhāwī (d. 902/1497), *al-Ḍaw' al-Lāmiʿ*, Cairo: 1353 AH, Vol. 8, p. 178).

ʿAyn al-ʿIlm wa Zayn al-Ḥilm
Muḥammad b. ʿUmar b. ʿUthmām al-Balkhī (d. 830/1426f.), Indian Ḥanafī.
An eleventh summary for which the Meccan Ḥanafī al-Mullā ʿAlī al-Qārī (d. 1014/1606) wrote a commentary entitled *Sharḥ ʿAyn*

al-ʿIlm. (Ḥājjī Khalīfah (d. 1067/1657), *Kashf al-Ẓunūn ʿan Asāmī al-Kutub wa al-Funūn*, Beirut: Dār al-Kutub al-ʿIlmīyah, 1992,).

Mukhataṣar al-Iḥyāʾ
Jalāl al-Dīn ʿAbd al-Raḥmān b. Abū Bakr al-Suyūṭī (d. 911/1505), Shāfiʿī from Cairo.
A twelfth summary. (Murtaḍā al-Zabīdī, *Ithāf*, Vol. 1. p. 56).

Al-Maḥajjah al-Baydāʾ fī Tahdhīb al-Iḥyāʾ
Muḥammad Muḥsin b. Murtaḍā known as al-Fayḍ al-Kāshānī (d. 1091/1680), Persian Imāmī-Shīʿī.
This is another recension of the *Iḥyāʾ* but in Imāmī version. (Cook, *Commanding Good*, 246).

Ithāf al-Sādah al-Muttaqqīn bi Sharḥ Iḥyāʾ ʿUlūm al-Dīn
Muḥammad b.Muḥammd al-Ḥusaynī al-Zabīdī, widely known as Murtaḍā al-Zabīdī (d. 1205/1791), Indian Sufi Ḥanafī lived in Zabīd (Yemen) for long time and then in Cairo where he died.
This is an extensive commentary on the *Iḥyāʾ*. In addition to its lengthy explanations and comments on al-Ghazālī's words, it includes the author's extended *takhārīj* (Ḥadīth verification) of the Prophetic traditions mentioned in the *Iḥyāʾ*. (See Murtaḍā al-Zabīdī, *Ithāf*, Vol. 1, p. 3).

Mawʿiẓah al-Muʾminīn min Iḥyāʾ ʿUlūm al-Dīn
Muḥamma Jamāl al-Dīn al-Qāsimī (d. 1332/1914), Syrian Salafī.
A thirteenth summary the author of which states in the introduction that in his long experience in teaching, he has found that the most useful source from which preaching topics can be selected is the *Iḥyāʾ*. (al-Qāsimī, *Tahdhīb Mawʿiẓah al-Muʾminīn*, n.p., n.d., p. 31.).

Iḥyāʾ ʿUlūm al-Dīn fī al-Qarn al-Wāḥid wa al-ʿIshrīn
Suʿād al-Ḥakīm (contemprary author), Lebanese academic specialized in Sufi traditions particularly Ibn al-ʿArabī's thoughts.
This is a contemporary rewrite of the *Iḥyāʾ*. The purpose of this work, as the author states, is to show that there is "a consensus Islam" (Islām *muttafaq ʿalayh*) which suits "an absolute man" (*insān mutlaq*). To achieve this purpose, she has put for herself a number of guidelines, namely: (1) simplifying al-Ghazālī's wording, (2) omitting issues which have been criticized by distinguished scholars, (3) rearranging the topics of the *Iḥyāʾ*, and (4) recording al-ʿIrāqī's verification of the Prophetic traditions cited in the *Iḥyāʾ*. (Suʿād al-

Ḥakīm, *Iḥyā' 'Ulūm al-Dīn fī al-Qarn al-Wāḥīd wa al-'Ishrīn*, Cairo: Dār al-Shurūq, 2004, pp. 8 & 45).

Al-Mustakhlaṣ fī Tazkiyah al-Anfus

Sa'īd Ḥawwā (d. 1409/1989), One of the leaders of the Syrian Muslim Brotherhood in the last century.

A fourteenth summary but with modifications and rearrangement of the selected materials. The author states in the introduction that he summarized from the *Iḥyā'* the uncontroversial elements on purifying the soul for which there is a real need in the modern age with some rearrangements and addition of some new topics. (Sa'īd Ḥawwā, *al-Mustakhlaṣ fī Tazkiyah al-Anfus*, Cairo: Dār al-Salām, 1984, p. 5).

Bibliography

Notes

- Dates of publications shown are Christion dates, unless they are followed by AH, which stands for *hijrī* date.
- Last names starting with "al-" are kept with "al-" but are listed under the letter following the "al-".
- Translated classical sources are in English, unless otherwise stated, and are listed under the name of the translators, but they are cross-referred to under the entries of the original authors.

'Abbūd, 'Abd al-Ghanī, *al-Fikr al-Tarbawī 'Ind al-Ghazālī*, Cairo: Dār al-Fikr al-'Arabī, 1982.
'Abd al-Bāqī, Muḥammad Fu'ād, *al-Mu'jam al-Mufahras li al-Fāẓ al-Qur'ān al-Karīm*, Cairo: Dār al-Ḥadīth, 1991.
'Abd al-Maqṣūd, Muḥammad al-Sa'īd, *Tarbiyah al-Ṣafwah 'ind al-Ghazālī: Dirāsah Tarbawiyyah li Risālah Ayyuhā al-Walad*, in Muḥammad Kamāl Ja'far (ed.), *al-Imām al-Ghazālī: al-Dhikrā al-Mi'awiyyah al-Tāsi'ah li Wafātih*, Doha: University of Qatar, 1986, pp. 481-437.
'Abd al-Rāziq, Abū Bakr, *Ma' al-Ghazālī fī Munqithih min al-Dalāl*, Cairo: al-Dār al-Qawmiyyah li al-Ṭibā'ah wa al-Nashir, n.d.

Abdel Haleem, Muhammad, *The Qur'an: A new translation*, Oxford: Oxford University Press, 2004.

—*Understanding the Qur'an: Themes and Style*, London: I.B. Tauris & Co Ltd., 1999.

Abdul Qayyum, *Letters of al-Ghazzali*, Lahore: Islamic Publications, 1976.

Abū Dāwūd al-Sijistānī, Sulaymān b. al-Ash'ath (d. 275/889), *Sunan*, ed. Muḥammad 'Abd al-'Azīz al-Khālidī, Beirut: Dār al-Kutub al-'Ilmiyyah, 1996.

Abul Quasem, Muhammad, *al-Ghazālī on Islamic Guidance*, Malaysia: National University of Malaysia, 1979.

—*The Ethics of al-Ghazālī: A Composite Ethics in Islam*, Selangor (Malaysia): Central Printing Sendirian Berhad, 1976.

—*The Jewels of the Qur'ān: al-Ghazālī's Theory*, translation of al-Ghazālī's *Kitāb Jawāhir al-Qur'ān*, Kuala Lumpur: The University of Malaya press, 1977.

—*The Recitation and Interpretation of the Qur'ān: al-Ghazālī's Theory*, translation of *Kitāb Ādāb Tilāwah al-Qur'ān* of al-Ghazālī's *Iḥyā'*, Kuala Lumpur: The University of Malaya press, 1979.

Abu-Sway, Mustafa, "al-Ghazālī's Spiritual Crisis Reconsidered," in *al-Shajarah*, Vol. 1, No. I, 1996, pp. 83-87.

—*al-Ghazzāliyy* [sic]: *A Study in Islamic Epistemology*, Kuala Lumpur: Diwan Bahasa dan Pustaka, 1996.

Aḥmad B. Ḥanbal (d. 241/855), *Musnad*, Beirut: Dār al-Kutub al-'Ilmiyyah, 1993.

Ahmad, Jamil, "Imām Ghazālī," in *Hundred Great Muslims*, pp. 126-132, Karachi: Ferozsons Ltd., 1977.

Al-'Allāf, Mashad, *Taṣānīf al-Imām Ḥujjah al-Islām*, 2002, electronic book: http://www.ghazali.org/articles/ma2.htm#d.

Al-Ālūsī, Maḥmūd (d. 1270/1854), *Ruḥ al-Ma'ānī fī Tafsīr al-Qur'ān al-'Azīm wa al-Sab' al-Mathānī*, Beirtu: Dār al-Fikr, 1997.

Ali, A. Yusuf, *The Holy Qur'ān: Text, Translation and Commentary*, Bierut: Dār al-Qur'ān, n.d.

Amīn, Aḥmad, *Ẓuhr al-Islām*, Cairo: Maktabah al-Nahḍah al-Miṣriyyah, 1955.

Amīn, Ḥusayn, *al-Ghazālī Faqīhā wa Faylasūfā wa Mutaṣawwifā*, Bagdad: Irshād Press, 1963.

Al-Anṣārī, Farīd, *al-Tawḥīd wa al-Waṣāṭah fī al-Tarbiyah al-Da'awiyyah*, Doha: Wazārah al-Awqāf, 1995.

Al-A'sam, 'Abd al-Amīr, *al-Faylasūf al-Ghazālī: I'ādah Taqwīm li Munḥanā Taṭawwrih al-Ruḥī*, Amzil (Tonisia): al-Dār al-Tūnisiyyah li al-Nashir, 1988.

Arberry, A.J. *Revelation and Reason in Islam*, London: George Allen & Unwin LTD., 1956.

—"Mysticism," in P.M. Holt and et al (eds.) *The Cambridge History of Islam*, Cambridge: The Cambridge University Press, 1970, Vol. 2, pp. 604-631.

—*Sufism: An Account of the Mystics of Islam*, London: George Allen & Unwin Ltd., 1969.

—*The Koran: Interpreted*, Oxford: Oxford University Press, 1982.

Arnaldez, R., "Falsafa" *EI²*, Vol. 2, pp. 769-775.

'Azzūz, Muḥī al-Dīn, *al-Lāma'qūl wa Falsafah al-Ghazālī*, Bin Arus (Tunisia): al-Dār al-'Arabiyyah li al-Kitāb, 1983.

Babbie, Earl, *The Practice of Social Research*, California: Wedswerth Inc., 1983.

Badawī, 'Abd al-Raḥmān, "*Awhām ḥawl al-Ghazālī*," a paper presented in a conference on al-Ghazālī in the University of Muḥammad al-Khāmis, Rabat, 1988, cited online: http://www.ghazali.org/articles/bd-whm.pdf, on 1/2/2007.

—*Mu'allafāt al-Ghazālī*, Kuwait: Wakālah al-Maṭbū'āt, 1977.

—*Shaṭaḥāt al-Ṣūfiyyah*, Kuwait: Wakālah al-Maṭbū'āt, 1978.

Bagley, F.R.C. *Ghazālī's Book of Councel for Kings*, translation of al-Ghazālī's *Naṣīḥah al-Mulūk*, London: Oxford Universtiy Press, 1964.

Bakar, Osman, *History and Philosophy of Islamic Science*, Cambridge: The Islamic Texts Society, 1999.

Al-Baqarī, 'Abd al-Dāym Abū al-'Aṭā, *I'tirāfāt al-Ghazālī*, Cairo: Dār al-Nahḍah al-'Arabiyyh, 1971.

Barakah, 'Abd al-Fattāḥ 'Abdullāh, *al-Ghazālī wa Tawajjuhuh al-Ijtimā'ī*, in Muḥammad Kamāl Ja'far (ed.), *al-Imām al-Ghazālī: al-Dhikrā al-Mi'awiyyah al-Tāsi'ah li Wafātih*, Doha: University of Qatar, 1986, pp. 197-219.

Al-Barāwī, Rāshid, *Qādah al-Fikr al-Islāmī fi Ḍaw' al-Fikr al-Ḥadīth*, Cairo: Maktabah al-Nahḍah al-Miṣriyyah, 1969.

Becker, C.H., "Badr al-Djamālī" *EI*, Vol. 1, pp. 860f.

Bel, A. "Almoravids," *EI*, Vol. 1, pp. 318-320.

—"'Alī b. Yūsūf b. Tāshafīn," *EI*, Vol. 1, pp. 290f.

Bello, Iysa A, *The Medieval Islamic Controversy between Philosophy and Orthodoxy: Ijmā' and Ta'wīl in the conflict between al-Ghazālī and Ibn Rushd*, Leiden: E.J. Brill, 1989.

Bisar, M.A.R., "al-Juwayni and al-Ghazali as theologians with special reference to al-Irshad and al-Iqtisad," a PhD thesis submitted to Edinburgh University in 1953.

Bosworth, C.E., "Saldjūḳids" in *EI²*, Vol. 8, pp. 936-959.

—"The Political and Dynastic History of the Iranian World (AD 1000-1217)," in *The Cambridge History of Iran*, Vol. 5, pp. 1-202.

Buehler, Arthur F, "Charismatic Versus Scriptual Authority: Naqshbadī Response to Deniers of Mediational Sufism in British India," in Frederick De Jong & Bernd Radtke (eds.) *Islamic Mysticism Contested*, Leiden: Brill, 1999, pp. 468-491.

Al-Bukhārī, Abū ʿAbdullāh Muḥammad b. Ismāʿīl (d. 256/870), *Ṣaḥīḥ*, Riyadh: Dār al-Salām, 1999.

Calverly, Edwin Elliot, *The Mysteries of Worship in Islam*, translation of *Kitāb Asrār al-Ṣalāh* of al-Ghazālī's *Iḥyā'*, New Delhi: Kitab Bhavan Exporters & Importers, 1992.

Chertoff, Gershon B, "The Logical Part of al-Ghazālī's Maqāṣid al-Falāsifah: In an anonymous Hebrew translation with the Hebrew commentary of Moses of Narbonee, edited and translated with notes and an introduction and translated into English," a PhD thesis, Columbia Universtiy,1952, part II, pp. 1-110, available on line in PDF: http://www.ghazali.org/books/chertoff.pdf.

Cook, Michael, *Commanding Right and Forbidding Wrong in Islamic Thought*, Cambridge: Cambridge University Press, 2000.

Dawood, N.J., *The Koran: Translated with Notes*, London: Penguin Books Ltd., 1999.

Al-Dhahabī, Shams al-Dīn Muḥammad b. Aḥmad b. ʿUthmān (d. 748/1348), *al-ʿIbar fī Khabar man Ghabar*, Beirut: Dār al-Kutub al-ʿIlmiyyah, n.d.

—*Siyar Aʿlām al-Nubalā'*, ed. Muḥī al-Dīn Abū Saʿīd ʿUmar b. Gharāmah al-ʿAmrawī, Beirut: Dār al-Fikr, 1997.

—*Tārīkh al-Islām wa Wafiyyāt al-Mashāhīr wa al-Aʿlām*, Beirut: Dār al-Kitāb al-ʿArabī, 1997.

Al-Dīb, ʿAbd al-ʿAẓīm, *al-Ghazālī wa Uṣūl al-Fiqh*, in Muḥammad Kamāl Jaʿfar (ed.), *al-Imām al-Ghazālī: al-Dhikrā al-Miʾawiyyah al-Tāsiʿah li Wafātih*, Doha: University of Qatar, 1986, pp. 331-376.

Dodge, Bayard, *The Fihrist of al-Nadīm*, New York: Columbia University Press, 1970. [Trans. of *Ibn al-Nadīm's Kitāb al-Fihrist*].

Donaldson, Dwight M. *Studies in Muslim Ethics*, London: S.P.C.K., 1953.

Donzel, E. Van, "Mudjaddid," in *EI²*.

Doutté, E. "ʿAbd-Allāh b. Yāsīn," *EI*, Vol. 1, pp. 32f.

Duggan, Alfred, *The Story of the Crusades*, London: Faber and Faber, 1963.

Dunyā, Sulaymān, *al-Ḥaqīqah fī Naẓar al-Ghazālī*, Cairo: Dār al-Maʿārif, 1965.

El-Ehwany, Ahmed Fouad, "Ibn Rushd" in *History of Muslim Philosophy*, Wiesbaden: Otto Harrassowitz, 1963, pp. 540-564.

Fakhry, Majid, *A History of Islamic Philosophy*, New York: Columbia University Press, 1970.

Faris, Nabih Amin, *The Book of Knowledge*, translation of *Kitāb al-'Ilm* of al-Ghazālī's *Iḥyā'*, New Delhi: Islamic Book Service, n.d, available online in PDF: http://www.ghazali.org/books/knowledge.pdf.

Farrūkh, 'Umar, *Tarīkh al-Fikr al-'Arabī ilā Ayyām Ibn Khaldūn*, Beirut: Dār al-'Ilm li al-Malāyīn, 1983.

Ferhat, Halima, "Yūsūf b. Tāshufīn," *EI²*, Vol. 11, pp. 355f.

Fierro, Maribel, "Opposition to Sufism in al-Andalus," in Frederick De Jong & Bernd Radtke (eds.), *Islamic Mysticism Contested*, Leiden: Brill, 1999, pp. 174-206.

Frank, Richard M., *Creation and the Cosmic system: al-Ghazālī and Avicenna*, Heidelberg: Carl Winter, 1992.

—*al-Ghazālī and the Ash'arite School*, Durham: Duke University Press, 1994.

Gardet, L., "'Ilm al-Kalām", *EI²*, Vol. 3, pp. 1141-1150.

Gardner, W.R.W., *al-Ghazālī*, Madras: Christian literature For India, 1919.

Al-Ghazālī, Abū Ḥāmid Muḥammad (d. 505/1111), *Faḍā'iḥ al-Bāṭiniyyah*, ed. 'Abd al-Raḥmān Badawī, Cairo: al-Dār al-Qawmiyyah, 1964; trans., see McCarthy, *Faḍ'iḥ*.

—*Fayṣal al-Tafriqah bayn al-Islām wa al-Zandaqah*, compacted with other works of al-Ghazālī in *Majmū'ah Rasā'il al-Imām al-Ghazālī*, Beirut: Dār al-Kutub al-'Ilmiyyah, n.d. Part 3, pp. 75-99.

—*Iḥyā' 'Ulūm al-Dīn*, Beirut: Dār Iḥyā' al-Turāth al-'Arabī, n.d.; trans.: *Kitāb Ādāb al-Akl*, see Johnson-Davies, Denys. *Al-Ghazālī*,

Kitāb Ādāb Tilāwah al-Qur'ān, see Abul Quasem, Muhammad. *The Recitation*,

Kitāb al-Adhkār wa al-Da'wāt, see Nakamura, Kojiro. *Al-Ghazālī*.

Kitāb Asrār al-Ṣalāh, see Calverly, Edwin Elliot. *The Mysteries*,

Kitāb Asrār al-Ṣawm, see Faris, Nabih Amin. *The Mysteries of Fasting*,

Kitāb Asrār al-Ṭahārah, see Faris, Nabih Amin. *The Mysteries of Purity*,

Kitāb Asrār al-Zakāh, see Faris, Nabih Amin. *The Mysteries of Almsgiving*,

Kitāb Dhikr al-Mawt wa mā Ba'dah, see Winter, T.J. *The Remembrance*.

Kitāb al-'Ilm, see Faris, *The Book of Knowledge*, and also MaCall, "The Book of Knowledge",

Kitāb Riyāḍah al-Nafs and *Kitāb Kasr al-Shahwatayn*, see Winter, T.J. *Al-Ghazālī*,

Kitāb Sharḥ 'Ajā'ib al-Qalb, see Skellie, "The Religious Psychology"; and also McCarthy, "Kitāb Sharḥ 'Ajā'ib al-Qalb".

Kitāb al-Tawbah, see Stern, M. *Al-Ghazālī*,

—*Iljām al-'Awāmm 'an 'Ilm al-Kalām*, compacted with other works of al-Ghazālī in *Majmū'ah Rasā'il al-Imām al-Ghazālī*, Beirut: Dār al-Kutub al-'Ilmiyyah, n.d. Part 4, pp. 41-83.

—*Jawāhir al-Qur'ān*, ed. Muḥamed Rashīd al-Qabbānī, Beirut: Dār Iḥyā' al-'Ulūm, 1990; trans., see Abul Quasem, *The Jewels*.

—*al-Kashf wa al-Tabyīn fī Ghurūr al-Khalq Ajma'īn*, compacted with other works of al-Ghazālī in *Majmū'ah Rasā'il al-Imām al-Ghazālī*, Beirut: Dār al-Kutub al-'Ilmiyyah, n.d. Part 5, pp. 157-185.

—*Makātīb Fārsī Ghazzālī banām Faḍā'il al-Anām min Rasā'il Ḥujjah al-Islām*, 'Abbās Iqbāl (ed.), Tehran: Majlis, 1333 P.C.: available online in PDF: http://www.ghazali.org/books/let-gz-prsn.pdf.

—*al-Mankhūl min Ta'līqāt al-Uṣūl*, Muḥammad Ḥasan Hītū (ed.), Damascus, n.p., 1970.

—*Maqāṣid al-Falāsifah*, ed. Maḥmūd Bījū, Damascus: Maṭba'ah al-Ṣabāḥ, 2000.

—*al-Maqṣad al-Asnā fī Sharḥ Ma'ānī Asmā' Allāh al-Ḥusnā*, ed. Faḍlah Shaḥādah, Beirut: Dār al-Mashriq, 1971; partial trans., see Robert Stade, *Ninty-Nine Names*.

—*Mi'yār al-'Ilm*, ed. Sulaymān Dunyā, Cairo: Dār al-Ma'ārif, 1961.

—*Mīzān al-'Amal*, ed. Sulaymān Dunyā, Cairo: Dār al-Ma'ārif, 1964.

—*al-Munqidh min al-Ḍalāl*, ed. Jamīl Ṣulībā and Kāmil 'Ayyād, Beirut: Dār al-Andalus, 1967; trans., see McCarthy, *Deliverance*, and Watt, *The Faith*.

—*al-Mustaṣfā min 'Ilm al-Uṣūl*, ed., Ḥamzah Zuhayr Ḥāfiẓ, Jeddah: Sharikah al-Madīnah al-Munawwarah li al-Ṭibā'ah, n.d.; trans., see Ḥammād, "Abū Ḥāmid al-Ghazālī's Jurist Doctrine in al-Mustaṣfā".

—*Naṣīḥah al-Mulūk*, trans., see Bagley, F.R.C. *Ghazālī's*.

—*Qānūn al-Ta'wīl*, ed. Maḥmūd Bījū, Damascus: n.p. 1993.

—*al-Qisṭās al-Mustaqīm*, ed. Maḥmūd Bījū, Damascus: al-Maṭba'ah al-'Ilmiyyah, 1983; trans., see McCarthy, *Deliverance*.

—*Sirr al-'Ālamīn*, compacted with other works of al-Ghazālī in *Majmū'ah Rasā'il al-Imām al-Ghazālī*, Beirut: Dār al-Kutub al-'Ilmiyyah, n.d. Part 6, pp. 3-95.

—*Tahāfut al-Falāsifah*, ed. Sulaymān Dunyā, Cairo: Dār al-Ma'ārif, 1980; trans., see Kamali, Sabih Ahmad. *Al-Ghazali's*.

—*al-Wasīṭ fī al-Madhhab*, ed. 'Alī Muḥī al-Dīn al-Qurrah-Dāghī, Qatar: Wazārah al-Awqāf, 1993; and also *al-Wasīṭ fī al-Madhhab*, ed. Aḥmad Maḥmūd Ibrāhīm, Cairo: Dār al-Salām, 1997.

Gianotti, Timothy J., *al-Ghazālī's Unspeakable Doctrine of the Soul: Unveiling the Esoteric Psychology and Eschatology of the Iḥyā'*, Leiden: Koninklijke Brill Nv, 2001.

Grafe, E, "Fāṭimids", *EI*, Vol. 2, pp. 88-92.

Greenland, Peter A.W. "al-Ghazālī and the Contemporary Age," MA Dissertation, King Alfred College, 2000, available online: http://www.btinternet.com/~petergreenland/al-ghazali_2000_ Dissertation.htm.

Grunebaum, Gustave E. Von, "The Concept of Plagiarism in Arabic Theory," in Journal of Near Eastern Studies, vol. 3 (4), pp. 234-253.

Ḥājjī Khalīfah (d. 1067/1657), *Kashf al-Ẓunūn 'an Asāmī al-Kutub wa al-Funūn*, Beirut: Dār al-Kutub al-'Ilmīyah, 1992.

Al-Ḥakīm, Su'ād, *Iḥyā' 'Ulūm al-Dīn fī al-Qarn al-Wāḥid wa al-'Ishrīn*, Cairo: Dār al-Shurūq, 2004.

—*Makanah al-Ghazālī min al-'Ulūm al-Ṣūfiyyah*, in *Majalah al-Turāth al-'Arabī*, Damasqus: Itiḥḥād al-Kuttāb al-'Arab, Issue 22, year 6, Jan. 1996, available online: http://www.awu-dam.org/trath/22/ turath22-009.htm.

Hallaq, Wael B., "Was the Gate of Ijtihad Closed?" in Wael B. Hallaq, *Law and Legal Theory in Classical and Medieval Islam*, Hampshire: Ashgate Publishing Limited, 1994, Part V, pp. 3-42.

Ḥammād, Aḥmad Z.M., "Abū Ḥāmid al-Ghazālī's Jurist Doctrine in al-Mustaṣfā Min 'Ilm al-Uṣūl with a translation of volume one of al-Mustaṣfā Min 'Ilm al-Uṣūl," a PhD thesis submitted to the University of Chicago in 1987, available online in PDF: http://www. ghazali.org/books/azhmd-p2.pdf.

Ḥanashī, Muḥammad 'Umrānī, *Shaṭaḥāt li Fuqahā'*, electronic book: http://www.alhiwar.org/ar/content/view/208/29/.

Ḥasan, Ḥasan Ibrāhīm, *Tārīkh al-Islām*, Cairo: Maktabah al-Nahḍah al-Miṣriyyah, 1967.

Ḥawwā, Sa'īd, *al-Mustakhlaṣ fī Tazkiyah al-Anfus*, Cairo: Dār al-Salām, 1984.

Heer, Nicholas L., "Moral Deliberation in al-Ghazālī's *Iḥyā' 'Ulūm al-Dīn*," in Parivis Morewedge (ed.), *Islamic Philosophy and Mysticism*, New York: Carvan Book, 1981, pp. 163-176

Al-Ḥijjī, 'Abd al-Raḥmān 'Alī, *al-Tārīkh al-Andalusī*, Damascus: Dār al-Qalam, 1987.

Hillenbrand, Carole, *The Crusades: Islamic Perspectives*, Edinburgh: Edinburgh University Press, 1999.

Hodgson, M.G.S. "Baṭiniyya," *EI²*, Vol. 1, pp. 1098-1110.

—*The Venture of Islam*, Chicago: The University of Chicago Press, 1974.

Hourani, Albert, *A History of Arab Peoples*, London: Faber and Faber Ltd., 1991.

Hourani, George F., "A Revised Chronology of Ghazālī's Writings," in *JAOS*, Vol. 104, No. 2, Apr.-June 1984, pp. 289-302.

Hrbek, I. and J. Devisse., "The Almoravids," in Elfasi, M. (ed.) *General History of Africa*, California: University of California Press, 1988, Vol. 3, pp. 337-366.

Hurat, Cl., "Ismā'īlliyya", *EI*, Vol. 2, pp. 549-552.

—"Seldjuḳs", in *EI*, Vol. 4, pp. 208-213.

Ibn 'Abbās, *Tafsīr*, online version: http://altafsir.com/Tafasir.asp?tMadh No=0&tTafsirNo=10&tSoraNo=11&tAyahNo=117&tDisplay=yes& UserProfile=0.

Ibn 'Asākir al-Dimashqī, Abū al-Qāsim 'Alī b. al-Ḥasan (d. 571/1176). *Tabyīn Kadhib al-Muftarī*, Damascus: al-Qudsī, 1347 AH

Ibn al-Athīr, Abū al-Ḥasan 'Alī b. Abī al-Karam Muḥammad al-Shibānī (d. 630/1233), *al-Kāmil fī al-Tārīkh*, Beirut: Dār al-Kutub al-'Ilmīyah, 1998; trans.: of sections related to the history of the Seljuk Turks over the year 420/1029 to the year 490/1096-1097, see, Richard, D.S. *The Annals*.

Ibn Durayd, Abū Bakr Muḥammad b. al-Ḥasan (d. 321/933), *Jamharah al-Lughah*, Hyder Abad: Dā'irah al-Ma'ārif, 1344-5 AH

Ibn Ḥanbal (d. 241/855), see Aḥmad b. Ḥanbal.

Ibn 'Idhārī al-Marrākūshī, Abū al-'Abbās Aḥmad b. Muḥammad, *al-Bayān al-Mughrib fī Akhbār Mulūk al-Andalus wa al-Maghrib*, Paris: Paul Euthner, 1930.

Ibn Jarīr al-Ṭabarī, Abū Ja'far Muḥammad (d. 310/923), *Tafsīr*, ed. Aḥmad Muḥammad Shākir, Beirut: Mu'assasah al-Risālah, 2000. The same edition available online on: http://www.qurancomplex. com/Quran/tafseer/Tafseer.asp?t=TABARY&TabID=3&SubItemID =1&l=arb.

Ibn al-Jawzī, Abū al-Faraj 'Abd al-Raḥmān b. 'Alī b. Muḥammad (d. 597/ 1201), *al-Muntaẓam fī Tārīkh al-Mulūk wa al-Umam*, Hyderabad: Dā'irah al-Ma'ārif al-'Uthmāniyyah, 1359 AH

—*Talbīs Iblīs*, Riyadh: Dar al-Mughnī, 2000.

Ibn Kathīr, Abū al-Fidā' Ismā'īl b. 'Umar (d. 774/1373), *Tafsīr al-Qur'ān al-'Aẓīm*, ed. Sāmī b. Muḥammad al-Salāmah, Riadh: Dār Ṭaybah, 1999; the same eddition vailable online on: http://www.qurancomplex. com/Quran/tafseer/Tafseer.asp?t=KATHEER&TabID=3&SubItemID =1&l=arb.

Ibn Khaldūn, 'Abd al-Raḥamān b. Muḥammad (d. 808/1406), *Kitāb al-'Ibar*, Beirut: Dār al-Kutub al-'Ilmiyyah, 1992.

—*Muqaddimah*, Beirut: Dār Iḥyā' al-Turāth, n.d; trans., see Rosenthal, *The Muqaddimah*.

Ibn Khallikān, Abū al-'Abbās Aḥmad b. Muḥammad b. Ibrāhīm (d. 681/1281), *Wafayāt al-A'yān*, Beirut: Dār al-Kutub al-'Ilmiyyah, 1998; trans., see Slane, *Ibn Khallikān's*.

Ibn Mājaḥ Abū ʿAbdullāh Muḥammad b. Yazīd al-Qazwīnī (d. 273/887), ed., Muḥammad Fuʾād ʿAbd al-Bāqī, Beirut: Dār al-Kutub al-ʿIlmiyyah, 1995.

Ibn Manẓūr, Abū al-Faḍl Jamāl al-Dīn Muḥammad b. Mukrram (d. 711/1311), *Lisān al-ʿArab*, Beirut: Dār Ṣādir, 1997.

Ibn al-Nadīm, *Kitāb al-Fihrist*, ed. Gustav Flügel, Leipzig (Germany): Verlag Von F.C.W. Vogel, 1871; trans., see Dodge, *The Fihrist*.

Ibn Qudāmah, Aḥmad b. ʿAbd al-Raḥamān al-Maqdisī (d. 689/1290), *Mukhtaṣar Minhāj al-Qāṣidīn*, Beirut and Damascus: Dār al-Khayr, 1998.

Ibn Sīdah, Abū al-Ḥasan ʿAlī b. Ismāʿīl (d. 458/1066), *al-Muḥkam wa al-Muḥīt, al-Aʿẓam fī al-Lughah*, eds. Muṣṭafā al-Saqqā et al., Cairo: Maʿhad al-Makhṭūṭāt bi Jāmiʿah al-Duwal al-ʿArabiyyah, 1958-1973.

Ibn Taghrībardī, Jamāl al-Dīn Abī al-Maḥāsin Yusūf (874/1470), *al-Nunjūm al-Zāhirah fī Mulūk Miṣr wa al-Qāhirah*, Cairo: al-Muʾassasah al-Miṣrīyah al-ʿĀmmah li al-Taʾlīf wa al-Tarjamah wa al-Ṭibāʿah wa al-Nashr, 1964.

Imām al-Ḥaramayn al-Juwaynī, *al-Burhān fī Uṣūl al-Fiqh*, ed. ʿAbd al-ʿAẓīm al-Dīb, Doha (Qatar): Maṭābiʿ al-Dūḥah al-Ḥadīthah, 1399 AH

Jaʿfar, Muḥammad Kamāl, *al-Miʿyār al-Khuluqī wa Nasaq al-Faḍāʾil ʿind al-Imām al-Ghazālī*, in Muḥammad Kamāl Jaʿfar (ed.), *al-Imām al-Ghazālī: al-dhikrā al-miʾawiyyah al-tāsiʿah li wafātih*, Doha: University of Qatar, 1986, pp. 378-436.

Janssens, Jules, "al-Ghazālī's Tahāfut: Is it really a rejection of Ibn Sīnā's Philosophy?," in *Journal of Islamic Studies*, 12:1, pp. 1-17, Oxford: Oxford Centre for Islamic Studies, 2001.

Al-Jawharī, Abū Naṣr Ismāʿīl b. Ḥammād (d. 393/1003), *al-Ṣiḥāḥ fī al-Lughah*, ed. Aḥmad ʿAbd al-Ghafūr ʿAṭṭār, Cairo: Dār al-Kitāb al-ʿArabī, 1377 AH

Johnson-Davies, Denys. *Al-Ghazālī on the Manners Relating to Eating*, translation of *Kitāb Ādāb al-Akl* of al-Ghazālī 's *Iḥyāʾ*, Cambridge: The Islamic Texts Society, 2002.

Juḥā, Farīd, *Abū Ḥāmid al-Ghazālī*, Damascus: Ṭilās li al-Dirāsāt wa al-Tarjamah wa al-Nashir, 1986.

Al-Juwaynī, see Imām al-Ḥaramayn.

Kamali, Sabih Ahmad, *al-Ghazali's Tahafut al-Falasifah*, Lahore: Pakistan Philosophical Congress, 1963.

Karra de Vaux (Bernard), Baro, *al-Ghazālī*, Translated into Arabic by ʿĀdil Zuʿaytar, Cairo: Dār Iḥyāʾ al-Kutub al-ʿArabiyyah, 1959.

Kazi, A.K. and J.G. Flynn, *Muslim Sects and Divisions: The section on Muslim Sects in Kitāb al-Milal wa al-Niḥal*, London: Kegan Paul International, 1984.

Kennedy, Hugh, *Muslim Spain and Portugal: A Political History of al-Andalus*, New York: Addison Wesley Longman Limited, 1996.

Al-Khalīl b. Aḥmad al-Farāhīdī, Abū ʿAbd al-Raḥmān (d. 170/786), *Kitāb al-ʿAyn*, ed. Mahdī al-Makhzūmī and Ibrāhīm al-Sāmarrāʾī, Baghdad: Wazārah al-Thaqāfah wa al-Iʿlām, 1980-1985.

Al-Khuḍarī, Muḥammad, *Tarīkh al-Tashrīʾ al-Islāmī*, Beirut: Dār al-Kutub al-ʿIlmiyyah, n.d.

Al-Kīlānī, Mājid ʿIrsān, *Hākadhā Ẓahr Jīl Ṣalāḥ al-Dīn wa Hākadhā ʿĀdat al-Quds*, Dubai: Dār al-Qalam, 2002.

Klausner, Carla L., *The Seljuk Vezirate: A Study of Civil Administration*, Massachusetts: Harvard University Press, 1973.

Knysh, Alexander, *Islamic Mysticism: A Short History*, Leiden: Brill, 2000.

Kogan, Barry S., "The Philosophers al-Ghazālī and Averroseon Necessary connection and the Problem of the Miraculous," in Parivis Morewedge (ed.), *Islamic Philosophy and Mysticism*, New York: Carvan Book, 1981, pp. 113-150

Lambton, A.K.S., "The Internal Structure of the Saljuq Empire," in *The Cambridge History of Iran*, Vol. 5, pp. 203-282.

Lane, Edward William, *Madd al-Qāmūs*: an Arabic-English Lexicon, Cambridge: Islamic Texts Society, 2003.

Lazarus-Yafeh, Hava, *Studies in al-Ghazzali*, Jerusalem: The Magnes Press, The Hebrew University, 1975.

Lévi-Provencal, E., "'Alī b. Yūsuf b. Tāshufīn" *EI²*, Vol. 1, pp. 389f.

Levtzion, Nehemia, "'Abd Allāh b. Yāsīn and the Almoravids," in John Ralph Willis (ed.), *Studies in West African Islamic History*, London: Frank Cass, 1979, pp. 78-112.

—"The Western Maghrib and Sudan: Almoravids and Almohads to c. 1250." in Roland Oliver (ed.), *The Cambridge History of Africa*, Cambridge: Cambridge University Press, Vol. 3, pp. 331-348.

MaCall, Willian Alexander, "The Book of Knowledge: Being a Translation, with Introduction and Notes of al-Ghazzālī's Book of the *Ihyāʾ*, Kitāb al-ʿIlm," a PhD thesis, Hartford Seminary Foundation, May, 1940, available online in PDF: http://www.ghazali.org/books/McCall-1940.pdf.

Macdonald, Duncan B., *Development of Muslim Theology, Jurisprudence and Constitutional Theory*, Beirut: Khayats Oriental Reprints, 1965.

—"al-Ghazālī, " in *EI¹*, Vol. 2, pp. 146-149.

—"Kalām," *EI*, Vol. 2, pp. 672-675.

—"Māturīdī," , *EI*, Vol. 3, p. 414.

—"The Life of al-Ghazālī, with Especial Reference to His Religious Experiences and Opinions," in *JAOS* (*Journal of the American Oriental Society*), Vol. 20, (1899), pp. 71-132.

—"The Meanings of the Philosophers by al-Ghazzali," *Isis*, Vol. 25, No. 1, May 1936, pp. 9-15, available online in PDF: http://www.ghazali. org/articles/dbm1.pdf.

Madelung, W. "Ismāʿīlliyya", *EI²*, Vol. 4, pp. 198-206.

—"Māturīdiyya," *EI²*, Vol. 6, pp. 847f.

Al-Mahdalī, Muḥammad ʿAqīl b. ʿAlī, *al-Imām al-Ghazālī wa ʿIlm al-Ḥadīth*, Cairo: Dār al-Ḥadīth, 1998.

Al-Mahdāwī, Ismāʿīl, *Abū Ḥāmid al-Ghazālī: al-Falsafah al-Taṣawwuf wa ʿIlm al-Kalām*, Marrakesh: Tansift, 1993.

Makdisi, George, "Authority in the Islamic Community," in George Makdisi, *History and Politics in Eleventh-Century Baghdad*, Hampshire: Variorum, 1990, part VIII, pp. 117-126.

Maʿlūf, Amīn, *al-Ḥurūb al-Ṣalībiyyah Kamā Ra'āhā al-ʿArab*, trans. from French to Arabic by ʿAfīf Dimashqiyyah, Beirut: Dār al-Fārābī, 1989.

Al-Maqdisī (d. 689/1290), see Ibn Qudāmah.

Marḥabā, Muḥammad ʿAbd al-Raḥmān, *Min al-Falsafah al-Yūnāniyyah ilā al-Falsafah al-Islāmiyyah*, Beirut: Manshūrāt ʿŪwaydāt, 1983.

Marmura, Michael E, ʿal-Ghazālī's Second causal Theory in the 17th discussion of his tahafut,' in Parivis Morewedge (ed.), *Islamic Philosophy and Mysticism*. New York: Carvan Book, 1981, pp. 85-112.

Al-Marzūqī, Abū Yaʿrub, *Mafhūm al-Sababiyyah ʿind al-Ghazālī*, Tunisia: Dār bu Salāmah li al-Ṭibāʿah wa al-Nashir, 1978.

Massignon, L. "Taṣawwuf," *EI²*, Vol. 10, pp. 314-316.

—*The Passion of al-Hallaj*, trans., Herbert Mason, Princeton: Princeton University Press, 1994.

Maududi, S. Abul A'la, *Four Basic Qur'anic Terms*, translated from Urdu to English by Abu Asad, Lahore (Pakistan): Islamic Publications Ltd., 1982.

Mayer, Hans Eberhard, *The Crusades*, translated from German by John Gillingham, Oxford: Oxford University Press, 1988.

McCarthy, Richard Joseph, *Deliverance from Error*, translation of *al-Munqidh min al-Ḍalāl* and other relevant works of al-Ghazālī, Louisville, KY: Fons Vitae, 1980.

—*Faḍā'iḥ al-Bāṭiniyya*, in McCarthy, *Deliverance*, pp. 152-244. [Trans. of al-Ghazālī's *Faḍā'iḥ al-Bāṭiniyya*]

—*Kitāb Sharḥ ʿAjā'ib al-Qalb*, in McCarthy, *Deliverance*, pp. 310-325. [Partial trans. of al-Ghazālī's *Kitāb Sharḥ ʿAjā'ib al-Qalb* of the *Iḥyā'*]

Merad, A., "Iṣlāḥ" in *EI²*, Leiden: E.J. Brill, 1978, vol. 4, pp. 141-163.

Mitha, Farouk, *al-Ghazālī and the Ismailis: A Debate on Reason and Authority in Medieval Islam*, London: I.B. Tauris & Co Ltd., 2001.

Muir, Sir William, *The Caliphate: Its Rise, Decline, and Fall*, ed. T.H. Weir, Edinburgh: John Grant, 1924.

Murtaḍā al-Zabīdī, Muḥammad b. Muḥammad al-Ḥusaynī (d. 1205/1791), *Tāj al-'Arūs*, ed. 'Abd al-Sattār Aḥmad Farrāj et al., Kuwait: Wazārh al-Irshād wa al-Anbā', 1965-1989.

—*Itḥāf al-Sādah al-Muttaqīn bi Sharḥ Iḥyā' 'Ulūm al-Dīn*, Beirut: Dār al-Kutub al-'Ilmiyyah, 2005.

Muslim b. al-Ḥajjāj, (d. 261/875). *Ṣaḥīḥ*, an edition with the commentary of al-Nawawī (d.676/1277), *al-Minhāj Sharḥ Ṣaḥīḥ Muslim B. al-Ḥajjāj*, ed. Khalīl Ma'mūn Shayḥā, Beirut: Dār al-Ma'rifah, 1996.

Muṣṭafā, Ibrāhīm et al. (eds.), *al-Mu'jam al-Waṣīṭ*, Istanbul: Dār al-Da'wah, 1989.

Al-Nadwī, al-sayyid Abū al-Ḥasan 'Alī, *Rijāl al-Fikr wa al-Da'wah fī al-Islām*, Damascus: Dār al-Qalam, 2002.

Nafi, Basheer M. *The Rise and Decline of the Arab-Islamic Reform Movement*, London: The Institute of Contemporary of Islamic Thought, 2000.

Al-Najjār, 'Āmir, *Naẓarāt fī Fikr al-Ghazālī*, Cairo: Sharikah al-Ṣafā li al-Ṭibā'ah wa al-Tarjamah wa al-Nashr, 1989.

Nakamura, Kojiro, "An Approach to Ghazālī's Conversion," *Orient*, Vol. 21, 1985, pp. 46-59.

—*Ghazali and Prayer*, Kuala Lumpur: Islamic Book Trust, 2001.

—"al-Ghazālī," in *Concise Routledge Encyclopaedia of Philosophy*, London & New York: Routledge, 2000, p. 314.

—*al-Ghazālī Invocations and Supplications*, translation of *Kitāb al-Adhkār wa al-Da'wāt* of al-Ghazālī's *Iḥyā'*, Cambridge: The Islamic Texts Society, 1996.

Al-Nasā'ī, Abū 'Abd al-Raḥmān Aḥmad b. Shu'ayb b. 'Alī (d. 303/915), *Sunan*, an edition with the commentary of Jalāl al-Dīn al-Suyūṭī and the marginal notes of al-Sindī, Beirut: Dār al-Kutub al-'Ilmiyyah, n.d.

Nasr, Seyyed Hossein, *Science and Civilization in Islam*, Cambridge: The Islamic Texts Society, 1987.

Nicholson, Reynold A., *The Mystics of Islam*, London: Routledge and Kegan Paul LTD, 1963.

Nīshāpūrī, Ẓahīr al-Dīn (579/1184 or 80/1185), *The History of the Seljuq Turks From the Jāmi' al-Tawārīkh: An Ilkhanid Adaption of the Saljūq Nāma of Ẓahīr al-Dīn Nīshāpūrī*, translated from Persian by Kenneth Allin Luther, edited by C. Edmund Bosworth, Richmond (Surrey): Curzon Press, 2001.

Norris, H.T., "al-Murābiṭūn," *EI²*, Vol. 7, pp. 583-589.

Ormsby, Eric L., "The Taste of Truth: The Structure of Experience in al-Ghazali's al-Munqidh," in Wael B. Hallaq & Donald P. Little (eds.) *Islamic Studies Presented to Charles J. Adams*, Leiden: Brill, 1991, pp.

133-152, available online in PDF: http://www.ghazali.org/articles/eo1.pdf.

Othman, Ali Issa, *The concept of Man in Islam: In the writings of al-Ghazālī*, Cairo: Dār al-Ma'ārif Printing and Publishing House, 1960.

—*Oxford English Dictionary, The.* 2nd ed., Oxford: Oxford University Press, 1989; available online: http://dictionary.oed.com.

Pines, Shlomo. "Islamic Philosophy," in Sarah Stroumsa (ed.) *Studies in the History of Arabic Philosophy: The Collected Works of Shlomo Pines*, Jerusalem: The Magnes Press, The Hebrew University, 1996, Vol. 3, pp. 3-46.

Al-Qaradawi, Yusuf. *Al-Imām al-Ghazālī bayn Mādiḥīh wa Nāqidīh*, Beirut: Mu'assasah al-Risālah, 1994.

Al-Qāsimī, Muḥammad Jamāl al-Dīn (d. 1332/1914). *Tahdhīb Maw'iẓah al-Mu'minīn*, n.p., n.d.

Al-Qushayrī, Abū al-Qāsim 'Abd al-Karīm (d. 465/1072). *Al-Risālah al-Qushayriyyah*, edited by 'Abd al-Ḥalīm Maḥmūd and Maḥmūd b. al-Sharīf, Cairo: Maṭba'ah Ḥassān, n.d.

Al-Rāghib al-Aṣfhānī, Abū al-Qāsim Muḥammad b. al-Ḥasan (502/1108). *Mufradāt Alfāẓ al-Qur'ān*, ed. Ṣafwān Dāwūdī, Damascus: Dār al-Qalam and Beirut: al-Dār al-Shāmiyyah, 1997.

Repgen, Konrad. "Reform," translated from German to English by Robert E. Shillenn, in *The Oxford Encyclopaedia of the Reformation*, vol. 3, pp. 392-395, New York & Oxford: Oxford University Press, 1996.

Richard, D.S., *The Annals of the Saljuq Turks: Selections from al-Kāmil fī'l-Ta'rīkh of 'Izz al-Dīn Ibn al-Athīr*, London: RoutledgeCurzon, 2002.

Robinson, Richard, *Definition*, Oxford: Clarendon Press, 1962.

Rosenthal, Franz, *The Muqaddimah: An Introduction to History*, London: Routledge & Kegan Paul, 1958. [Trans. of Ibn Khaldūn *Muqaddimah*].

Runciman, Steven, *A History of the Crusades*, Cambridge: Cambridge University Press, 1951.

Al-Sabḥānī, Ja'far, *Buḥūth fī al-Milal wa al-Niḥal*, vol. 2, Beirut: al-Dār al-Islāmiyyah, 1991.

Al-Ṣafadī, Ṣalāḥ al-Dīn Khalīl b. Aybak, *al-Wafī bi al-Wafiyyyāt*, ed. Helmut Ryter, Visbaden: Frans Shtayz, 1962.

Al-Ṣaghīr, 'Abd al-Majīd, "*al-Bu'd al-Siyāsī fī Naqd al-Qāḍī Ibn al-'Arabī li Taṣawwuf al-Ghazālī*," in *Abū Ḥāmid al-Ghazālī: Dirāsāt fī fikrih wa 'Aṣrih wa T'thīrih*, pp. 173-193, Rabat: College of Arts and Humanities, Muḥammad al-Khāmis University, 1988.

Al-Ṣāḥib b. 'Abbād, Abū al-Qāsim Ismā'īl b. Abū al-Ḥasan 'Abbād al-Ṭāliqānī, most known as al-Ṣāḥib b. 'Abbād (d. 385/995). *Al-Muḥīṭ fī al-Lughah*, ed. Muḥammad Ḥasan Āl-Yāsīn, Baghdad: Maṭba'at al-Ma'ārif, 1975.

Al-Sakhāwī, Shams al-Dīn Muḥammad b. 'Abd al-Raḥmān (d. 902/1497), *al-Ḍaw' al-Lāmi'*, Cairo: 1354 AH.

Al-Ṣallābī, 'Alī Muḥammad, *'Ilām Ahl al-'ILm wa al-Dīn bi Aḥwāl Dawlah al-Muwaḥḥidīn*, Sharjah: Maktabah al-Ṣaḥābah, 2001.

—*al-Jawhar al-Thamīn bi Ma'rifah Dawlah al-Murābiṭīn*, Sharjah: Maktabah al-Ṣaḥābah, 2001.

Sayyd Bi, Jamāl Rajab, *Naẓariyāt al-Nafs bayn Ibn Sīna wa al-Ghazālī*, Egypt : al-Hay'ah al-Miṣriyyah al-'Āmmah il al-Kitāb, 2000.

Schacht, Joseph. *An Introduction To Islamic Law*, Oxford: Oxford University Press, 1964.

—"Law and Justice," in P.M. Holt and et al (eds.), *The Cambridge Histroy of Islām*, pp. 539-568.

Schimmel, Annemarie, *Mystical Dimensions of Islam*, Chapel Hill: The University of North Carolina Press, 1975.

Al-Shahristānī, Abū al-Fatḥ Muḥammad b. 'Abd al-Karīm b. Aḥmad (d. 548/1153), *al-Milal wa al-Niḥal*, Beirut: Dār Maktabah al-Mutanabbī, 1992; trans., see Kazi, *Muslim Sects*.

Al-Shāmī, Ṣāliḥ Aḥmad, *al-Imām al-Ghazālī: Ḥujjah al-Islām wa Mujaddid al-Mi'ah al-Khāmisah*, Damascus: Dār al-Qalam, 1993.

Shams al-Dīn, Muḥammad 'Alī, *al-Iṣlāḥ al-Hādi': Naẓra fī Fikr wa Sulūk al-Mujtahid al-Sayyid Muḥsin al-Amīn al-Ḥusaynī al-'Āmilī*, n.p. Awrāq Sharqiyyah, 1985.

Shehadi, Fadlou, *Ghazali's Unique Unknowable God*, Leiden: E.J. Brill, 1964.

Sherif, Mohamed Ahmed, *Ghazali's Theory of Virtue*, Albany: State University of New York Press, 1975.

Skellie, W.J., "The Religious Psychology of al-Gahzzālī: A Translation of his Book of the *Iḥyā'* on the Explanation of the Wonders of the Heart," a PhD thesis submitted to Hartford Seminary Foundation in 1938, available online in PDF: http://www.ghazali.org/books/skillie.pdf.

Slane, B Mac Guckin De, *Ibn Khallikān's Biographical Dictionary*, Paris: Oriental Translation Fund of Great Britain and Ireland, 1868. [Trans. of Ibn Khallikān's *Wafiyyāt*.]

Smith, Margaret, *Al-Ghazali the Mystic*, London: Luzac and co., 1944.

Stade, Robert, *Ninty-Nine Names of God in Islam*, translation of the major portion of al-Ghazālī's *al-Maqṣad al-Asnā*, Ibadan (Nigeria): Daystar Press, 1970.

Stern, M., *al-Ghazālī on Repentance*, translation of *Kitāb al-Tawbah* of al-Ghazālī's *Iḥyā'*, Michigan: University Microfilms International, 1978, available online in PDF: http://www.ghazali.org/books/gz-repent.pdf.

Al-Subkī, Tāj al-Dīn, (d. 771/1370). *Ṭabaqāt al-Shāfiʿiyyah al-Kubrā*, Cairo: al-Maṭbaʿah al-Ḥusayniyyah, 1906.

Al-Ṭabarī, (d. 310/923), see Ibn Jarīr al-Ṭabarī.

Al-Ṭāhir Būnābī, *Nash'ah wa Taṭwwur al-Adab al-Ṣūfī fī al-Maghrib al-Awsaṭ*, in *Ḥawliyyah al-Turāth*, Algeria: Mistiganim Univesity, Issue # 2, Sept. 2004, electronic version: http://annales.univ-mosta.dz/texte/ap02/15bounabi.htm.

Tamir, ʿĀrif, *al-Ghazālī bayn al-Falsafah wa al-Dīn*, London: Riyad el-Rayyes Books Ltd., 1987.

Al-Tiftazānī, Abū al-Wafā al-Ghunaymī, *Madhkal ilā al-Taṣawwuf al-Islāmī*, Cairo: Dār al-Thaqāfah wa al-Nashr wa al-Tawzīʿ, 1989.

Al-Tirmidhī, Abū ʿĪsā Muḥammad b. ʿĪsā (d. 279/892), *al-Jāmiʿ al-Ṣaḥīḥ*, ed. Muḥammad Muḥammad Naṣṣār, Beirut: Dār al-Kutub al-ʿIlmiyyah, 2000.

ʿUmaruddin, M., *The Ethical Philosophy of al-Ghazzālī*, Delhi: Adam Publishers & Distributers, 1996.

Al-ʿUthmān, ʿAbd al-Karīm, *Sīrah al-Ghazālī wa Aqwāl al-Mutaqaddimīn fīh*, Damascus: Dār al-Fikr, n.d.

Van Ess, Josef, "Sufism and its Opponents," in Frederick De Jong and Bernd Radtke (eds.), *Islamic Mysticism Contested: Thirteen Centuries of Controversies and Polemics*, Leiden: Brill, 1999, pp. 28ff.

Vaux, B. Carra de, "Falsafa," *EI*, Vol. 2, pp. 48-52.

Voll, John Obert, *Islam: Continuity and Change in the Modern World*, New York: Syracuse University Press, 1994.

—"Renewal and Reform in Islamic History: *Tajdid* and *Islah*," in John L. Esposito (ed.), *Voices of Resurgent Islam*, Oxford: Oxford University Press, 1983, pp. 32-47.

Al-Wāsiṭī, Muḥammad b. al-Ḥasan al-Ḥusaynī (d. 776/1374), *Tarjamah al-Ghazālī fī al-Ṭabaqāt al-ʿAliyyyah*, ed. ʿAbd al-Amīr al-Aʿsam, printed in the appednex of ʿAbd al-Amīr al-Aʿsam's *al-Faylasūf al-Ghazālī: Iʿādah Taqwīm li Munḥanā Taṭawwrih al-Rūḥī*, Amzil (Tonisia): al-Dār al-Tūnisiyyah li al-Nashir, 1988.

Wasserstein, D.J., "Mulūk al-Ṭawāif: In Muslim Spain," *EI²*, Vol. 7, pp. 552-554.

—*The Rise and Fall of the Party-Kings: Politics and Society in Islamic Spain 1002-1068*, Princeton: Princeton University Press, 1985.

Watt, W. Montgomery, *A History of Islamic Spain*, Edinburgh University Press, 1965.

—"al-Ash'arī, Abu'l-Ḥasn," *EI²*, Vol. 1, pp. 694f.

—"al-Ash'ariyya," *EI²*, Vol. 1, p. 696

—*Islamic Philosophy and Theology*, Edinburgh: The University Press, 1985.

—*Muslim Intellectual: A Study of al-Ghazali*, Edinburgh: The University Press, 1963.

—"The Authenticity of the Works Attributed to al-Ghazālī," in *Journal of the Royal Asiatic Society*, 1952, pp. 24-45.

—*The Faith and Practice of al-Ghazālī*, translation of al-Ghazali's *al-Munqidh* and *Bidāyah al-Hidāyah*, London: George Allen and Unwin Ltd., 1953.

Wensinck, A.J., *On the Relation between Ghazāli's Cosmology and it's Mysticism*, Amsterdam: Uigave van De N.V. Noord-Hollandsche, 1933.

Wilson, John, *Thinking with Concepts*, Cambridge: The University Press, 1969.

Winter, T.J., *The Remembrance of Death and the Afterlife*, translation of *Kitāb Dhikr al-Mawt wa ma Ba'dah* of al-Ghazālī's *Iḥyā'*, Cambridge: The Islamic Texts Society, 1989.

—*al-Ghazālī on Disciplining the Soul and on Breaking the Two Desires*, translation of *Kitāb Riyāḍah al-Nafs* and *Kitāb Kasr al-Shahwatayn* of al-Ghazālī's *Iḥyā'*, Cambridge: The Islamic Texts Society, 2001.

Al-Yāfi'ī, Abū Muḥammad 'Abdullāh b. As'ad (d. 768/1367), *Mir'āh al-Jinān wa 'Ibrah al-Yaqẓān*, Hyderabad: Dā'irah al-Ma'ārif al-Niẓāmiyyah, 1338 AH

Al-Zabīdī, see Murtaḍā al-Zabīdī.

Al-Zamakhsharī, Jārullāh Abū al-Qāsim Maḥmūd b. 'Umar (d. 538/1144), *Asās al-Balāghah*, Beirut: Dār Iḥyā' al-Turāth al-'Arabī, 2001.

Zambaur, E.V., "Ḥisba," in *EI¹*.

Zettersteen, K.V., "Barkiyārūk" in *EI*, Vol. 1, pp. 661f.

Zuberi, Masarrat Husain, *Aristotle and al-Ghazali* [sic], Delhi: Noor Publishing House, 1992.

Zwemer, Samuel M., *A Moslem Seeker after God*, New York: Fleming H. Revell Company, 1920.

Index

www.ingramcontent.com/pod-product-compliance
Lightning Source LLC
Chambersburg PA
CBHW020311160726
47992CB00004B/1483